Cloud Computing Solutions

Scrivener Publishing
100 Cummings Center, Suite 541J
Beverly, MA 01915-6106

Publishers at Scrivener
Martin Scrivener (martin@scrivenerpublishing.com)
Phillip Carmical (pcarmical@scrivenerpublishing.com)

Cloud Computing Solutions

Architecture, Data Storage, Implementation and Security

Souvik Pal
Sister Nivedita University, Kolkata, India

Dac-Nhuong Le
Haiphong University, Haiphong, Vietnam

Prasant Kumar Pattnai
Kalinga Institute of Industrial Technology (KIIT), Deemed to be University, India

Scrivener
Publishing

This edition first published 2022 by John Wiley & Sons, Inc., 111 River Street, Hoboken, NJ 07030, USA and Scrivener Publishing LLC, 100 Cummings Center, Suite 541J, Beverly, MA 01915, USA
© 2022 Scrivener Publishing LLC
For more information about Scrivener publications please visit www.scrivenerpublishing.com.

Wiley Global Headquarters
111 River Street, Hoboken, NJ 07030, USA

For details of our global editorial offices, customer services, and more information about Wiley products visit us at www. wiley.com.

Limit of Liability/Disclaimer of Warranty

Library of Congress Cataloging-in-Publication Data

ISBN 978-1-119-68165-6

Cover image: Pixabay.Com
Cover design by Russell Richardson

Set in size of 11pt and Minion Pro by Manila Typesetting Company, Makati, Philippines

Printed in the USA

10 9 8 7 6 5 4 3 2 1

*Dedicated to our friends
and family for their
constant support during the
course of this book*

Contents

Part IV: Cloud Computing Simulator Tools 269

List of Figures

List of Tables

Foreword

This book discusses the evolution of cloud computing through grid computing and cluster computing. The main purpose of this book is to include all the cloud-related technologies in a single platform, so that undergraduate and postgraduate students, researchers, academicians, and those in industry can easily understand the cloud-based ecosystems. This book will take the reader on a journey that begins with understanding the cloud infrastructure paradigm in cloud-enabled technologies and how it can be applied in various ways. It will help researchers and practitioners to understand grid and distributed computing, cloud infrastructure, virtual machine, virtualization, live migration, scheduling techniques, auditing concept, security and privacy, business models, and case studies through the state-of-the-art in cloud computing countermeasures.

This book covers a wide range of cloud computing-related technologies. The wide-ranging contents will differentiate this book from others. The topics are likely to be embedded with various aspects of cloud business model-enabled technologies. It aims to provide the concepts of related technologies based on novel findings of the researchers through its chapter organization. The primary audience for the book includes specialists, researchers, undergraduate students, designers, experts and engineers who are occupied with research.

The book is organized in independent chapters to provide greater readability, adaptability and flexibility to readers.

Souvik Pal
Dac-Nhuong Le
Prasant Kumar Pattnaik

Preface

Recently, cloud computing has been one of the emerging technologies in the fields of computer science and information technology (IT). The advancement of cloud computing has resulted from the fast-growing use of the internet among people. This book is intended for readers who have no prior knowledge of this subject. Some topics in this book are unique and based on published information, both current and timely, which will be helpful to research scholars as well as specialists working in cloud computing-related issues. It is suitable as an introductory text for a semester-length course in cloud computing for undergraduate and postgraduate science courses in computer science and information technology. The authors decided to work on an introductory textbook on this subject for the benefit of students and teachers. Some topics in this book are unique and based on published information which is both current and timely.

The key features of the book are as follows:

- Discusses the evolution of cloud computing from grid computing, cluster computing, and distributed system.
- Provides coverage of cloud computing environments and popular views of them.
- Incorporates a survey of the virtualization environment and its latest developments.
- Discusses live migration, database, auditing and applications as part of the materials related to cloud computing.
- Provides concepts of cloud storage, cloud strategy planning and management, cloud security and privacy issues.
- Explains complex concepts in a very simple manner.
- Covers information appropriate for beginners as well as advanced users.
- Presents information using layman's terms and clear language.
- Widely covers the latest topics.
- Extensively uses analogies.

Souvik Pal
Dac-Nhuong Le
Prasant Kumar Pattnaik
March 2022

Acknowledgments

First of all, we would like to thank all our colleagues and friends for sharing our happiness at the start of this project and following up with their encouragement when it seemed too difficult to complete. We are thankful to all the members of Scrivener Publishing, especially Martin Scrivener and Phillip Carmical, for giving us the opportunity to write this book.

Dr. Pal is grateful to his father, Prof. Bharat Kumar Pal, and mother, Smt. Tandra Pal, for their blessings and constant support. He is also grateful to his grandmother, the late Sakhi Rani Pal, and grandfater, the late Ajit Kumar Pal, for their affection and motivation. He is thankful to his beloved wife, Smita, and son, Binayak, for their love and encouragement.

Dr. Dac-Nhuong Le would like to acknowledge and thank the most important people in his life, his patents and his partner, for their support. This book has been a long-cherished dream which would not have been turned into reality without the support and love of these amazing people, who encouraged him with the right amount of time and attention. He is also grateful to his best friends for their blessings and unconditional love, patience and encouragement.

Prof. Pattnaik is grateful to his father, the late Ramanarayan Patnaik, his mother, Smt. Jayalakshimi Patnaik, his father-in-law, Er. Chittaranjan Mohanty, and mother-in-law, the late Renubala Mohanty, for their blessings. He is also thankful to his wife, Bismita, and daughter, Prasannakshi, for their love and support.

And above all, the God Almighty.

Souvik Pal
Dac-Nhuong Le
Prasant Kumar Pattnaik

Acronyms

5G	The Next (5*th*) Generation
ACID	Atomicity, Consistency, Isolation, Durability
ACL	Access Control List
AI	Artificial Intelligence
AIIOT	Artificial Intelligence and Internet of Things
AKS	Azure Kubernetes Service
ALB	Adaptive Load Balancing
AMQP	Advanced Message Queuing Protocol
ANSI	American National Standards Institute
API	Application Programming Interface
ARP	Address Resolution Protocol
ARPA	Advanced Research Projects Agency
AS	Autonomous System
ATL	Atlas Transformation Language
AWS	Amazon Web Services
BGP	Border Gateway Protocol
BSM	Business Service Management
BSP	Business Service Provider
BSON	Binary JSON
CAA	Cloud Application Architecture
CAM	Content Addressable Memory
CAP	Consistency, Availability, and Partition
CapEx	Capital Expenditure
CC	Cluster Controller
CDP	Continuous Data Protection
CDS	Content Delivery Servers
CCE	Cloud Computing Environment
CERN	European Organization for Nuclear Research
CFI	Control Flow Integrity
CIDR	Classless Inter-Domain Routing
CIS	Cloud Information Service
CLC	Cloud Controller
CMR	Customer Relationship Management
CODINE	Computing in Distributed Networked Environments

COI	Community of Interest
CPA	Cloud Platform Architecture
CPU	Central Processing Unit
CSA	Cloud Protection Alliance
CSLB	Central Scheduler Load Balancing
CSP	Cloud Service Provider
DAM	Database Activity Monitoring
DaaS	Database as a Service
DBMS	Database Management System
DCE	Data Center Efficiency
DC	Distributed Computing
DDoS	Distributed Denial of Service
DoS	Denial of Service
DHCP	Dynamic Host Configuration Protocol
DLP	Data Loss Prevention
DNS	Domain Name Server
DNSSEC	Domain Name System Security Extensions
DPM	Distributed Power Management
DRS	Distributed Resource Scheduler
DSM	Distributed Shared Memory
DVFS	Dynamic Frequency Voltage Scaling
ECMP	Equal-Cost Multi-Path
EC2	Elastic Compute Cloud
ECN	Explicit Congestion Notification
EPPKS	Efficient Privacy Preserving Keyword Search Scheme
FAM	File Activity Monitoring
FGBI	Fine-Grained Block Identification
FCAPS	Fault, Configuration, Account, Performance, Security
FC	Fiber Channel
FC-SAN	FC-Based Storage Area Networks
GA	Genetic Algorithm
GAE	Google App Engine
GVMI	Generic Virtual Machine Image
GOC	Green Open Cloud
GPS	Global Positioning System
GPLv2	General Public License
GUI	Graphical User Interface
HA	Homomorphic Authenticator
HDFS	Hadoop Distributed File System
HMAC	Hash Message Authentication Code
HIPS	Host Intrusion Prevention System

HME	Hypervisor Monitoring Environment
HPC	Hardware Performance Computing
HTTP	Hypertext Transfer Protocol
HVM	Hardware-Assisted Virtual Machine
IaaS	Infrastructure as a Service
IDC	international Information Enterprise
IDS	Intrusion Detection System
IDS/IPS	Intrusion Detection System/Intrusion Prevention System
IMA	Integrity Management Architecture
IoT	Internet of Things
IP	Internet Protocol
IPsec	IP-Level Security
IPS	Intrusion Prevention System
IRM	In-Lined Reference Monitors
ISA	Instruction Set Architecture
IT	Information Technology
I/O	Input/Output
JSON	JavaScript Object Notation
KVM	Kernel-Based Virtual Machine
KBA	Knowledge-Based Answers/Questions
LAN	Local Area Network
LGPL	Lesser General Public License
LLFC	Link Layer Flow Control
LLM	Lightweight Live Migration
LVM	Logical Volume Manager
LVMM	Live Virtual Machine Migration
MaaS	Model as a Service
MAC	Media Access Control
MCC	Mobile Cloud Computing
MFA	Multi-Factor Authentication
MiTM	Man-in-the-Middle Attack
MP	Microprocessor
MPI	Message Passing Interface
MPLS	Multi-Protocol Label Switching
MSN	Mobile Social Networking
MVCC	Multi-Version Concurrency Control
NAS	Network-Attached Storage
NAC	Network Access Control
NC	Node Controller
NFS	Network File Server

NSF	National Science Foundation
NSFC	National Natural Science Foundation of China
NIPS	Network Intrusion Prevention System
NIC	Network Interface Controller
NoSQL	Not-only-SQL
NOW	Networks of Workstations
NICs	Network Interface Cards
NRDC	Natural Resources Defense Council
OCR	Optical Character Recognition
OLTP	Online Transaction Processing
ONF	Open Networking Foundation
OS	Operating System
OSG	Object Storage Gateway
OSP	Object Storage Provider
OVS	Open vSwitch
P2P	Peer-to-Peer
PaaS	Platform as a Service
PAP	Policy Access Points
PC	Personal Computer
PCB	Process Control Block
PDT	Performance Degradation Time
PDP	Policy Decision Points
PEP	Policy Enforcement Points
PKI	Public Key Infrastructure
PMC	Performance Monitoring Counters
POR	Proof of Retrievability
POC	Proof of Concept
PPW	Performance Per Watt
PUE	Power Usage Effectiveness
PVM	Parallel Virtual Machine
PV	Public Verifiability
QoS	Quality of Service
RaaS	Resources as a Service
RBAC	Role-Based Access Control
RDBMS	Relationship Database Management System
RDPC	Remote Data Processing Scheme
RDS	Relational Database System
RED	Random Early Detection
RLE	Run-Length Encoding
RPC	Remote Procedure Call Protocol
RPM	Red Hat Package Manager

RSA	Rivest–Shamir–Adleman
RTT	Round-Trip Time
S3	Simple Storage Service
SAN	Storage Area Network
SaaS	Software as a Service
SAML	Security Assertion Markup Language
SC	Storage Controller
SDN	Software-Defined Networks
SECaaS	Security as a Service
SEaaS	Sensor Event as a Service
SFI	Software Fault Isolation
SIEM	Security Information and Event Management
SLA	Service-Level Agreements
SMC	Secure Multi-Party Computation
SME	Small Medium Enterprise
SMP	Symmetric Multi-Processing
SOAP	Simple Object Access Protocol
SOA	Service-Oriented Architecture
SPT	Shadow Page Table
SQL	Structured Query Language
SSC	SQL Server Compact
SSH	Password-Based Auth
SSI	Single System Image
STP	Spanning Tree Protocol
TCSEC	Trusted Computer System Evaluation Criteria
TDS	Tabular Data Stream
TPA	Third-Party Auditor
TPAS	Third-Party Auditing Service
TPM	Trusted Platform Module
TTP	Trusted Third Party
TCG	Trusted Computing Group
TCP/IP	Transmission Control Protocol/Internet Protocol
UDB	User Database
UFS	User-Facing Service
VDCs	Virtual Data Centers
VDI	Virtual Desktop Infrastructure
VEE	Virtual Environment Extension
VLAN	Virtual Local Area Network
VLB	Valiant Load Balancing
VM	Virtual Machine
VMLM	Virtual Machine Live Migration

VMM	Virtual Machine Migration
VO	Virtual Organization
VPC	Virtual Predict Checkpointing
VPN	Virtual Private Network
WaaS	Workflow as a Service
WAN	Wide Area Network
WSN	Wireless Sensor Network
WWS	Writable Working Set
WWW	World Wide Web
XSS	Cross-Site Scripting
XML	Extensible Markup Language
YARN	Yet Another Resource Negotiator

PART I

Cloud Computing Architecture

Basic Computing Architecture

1

BASICS OF CLOUD COMPUTING

Souvik Pal[1], Dac-Nhuong Le[2], Prasant Kumar Pattnaik[3]

[1] Sister Nivedita University, Kolkata, India
[2] Haiphong University, Haiphong, Vietnam
[3] KIIT, Deemed to be University, India
 Email: souvikpal22@gmail.com, nhuongld@dhhp.edu.vn, patnaikprasant@gmail.com

Abstract
Consider an analogy where personal computer users are not required to run, install or store their applications on their personal computers. Consider a situation where every piece of your information and data may be stored on the cloud (Internet). As an allegory for the Internet, cloud is a very popular word but when integrated with the word "computing," it becomes more important and uncertain. Cloud computing comes into focus only when users think about what they always need, which leads to the concept of an updated version of utility computing. The advancement of cloud computing came about because of the quickly developing utilization of the web among the general population. Cloud computing is anything but an absolutely new innovation; it's actually a voyage through distributed, cluster, grid and presently cloud computing. Before the increasing utilization of the web everywhere throughout the globe, cloud computing had just been used in the IT business. Cloud computing is transforming the computing landscape. The cloud concept and its computing process is an emerging topic in internet-centric and IT-market-oriented businesses. The goal required for the IT industry should be a direct conversation about how this new computing worldview will put an effect the associations, how it can be utilized with the current advancements. Cloud computing needs a third-party vendor through which a client or an end user or a customer may use the cloud provided by a cloud service provider (CSP) on demand.

Keywords: Cloud service provider, cloud computing

1.1   Evolution of Cloud Computing

Cloud computing isn't new. Truth be told, a lot of what we do on our personal computers today requires it. What is changing is the way that we look at what cloud computing is able to do for us today. The idea of cloud computing came after the period of mainframe computers of the 1960s when the likelihood of utility computing had already been proposed by MIT personal computer researcher John McCarthy, who opined that "Calculation may some time or another be sorted out as an open utility."

> In 1961, John McCarthy proposed [1]: "If personal computers of the kind I have supported turned into the personal computers without bounds, at that point computing may some time or another be sorted out as an open utility similarly as the phone framework is an open utility... The personal computer utility could turn into the premise of another critical industry. Utility Computing is called a service providing model. Here, the service provider ensures the accessibility of computing resources and framework administration to the client as per requirement. This method is just like the pay per use service and that of the metered services, which implies that clients can pay according to their use of network access, sharing of records and several other applications. In 1966, Douglas F Parkhill published the book *The Challenge of the Computer Utility*. In his book, he investigated the idea of versatile provisioning and resource sharing."

The sequential development of the computing environment may be arranged in a year-wise manner as shown in Figure 1.1. IBM System/360 entered the global market in 1964.This model and other items of the same family attracted attention from the business community because the fringe parts were movable and the item unit was implemented in all systems of the family [1]. The scaling down of the mainframe systems and more improvements over time prompted the free machines, the reported minicomputers; for example, DEC's PDP-8 minicomputer introduced in 1964 and Xerox's Alto in 1974 [2].

The computer era began in the early 1970s with the release of the first Intel 4004 microprocessor (MP) in 1971, followed by the release of the Intel 8008 MP in 1972. The first personal home computer, the Micral, was created by André Truong Trong Thi [2] based on the Intel 8008 MP. Development of the Mark-8 or TV-Typewriter was the first project for microcomputer hobbyists. In 1975, the MITS Altair 8800 microcomputer kit advertised in several scientific and hobby magazines is credited with having popularized microcomputers. This personal computer was supposed to be the underlying idea behind home computers. The first programming language for the machine was Microsoft's founding product, Altair BASIC. Successively, Apple, Commodore, Atari and others entered the personal home computer market. IBM introduced its first personal computer to the market, which was commonly known as the IBM PC. Microsoft engineered the operating system (OS) for IBM PCs, which was built up and standardized and wound up being used by numerous PC makers. There have been numerous consecutive periods of improvement with headway being made in the advancements whipping up the market. With the creation of graphical user interface (GUI), the next stage of improvements is being prompted.

While thinking about how to significantly improve interactions among numerous personal computers, another point of reference began in the business sector, which was the Internet. The Advanced Research Projects Agency (ARPA)[1] presented the idea of the In-

---

[1] https://www.darpa.mil

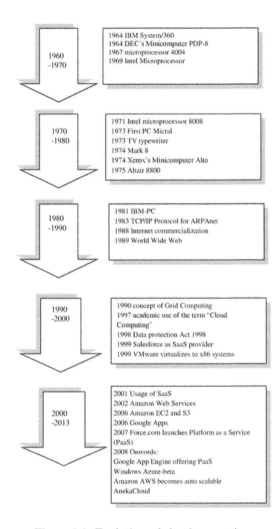

Figure 1.1: Evolution of cloud computing.

ternet as an exploratory venture. Each interfacing point is known as a node in a web. With the help of the U.S. Department of Homeland Security, a correspondence framework has been made with the end goal that in case any of the nodes get broken, the correspondence framework remains connected. In the long run, from this endeavor, the ARPANET was created and nearly 200 foundations were connected to this system. The thought of TCP/IP in 1983 has been exhibited, and the internet was changed to TCP/IP, which relates the entire subnet to the ARPANET. By and by the internet has become known as a system of systems. With the advancement of the World Wide Web (WWW) by British expert and personal computer researcher Sir Timothy John Berners-Lee in 1989, the web accomplished its definitive leap forward. Berners-Lee proposed an information administration framework for CERN (European Organization for Nuclear Research)[2] where hyperlinks were

[2]https://home.cern

utilized. In the end, with respect to the end clients there was a necessity for web programs. Thus, the WWW became ubiquitous when the web browser Mosaic was introduced in the market.

Today, the entire information technology sector is putting effort into outlining the quality of web programming by increasing the bandwidth and also by using some innovative ideas to build up programs. We can easily develop user interactive websites with the use of Java, PHP or AJAX. These advancements result in the development of different multimedia websites and interactive applications for the business sector.

Meanwhile, in the 1990s, the idea of grid computing was presented in academia. Carl Kesselman and Ian Foster disseminated their book *The Grid: Blueprint for a New Computing Infrastructure*. The new linkage was related to the idea of an electric grid. We can relate the idea of grid computing with our day-to-day example. When a device is connected to a power outlet, we are unaware of how electric power is generated and reaches the outlet, we just use it. This is what is known as virtualization. Here, we don't know the basic architecture or method behind the scene. We don't know how things are made available to the users, but we are aware that they are actively using it. We can predict that power is virtualized; virtualization conceals a gigantic scattering grid and power generation stations. This idea may be adapted in computing, where distinctive conveyed segments, such as storage, data management, and software assets, are incorporated [3]. In innovations like cluster, grid and now cloud computing, every one of the developments have focused on enabling access to an enormous amount of computing assets in a totally virtualized design. It influences a singular framework for examining social occasions involving resources in a total example. These are all given to the users or the organizations or to customers on the basis of "pay-per-use" or "pay-as-you-go" design (payment based on utilization).

In 1997, the term "cloud computing" was introduced in academia by Ramnath Chellappa, who defined it as a "computing paradigm where the boundaries of computing will be determined by economic rationale rather than technical limits alone." In 1999, Salesforce started conveying applications to their clients utilizing basic websites. The actual applications were undertaken and dispersed over the web; in this manner, utility-based computing began being used in the real world. Amazon started its point of reference by creating Amazon Web Services (AWS) and conveying storage services, estimations and so on in 2002. Amazon allows clients to integrate its immense online substance with their own website. Its web services and computing facility have expanded slowly upon request. In 2006, Amazon initially launched its Elastic Compute Cloud (Amazon EC2)[3] as a commercial internet benefit that allows small enterprises and individuals to lease infrastructure (resources, storage, memory) upon which they can carry and run their own applications. With the implementation of Amazon storage (Amazon S3), a "pay-per-use" model was also implemented. Cloud's Google App Engine,[4] Force.com, Eucalyptus,[5] Windows Azure,[6] Aneka[7] and a lot more of their kind are capturing the cloud business.

The next section is about cluster, grid and mobile computing.

---

[3]https://aws.amazon.com/ec2
[4]https://cloud.google.com/appengine
[5]https://www.eucalyptus.cloud
[6]https://azure.microsoft.com
[7]www.manjrasoft.com/aneka_architecture

1.2 Cluster Computing

A computer cluster can be characterized as an arrangement of several coupled computers cooperating in such a way that every machine can be viewed as a single system image (SSI). Computer clusters are developed by merging a colossal number of computer developments, including access to fast networks, low-cost MPs, and software that delivers high-performance computing.

According to Sadashiv and Kumar [4], a cluster can be defined as the collection of distributed or parallel computers attached among themselves with the help of high-speed networks such as SCI, Myrinet, Gigabit Ethernet and InfiniBand. They function collectively in the execution of data- and compute-intensive tasks that would not be feasible for a single computer to execute alone. The clusters are mostly used for load balancing (to distribute the task over the different interconnected computers), high availability of the required data, and for compute purpose. The interconnected computers are used due to their high availability as they maintain the redundant nodes which are being utilized to convey the required service when the system components fail.

The performance of the system is upgraded enough and enhanced in that case because regardless of whether one node neglects to figure out the task, there is another backup node which will be ready to convey the task and takes on the simple single purpose without any snags [5]. At the point when numerous computers are connected in a computer cluster, they can easily share computational workload as a single virtual computer. From the client's perspective, they are numerous machines, yet they are working as a single virtual machine. The client's demand is received and appropriated among all the independent computers to shape a computer cluster. This outcome is adjusted and reasonable computational workload is shared among various machines, enhancing and improving the computational performance of the cluster systems. Frequently clusters are used for the most part for computational purposes, and than for taking care of IO-based exercises.

1.2.1 The Architecture of Cluster Computing Environment

Figure 1.2 represents the cluster where numerous independent computers, an operating system, a correspondence or networked system and an elite interconnecting medium, middleware and diverse application are incorporated. A computer is either a single or a multiprocessor system with memory, Input/Output provisions and operating system. A computer cluster for the most part alludes to at least two quantities of computers (nodes) interconnected. The nodes can remain in a specific bureau or can be physically particular and associated through fast LAN. The network interface equipment fills in as a correspondence processor; however, it transmits and gets packets of information between cluster nodes via a system/switch. Correspondence programming is in charge of fast and dependable information exchange among cluster nodes and the exterior. The cluster middleware remains in the middle of the numerous personal computers or workstations and several applications. It fills in like single system image producer and accessibility infrastructure. Programming situations offer proficient, compact and easy-to-use apparatuses for application improvement. Computer clusters are also being used for the execution of parallel and consecutive applications.

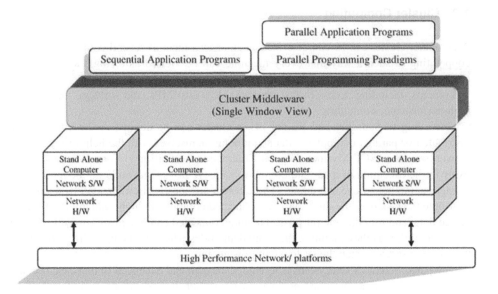

Figure 1.2: Architecture of computer cluster.

1.2.2 Components of Computer Cluster

A typical computer cluster has some prominent components which are used to do a specific task [6]. The components are as follows:

1. Multiple high-performance computers (PCs, workstations or SMPs)

2. State-of-the-art operating systems (layered or micro-kernel based)

3. High-performance networks/switches (such as Gigabit Ethernet and Myrinet)

4. Network interface cards (NICs)

5. Fast communication protocols and services (such as active and fast messages)

6. Cluster middleware (single system image (SSI) and system availability infrastructure):

   - Hardware (such as digital (DEC) memory channel, hardware DSM, and SMP techniques),

   - Operating system kernel or gluing layer (such as Solaris MC and GLUnix),

   - Applications and subsystems applications (such as system management tools and electronic forms),

   - Runtime systems (such as software DSM and parallel file system),

   - Resource management and scheduling software, such as ISF (load sharing facility),

   - CODINE (computing in distributed networked environments)

7. Parallel programming environments and tools (such as compilers, PVM (parallel virtual machine), and MPI (message passing interface)), and

8. Applications of sequential, parallel or distributed computing.

1.3 Grid Computing

Carl Kesselman and Ian Foster first coined the term grid computing in the 1990s, which is characterized as resource sharing and critical thinking in unique, multi-institutional virtual associations [7]. We have to contrast grid computing's classification with cluster. While clusters use the same operating system and hardware and run locally, grids involve heterogeneous computer systems that are interconnected with one another and distributed globally. The hardware and OSs run on the machines could also be distinct from each other [5, 8].

Grid computing is a convoluted component which has progressed by means of earlier advancements in parallel, dispersed and high-performance computing (HPC) [9, 10].

> The real and specific problem that underlies the Grid concept is coordinated resource sharing and problem solving in dynamic, multi-institutional virtual organizations. The sharing that we are concerned with is not primarily file exchange but rather direct access to computers, software, data, and other resources, as is required by a range of collaborative problem-solving and resource-brokering strategies emerging in industry, science, and engineering. This sharing is, necessarily, highly controlled, with resource providers and consumers defining clearly and carefully just what is shared, who is allowed to share, and the conditions under which sharing occurs. A set of individuals and/or institutions defined by such sharing rules form what we call a virtual organization (VO) [2].

Computing grids are conceptually and logically like electrical grids. In an electrical grid, wall outlets allow us to connect to an infrastructure of resources which generate and distribute the electricity. When we connect to the electrical grid, we don't even need to know where the power plant is situated or how the electricity gets to us. Likewise, in the IT industry, grid computing uses middleware to coordinate distinct IT resources over the network, allowing them to function and work as a virtual whole. The goal of a computing grid, like that of the electrical grid, is to provide users with access to the resources they need when they need them, and to provide remote access to IT assets, and aggregating processing power.

According to Zhang *et al.* [8], grid provides a series of distributed computing resources via LAN or WAN to the terminal user's application, as if he/she is using a super virtual computer. This basic idea will realize safe and secure use and coordinate and organize resource sharing among the person, business group, organization and resources, and will produce virtual and dynamic organization. Grid computing is a technique of distributed computing. It also includes location and organization software and hardware to provide unlimited power. Its goal is to allow anyone in the grid to cooperate and access each other's information. But cloud computing is better; it has many advantages over grid computing. Cloud computing grows from grid computing and provides the users with on-demand resources that are provisioned according to their application.

1.3.1 Grid-Related Technologies

Grid computing engages in linking different geographically remote machines and servers into one individual network to create (from client's perspective) a virtual supercomputer aided by joining the resource and computational control of all computers on the grid. A system of geologically and physically distributed resources having machines, switches, devices, connecting cables, appliances and data make up the grid computing environment. Every resource can be utilized by every user with only one login account. Diverse artifaces may possess the physical artifaces. The related terminologies in grid computing are distributed computing and peer-to-peer computing [9].

- **Distributed Computing (DC)**: Distributed computing uses the procedure of dispersing the workload of a program across at least two procedures. The prime goal of distributed computing is separating and dealing with issues in various computers associated through a typical network. A distributing system involves different self-governing computers, self-communicating with each other by means of a personal computer network. The personal computer cooperates keeping in mind the end goal to attain a shared objective. A few characteristics of a distributed system are given below:

- **Fault Tolerance**: All personal computers inside the shared system have to cope with crashes, i.e., the system needs to tolerate the faults.

- **Heterogeneous Atmosphere**: The disseminated framework (network latency, network topology, network associations and several involved personal computers) isn't predefined. The disseminated framework may incorporate specific types of personal computers and heterogeneous network joins. When running a program, framework structure could change with a specific end goal to achieve that goal. This is known as "heterogeneous atmosphere."

- **Separate Participation**: Separate participation is an instance where each and every personal computer has its particular participation and has a constrained perspective of the final system. All personal computers may just know a few modules or a few parts of the entire program or information.

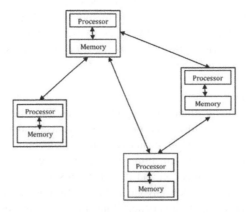

Figure 1.3: Schematic diagram of distributed system.

The above Figure 1.3 shows disseminated frameworks as a group of personal computers connected with each other by a correspondence network with all personal computers having a processor and memory with a similar kind of end goal for the work. Depending upon the workload and the execution time, the network topology and aggregate number of contributing personal computers can be progressively orchestrated.

- **Peer-to-Peer Computing (P2P)**: In this strategy, every personal computer shares the physical resources and services by specifically interchanging among the systems and every personal computer could perform as servers and client for other personal computers associated with the network. Which personal computer could perform as a client or server depends upon which part is more dependable and proficient for that network. In P2P, data is commonly interchanged immediately and maintain the basic internet protocol (IP) network. The main priority of P2P is decentralized coordination which avoids single dependency.

Figure 1.4 below shows 6 nodes, Node *A*, *B*, *C*, *D*, *E*, and *F*. Every node speaks for itself in a machine and could distribute the physical artifacts and organizations specifically trading between the nodes and communicating with all others. Every node could act as server and client for alternate nodes associated with the system.

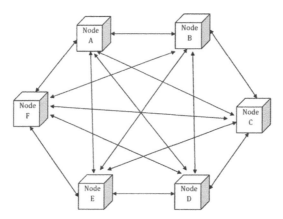

Figure 1.4: Peer-to-peer communication scenario.

In P2P frameworks, resources such as storage, estimations and bandwidth are given by clients. The main advantage of P2P network is the decentralized system. Subsequently, there is an arrangement of information and framework backup among the nodes. In any case, the fundamental proviso of P2P framework is the security issue. A node can download an infection document that could contaminate alternate frameworks; in that worry, P2P framework is powerless against unsigned and unsecured codes which prompt unsecured conditions because of the absence of a unified executive.

1.3.2   Levels of Deployment

Cluster grids, enterprise grids, and global grids are three logical levels in the deployment of grid computing environment [10]:

- *Cluster Grids*: The cluster grids are the basic form of a grid environment which consists of multiple computer systems interrelated by means of a network. Cluster grids might include distributed workstations and servers, and also contain centralized physical resources in a datacenter environment. High-performance jobs and high throughput is supported by cluster grid. Some examples of the cluster grid framework are groups of multi-processor high-performance computing (HPC), compute farms, and networks of workstations (NOW).

- *Enterprise Grids*: Enterprise grids may be formed by combining multiple cluster grids. Multiple projects or departments can be enabled by enterprise grids to distribute computing and physical resources in a supportive way. Enterprise grids generally may have the resources from multiple domains situated in a similar region.

- *Global Grids*: Global grids are a group of enterprise grids, each having different agreed upon protocols and universal usage policies, but not necessarily a similar manner of execution. Computing and physical resources might be geographically distributed, and they are used for connecting different sites throughout the globe. Global grids give the intensity of appropriated resources to users anywhere on the planet.

Figure 1.5 deals with cluster grids, enterprise grids and global grids. Cluster grids consist of multiple systems denoted as Node 1...., with Node *N* interconnected via the network.

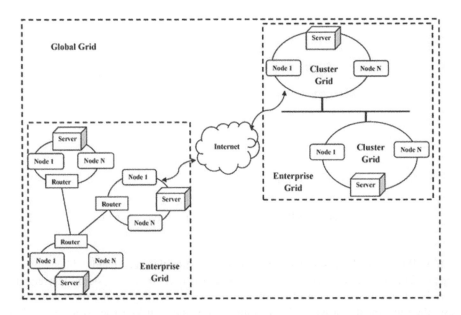

Figure 1.5: Scenario of global grid consisting of cluster and enterprise grid.

This kind of grid may contain servers, workstations, and data centers. All the components are acquired and used by a single department or administrative domain. When the need for resources increases, multiple cluster grids work together to make an enterprise grid. Multiple administrative domains may share the resources when they are in enterprise grids located in the same geographic location. Meanwhile, in contrast to enterprise grids, global grids are a compilation of enterprise grids. Each of them agree upon universal usage policies and protocols but it is not mandatory that executions will be the same. Users have the authority to use the distributed resources anywhere in the world.

1.3.3 Architecture of Grid Computing Environment

This subsection describes the layered grid architecture used to distinguish prerequisites for general classes of parts. Parts inside each layer share regular qualities yet can expand upon the capacities and practices given by any lower layer.

Figure 1.6 depicts the layered framework, namely the fabric layer (interfacing local control), connectivity layer (communicating layer), resource layer (sharing single resources), collective layer (coordinates several resources), and application and protocol layer [11-18]. Each of the layers is discussed below.

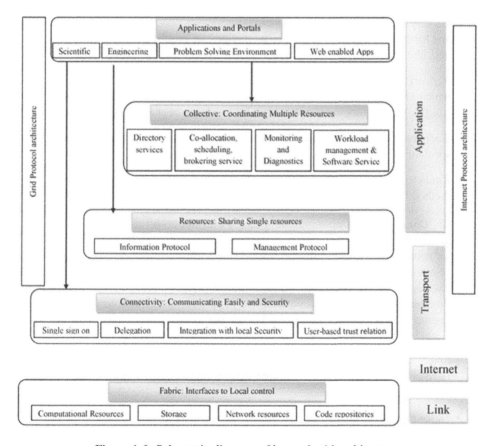

Figure 1.6: Schematic diagram of layered grid architecture.

1.3.3.1 Fabric: Interfaces to Local Control

Fabric interface and local control provide the physical resources that are distributed and are the intermediate layer of grid protocols such as storage systems, computable artifacts, network resources, catalogs and sensors. A "resource" is defined as a logical part, like a computer cluster, distributed file system, or distributed computing pool; particularly in some areas, a resource execution might include internal protocol. In any case, these are not the concern of the grid framework.

- *Computational resources*: Techniques are fundamental for initializing projects and for observing and governing the implementation of the subsequent processes. Administration instruments which permit screening and taking over the physical and computational resources designated for processes are required, as are time components approved ahead of time. Inquiry capacities are attractive for deciding equipment and programming qualities and pertinent state data; for example, current load and queue state due to scheduler-managed artifacts.

- *Storage resources*: Methods are necessary for using and taking over files. Management methods that permit taking over the physical resources distributed and provisioned for information exchanges (network bandwidth, space, disk bandwidth, CPU) are very functional, and are an advanced reservation policy. For determining software and hardware characteristics, inquiry functions are required and an applicable load of data like bandwidth utilization and available storage is also needed for those reasons.

- *Network resources*: Management methods that confer the authority of the resources which are assigned to network transfers (e.g., reservation, prioritization) might be fruitful. Inquiry functions are required for resolving network features and load.

- *Code repositories*: This method for managing source and object coding is used by the specialized form of storage resource, e.g., a control system.

- *Catalogs*: They are a particular type of repository that store resources and require a method for executing catalog query and update operations, e.g., a relational database.

1.3.3.2   Connectivity: Communicating Easily and Securely

Connectivity layer has validation and approval protocols which are required for grid-specific network exchanges and furthermore characterizes center correspondence strategies. Correspondence protocols are required for the trading of information between texture layer assets. Correspondence necessities incorporate routing, transport and naming. Confirmation protocols are required for correspondence administrations for giving secure instruments to approve the validation of clients and assets. Connectivity layer gives validation administrations which have the accompanying qualities:

- *Single sign on*: Clients must have the capacity to approve themselves ("sign on") just once and after that they simply approach numerous grid assets depicted in texture layer.

- *Delegation*: The user should have the ability to run a program for its own benefit, with the goal of finding out whether the program is fit to get the grid resources which the verified user is entitled to.

- *Integration with various local security solutions*: All sites and resource suppliers ought to be incorporated with different nearby security arrangements. Grid security arrangements must have the capacity to consolidate with different nearby security arrangements and enable mapping to the local condition.

- *User-based trust relationships*: In the event that the user has the privilege to utilize the artifacts from unmistakable locales or resource suppliers, the user ought to have the capability of using destinations together without requiring connection with the overseers of suppliers.

1.3.3.3 Resource: Sharing Single Resources

The resource layer lies above the connectivity layer correspondence and verification conventions to recognize conventions for the inception, checking, secure negotiation, accounting, control and payment of distributed operations of singular resources. Resource layer executes these conventions in the texture layer for controlling neighborhood resources. Two key classes of resource layer conventions could be striking:

- *Information protocol*: These conventions are used in getting information of the structure and states of assets like the use governing policy, current load and its outline.

- *Management protocols*: These protocols are used in negotiating access to shared physical resources, specifying resource requirements and monitoring tasks to be executed. A protocol might hold up monitoring the current state of an operation and while executing controlling operations.

1.3.3.4 Collective: Coordinating Multiple Resources

The following layers are engaged towards the protocols and services which are related along universal resource and cooperate with assembling of resources. This is the reason we called the following layer of the grid engineering the collective layer.

- *Directory services*: Enables its clients to ask questions for artifacts by type, accessibility or load-sharing demand. Resource-level protocol is utilized in building indexes.

- *Scheduling, co-allocation and brokering service*: This service enables members to ask for distribution of assignments of at least one physical resource for a specific reason and the scheduling of undertakings for appropriate resources.

- *Monitoring and diagnostic services*: These specific applications screen asset designation, overload management, and additionally keep considerations regarding the assaults.

- *Data replication services*: It supports the capacity management to expand the data received to execute and limit the reaction time and money.

- *Workload management systems*: These systems deal with the utilization, depiction, status of the errand and multi-component work processes.

1.3.3.5 Application Layer

The end layer of grid framework is the application layer which interacts with the end users. According to the user applications, physical resources are provisioned and properly used by the applications.

- *Scientific and engineering*: In the scientific and engineering fields, various application-specific and user-specific requirements are entertained and physical and computing resources are provisioned accordingly.

- *Problem-solving statement*: Application layer directly interacts with the problem-solving area. Application layer solves the problem module-wise.

- *Web-based apps*: Application layer handles the Web-based apps and provides access to services like resource management, data access and so forth.

1.3.3.6 Comparison-Based Study of Cluster, Grid and Cloud Computing
Table 1.1 below describes a comparison-based study of cluster, grid and cloud.

Table 1.1: A comparison-based study of cluster, grid and cloud.

Characteristic	Clusters	Grids	Clouds
Allocation	Centralized	Decentralized	Both
Resource Handling	Centralized	Distributed	Both
Computation Service	Computing	Maximum computing	On-demand
Scalability	No	Partial scalable	Full scalable
Virtualization	Partial	Partial	Full
Business Model	No	No	Yes

1.4 Mobile Computing

Two major developments over the last decade have revolutionized the way people use their computers. First, advances in the miniaturization of circuits and components have made it possible to pack powerful processing units into portable laptops and more recently in palmtop computers. As a result, people from all walks of life have started carrying personal computers wherever they go. The second major development concerns computer communication and wireless networking of portable computers becoming a reality. These two developments have merged portable personal computing and communication to form the discipline of mobile computing [19-25].

Figure 1.7: Mobile computing.

Mobile computing is widely described as the ability to compute and communicate while on the move. This new emerging discipline has made it possible for people to get information from anywhere and at any time. Mobile computing means two separate and distinct concepts: mobility and computing. Computing denotes the capability to automatically carry out certain processing. Mobility, on the other hand, provides the capability to change a portable location during communication and computing. The main advantage of this mobility is the flexibility that it provides to the user. The user need not necessarily sit in front of his desktop, but can either move locally or even to faraway places.

1.4.1 Characteristics of Mobile Computing

A computing environment is said to be "mobile" when either the sender or receiver of information can move (mobile) while transmitting or receiving information. The following are the important characteristics of a mobile computing environment.

- *Ubiquity*: The definition of ubiquity is "the state of being everywhere all the time." Mobile computing allows a user to perform computation from anywhere, anytime. For example, a business executive can receive business notifications and issue business transactions as long he/she is in wireless coverage area.

- *Location awareness*: A handheld device equipped with a global positioning system (GPS) can provide information about the current location of a user. Many applications ranging from strategic to personalized services require or get value additions with location-based services. For example, while a person is on the move, he/she may be on the lookout for car maintenance services available nearby. This can be very easily achieved through mobile computing. Of the numerous applications, a few example applications are traffic control, fleet management and emergency and security services.

- *Adaptation*: Adaptation implies the ability of a system to adjust to bandwidth fluctuation without inconveniencing the user. In a mobile environment, adaptation is crucial because of intermittent disconnections and bandwidth fluctuations that arise due to handoff, obstacles, environmental noise, etc.

- *Broadcasting*: Efficient delivery of data to hundreds of mobile users simultaneously is possible in the mobile environment due to the fundamental broadcast nature of the underlying communication.

- *Personalization*: Services in the mobile environment can be tailored to the user's profile. This is required to let users easily avail information with handheld devices. For example, a mobile user may need certain information from specific sources, which can be easily achieved through personalization.

1.4.2 Characteristics of Mobile Networks

A few important characteristics of a mobile network are the following:

- *Dynamic topologies*: Since systems can be moved subjectively, the system topology may change capriciously.

- *Bandwidth constrained, variable capacity links*: Connecting wireless devices all together brings down connection limits compared with their wired alternative. Likewise, because of issues, for example, multi-access, fading, commotion and impedance conditions, the data transfer capacity of the remote connections can change discretionarily with time.

- *Energy constrained operation*: The nodes in a MANET rely on battery power source. Mobile node batteries are small and normally store a very limited amount of energy. Inefficient network operations, such as routing, network initialization, etc., can rapidly drain batteries. In this situation, the most essential basic system paradigm should be vitality preservation.

- *Limited physical security*: Mobile networks are prone to many more types of security threats than fixed networks, mainly due to wireless transmissions and collaborative routing. There are increased possibilities of eavesdropping, spoofing, and DOS attacks in these networks. Also, nodes are vulnerable to capture and compromise.

1.5 Summary

The basics of cloud computing have been described in this introductory chapter. The chapter began with a description of the evolution of cloud computing, including the historical advancement of cloud and how different computer systems are linked to form a cloud infrastructure. The concept of grid computing and its architecture and also cluster computing and its architecture were discussed. This chapter also presented a comparison-based study of cluster, grid and cloud, and concluded with a discussion of mobile computing.

EXERCISES

1. What is cloud computing? How do you differentiate it from internet computing?

2. Differentiate between a tightly coupled and a loosely coupled system with examples.

3. Define the cluster of computer environment. How can the cluster be used for high availability purposes?

4. What are the benefits of cloud computing?

5. What is a cloud?

6. Explain the architecture of the cluster of computers with neat sketches.

7. What is computer grid? How does the concept of grid computing mimic the electric grid?

8. Differentiate between distributed computing and peer-to-peer computing. What are the major challenges in distributed computing and peer-to-peer computing?

9. Explain how the grid computing environment is deployed.

10. What is mobile computing? Explain the three-tier structure of the mobile computing environment.

11. Briefly discuss the structure of mobile peer-to-peer computing. What are the characteristics of mobile peer-to-peer computing?

12. What is an ad-hoc network? Is it always mobile? Briefly discuss the major application of mobile ad-hoc network.

13. Which are the different layers that define cloud architecture?

14. What are the different data types used in cloud computing?

15. What are the different layers in cloud computing? Explain how they work.

References

1. Garfinkel, S. (1999). *Architects of the information society: 35 years of the Laboratory for Computer Science at MIT*. MIT press. ISBN 978-0-262-07196-3.

2. Paul, F., & Michael, S. (2000). *Fire in the valley: The making of the personal computer*. New York: Osborne-McGraw-Hill.

3. Foster, I. (2003). *The grid: Computing without bounds. Scientific American*, 288(4), 78-85.

4. Sadashiv, N., & Kumar, S. D. (2011, August). Cluster, grid and cloud computing: A detailed comparison. In 2011 6th *International Conference on Computer Science & Education (ICCSE)* (pp. 477-482). IEEE.

5. Buyya, R. (1999). *High performance cluster computing: Architectures and systems* (volume 1). Prentice Hall, Upper SaddleRiver, NJ, USA, 1, 999.

6. Mark baker and Rajkumar Buyya, "Cluster Computing at a Glance"

7. Foster, I., & Kesselman, C. (Eds.). (2003). *The Grid 2: Blueprint for a new computing infrastructure*. Elsevier.

8. Zhang, S., Chen, X., Zhang, S., & Huo, X. (2010, October). The comparison between cloud computing and grid computing. In 2010 *International Conference on Computer Application and System Modeling (ICCASM 2010)* (Vol. 11, pp. V11-72). IEEE.

9. Weishaupl, T., & Schikuta, E. (2004, October). Towards the merger of grid and economy. In *International Conference on Grid and Cooperative Computing* (pp. 563-570). Springer, Berlin, Heidelberg.

10. Jackson, K. R., Ramakrishnan, L., Muriki, K., Canon, S., Cholia, S., Shalf, J., ... & Wright, N. J. (2010, November). Performance analysis of high performance computing applications on the amazon web services cloud. In *2010 IEEE second international conference on cloud computing technology and science* (pp. 159-168). IEEE.

11. Le, D. N., Kumar, R., Nguyen, G. N., & Chatterjee, J. M. (2018). *Cloud Computing and Virtualization*. John Wiley & Sons.

12. Le, D. N., Bhatt, C. M., & Madhukar, M. (Eds.). (2019). *Security Designs for the Cloud, IoT, and Social Networking*. John Wiley & Sons.

13. Hurwitz, J. S., & Kirsch, D. (2020). *Cloud Computing for Dummies*. John Wiley & Sons.

14. Ruan, L., Guo, S., Qiu, X., & Buyya, R. (2020). Fog Computing for Smart Grids: Challenges and Solutions. *arXiv preprint arXiv:2006.00812*.

15. Huth, A., & Cebula, J. (2011). *The Basics of Cloud Computing*. United States Computer.

16. Allahvirdizadeh, Y., Moghaddam, M. P., & Shayanfar, H. (2019). A survey on cloud computing in energy management of the smart grids. *International Transactions on Electrical Energy Systems*, 29(10), e12094.

17. Srinivasan, S. (2014). *Cloud Computing Basics*. Springer.

18. Pattnaik, P. K., & Mall, R. (2015). Fundamentals of Mobile Computing. PHI Learning Pvt. Ltd..

19. Rountree, D., & Castrillo, I. (2013). *The basics of cloud computing: Understanding the fundamentals of cloud computing in theory and practice*. Newnes.

20. Machidon, O., Fajfar, T., & Pejovic, V. (2020). Implementing Approximate Mobile Computing. In *Proc. of the 2020 Workshop on Approximate Computing Across the Stack* (WAX) (pp. 1-3).

21. Van, V. N., Long, N. Q., Nguyen, G. N., & Le, D. N. (2016). A performance analysis of openstack open-source solution for IaaS cloud computing. In *Proceedings of the Second International Conference on Computer and Communication Technologies* (pp. 141-150). Springer, New Delhi.

22. Van, V. N., Long, N. Q., & Le, D. N. (2016). Performance analysis of network virtualization in cloud computing infrastructures on openstack. In *Innovations in Computer Science and Engineering* (pp. 95-103). Springer, Singapore.

23. Hurwitz, J. S., & Kirsch, D. (2020). *Cloud computing for Dummies*. John Wiley & Sons.

24. Seth, B., Dalal, S., Jaglan, V., Le, D. N., Mohan, S., & Srivastava, G. (2020). Integrating encryption techniques for secure data storage in the cloud. *Transactions on Emerging Telecommunications Technologies*, e4108.

25. Bohu, L., Lin, Z., & Xudong, C. (2020). Introduction to cloud manufacturing. *ZTE Communications*, 8(4), 6-9.

2

INTRODUCTION TO CLOUD COMPUTING

SOUVIK PAL[1], DAC-NHUONG LE[2], PRASANT KUMAR PATTNAIK[3]

[1] Sister Nivedita University, Kolkata, India
[2] Haiphong University, Haiphong, Vietnam
[3] KIIT, Deemed to be University, India
Email: souvikpal22@gmail.com, nhuongld@dhhp.edu.vn, patnaikprasant@gmail.com

Abstract

This chapter presents the basics of cloud computing and its related advances. Computing itself, to be considered absolutely virtualized, must give personal computers working from physically conveyed parts the ability to store and process information and program artifices. The end clients access computational and physical assets with utility computing, which portrays a business system for conveying the services and computational power upon request. Furthermore, as indicated by the need of the client, the intent of CSPs is to convey the services and cloud clients needed to pay the CSPs in view of their use. In cloud computing, clients are not required to know the basic design for getting services; they simply need to pay as per their utilization. Cloud is fundamentally a foundation which is kept up by some CSPs and end-clients are getting the services on request from the CSPs and need to pay the required cash for their utilization. Service providers like Amazon, Microsoft, Google, and IBM offer on-request resource and computational services to the client industrially.

Keywords: Cloud computing, cloud service provider

2.1   Definition of Cloud Computing

Numerous specialists from industry and scholarly circles have given numerous perspectives on cloud and its computational highlights. Some of them are given below.

> Buyya *et al.* have stated that *"Cloud is a parallel and dispensed framework consisting of a group of associated and virtualized personal computers that are progressively allocated and introduced as at least one bound together computational artifice in view of service-level agreements (SLA) built up through arrangement amongst the CSPs and shoppers."* [2].

> McKinsey & Company expressed that *"Clouds are hardware-based services offering compute, network and storage capacity where: 1) Hardware management is highly abstracted from the buyer. 2) Buyers incur infrastructure costs as variable OPEX. 3) Infrastructure capacity is highly elastic (up or down)."* [3].

> As per Vaquero *et al.,*: *"Clouds are a large pool of easily usable and accessible virtualized resources (such as hardware, development platforms and/or services). These resources can be dynamically assigned to adjust to a variable load, allowing also for an optimum resource utilization. This pool of resources is typically exploited by a pay-per-use model in which guarantees are offered by the Infrastructure Provider by means of customized SLAs."* [4].

> The National Institute of Standards and Technology (NIST)[a] characterizes cloud computing as *"a model for enabling ubiquitous, convenient, on-demand network access to a shared pool of configurable computing resources (e.g., networks, servers, storage, applications, and services) that can be rapidly provisioned and released with minimal management effort or service provider interaction."* [5].
>
> [a]https://www.nist.gov

> Armbrust *et al.* called cloud *"datacenter hardware and software"* which provide services [6]. The fundamental point of cloud computing is to consolidate the physical and computational resources and to send appropriate computational tasks to numerous dispersed personal computers.

In this digital period, customers basically prefer the pay-per-use method [7, 8].

2.2   Characteristics of Cloud

Some essential qualities of cloud computing that make it so admired are discussed below.

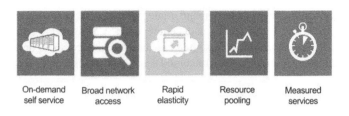

| On-demand self service | Broad network access | Rapid elasticity | Resource pooling | Measured services |

Figure 2.1: Characteristics of cloud.

2.2.1 Elasticity and Scalability

Cloud computing helps fulfill the dream of unending hardware and computational resources which are accessible upon request [6]. Consequently, from the user's perspective, computational and physical resources can be maintained whenever the amount of resources are required. A cloud framework should be able to provide sufficient computational resources in a flexible manner, expanding along with the number of clients or application stacks, and can discharge the resources when its job is over.

Scalability additionally characterizes an application that is fit for scaling itself when many customers and applications are included and furthermore when the design of utilization or application necessitates changes. It ought to be equipped for discharging the resources when the clients or applications are through with the service. Scalability allows the cloud framework to scale-up and downsize as per the prerequisites of the applications.

2.2.2 Metered and Billing of Service

While utilizing cloud framework, cloud subscribers don't need to know the fundamental engineering or the setup abilities. They don't have to keep up the hardware and framework resources. In any case, they utilize each of those hardware or framework or calculation resources and services. Obviously, these are not free under any condition. Cloud innovation enables the clients to ask for and encourages customers to use just the required amount of resources. Services should be asked for and valued according to the appropriate premise, such as continuously or constantly, which frees up resources when their job is done [6]. Accordingly, clouds should be equipped to permit exchanging services which incorporate accounting, payment and charging services [2]. Metering ought to be classified by the type of required services, for example, processing resources, storage, appliances and framework artifices. Hence, customers need to pay according to the amount of resources and services they utilize, which is the "pay-as-you-utilize" model. In this model, the amount of resources utilized are instantly revealed by metering and charged accordingly.

2.2.3 Self-Service Allocation of Resources

Cloud users basically require the services as per their requirements. The cloud customers are essentially asking for a specific measure of services, storage, processing capacities, and computational services from the CSPs. What's more, to service that demand, CSPs must provide a climate that encourages self-service. Self-service encourages customers to request and tweak payments as they utilize resources and services without manual intervention [5]. Assume an association is taking a shot at an application utilizing a cloud and the association needs to actualize the new application or include more enhancements to the current application; it needs to demand contemporary computational and hardware resources from the CSPs. Furthermore, data centers inside CSPs need to arrange themselves as per demand. So, allocation of resource capacities and services upon request reduces wait times and the customer receives the cloud service in almost a split second.

2.2.4   Application Programming Interface (APIs)

Cloud services need to fabricate an institutionalized interface that would encourage the clients to deal with the connections between monetary administration framework, auditing administration framework and restructuring administration framework. The standard is implied by an arrangement of normal, configurable and repeatable conventions which are resolved and shared by a few associations. So, these institutionalized stages, or then again interfaces, help the cloud customers benefit from the typical ways in which various applications or different data sources can be prepared to associate with each other.

2.2.5   Efficiency Measurement Service

The CSPs should have the capacity to to keep up the management system that screens the retrievals from data centers and IT services. For example, an affiliation is using a cloud service from an administration provider and this affiliation has composed its own data and administrations with the cloud. So, it requires some security with the goal that the inside information of the association must be securely kept. At the point when the association requires some more resources for upkeep of the extra enhancements and applications, it solicits the data centers, and the CSP runs a monitoring framework which screens the accessibility of the resources and the resources are maintained as required by the user. The administration framework screens the services, measures the efficiency, decreases time delays and enhances services.

2.2.6   Device and Location Interdependency

Cloud services encourage clients to get the calculation and appliance resources utilizing just an internet browser with no reliance on their area or what sort of gadget they are utilizing. A cloud foundation is arranged offsite and resources are received via the internet by the cloud customers. Without much stretch, interface with the foundation and resources can take place anywhere, paying little mind to the area they are in.

2.2.7   Customization

The framework and calculation resources must have a high degree of adaptability when the cloud customers lease a particular resource from the providers. Customization promotes an environment in which customers are permitted to send their applications onto cloud and resources are modified and arranged according to the needs of the customers. For instance, when an association conveys more enhancements and customers for a specific amount of time, it needs additional resources such as additional processing, information transfer capacity, computational resources and more CPU centers for that time period. And every one of the resources are arranged and modified, thereby having the enhancements and customers for that length of time.

2.2.8 Security

At the point when security is considered, it is enhanced due to information being consolidated. Be that as it may, the loss of control over certain delicate information is an annoyance. On the off chance that we take a look at the system level of security, we need to guarantee the privacy and trustworthiness of the information being transmitted to and from the cloud supplier. In any case, in a cloud framework, privacy can be a concern as the CSPs have access to the sensitive and private information of their customers.

2.3 Cloud Computing Environment

From a business perspective, each cloud administration considers the maximization of profit, but at the same time, the cloud providers need to satisfy the customers also.

2.3.1 Access to Supporting Business Agility

A standout amongst the most obvious repayments of cloud framework services is to affix or include a new foundation limit quickly and at an insignificant price. By and large, self-service allocation of resources enables customers to get resources in a self-service way with no human collaboration. Hence, computerized self-service prompts more adaptable cloud framework.

A regular service provider needs to stay on the leading edge of pricing to safeguard the economies of the organizations assisting the association with enough growth capacity.

2.3.2 Minimizing Investment Expenditures

An association needs to fabricate new business applications with the least amount of venture capital for computational and hardware resources for supporting its customers. The association may lease the computational and framework resources on a per-hour or per-storage-unit basis from a CSP who supplies this type of office.

Organization management is influenced when more customers or extra enhancements are increasingly added there to expend the service. To conceal the circumstance, the association either may develop new foundation or may lease resources from some CSPs with pay-as-you-go pricing. According to one cloud service provider, "it's smarter to lease than to purchase." In this way, the association can lessen its consumption by leasing the services from the CSPs.

While a client is going to get services from the CSP, the CSP may guarantee the security and privacy of clients. There are motivations for maintaining a few types of clouds for specific reasons, particularly the public cloud, private cloud, hybrid cloud and community cloud discussed below.

2.3.3 Public Cloud Computing Environment

As indicated by Armbrust *et al.* [3], a public cloud is a type of cloud computing made available in a pay-as-you-go manner to the public. In this public cloud architecture, hardware and computational resources and also the same foundation are used by the various customers. Public cloud forces some essential measures that make it so mainstream, which are given below:

- *Usable systematic load for application*: When an ever-increasing number of applications are sent into the cloud, hardware resources ought to be allocated in a proficient way and the cloud foundation ought to be fit for maintaining the load so the customers can utilize the administration with no interference.

- *High scalability*: Cloud has the property of being very adaptable. A gigantic number of customers utilize the general population cloud at a time and the public cloud is exceedingly equipped for giving every one of the services to the customers.

- *Testing and creating application*: Public cloud encourages customers to analyze and build up the applications.

- *Collaborating ventures*: Public clouds provide an architecture where the customers are encouraged to blend their activities and customers work together to develop a greater and more astute undertaking.

Public cloud gives the customers conventional standard services where resources are progressively allocated and used in light of the well-tuned, self-service premise of the internet, with the help of web applications/services. The email framework is a decent example of public cloud. For instance, when customers use email services like Yahoo or Gmail, they just need a personal computer with web association. Users don't have to bother with fundamental procedures. They are simply utilizing the Google/Yahoo cloud. Every kind of analysis and errand creation is finished by Yahoo/Google itself.

2.3.4   Private Cloud Computing Environment

At the point when customers need to anchor their own particular information, yet at the same time need to pick up cloud framework, they require private cloud. For example, suppose an association is maintaining a database of customers and empowers the customers to present their private data to the database. Furthermore, the association needs to manage the database privately and maintains its security. Consequently, the association needs to put its critical and private information in the private cloud that previously stayed within the organization's firewall. A few of the attributes built into the private cloud that make it very usable are given below.

- *Optimizes use of calculation ability and resource allocation*: It enables the IT business to provide customers with resource allocation and calculation capacity in a self-service and enhanced way to gain the most extreme output.

- *Less expensive*: Utilizing a private cloud makes the association very beneficial. For example, assume an association with an enormous datacenter is utilizing public cloud framework, during which time it needs to put radical enhancements into the current plan, and needs to lease the necessary resources from CSPs, which as a rule is very expensive. Hence, the association can use a private cloud in its firewall which is accommodating in order to decrease the price unpredictability of using a public cloud.

- *Supports particular loads*: Private cloud is harmoniously equipped for managing the particular loads inside the association. Restricted load encourages the private cloud to increase quick retrieval of resources.

- *Privacy*: With private cloud, an association can place particular information behind the association's firewall that drives the organization to maintain security and protect its information. The association needs to review the parts of information security; for example, information in transit (amid transmission), static information (in storage), information provenance (information trustworthiness and computational exactness), and information remanence (lingering information ostensibly being deleted or evacuated) [9]. Consequently, private cloud encourages the association and its customers to be casual about their information security.

- *Management control*: As each piece of information exists inside the association, it can proficiently deal with every piece of information itself. Furthermore, it has the expertise to control who gets the information. This means that the association controls every issue.

2.3.5 Hybrid Cloud Computing Environment

While public cloud manages general customers and private cloud connects with the clients devoted to a specific association, cloud providers consider blending the best of both to fulfill numerous business needs, which is known as hybrid cloud. A hybrid cloud is used in a circumstance where a private cloud is augmented with resources and computational power from public clouds [10]. A hybrid cloud foundation is a blend of public and private cloud. Hybrid cloud refers to a mixed computing, storage, and services environment made up of on-premises infrastructure, private cloud services, and a public cloud with orchestration among the various platforms.

For example, when an organization needs to utilize an SaaS application that would understand what is needed by the organization, i.e., security, protection and institutionalized use throughout the organization, the SaaS supplier makes a private cloud for the specific organization in their firewall with the goal that the whole organization may utilize the cloud as a benchmark. Currently, they give the organization a virtual private network (VPN) for greater security [11, 12].

Hybrid cloud has the qualities of both private and public cloud. Hybrid cloud is equipped to maintain the protection and security of the user information of its customers.

As another example, suppose an association provides services based on what various merchandisers need. Diverse customers may have to deal with delivery services for producers, payments for protection specialists, credit analysis services or some additional services. The association may need a public cloud in order to create an online domain where every client could access services and check on how things stand. Nevertheless, any user information the association has needs to remain in its own private cloud in order to keep it secure and deal with any problems that may come up.

2.3.6 Community Cloud Computing Environment

In the event of a joint undertaking application, an equivalent cloud foundation should be developed and shared by a few associations mutually, with the goal that they may have use of an indistinguishable structure as well as arrangements, services, necessities, applications, and problems [13]. A mixed-cloud approach is profoundly versatile and lessens the toll taken on multifaceted quality. The outsider seller or any of the merchants inside the network may have access to and maintain the network cloud framework [12]. At the point when an expansive application or huge task is to be completed that takes a significant amount of time, the network cloud foundation is in effect extremely useful for that reason, and as one of the sellers is maintaining the cloud framework, the intricacies of pricing are also lessened.

2.4 Cloud Services

Customers use the cloud services as per their requirements. CSPs convey the service on an on-demand basis. The cloud service model, shown in Figure 2.2, consists of RaaS, IaaS, PaaS and SaaS. Each of these is briefly discussed below.

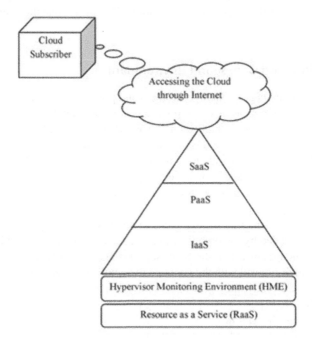

Figure 2.2: Cloud service model.

2.4.1 Resources as a Service (RaaS)

At the base of the cloud service stack, there is an accumulation of hardware components, such as storage, servers, transfer speed, data center space, and networks, that might be accessed and distributed by various CSPs. Presently, in the IT industry, resource virtualization is the key element of cloud computing and fast development of hardware and computational resource virtualization encourages the CSPs to use RaaS service needed for specific services. Later on we will discuss virtualization methods and various types of virtualization. In this flood of quickly developed resource virtualization, computational and framework resources are allocated according to the need of the cloud user.

2.4.2 Infrastructure as a Service (IaaS)

Infrastructure as a Service (IaaS) manages the foundation in which RaaS might be extended because of resource virtualization. IaaS provides virtualization innovation which includes the allocation of framework to the cloud customers. Customers may lease framework services as opposed to purchasing those services to diminish the multifaceted nature of pricing, and resource virtualization may encourage them to get those services. The ability to arrange processing, networks, storage and additional enforced computational resources, the endorsers can send their application and can run self-assertive programming that incorporates operating frameworks and applications. The purchaser of cloud services doesn't control/deal with the fundamental cloud framework but rather has control over the sent applications, operating frameworks, some systems administration segments, information transfer capacity and so on. The IaaS service underpins dynamic scaling and the distribution of resources. This cloud has ordinarily proved to be useful when the request-compose is unstable, which implies that when the specific undertaking is done, every one of the resources are returned to the resource storage area. What's more, this service is most productive when an association needs to build up a modern business and wouldn't like to spend an ample amount of time on developing resources in order to create another computational framework. Along these lines, we can state that from a business point of view, IaaS is extremely useful for diminishing price intricacy.

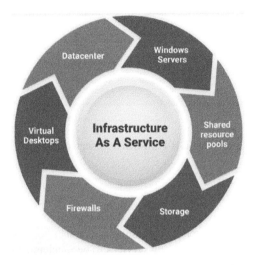

Figure 2.3: Infrastructure as a service (IaaS).

A standout among the most critical elements of IaaS is virtualization, which for the most part manages system, storage and calculation virtualization. The fundamental idea of virtualization is to store hidden foundation by creating an intelligent interface. Resources are virtualized and consistently spoken to in this layer. We will talk about various kinds of virtualization in Chapter 4 of this book.

2.4.3 Platform as a Service (PaaS)

Platform as a Service (PaaS), which has the ability to provide self-reliant framework having distribution capacities, might be fit for executing numerous applications on a sole framework simultaneously. The client might be allowed to make their own applications that could be kept running on the CSP's framework. PaaS provides interface to convey customer-created or distinctively obtained applications using different programming languages and different resources that are sustained by the CSPs. The customers do not have permission to restrain or deal with the basic cloud framework; however, they have control over their sent applications. Platform services incorporate gadget movement, gadget reconciliation, session administration, instrumentation and testing, condition arrangement, content administration, universal description, discovery, and integration (UDDI), and an extensible markup language (XML) registry that provides components for enrolling and finding web service applications.

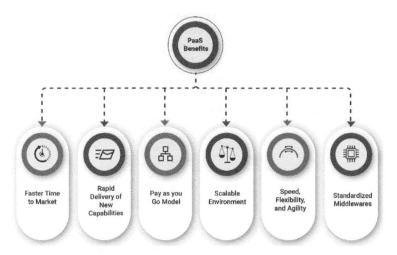

Figure 2.4: Platform as a service (PaaS).

Generally, PaaS is used where a substantial programming venture is working and when various developers and customers are planning to connect various programming modules in order for the organization and testing services to be mechanized. All things considered, cloud customers aren't required to understand the basic foundation of the cloud; however, they are eager to utilize the services and tweak the services further.

2.4.4   Software as a Service (SaaS)

Software as a Service (SaaS) utilizes applications conveyed by the CSPs in a specific cloud framework, which were available via different devices by means of a user interface similar to electronic mail. SaaS gives the architecture for programming use. Customers simply use the product service without Ariel software to maintain and refresh the product. It decreases the multifaceted nature of pricing as customers don't want to worry about each one of these problems. For example, perhaps customers can use Salesforce.com as their SaaS provider. The layer might provide prepared for use programming service and the customers don't have the stress involved in buying and maintaining the product [12]. Cloud customers don't need to understand the fundamental engineering of cloud foundation; they simply use the product. Essential modules of programming services may encourage the creation, conveyance and utilization of the product [14].

Figure 2.5: Software as a service (SaaS).

Programming services provided to the customers incorporate enterprise services close to work process administration, coordinated effort administration, digitized signature, supply chain management, programming conveyance services, financial administration, customer relationship management (CRM) and so on. Web 2.0 applications can include metadata administration, gateway services, social networking, blogs, etc.

To assist these service conveyance models, a few important services ought to be incorporated:

- Service management and resource allocation, operations administration, SLA administration, QoS administration, specialized help and reinforcements.

- Security administration which incorporates approval and confirmation, interruption avoidance, affirmation, control, review, infection insurance and firewalls.

- Allied online support based on the client's inclinations, personalized announcements.

- Collaborating with and incorporating the services through heterogeneous field is also something to think about.

2.4.5 Network as a Service (NaaS)

Although not a hosted server/application cloud-based service model, we feel Network as a Service (NaaS) needs a quick introduction at this point. The NaaS model allows your business to outsource the day-to-day burden of running your wide area network (WAN) connectivity. You can even outsource your LAN infrastructure if required. The network provider becomes responsible for your overall network connectivity when using NaaS; theretofore, you can enjoy time and cost savings due to overall simplification and performance gains.

NaaS providers, such as Amber Networks, are also capable of providing hosted cloud services over high speed connections directly from their core network ("on net"). This means that the traffic for your hosted cloud services does not have to traverse the public internet, but rather travels directly from your site to your NaaS provider's network, and then directly to your hosted cloud service.

2.4.6 Desktop as a Service (DaaS/VDI)

One further step that is becoming increasingly popular is removing most of the desktop support element from your local IT team by using the Desktop as a Service (DaaS) model. In this service model the provider hosts, manages and supports the virtual desktop infrastructure (VDI) environment and delivers that service securely either over the public internet or via a private network.

Your IT team can manage your own virtual desktop images and applications or have the provider perform that function for you.

2.4.7 Recovery as a Service (DRaaS)

The Recovery as a Service (RaaS) model (also known as DRaaS) allows you to use a single managed platform for all of your backup and disaster recovery needs. The RaaS provider's platform will allow you to backup and recover server operating systems, applications and databases.

RaaS is a cost-effective backup model that can help your business reduce the impact of downtime due to hardware and application failure by providing backup services for critical data and applications. RaaS can replicate your production services to a diverse backup infrastructure, so transitioning to the backup environment is quick and seamless.

2.5 Security Paradigms and Issues of Cloud Computing

Cloud computing relies on a change in perspective with ramifications in computational issues. Ideal models moving to cloud computing are the fundamental mainstay of progress in traditional computational models for addressing problems concerning information security and protection. The various components concerned with security and protection types of problems are shown in Table 2.1 and discussed below.

Table 2.1: Shared responsibility model for security of cloud computing.

On-Premises (for reference)	IaaS (infrastructure-as-a-service)	PaaS (platform-as-a-service)	SaaS (software-as-a-service)
User Access	User Access	User Access	User Access
Data	Data	Data	Data
Applications	Applications	Applications	Applications
Operating System	Operating System	Operating System	Operating System
Network Traffic	Network Traffic	Network Traffic	Network Traffic
Hypervisor	Hypervisor	Hypervisor	Hypervisor
Infrastructure	Infrastructure	Infrastructure	Infrastructure
Physical	Physical	Physical	Physical

| Customer Responsibility | Cloud Provider Responsibility |

- *User information restrained by third-party service*: Currently, domination is surrendered to the third-party services; thus, extraordinary security and protection problems concern allied unapproved ingress, information ingress restraint, information debasement, upgrading non-static allotment methodologies, restraining sensitive data stream and so forth. As far as third-party service is concerned, customers store their precise information in the database and storage service provided by a third party.

Thus, outsiders have the obligation to keep up the security and protection of the information, which is the reason why outsiders need to empower an inspecting service. As per information systems control and audit, IT reviewing could be characterized as a procedure of conglomerating and assessing confirmation to choose whether a computational information framework shields resources, maintains information trustworthiness and secures sensitive user information, accomplishes hierarchical goals adequately and expends physical and computational resources proficiently.

- *Information is stored in different locations which are regulated by numerous associations*: Cloud services are provided by various CSPs, which maintain hardware components, such as processors, memory and storage, in individualized parts. Therefore, the user information is stored in numerous locales which are controlled by a few associations. Thus, the purported "issue of numerous ways" could emerge based on the capacity of specialists and/or people to process and manage the administration by the accumulation, utilization, distribution and revealing of their personal information by others. Boundless universal information utilization, information sharing and pools of information storage among the associations would become an issue in the perplexing association of cloud services. It is very hard to verify who will assume the liability if anything undesirable happens to stored information. All the logging information must be checked and should keep information acquisition, information transmission or information change.

- *Accountability*: This is another part of protection and security. Sufficient data is needed with respect to how information is overseen by the CSPs so they can keep track of information acquisition, information transmission or information change. That is the reason why the representatives of associations authorize the standards and directions used to maintain bookkeeping records.

2.6 Major Cloud Service Providers

This section discusses some popular CSPs, including Amazon, Microsoft, Google, Sun and Yahoo, which epitomize utilization of cloud computing. These CSPs are being used by individual customers having the extensive ventures discussed below.

2.6.1 IaaS CSPs

Amazon Elastic Compute Cloud (EC2): This is a business web service which enables clients to lease personal computers on which to run and convey their personal computer applications. EC2 permits versatile arrangement of office applications by providing a web services interface and an organization platform over which a client can make virtual machines (VM), for example, server cases, where the client can put and run the product of their choice.

Amazon announced a limited public beta test of EC2 on August 25, 2006. Access to EC2 was allowed on a first-come, first-served basis. For the most part, EC2 turned out to be accessible on October 23, 2008 with the help of Microsoft Windows Server.

Amazon.com facilitates customer access with EC2 cloud as one of a few web services advertised under the sweeping title Amazon Web Services (AWS).[1] It started its service as

---

[1] http://aws.amazon.com

IaaS clouds with a variety of services, including S3 (for storage), CloudFront (content delivery), SimpleDB (for structured data storage), SQS (for reliable messaging), CloudFront Streaming (for video streaming), RDS (for relational database), and Elastic MapReduce (for information processing).

- *Small Instance*: The small instance (default) likens to "a framework with 1.7 GB of memory, 1 EC2 Compute Unit (1 virtual center with 1 EC2 Compute Unit), 160 GB of storage space, 32-bit framework."

- *Large Instance*: The large instance depicts "a framework with 7.5 GB of memory, 4 EC2 Compute Units (2 virtual cores with 2 EC2 Compute Units each), 850 GB of storage space, 64-bit framework."

- *Extra Large Instance*: The extra-large occurrence offers "what might as well be called a framework with 15 GB of memory, 8 EC2 Compute Units (4 virtual cores with 2 EC2 Compute Units each), 1690 GB of storage space, 64-bit framework."

Amazon charges customers in two primary ways:

- Hourly cost/VM.

- Information exchange cost.

The hourly VM rate is arrived at in view of the limit and enhancements of the VM. Amazon publicizes the evaluation plan as "pay for resources you consume."

Clients can begin and stop VMs to manage costs without much trouble, with Amazon estimating with hourly granularity. Few are ready to keep each virtual machine running close to the limit and pay just for CPU time really used.

FlexiScale: This is a UK-based CSP that offers services which are equivalent to Amazon Web Services. The virtual servers of this cloud provider offer features such as persistent storage by default, dedicated VLAN, fixed IP address, runtime adjustment of CPU, and a wider range of server sizes. FlexiScale cloud services are also priced by the hour.

In the current scenario in the UK, FlexiScale cloud is providing services such as Web service (SOAP), access to virtual server through SSH (Linux), web-based user interfaces, Remote Desktop (Windows), per hour pricing, automatic scaling, and in case of hardware failure, automatic recovery of VMs as per SLA.

GoGrid:[2] Similar to other IaaS CSPs, GoGrid permits its clients to use a wide range of Windows and Linux images, with a scope of fixed instance sizes. GoGrid provides the services like "value-added" stacks, which are prioritized more for various applications like e-commerce, web hosting and database services.

It also provides a new feature which makes it easier for customers to combine traditional dedicated hosts with the autoscaling infrastructure facility. Customers can take the benefits of dedicated hosting combined with on-demand cloud infrastructure, which leads to the user getting the advantages of each paradigm of computation.

Rackspace Cloud:[3] Rackspace provides infrastructure service that offers fixed instances of VMs in the cloud. Rackspace provides a wide scope of pre-made Linux-based images. In this cloud, RAM is measured per user-requested images. Like GoGrid, Rackspace servers combine dedicated hosts with cloud infrastructure to facilitate the customers accessing all of the features of automated cloud computing. It offers advantages such as enabling static (fixed) IP address, load balancing, and persistent storage.

---

[2]http://gogrid.com/
[3]https://www.rackspace.com

2.6.2 PaaS CSPs

Aneka:[4] the Aneka [16] cloud is an example of PaaS, which is a .NET-utilized platform which supports resource management and development. Each and every server acts like a cloud node and hosts Aneka container that provides the platform consisting of security and privacy, services for persistence, and control over communication. Customers request the required resources through a client to the Aneka master node, which acts as a reservation service manager and controls all the cloud nodes. Master node has the responsibility for scheduling the requests and distributing them.

The Aneka container is capable of hosting n number of other services which could be included by the developers to get the functionalities of an Aneka node.

App Engine:[5] Google App Engine lets the customers run their Python program and Java applications on the cloud infrastructures provided by Google. App Engine allows the customers to deploy their applications to scale dynamically and it supports the need for information storage scaling up and down according to the requirements of the customers. Google API (application programming interface) gives autonomous framework which has arrangement capacities and multi-tenure (fit for running numerous applications on a single framework simultaneously) engineering. The customer has the flexibility to make his own particular applications, which keep running on the supplier's foundation. PaaS providers offer a predefined course of action of OS and application servers [6, 17-25].

2.6.3 SaaS CSPs

Salesforce is a customer relationship management (CRM) platform, that conveys to organizations on the web utilizing the SaaS model.

Salesforce.com was established in 1999 by the previous Oracle official Marc Benioff. In June 2004, the organization opened up to the world on the New York Stock Exchange underneath the stock image CRM. Beginning speculators in Salesforce.com were Marc Benioff, Larry Ellison, Halsey Minor, Magdalena Yesil and Igor Sill of Geneva Venture Partners.

Salesforce is headquartered in San Francisco, California, and has home offices in Dublin, Singapore and Tokyo (covering Japan). Salesforce.com has its services converted into 15 distinct dialects and as of now has 43,600 clients and more than 1,000,000 endorsers.

2.7 Summary

Cloud computing has become a buzzword in the current IT industry as well as in academic research, which is strongly concerned with customer involvement with cloud service providers. The main concept behind cloud computing is on-demand sharing of resources available in the resource pool, which implies new emerging and promising business models. This chapter has described different perspectives on cloud computing along with the characteristics of cloud computing. Cloud service models and cloud deployment models have also been described. In the later part of the chapter, some examples of cloud CSPs were also discussed.

---

[4]www.manjrasoft.com/aneka_architecture
[5]https://cloud.google.com/appengine

EXERCISES

1. State the basic principles of cloud computing.

2. Why is cloud computing so popular in the era of the internet? Justify your answer with an appropriate example.

3. Explain how the cloud computing environment caters to the needs of customers and providers.

4. Are the cloud deployment models based on security and privacy issues or not? Justify your answer with suitable examples.

5. Justify the following: "Cloud is more suitable for the large organizations."

6. State some commercially available clouds for public, private and hybrid clouds.

7. State the characteristics of public cloud.

8. Are the cloud services used by the cloud user according to their requirements? Explain with suitable examples.

9. State the characteristics of private cloud.

10. How is the hybrid cloud infrastructure a combination of public and private cloud?

11. What is community cloud and how is it different from private and public clouds?

12. Give at least two examples where virtualization plays a significant role in RaaS and IaaS.

13. State the applications of PaaS and SaaS. And also give some examples of PaaS and SaaS.

14. What is IaaS? Give at least one commercially available service provider that allows the user to rent computers to run and deploy their applications.

15. Write short notes on:

    (a) Aneka Cloud
    (b) Salesforce.com
    (c) Google App Engine.

16. What is on-demand functionality? How is it provided in cloud computing?

17. What are the platforms used for large-scale cloud computing?

18. What are the different models for deployment in cloud computing?

19. What is the difference between cloud computing and mobile computing?

20. What is the difference between scalability and elasticity?

References

1. Foster, I. (2003). The grid: Computing without bounds. *Scientific American*, 288(4), 78-85.

2. Buyya, R., Yeo, C. S., Venugopal, S., Broberg, J., & Brandic, I. (2009). Cloud computing and emerging IT platforms: Vision, hype, and reality for delivering computing as the 5th utility. *Future Generation computer systems*, 25(6), 599-616.

3. McKinsey & Co. (2009). Clearing the Air on Cloud Computing, Technical Report, 2009. REFEREN CES 37

4. Vaquero, L. M., Rodero-Merino, L., Caceres, J., & Lindner, M. (2008). A break in the clouds: towards a cloud definition. *ACM SIGCOMM Computer Communication Review*, 39(1), 50-55.

5. Mell, P., & Grance, T. (2011). The NIST definition of cloud computing., *Information Technology Laboratory, Technical Report.*

6. Fox, A., Griffith, R., Joseph, A., Katz, R., Konwinski, A., Lee, G., ... & Stoica, I. (2009). Above the clouds: A berkeley view of cloud computing. Dept. *Electrical Eng. and Comput. Sciences, University of California*, Berkeley, Rep. UCB/EECS, 28(13), 2009.

7. L. Silva and R. Buyya (1999). *Parallel Programming Models and Paradigms*, High Performance Cluster Computing: Programming and Applications, Rajkumar Buyya (editor), ISBN 0-13-013785-5, Prentice Hall PTR, NJ, USA.

8. O'reilly, T. (2007). What is Web 2.0: Design patterns and business models for the next generation of software. *Communications & strategies*, (1), 17.

9. Mather, T., Kumaraswamy, S., & Latif, S. (2009). *Cloud security and privacy: an enterprise perspective on risks and compliance*. O'Reilly Media, Inc.

10. Sotomayor, B., Montero, R. S., Llorente, I. M., & Foster, I. (2009). Virtual infrastructure management in private and hybrid clouds. *IEEE Internet computing*, 13(5), 14-22.

11. Hurwitz, J. S., Bloor, R., Kaufman, M., & Halper, F. (2010). *Cloud computing for dummies*. John Wiley & Sons.

12. Pal, S., & Pattnaik, P. K. (2012). Efficient architectural framework for cloud computing. *International Journal of Cloud Computing and Services Science*, 1(2), 66.

13. Yang, J., & Chen, Z. (2010, December). Cloud computing research and security issues. In 2010 *International Conference on Computational Intelligence and Software Engineering* (pp. 1-3). IEEE.

14. Sarathy, V., Narayan, P., & Mikkilineni, R. (2010, June). Next generation cloud computing architecture: Enabling real-time dynamism for shared distributed physical infrastructure. *In 2010 19th IEEE International Workshops on Enabling Technologies: Infrastructures for Collaborative Enterprises* (pp. 48-53). IEEE.

15. Pal, S., Mohanty, S., Pattnaik, P. K., & Mund, G. B. (2012). A Virtualization Model for Cloud Computing, in the *Proceedings of International Conference on Advances in Computer Science* (AET_ACS_2012), December 2012, pp.10-16.

16. Vecchiola, C., Chu, X., & Buyya, R. (2009). Aneka: a software platform for .NET-based cloud computing. *High Speed and Large Scale Scientific Computing*, 18, 267-295.

17. Le, D. N., Kumar, R., Nguyen, G. N., & Chatterjee, J. M. (2018). *Cloud Computing and Virtualization*. John Wiley & Sons.

18. Le, D. N., Bhatt, C. M., & Madhukar, M. (Eds.). (2019). *Security Designs for the Cloud, IoT, and Social Networking*. John Wiley & Sons.

19. Mansouri, N., Ghafari, R., & Zade, B. M. H. (2020). Cloud computing simulators: A comprehensive review. *Simulation Modelling Practice and Theory*, 104, 102144.

20. Van, V. N., Long, N. Q., Nguyen, G. N., & Le, D. N. (2016). A performance analysis of openstack open-source solution for IaaS cloud computing. In *Proceedings of the Second International Conference on Computer and Communication Technologies* (pp. 141-150). Springer, New Delhi.

21. Van, V. N., Long, N. Q., & Le, D. N. (2016). Performance analysis of network virtualization in cloud computing infrastructures on openstack. In *Innovations in Computer Science and Engineering* (pp. 95-103). Springer, Singapore.

22. Hurwitz, J. S., & Kirsch, D. (2020). *Cloud computing for Dummies*. John Wiley & Sons.

23. Seth, B., Dalal, S., Jaglan, V., Le, D. N., Mohan, S., & Srivastava, G. (2020). Integrating encryption techniques for secure data storage in the cloud. *Transactions on Emerging Telecommunications Technologies*, e4108.

24. Prokhorenko, V., & Babar, M. A. (2020). Architectural resilience in cloud, fog and edge systems: A survey. *IEEE Access*, 8, 28078-28095.

25. Bohu, L., Lin, Z., & Xudong, C. (2020). Introduction to cloud manufacturing. *ZTE Communications*, 8(4), 6-9.

3

ARCHITECTURAL FRAMEWORK FOR CLOUD COMPUTING

Souvik Pal[1], Dac-Nhuong Le[2], Prasant Kumar Pattnaik[3]

[1] Sister Nivedita University, Kolkata, India
[2] Haiphong University, Haiphong, Vietnam
[3] KIIT, Deemed to be University, India
Email: souvikpal22@gmail.com, nhuongld@dhhp.edu.vn, patnaikprasant@gmail.com

Abstract
Cloud is an internet-based concept that tries to hide its underlying complexity from end users. Cloud service providers (CSPs) use many structural designs combined with self-service capabilities and ready-to-use facilities for computing resources, which are enabled through network infrastructure, especially in the internet, which is an important consideration. This chapter elaborately describes an efficient architectural framework for cloud computing that may lead to better performance and faster access.

This chapter focuses on the architectural framework along with the economic reasons like minimum investment on infrastructure, no need to assemble and maintain a large-scale system, low computing costs and no need for employee investments. Due to these economic advantages, clients benefit from minimizing the execution time of user applications, including data-intensive and compute-intensive applications. Moreover, the application developers can get an interface or platform where they can derive pleasure from the use of immediate and ready-made infrastructure and can feel free to design the related applications without any overhead in terms of where the application will be executed.

From a business point of view, cloud computing has a great advantage of reducing setup cost for service providers. Cloud service providers set up the cloud infrastructure, including bare metal hardware resources, system and computing resources in the primary level. And after that they are able to provide the services to the clients according their requirements. On the other side, the cloud users get the services from the providers without setting up any cloud infrastructure and also without making any investments in that particular service; only they have to provide the payment according to their usage.

The aim of cloud computing is to make the relation easy between the clients and providers. Hence, a good cloud architectural framework is needed so that the clients can easily deploy their application on the cloud platform and get the chance to design and test their applications. Therefore, this chapter focuses on the cloud framework where multiple users can get cloud service from the providers and also can deploy their application on the cloud platform irrespective of which operating system they are using. The main hold of cloud computing is the ability to use several servers according to the requirements of the users to provide an optimal response to the cost and time constraints of an application. It can be possible when the workload can be divided into different data centers using the virtual machines discussed in this chapter.

Keywords: Cloud service providers, service-oriented architecture, virtual machine

3.1 Challenges of Cloud Computing Environment

Cloud computing presents itself as a good servant to the end user, but it has some challenges and issues.

In the real-time system, it is too difficult to isolate the performance of the virtual machines, especially if the system is highly loaded. If the performance of virtual machines cannot be determined, cloud designers won't be able to distribute the workload among the several data centers.

Cloud computing involves shared networks, fluctuations in bandwidth and various topologies. Due to these constraints, cloud computing infrastructure reveals latency while transferring the data from one virtual machine to another. Therefore, it affects the performance of the deployed applications.

Security issues are also issues of cloud computing. It's very risky to put all the data of an organization in the hands of a cloud provider and running an application in another place is also at risky. A common problem is the threat of data loss due to a phishing attack. Therefore, privacy and reliability should be maintained during transportation and storage of the data. Cloud is made for sharing the workload in a common infrastructure and users have to rely on the cloud provider for their identity information, operation histories and perceptive data. Cloud is not responsible for unauthorized usage and its retrieval, lack of user administration and third-party access. From a piracy aspect, there is a pool of resources and millions of software applications and services being run publicly. So it's very easy to pirate floating data from all those things and use it in an unauthorized way without any identification and authentication. It irritates a customer when CSPs promise to deliver a service but due to over-utilization are not able to meet their needs. Internet latency is also a drawback of cloud computing, which hampers the CSPs ability to deliver services on time. In regard to auditing, in a particular service or application, the CSP and the end user have the authoritative control over the data. CSP has the authority to replicate, shift and alter the data. That's why the clients need to keep watch over all those activities so that the CSP can't act beyond its domain. But it is not practical to audit all the data and also complicated to decide which data needs to be audited [1]. Moreover, multi-tenancy is also a problem if the number of applications running on a particular node is going to increase, in which case the bandwidth allocated to each application decreases, which means that the number of applications and allocated bandwidth is inversely proportional. This reduces the performance of the system.

3.2   Architectural Framework for Cloud Computing

Cloud computing involves request-response communication between the clients and stateless server. In the case of stateless server, a client doesn't need to first establish a communication to the server; instead, the server views a client request as an autonomous transaction and responds to the client.

Cloud computing uses a stateless server due to some of the following obvious reasons:

- If the server node fails due to some technical faults or natural disaster, it will create a considerable overhead because of maintenance of the state of all the connections.

- If a stateless server goes down, the clients won't be affected because no data or no information from the client's side will be lost.

- The clients need not be concerned about all the states of the server; if a client gets a response to a request, that indicates the server is running and quite capable of handling a request.

- A stateless server is more advantageous than a connection-oriented service. In the connection-oriented service, the states of all the connections have to be stored and that will take up space in the memory. So, the stateless server is also memory efficient.

The common example of a stateless server is a web server. The web server need not keep the history and states of the past interactions with client; it just responds to the HTTP (Hypertext Transfer Protocol) request made by the clients. HTTP is basically a request-response application protocol which is used to communicate between the web servers and the clients, i.e., a web browser. Web browsers are also stateless; neither the clients nor the web browsers need to reserve the state of the server; they just send the requests and wait for the reply from the web server.

The following subsections deal with the service-oriented architecture (SOA), the need for SOA in cloud computing, its characteristics, and combining the strategy of SOA and cloud architecture.

3.2.1   Service-Oriented Architecture (SOA)

Cloud computing environment has basic characteristics like self-service provisioning, pay-as-go, elasticity, and on-demand usage. The main concept behind the cloud architecture is its of modular framework-based approach which makes cloud so popular. A component-based and modular-based approach of cloud architecture enables the cloud characteristics. What lies under the cloud framework or cloud flexibility is the modular approach of service-oriented architecture (SOA). So, this subsection presents a basic overview of service-oriented architecture.

Jothy Rosenberg and Arthur Mateos have defined SOA as follows [10]:

> *"A flexible set of design principles used during the phases of systems development and integration. A deployed SOA-based architecture provides a loosely coupled suite of services that can be used in multiple business domains. SOA separates functions into distinct units, or services, which developers make accessible over a network (usually the internet) in order to allow users to combine and reuse them in the production of applications. These services, and their corresponding consumers, communicate with each other by passing data in a well-defined, shared format (usually XML), or by coordinating an activity between two or more services."*

Service-oriented architecture is a paradigm for organizing and utilizing distributed capabilities that may be under the control of different ownership domains. Service is a mechanism to enable access to one or more capabilities, where the access is provided using a prescribed interface and is exercised consistent with constraints and policies as specified by the service description [11]. In a service-oriented architecture environment, end-users request an IT service (or an integrated collection of such services) at the desired functional, quality and capacity level, and receive it either at the time requested or at a specified later time. Service discovery, brokering, and reliability are important, and services are usually designed to interoperate, as are the composites made of services. In the service-oriented architecture approach, service-based solutions are the major vehicle for delivery of information and other IT-assisted functions at both individual and organizational levels, e.g., software applications, web-based services, personal and business computing.

> *Consider an example to understand the application of SOA and also get an idea of how SOA and cloud computing are combined to provide services to customers. Let's take a corporate travel reservation system which requires the SOA approach and SaaS service. A corporate travel reservation system is required to fulfill requests for reservations with multiple airlines and hotels for corporate employees traveling on business trips. An approach for design of travel reservations solution for use by corporate business travelers based on service-oriented architecture, software as a service, and cloud computing paradigms can be taken as an example of cloud. Here a single copy of software can be made available to consumers on demand as a shared service accessible over remote network location and charged on subscription or pay-per-use basis. The term SaaS denotes application software provided in such a way [12].*

3.2.2   SOA Characterization

The main features and key characteristics of SOA are described below so that the readers can easily understand the real use of SOA in cloud computing and why the SOA characteristics are combined with cloud architecture.

- *Black-box component concept in SOA*: The main feature of black box is reusability of existing business applications. When the developers are mounting new applications, they feel free to reuse the advantages of existing applications; black box is simply adding adapter to them. The service consumers don't really need to be on familiar terms with the details of what is going on inside each component. SOA hides the underlying structure and the complexity.

- *Loose coupling*: Previously, in traditional structure, the different software components are extremely dependent on each other and that makes the applications more complex and time-consuming. A bit change on one component makes lots of changes in others. So, to make the applications more feasible to the customers, the components of SOA have been made loosely coupled, which is the independent modular approach which makes the developer feel free to keep the software modules together and reuse them according to the needs of the user. Loosely coupled components can interchange the data between them after processing. One component does its task and passes the data to another neighboring component which carries out the job and either keeps the data or passes on the data accordingly. You might be a bit confused regarding the software module. What is a software module? How is it used? How can it be reused? However, we will consider an example so that we can understand the concept of software module. Software module is nothing but a collection of coding. If users want to access resources from their service provider, they make a request to the provider. The provider handles the request and gives permission. So, there is a need for authentication and authorization. This is done with a coding component. This code can be done in an application-specific or independent coding way. The latter is more useful because we can use this type of independent coding as a software module and with some modification of this coding module we are able to reuse that component.

- *Service-oriented architecture*: SOA supports an environment where different components are arranged in such a way that SOA is able to deliver a business service. While designing SOA service, developers incorporate some service-level agreements (SLA) so that a standard platform can be built for business management. This is called business process management (BPM). BPM is highly required to maintain the alignment of business service.

3.2.3 Life Cycle of Services in SOA

Now we are moving on to the life cycle of services in SOA. A service life cycle is required to understand the sequential activities, processes and the physical and computing resources necessary for designing, building, developing, deploying and finally executing and delivering the services that make up SOA.

When a service is requested, then it has to be realized in a business process and has to be processed in a particular service life cycle. To understand how a business service can be realized in real-time procedure, Figure 3.1 shows a schematic diagram of the service life cycle in SOA.

- *Service analysis*: This is the analytical study of a particular business process and its rationalization of capabilities in different fields of business service like service contracts, agreements, globalization, etc. Driven by the different strategies and policies of the service provider, the business case is established, and those strategies and policies will be used in future stages.

- *Service development*: After the analysis phase, the development phase creates the business service as required by the customers. It is the phase where service developers write the coding part which leads to rationalization of different contracts and business service is implemented through this phase. Service developers also create the web-based interface through which the customers can easily get the services.

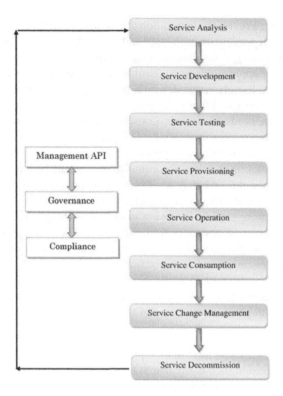

Figure 3.1: Life cycle of SOA.

- *Service testing*: Service testing is the phase which comes after the development phase and it contains a test data module for testing purpose. In this phase, in-progress software can be periodically checked for errors, regressions, and also for debugging. Sometimes, performance testing and functional testing is also done in this phase for maintaining quality of service (QoS).

- *Service provisioning*: When the testing phase is completed, service is ready to be utilized and the service is provisioned to the users. While consuming the service, the users have to maintain the service-level agreements (SLA) because they are using properly designed production infrastructure. When each term and all the rules and regulations of SLAs are found satisfactory, dedicated business service is successfully provisioned to the customers.

- *Service operation*: This is a key phase in the life cycle. There are various types of activities done by the Management API, which is the management infrastructure responsible for the following operations: metered usage of services, performance optimization, service updating, enabling authentication, authorization procedure, maintaining data privacy, generating business strategies, providing dynamic provisioning, monitoring transactions, reporting, and keeping metadata.

- *Service consumption*: This can be understood by its name alone. A business service is consumed by the users. Service is getting consumed through web services; whenever service providers validate some business services, the customers as well as the providers maintain some regulations, which are as follows: security policies, service dependencies, agreement level policies, resource provisioning rules, service syntax and semantics, and also capability.

- *Service change management*: In any IT business application or business service, there may be a sudden change while interacting with the customer. So there is a phase that has the authority to control the service change management, keeping in mind that the existing customers should not be affected. In addition to security, privacy as well as SLA policies, the technology platform change is of primary concern in this phase. This phase leads the service developers to be more flexible.

- *Service decommissions*: In this phase of the cycle, data is transferred and unused data are cleaned up. An acknowledgment message is also transferred from the user and even from the related organization's end. As there are changes in different business strategies, service providers try their best to provide better services. And this phase also has the ability to decommission services.

3.2.4 Integrating SOA and the Cloud

We have already discussed the cloud services and also basic concepts of SOA. Cloud services benefit from service-oriented orchestration. The modular approach of SOA is advantageous and getting attached with cloud services. When cloud services and the service-oriented approach are combined, service providers benefit because they can provide the services according to the requirements of the cloud users. Moreover, cloud users also get the advantages of this combinatorial approach because they are getting services according to how much they need. So, they have to pay for how much they have used. And this is the concept of "pay-per-use."

Cloud architectures are built in such a way that components can be reused in an efficient way and those will be effectively compatible with the service-oriented approach. In the SOA approach to modeling software, software is organized in terms of services, each capturing reusable functionality that can be discovered at run time and accessed in a location transparent manner through well-defined, open standards technology-based interfaces. Although SOA is not a new concept, it has been receiving considerable attention in recent years [8].

In an SOA environment, end users request an IT service (or an integrated collection of such services) at the desired functional, quality and capacity level, and receive it either at the time requested or at a specified later time. Service discovery, brokering, and reliability are important, and services are usually designed to interoperate, as are the composites made of services [8].

Hence, we can see that the SOA-based approach is quite suitable for designing cloud services. While designing the cloud architecture, the cloud architects and cloud developers can easily get the benefits of SOA and are able to provide the services according to the needs of the users. The main purpose of this approach is to deliver the business service to the customers with minimal cost and also efficient use of resources.

In the next subsection, we will focus on the architectural framework of cloud computing. We will describe the modular approach of cloud computing which is the combination of cloud services and SOA.

3.2.5   Cloud Architecture

This subsection, deals with hybrid architecture issues of the cloud. Each cloud client or end user or employee of an organization accesses the operating system, software application, network, bandwidth, and storage via the internet, as shown in Figure 3.2.

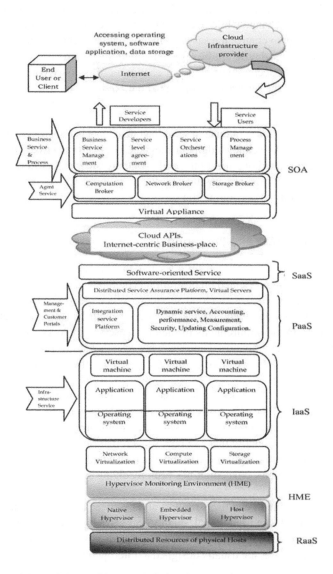

Figure 3.2: Architecture of cloud computing environment.

The entire hybrid framework may be subdivided into two important layers [5] as cloud platform architecture (CPA) and cloud application architecture (CAA). In between the CPA and CAA layer, there is a connecting layer which is the cloud provider, which is associated with cloud APIs and is available in the internet-oriented business area of the IT industry. The significance of two layers is discussed below.

3.2.5.1 Cloud Platform Architecture

Cloud platform architecture is the base architecture of cloud, which includes the cloud service-oriented architecture. In a CPA reference model, we classified the CPA model into the following sublayers:

1. *Distributed resources of physical hosts*: Resources of physical hosts are distributed over the lowest level of the framework. These resources are logically represented as a multiple numbers of virtual machines (VMs) through resource virtualization. Resources are basically a pool of processors, memory, CPU cores, storage, networking components, etc. All those resources are efficiently provisioned to the cloud users through virtualization technique. Resources virtualization is discussed in the fourth layer.

2. *Cloud hypervisor*: Cloud hypervisor is designed like a mainframe operating system that allows other operating systems to run on the same machine concurrently. It monitors the access of guest operating systems (users' operating systems). Hypervisor monitoring environment (HME) administrates the system by letting the guest node enter the system and handle the memory management of the VMs, e.g., VMware, Hyper-V, KMV, Xen.

3. *Resources virtualization*: The concept of virtualization is the most important basic sub-block of the cloud framework. Virtualization is the process by which we can hide the underlying infrastructure by inserting a logical layer. The three basic resources, i.e., computation, network and storage, are virtualized and represented logically in this layer. Resource virtualization can be considered as the most important layer of the cloud stack. Resource virtualization is that which mainly deals with network, storage and computation virtualization. The basic concept of virtualization is to hide underlying infrastructure by creating a logical interface which helps customers deploy their application onto their respective VMs and also makes provisioning the resources to users easier. We will elaborately discuss different types of virtualization in the next chapter.

4. *Virtual machines (VMs)*: These are the abstraction level of real host machines and each VM is dedicated to each application. Multiple numbers of virtual machines are there to support multiple operating system and application instances. These VMs provide greater scalability, flexibility, and better performance. The details of VMs are presented in the subsequent chapter.

5. *Distributed service assurance platform*: This platform helps to create FCAPS (Fault, Configuration, Account, Performance, Security) virtual servers [6] that allow hosting the operating systems and executing the applications. It provides dynamic service, accounting, and performance optimization, enabling security and updating configuration. Creation of FCAPS virtual servers provide automated mediation services to ensure better performance, reliability and fault management.

> *Automated mediation service is that which provides the capability to compose logical virtual servers which assures Quality of Service (QoS) and proper resource provisioning. Cloud service providers offer these virtual machines or the virtual servers including proper management API (application programming interface) component to the developers so that they can easily develop self-optimized and self-configured business services.*

6. *Software-oriented service*: This module provides ready-to-use software service. The end users do not incur any overhead for purchasing and maintaining the software.

3.2.5.2 Cloud Application Architecture

Cloud application architecture is basically service-oriented architecture (SOA), which helps users/clients get their on-demand service. This reference model will help the service providers and end users maintain controlled access and dynamism in real-time applications. This architecture includes three sublayers, namely virtual appliances, agent-based layer and business service provider. Each of these sublayers is discussed below.

1. *Virtual appliances*: These run with the APIs (application programming interface) of various customer service providers (CSPs) or platforms. It is an instance of virtual environment extension (VEE). Cloud applications are deployed as virtual appliances to make management better. Virtual appliance configuration should be done in such a way that the application and services continue to grow but management overheads do not grow proportionally.

> *VEE (virtual environment extension): Basically, it is fully isolated runtime environment which abstracts away the physical characteristics of the resource and also enables sharing. The VEEs create partitioning by the virtualization layer within a site to optimize the resource utilization.*

2. *Agent-based layer*: In this layer, cloud agents are like brokers between the virtual appliances layer and business service and provider (BSP) layer. The main aim of the cloud agents is the optimal arrangement of VEEs into CSPs configured and managed by the service manager. What does optimal arrangement mean? Suppose there are multiple users in a particular instance of time and all are intended to get the services. Then the cloud broker places the VEEs optimally so that resources can be provisioned in a maximized way. And from the perspective of cost complexity, both cloud provider and cloud user also benefit from this optimal arrangement or optimal placement of VEEs.

> *Cloud brokers have the authority to move throughout the VEEs and are also free to place and move different sites, even remote sites, until the arrangement is satisfied. At broker level, when a service is deployed on the cloud, it is realized as a set of interrelated virtual environment extension or as a VEE group. Hence, all the activities can be done as a whole. Simply put, we can say that cloud brokers are responsible for arranging the deployment order and rollback policies, and maintaining the service workload depending upon the dynamic nature of the applications. And cloud brokers also have the authority to change the capacity of a single VEE or to add and remove the present VEEs from existing group [9].*

3. *Business service provider (BSP)*: The BSP layer consists of business service management (BSM), service-level agreement (SLA), service orchestration, and process management. It provides common infrastructure elements for service-level management, metered usage, policy management, license management, and disaster recovery [7].

> *BSM handles the business service policies. It manages the different services requested by the clients. It also provides the different quality of service (QoS) parameters negotiated in SLA when the business agreement was established. SLA is concerned about business-oriented agreements and laws. SLA contains some specific rules and regulations which are established between the service provider and service user. According to their agreement, cloud users can access the resources and can also renew the agreement for getting further service. Process management schedules and manages the processes. Service orchestration is the component which is responsible for ordered arrangements of the requests. Process management system schedules the processes according to their priority or provisioning strategy of computing and physical resources.*

3.2.5.3 Framework Constraints

The cloud model delivers quality service to the customers, but not free from some of the constraints given below:

- *Dependability on hypervisor*: As hypervisor controls all access to VMs and monitors the environment, the hypervisor failing or crashing or an attack on it by hackers may lead to performance degradation.

- *Standardized platform*: Each organization has its own APIs, services, policies and different rules and regulations. So in a cloud platform, it's quite difficult to maintain the combination of all those things from various organizations and interoperability of all the applications is also a mammoth task.

- *Energy efficiency*: Although cloud computing provide various types of on-demand services and running applications, it requires a lot of power. And hypervisor monitoring system also requires a huge amount of electricity to monitor the access to VMs. So, energy efficiency is also a concern in cloud computing.

3.3 Architectural Workflow and Co-ordination of Multiple Activities

This section includes architectural workflow when an application is deployed on the cloud platform. Workflow style is presented here to help you easily understand the steps involved in executing and managing an application. The concept of workflow is not new. Workflow technologies first emerged in the mid-1970s with simple office automation prototypes at Xerox PARC and the Wharton School of the University of Pennsylvania. In the early 1990s, workflow and office automation gained new life.

According to Dave Green and John Evdemon, workflow is defined as follows:

> *"Workflow is fundamentally about the organization of work. It is a set of activities that coordinate people and/or software. Communicating this organization to humans and automated processes is the value-add that workflow provides to our solutions. Workflows are fractal. This means a workflow may consist of other workflows (each of which may consist of aggregated services). The workflow model encourages reuse and agility, leading to more flexible business processes."*

In their research article, Monika Bharti and Anju Bala [15] have described different categories and different functionalities. They are as follows:

> "*Workflow works behind cloud to manage resources, various clients, cost constraints. The concept of workflow is proposed by fixed work procedures with conformist activities. The tasks are divided into subtasks, roles, rules and processes to execute and observe the workflow; workflow system boosts the level of production of organization and work efficiency. Various types of workflows are business workflow, abstract workflow, concrete workflow, scientific workflow and so on. Business workflow allows controlled flow of execution and simplifies workflow management. It provides support for security, reliability, transactions, and performance. Its performance can be increased by use of faster server. Its workflow lifecycle is design, deployment, execution, monitoring and finally refinement. Scientific workflow supports large data flows and needs to do parameterized execution of large number of jobs. It is also to monitor and control workflow execution including ad-hoc changes. The input given to workflow is written in languages like Java, Perl, Python and the output generated is the workflow. These workflows are managed and coordinated by workflow management system, which provides the end users with the required data and the appropriate application program for their tasks. It allocates tasks to end-user based only on the performance of constraints like control flow, data flow, transition conditions or pre- and post-conditions. The issues that arise with workflow and its management are workflow scheduling, fault tolerance, energy efficiency and so on. Workflow scheduling maps and manages the execution of inter-dependent tasks on the distributed resources. Fault tolerant is when a system's service failure can be avoided when faults are present in the system.*"

3.3.1 Characteristics of Workflow

The key characteristics of workflow are co-ordination and interaction between different modules, duration of a process, and human interaction. Already we have gone through the modular approach of cloud computing architecture; there are different software-based components or modules which are assigned to different tasks. So, there is a need for workflow co-ordination and proper interaction between different modules. We can also predetermine or measure the approximate duration that can be calculated in weeks, days, hours, and even minutes. Human interaction is a considerable part of the process because, after all, cumulative work of human interaction has made all of this possible.

3.3.2 Need for Workflow

This section discusses the need for workflow.

- Workflow modeling is required for monitoring schema, insight, and performance optimization. For monitoring schema, knowing which individuals are contributing work to which business process is very useful when trying to understand costs and workloads. A group of interrelated workflow models is there to be used to gain insight into the stream of the work. Through this workflow model, the service developers can provide the module-wise functionalities; so they can bring the modules together for a particular task to optimize the business process which leads to the performance optimization.

- A model-driven approach describes the workflow system. Service developers are using UML diagram and other modeling techniques for implementing the workflow system. Many workflow tools are also used for that purpose only. Workflow system also provides a state machine model and sequential model; these provide an overview of how workflow is going on in the system.

Apart from that, at the end of this discussion, we can conclude that workflow management is also responsible for the following functionalities: Automation of individual business process, compliance report, customization of predefined workflows, ready-to-use forms and workflows, development and integration of company-specific processes, tool sets for graphical process modeling and simulation, transparent workflow process, and email notification for workflow process.

However, in a workflow system, one term is often used, and that is business process, which is defined as a collection of related, structured activities which provide a particular service for the customer.

Davenport [16] defines a (business) process as:

> *"A structured, measured set of activities designed to produce a specific output for a particular customer or market. It implies a strong emphasis on how work is done within an organization, in contrast to a product's emphasis on what. A process is thus a specific ordering of work activities across time and space, with a beginning and an end, and clearly defined inputs and outputs: a structure for action... Taking a process approach implies adopting the customer's point of view. Processes are the structure by which an organization does what is necessary to produce value for its customers."*

Rummler and Brache [17] use a definition that clearly encompasses a focus on the organization's external customers, when stating that

> *"A business process is a series of steps designed to produce a product or service. Most processes (...) are cross-functional, spanning the 'white space' between the boxes on the organization chart. Some processes result in a product or service that is received by an organization's external customer. We call these primary processes. Other processes produce products that are invisible to the external customer but essential to the effective management of the business. We call these support processes."*

Following are the basic functionalities that support the workflow system:

- Build-time functions are concerned with defining, and possibly modeling, the workflow process and its constituent activities.

- Run-time control functions are concerned with managing the workflow processes in an operational environment and sequencing the various activities to be handled as part of each process.

- Run-time concerns interactions with human users and IT application tools for processing the various activity steps.

3.4 Examples of Workflow Tools

Various tools are used for the workflows in cloud computing environment. In their paper, Monika Bharti and Anju Bala [15] elaborately describe different workflow tools and their respective operating system, the language they are written in, year of release, developer of the tools, description of the tools, architectural style, database used, and respective companies [16-25].

Table 3.1: Workflow tools in cloud computing.

Tool	Language	Year	Link
UGENE	C++, QtScript	12/2011	ugene.net
Bonita Open Solution	Java	01/2011	www.bonitasoft.com
Google App Engine	Python, APIs, URL fetch	2008	cloud.google.com/appengine
OrangeScape	Java	2003	www.orangescape.com/
Kaavo	Java, PHP	2007	kaavo.com.cutestat.com/
Oozie	hpdl	2006	oozie.apache.org/
Pegasus	Java, Perl, Python	2003	www.pegasuscloud.cf/
YAWL	XML, XPath and XQuery	2002	www.yaug.org

- **UGENE**: It is a free open-source cross-platform bioinformatics software, which integrates a number of biological tools and algorithms, and provides both graphical user and command line interfaces. It was developed by UniPro in December 2011. Operating system used is cross-platform, C++ and QtScript is used in language background, it is based on client-server architecture and database used in UGENE is NCBI, PDB, UniProtKB/Swiss-Prot.

- **Bonita Open Solution**: The French National Institute for Research in Computer Science developed the Bonita Open Solution in January, 2011. The business processes can be graphically modified using Bonita Studio. The processes can also be connected to other pieces of the information system to generate an autonomous business application accessible as a web form. It creates high-tech workflows and spreadsheets. Like UGENE, cross platform is used and Java is the developing language. It is based on client-server architecture and ERP, ECM database is used.

- **Google App Engine**: Google developed Google App Engine in 2008, which allows the users to run web application. It is also in client-server pattern and the database used in App Engine is Python or Java. Windows OS is used and Python, APIs, and UrlFetch are used as languages.

- **OrangeScape**: It is an India-based software development company with its headquarters in Chennai, India. It was founded by Suresh Sambandam, who currently serves as chief executive officer at OrangeScape. In 2002, it was named the prime technology partner for Google App Engine.

- **Kaavo**: It provides a framework to mechanize the deployment and run-time management of applications and workloads on multiple clouds. It takes a top-down application-centric approach for deploying and managing applications in the cloud.

- **Oozie**: It is a Java web application that runs in a Java servlet container. Oozie work-flow is a collection of actions arranged in a control dependency DAG (direct acrylic graph), specifying a sequence of actions execution, specified in hPDL (a XML process definition language).

- **Pegasus**: Ewa Deelman developed Pegasus in 2003, which is based on client-server architecture. It translates complex computational tasks into workflows. Operating system used is Linux and Windows and language used is Java, Perl, and Python.

- **YAWL**: A new workflow language called YAWL (Yet Another Workflow Language) offers comprehensive support for the control-flow patterns and has a proper formal foundation. It also has unique support for dynamic workflow through the worklet approach. Workflows can thus develop over time to meet new and changing require-ments.

3.5 Summary

This chapter has presented the architecture of cloud computing. Cloud computing architectures are essentially subdivided into cloud platform architecture (CPA) and cloud application architecture (CAA), which are linked via the cloud services available on the IT utility marketplace. This chapter also discussed the SOA concept, life cycle of SOA and integration with cloud computing. Fundamentals of the workflow concept were also presented and some workflow tools were discussed at the end of the chapter.

EXERCISES

1. Discuss the framework of cloud computing environment with suitable schematic diagram.

2. What is service-oriented architecture? Explain its characteristics.

3. State and explain the life cycle of service-oriented architecture.

4. What is workflow? How does it coordinate multiple activities in cloud computing environment?

5. Discuss the importance of workflow and state at least one work tool and its working principle.

6. Discuss the challenges of cloud computing environment.

7. What are the various reasons for cloud computing using a stateless server?

8. Provide a real-time example where SOA and cloud computing work together.

9. What is black-box component in SOA?

10. How is the SOA and the cloud integrated and state its workflow principle.

11. Explain different types of hypervisors.

12. Explain network, compute and storage virtualization.

13. What is broker service? Explain different types of broker service.

14. What is distributed resources of physical host?

15. Explain the role of virtual appliance.

16. What are the differences between cloud platform architecture (CPA) and cloud application architecture (CAA)?

17. "Workflow is defined in different ways." Justify.

18. What is the usage of utility computing?

19. What are the security benefits of cloud computing?

20. What are the open source cloud computing platform databases?

References

1. Hall, J. A., & Liedtka, S. L. (2007). The Sarbanes-Oxley Act: implications for large-scale IT outsourcing. *Communications of the ACM*, 50(3), 95-100.

2. Buyya, R., Yeo, C. S., & Venugopal, S. (2008, September). Market-oriented cloud computing: Vision, hype, and reality for delivering it services as computing utilities. In 2008 *10th IEEE International Conference on High Performance Computing and Communications* (pp. 5-13). Ieee.

3. Pal, S., & Pattnaik, P. K. (2012). Efficient architectural framework for cloud computing. *International Journal of Cloud Computing and Services Science*, 1(2), 66.

4. Dash, S. K., Mohapatra, S., & Pattnaik, P. K. (2010). A survey on applications of wireless sensor network using cloud computing. *International Journal of Computer Science & Emerging Technologies*, 1(4), 50-55.

5. Tianfield, H. (2011, October). Cloud computing architectures. In 2011 IEEE International Conference on Systems, Man, and Cybernetics (pp. 1394-1399). IEEE.

6. Sarathy, V., Narayan, P., & Mikkilineni, R. (2010, June). Next generation cloud computing architecture: Enabling real-time dynamism for shared distributed physical infrastructure. In 2010 19th IEEE International Workshops on Enabling Technologies: Infrastructures for Collaborative Enterprises (pp. 48-53). IEEE.

7. Buyya, R., Yeo, C. S., Venugopal, S., Broberg, J., & Brandic, I. (2009). Cloud computing and emerging IT platforms: Vision, hype, and reality for delivering computing as the 5th utility. *Future Generation computer systems*, 25(6), 599-616.

8. Swagatika, S., & Pattnaik, P. K. (2011). Design Criteria of SOA for Cloud Based Infrastructure Resource Management as a Service. *International Journal of Instrumentation, Control & Automation (IJICA)*, 1(1).

9. Rochwerger, B., Breitgand, D., Levy, E., Galis, A., Nagin, K., Llorente, I. M., ... & Ben-Yehuda, M. (2009). The reservoir model and architecture for open federated cloud computing. *IBM Journal of Research and Development*, 53(4), 4-1.

10. Rosenberg, J., & Mateos, A. (2010). *The cloud at your service*. Manning Publications Co..

11. Pioneer Consulting Report (2006). *The WiMAX Report Emergence of Fixed & Mobile Solutions.*

12. ITU, S. (2004, March). 05, Broadband mobile communications towards a converged world, ITU. In MIC Workshop on shaping the future mobile information society, Seoul.

13. Marinescu, D. C. (2017). *Cloud computing: theory and practice.* Morgan Kaufmann.

14. Evdemon, J. (2007). *Service Oriented Architecture (SOA) in the Real World.*

15. Bharti, M., & Bala, A. (2012). Workflow management in cloud computing. *International Journal of Applied Information Systems (IJAIS).*

16. Thomas Davenport (1993). *Process Innovation: Reengineering work through information technology.* Harvard Business School Press, Boston.

17. Rummler & Brache (1995). *Improving Performance: How to manage the white space on the organizational chart.* Jossey-Bass, San Francisco.

18. Le, D. N., Kumar, R., Nguyen, G. N., & Chatterjee, J. M. (2018). *Cloud Computing and Virtualization.* John Wiley & Sons.

19. Le, D. N., Bhatt, C. M., & Madhukar, M. (Eds.). (2019). *Security Designs for the Cloud, IoT, and Social Networking.* John Wiley & Sons.

20. Van, V. N., Long, N. Q., Nguyen, G. N., & Le, D. N. (2016). A performance analysis of openstack open-source solution for IaaS cloud computing. In *Proceedings of the Second International Conference on Computer and Communication Technologies* (pp. 141-150). Springer, New Delhi.

21. Van, V. N., Long, N. Q., & Le, D. N. (2016). Performance analysis of network virtualization in cloud computing infrastructures on openstack. In *Innovations in Computer Science and Engineering* (pp. 95-103). Springer, Singapore.

22. Hurwitz, J. S., & Kirsch, D. (2020). *Cloud computing for Dummies.* John Wiley & Sons.

23. Seth, B., Dalal, S., Jaglan, V., Le, D. N., Mohan, S., & Srivastava, G. (2020). Integrating encryption techniques for secure data storage in the cloud. *Transactions on Emerging Telecommunications Technologies*, e4108.

24. Seth, B., Dalal, S., Le, D. N., Jaglan, V., Dahiya, N., Agrawal, A., Mayank M. S., Deo P. & Verma, K. D. (2021). Secure Cloud Data Storage System Using Hybrid Paillier-Blowfish Algorithm. *CMC-Computers Materials & Continua*, 67(1), 779-798.

25. Prokhorenko, V., & Babar, M. A. (2020). Architectural resilience in cloud, fog and edge systems: A survey. *IEEE Access*, 8, 28078-28095.

4

VIRTUALIZATION ENVIRONMENT IN CLOUD COMPUTING

Souvik Pal[1], Dac-Nhuong Le[2], Prasant Kumar Pattnaik[3]

[1] Sister Nivedita University, Kolkata, India
[2] Haiphong University, Haiphong, Vietnam
[3] KIIT, Deemed to be University, India
 Email: souvikpal22@gmail.com, nhuongld@dhhp.edu.vn, patnaikprasant@gmail.com

Abstract

This chapter deals with virtualization, which is the most important characteristic of cloud infrastructure. Virtualization presents a logical view of original things. In real-time scenario, when a user opens their computer icon, some hard drive partitions appear such as `Local Disk (: C)`, `Local Disk (: D)`, `Local Disk (: E)` and so on. The partition is the logical division of a hard disk drive to create a user-friendly view of multiple numbers of separate hard drives. Are there really multiple numbers of separate hard drives? No, not at all. You have probably seen your hard disk in your computer. It is only a single device. Hence, virtualization is a technique by which a logical view of actual things can be undertaken.

In cloud computing environment, there are a multiple number of servers connected through a network which make an environment through virtualization technique that creates an interface on which users can access data and deploy their applications without their needing to know the underlying process, such as our hard drive example.

Keywords: Virtualization, virtual machine, system virtual machine, distributed resources

4.1 Introduction

> For simplicity, take another example regarding virtualization, and that is virtual memory. Disk has much more memory than primary memory. When a large number of processes are running, it requires more memory to run all the processes. So, virtual memory mapping technique (mapping of primary memory to disk memory) is there to provide enough memory for all the processes to run effectively. Although the user doesn't know the underlying process, they can easily run all the processes. Logically they are using main memory but actually they are using disk memory.

4.1.1 Need of Virtualization in Cloud Computing Environment

In the IT industry, virtualization helps to create more dynamic and flexible datacenter with virtualization environment. This is going to help to meet enterprise application service-level agreements (SLAs) and increase the efficiency of application provisioning. Virtualization helps the small organization reduce the capital expenses by server consolidation and improve operational cost through automation.

Virtualization supports automated operations management which deals with newly created dynamic virtual infrastructures to deliver cost-efficient services, improve operational efficiency, and ensure compliance and privacy. The key facilities provided by virtualization are as follows:

- Virtualization helps to increase energy efficiency, which leads to reducing cost complexity.

- Virtualization requires less hardware component with server consolidation.

- It supports different SLAs from different organizations to deliver better performance.

- Virtualization reduces capital and operational expenses, which results in an organization being more profitable.

4.1.2 Virtualization versus Traditional Approach

Virtualization uses computer resources to imitate other computer resources or whole computers. A virtualization environment that enables the configuration of systems (i.e., compute power, bandwidth and storage) as well as helps the creation of individual virtual machines has become the essential technology of cloud computing environments. Virtualization provides a platform for optimizing complex IT resources in a scalable manner (efficiently growing), which is ideal for delivering services. At a fundamental level, virtualization technology enables the abstraction or decoupling of the application payload from the underlying physical resource [1]; that means machine resources can be changed or transformed into virtual or logical resources on-demand, which is known as provisioning.

In a traditional approach, there are mixed hardware environment, multiple management tools, frequent application patching and updating, complex workloads and multiple software architecture. But comparatively, in cloud data center there is the far better approach of homogeneous environment, standardized management tools, minimal application patching and updating, simple workloads and single standard software architecture [2]. Table 4.1

shows the advancements of the traditional approach due to virtualization in a tabular format so that the readers can understand the basic differences between traditional computing and cloud computing.

Table 4.1: Traditional computing vs. cloud computing.

Traditional Computing	Cloud Computing
1. Manually Provisioned	1. Self-provisioned
2. Dedicated Hardware	2. Shared hardware
3. Fixed Capacity	3. Elastic Capacity
4. Pay for entire capacity	4. Pay-per-use
5. Capital & Operational Expenses	5. Only Operational Expenses
6. Managed through system administration	6. Managed through Application Programming Interface (APIs)

4.2   Virtualization and Virtual Machine

This section deals with virtualization and virtual machines (VMs). A virtual machine is basically defined as "an efficient, isolated duplicate of a real machine." Virtual machines have no direct interaction with any real hardware. A virtual machine may be defined as a software implementation of a computing and operational environment on which system software like an operating system (OS) or application software like user programs can be installed and also run. The virtual machines typically emulate a physical computing environment, but requests for CPU, hard disk, memory, network, and other bare metal hardware resources are managed by a virtualization level that translates these requests to the underlying metallic physical hardware level infrastructure. VMs are created within the virtualization layer; the operating system, running on the servers or data centers, can be referred to as host operating system and the operating systems in each virtual machine partition are called guest operating systems. The operating systems that run on the virtualization platform can be referred to as virtual machine monitor (VMM). The operating systems communicate with the hardware via virtual machine monitor which can also be called the machine controller program (see Figure 4.1). The virtual machine monitor virtualizes the hardware for each virtual machine.

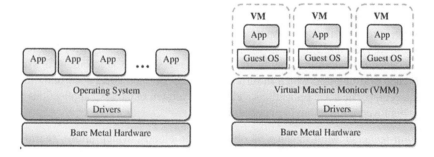

Figure 4.1: Virtual machine scenario.

Typically, guest operating systems and programs are not aware that they are running on a virtual platform. For example, the guest operating system might appear to have a physical hard disk attached to it, but actual I/O requests are translated by the virtualization layer so they actually occur against a file that is accessible by the host operating system. To help you understand, we present a schematic diagram of both virtualized and non-virtualized system.

Virtual machines can provide several advantages over the installation of operating systems and software directly on the physical hardware. Isolation ensures that applications and services that run within a virtual machine are not able to interfere with the host operating system or other virtual machines [3]. Virtual machines can also be easily moved, copied, migrated, and reassigned between the host servers to optimize the hardware resource utilization. Administrators may also use the advantages of the virtual environments to simplify backups, new deployments, disaster recovery, and basic system administration tasks. The use of virtual machines also comes with several important management considerations, many of which can be addressed through general systems administration best practices and tools that are designed to manage virtual machines [4].

An operating system along with one or more applications can run in an isolated partition within the computer [5]. It enables different operating systems to run in the same computer concurrently as well as prevents applications from interfering with each other. The virtual machine manager (VMM) starts at the time of system booting. All virtual machines run simultaneously. For simplicity, we can say that each virtual machine is like a "machine within the machine" and functions as if it owned the entire computer.

> The major characteristic of virtualization is the capability to make the abstraction of technical complexity from the cloud users, so that it can easily increase independence of cloud services. Secondly, physical and computing resources can be efficiently utilized after appropriate configuration, considering that on the same machine multiple applications are able to run. Thirdly, fault tolerance and quick recovery are also permitted. Virtual environment can be easily backed up and migrated with no interruption in service [6].

4.2.1 Advantages of Virtualization Technique in Cloud Computing Environment

Some of the advantages of virtualization technique in cloud computing environment are given below:

1. *Consolidation*: Various operating systems are able to run on the same particular server, reducing the requirement of a dedicated single machine to a particular application. New and existing applications can run simultaneously with their respective preloaded operating systems in multi-core servers which are combined with many threads of execution, which in turn saves space and also energy consumption in the datacenter. The new applications and the new version of existing applications can also be deployed without buying new hardware.

2. *Multi-tenancy*: Multi-tenancy is obligatory in clouds, which allows sharing of resources and costs across multiple users. Multi-tenancy is a principle in software architecture where a single instance of the software runs on a server, serving multiple client organizations (tenants). Multi-tenancy brings service providers several

benefits, such as centralization of infrastructure in different locations with minimized costs and increment of utilization and efficiency with high peak load. Tenancy information, which is stored in a separate database but altered concurrently, should be well maintained for isolated tenants. Otherwise, some problems such as data protection will arise.

3. *Stability and security*: Security is one of the major concerns for adoption of cloud computing. There is no reason to doubt the importance of security in any system dealing with sensitive and private data. In order to obtain the trust of potential clients, providers must supply the certificate of security. For example, data should be fully segregated from one to another, and an efficient replication and recovery mechanism should be prepared if disasters occur. The complexity of security is amplified when data is distributed over a wider area and also shared by unrelated users. However, the complexity minimization is necessary, due to the fact that ease-of-use capability can draw the attraction of more potential clients. Multiple virtual machines running essential user applications are kept safely isolated from each other. In addition, the process of isolation makes the system more secure because each virtual machine is isolated from the remainder of the others and therefore a security violation in one virtual machine does not affect the others. The security and fault tolerance brought about by the isolation of each virtual machine is a key advantage of virtualization.

4. *Development flexibility*: A virtualized machine can host several versions of an operating system, allowing developers to test their programs in different OS environments on the same machine. In addition, with each application running in its own individual virtual partition, one virtual machine crashing will not overthrow the system.

5. *Migration and cloning*: Virtual machine migration is a cloud infrastructure capability that is gradually being increasingly utilized. It is the key feature of virtualized technologies. Virtual machine live migration is basically transferring its instances that include the operating system, run-time memory pages, and active CPU states from a source host to the destination host. Virtual machines, each having their own operating systems and applications, perform respective tasks like self-contained packages, which is called "decoupled from the hardware." It is relatively easy to move a virtual machine from one host physical machine to another host machine that is either currently running or will be running or booted up after placing the new VMs as well as recovering from hardware failure.

4.2.2   Category of Virtual Machine

A virtual machine (VM) is a software implementation of a machine (i.e., a computer) that executes programs like a physical machine. Virtual machine can be categorized based on its relationship with the real machine. Each of them is capable of running multiple independent instances of one operating system or different operating systems, all of which behave as though they are solely in control of the system. Virtual machine may be classified as system virtual machine and process virtual machine.

4.2.2.1 *System Virtual Machine*

A system virtual machine enables one computer to behave like two or more computers by sharing the host's hardware resources. Multiple virtual machines, each running their own operating system (its operating system is called guest operating system), are frequently utilized in server consolidation, where different cloud services are used to execute on separate machines to avoid interference and instead are run in individual virtual machines on the same physical machine. The requirement to execute multiple operating systems was the actual inspiration for virtual machines, as it permitted time-sharing a single computer between numerous single-tasking operating systems. In some cases, a system virtual machine can easily be measured as a generalization of the idea of virtual memory that historically preceded it. The use of virtual machines to support different guest operating systems is becoming popular in embedded systems; a typical use is to support a real-time operating system at the same time as a high-level operating system such as Linux or Windows.

A schematic diagram of a system virtual machine is presented in Figure 4.2. On the hardware or host machine, virtualizing software is there to virtualize the resources, which can be referred to as VMM, and above the VMM, guest operating system is run and that operating system is quite capable of handling the user application. From the user's point of view, they are using the hardware infrastructure through virtual machine; and while the user request comes to the cloud service provider (CSP), according to the need of the user, a particular virtual machine is created and the resources are provisioned. When the task is completed, the virtual machine is also destroyed or we can say it shuts down.

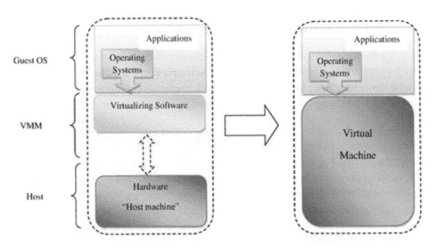

Figure 4.2: System virtual machine.

Common examples of system virtual machines are: Atlas Transformation Language (ATL), VMware (ESX Server, Fusion, Virtual Server, Workstation, Player and ACE), Xen (Opensource), Windows Virtual PC (formerly Microsoft Virtual PC), and Microsoft Virtual Server.

4.2.2.2 *System Virtual Machine Advantages*
The system virtual machine has some of the following advantages:

- Various OS instances may co-exist on the same particular computer, but in strong separation and also running time isolation from each other.

- The virtual machine may provide instruction set architecture (ISA) that is rather different and distinct from that of the real machine.

- The system virtual machine may be utilized in application provisioning, high availability of resources, maintenance, and disaster recovery.

4.2.2.3 Process Virtual Machine

A process virtual machine, sometimes referred to as an application virtual machine, runs as a normal application process inside operating systems and also supports a single process. A process virtual machine is created when that particular process is started and also destroyed when it exits. The process virtual machine aims to provide a platform-independent programming environment which abstracts away the details of the underlying infrastructure or hardware or operating system, and also allows a program to execute in the same way on any platform.

A process virtual machine is able to provide a high-level abstraction — that of a high-level programming language. Process virtual machines are implemented using an interpreter; performance comparable to compiled programming languages is gained by the use of just-in-time compilation.

A schematic diagram of a process virtual machine is presented in Figure 4.3 below. Above the bare metal hardware of host machine, a host operating system is installed and after that a virtualizing software is there to virtualize the hardware resources in run-time environment. Likewise, the system virtual machine creates a particular VM according to the needs of the user and the resources are provisioned. When the task is completed, the virtual machine is also destroyed or shut down.

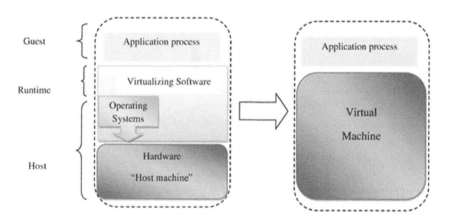

Figure 4.3: Process virtual machine.

The common examples of process VMs are Dalvik virtual machine, which is a part of Android operating systems, Java Virtual Machine, Macromedia Flash Player, SWF,[1] Vx32 virtual machine,[2] application-level virtualization for native code.

---

[1] SWF: It is an Adobe Flash file format which is used for graphics and multimedia.
[2] Vx32: It is an application level virtual machine which is implemented as user-mode library and is designed to run x86 code

4.3   Virtualization Model for Cloud Computing

An enhanced service model [12] involved in the mapping of virtual machines onto the host machines is presented in Figure 4.4 below. While accessing operating system, network, data storage or software applications through the internet from the service provider, cloud users have to send the request according to their needs and the hardware and computing resources are provisioned and virtual machines are mapped by the hypervisor administrator as shown in the Figure 4.4.

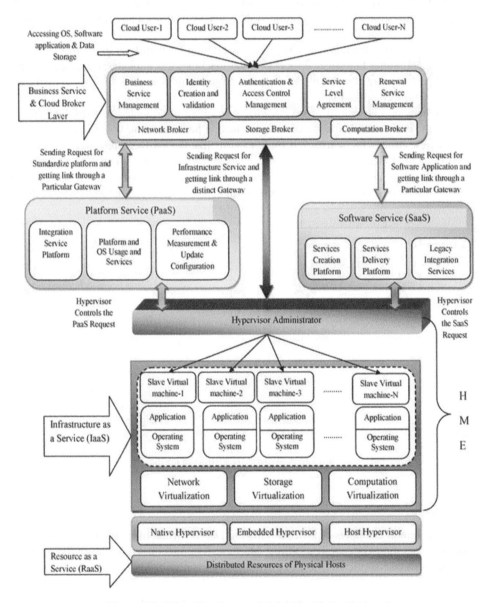

Figure 4.4: Virtualization model for cloud computing.

4.3.1 Distributed Resources of Physical Hosts

At the base level of the cloud stack, there is a pool of resources of physical hosts in the distributed manner. Physical hosts are nothing but a collection of processors, memory, CPU cores, and storage, which are provisioned to the user and logically presented as several members of VMs through the process of resource virtualization.

4.3.2 Hypervisor Monitoring Environment (HME)

Over the physical hosts, there is a hypervisor monitoring environment layer that consists of hypervisor, resource virtualization, VMs and hypervisor administrator. Suppose a cloud user needs an infrastructure-based service. While requesting infrastructure and resources, hypervisor is available from the booting time of the system to manage the allocation of physical and computing resources from the resource later across multiple VMs, which would be mapped depending on the availability of the physical hosts.

4.3.2.1 Hypervisor

Hypervisor is basically a mainframe operating system which allows other operating systems to run on the same system concurrently [7]. Access to VMs is controlled by the hypervisor. Hypervisors may be categorized into three types [8]:

- *Native hypervisor*: This type of hypervisor is designed to reside directly over the hardware platform for providing better performance.

- *Embedded or bare metal hypervisor*: To get high performance and reduce the time complexity, embedded hypervisors are integrated with processors on a separate chip.

- *Host hypervisor*: This kind of hypervisor acts as a separate software layer over both operating system and hardware to get improved performance.

4.3.2.2 Virtualization Layer

One of the most important layers of cloud stack is virtualization, which mainly deals with network, storage and computation virtualization. The basic concept of virtualization is to hide underlying infrastructure by creating a logical interface. Resources are virtualized and logically represented in this layer.

- *Network Virtualization*: Network virtualization involves in implementing virtual networks within the physical server for switching between all the virtual servers instead of multi-pathed or multiplexed network channels by directly trunking them to WAN transport, and multiple HBAs and NICs may be needed for each application provided with a high-speed single Ethernet connection [11].

- *Storage Virtualization*: The key driver of storage virtualization, storage networking and server virtualization is fiber channel (FC) and FC-based storage area networks (FC-SAN), which facilitate storage connectivity (very high speed) and storage solutions like point-to-point replication and serverless backup [11]. It also helps to optimize the performance of the servers on which multiple applications are running, and this technique has enabled numerous advancements in the datacenter.

- *Computation Virtualization*: This leads to virtualization of computing resources. Computing resources like server virtualization and operating system virtualization has enabled the transformation from the server-centric traditional computing to network and internet-centric computing. Operating system and server virtualization create the virtual (logical) servers which are free of constraints of the underlying physical location and physical infrastructure, and the virtualization may facilitate moving the workloads from source VM instance to target VM instance, which is called live migration [9, 11].

4.3.2.3 Virtual Machine (VM)

Virtual machines are like the interface to the user, which have their own operating system (Guest OS) hosted by the host operating system. Instead of interacting with a single computer, virtual machines should have the capability to facilitate the aggregation of system and computing resources from multiple machines and they should present a consistent and unified view to the users and the applications. The basic responsibility of VMs is to support multiple OS and application instances and to provide greater scalability and better performance.

4.3.2.4 Hypervisor Administrator

In a cloud computing environment, hypervisor administrator may have the main responsibility to control access to VMs. It should monitor how the computing and system resources are distributed and circulated for virtualization and how virtual machines are mapped onto the host machines so that the data and computing resources can easily be retrieved from the resource pool by the CSPs or the cloud user. When the system is booting up, hypervisor is accessible and hypervisor administrator may regulate the allocation of system and computing resources and VMs are mapped onto the host machine according to need of the user or the application. Hypervisor administrator should have the capability to manage both the resources within the server (locally) as well as the resources located in the other servers connected to the network [11].

4.3.3 Platform Service

Platform service should have the ability to create FCAPS-oriented (Fault, Configuration, Account, Performance, and Security) virtual servers [11], which should allow hosting the guest operating systems and executing user applications.

- *Integration platform as a service*: This block has the responsibility to integrate the resources for multiple applications and for the guest operating system. There will be different kinds of guest operating systems; hence, this should be platform independent.

- *Platform and OS usage and services*: In this block, virtual servers may load and host the preferred choice of operating systems that allow the loading and executing of the user application. In a cloud platform, application developers create and deploy applications and do not necessarily need to know the underlying resources or infrastructure.

- *Performance measurements and update configuration*: Virtual servers have the responsibility to manage performance measurements, performance optimization, fault management and reliability and accounting. This block allows the service developers to create self-managed and self-configuring business workflows.

4.3.4 Software Service

This layer may provide ready-to-use software service and the clients need not incur any overhead for buying and maintaining the software [7]. Cloud users need not understand the underlying architecture of cloud infrastructure; they just use and access the software. Basic blocks of software services may facilitate the creation, delivery and usage of the software discussed below [11].

- *Services creation platform*: This block may provide the tools which can be used for creation of applications. Applications are called collection of services and they can be created and distributed over the virtual servers created and controlled by the platform service.

- *Services delivery platform*: This can be defined as a workflow engine that should be capable of executing the application and management of the orchestration of multiple distributable workflow elements.

- *Legacy integration services*: This block may provide the services which can support integration of legacy or existing application. Support for inheritance or legacy of previous application is the key responsibility of this block.

4.3.5   Broker Service

Cloud brokers act as the agents between the virtual environment and business service layer. The main goal of the cloud broker is to create an optimal arrangement of virtual environment of CSPs, which is configured and managed by the service manager. In order to serve local requests the cloud broker would have the responsibility for the federation of remote sites [10]. Like the virtualization layer, there are network brokers, storage brokers, and computation brokers, each with their own responsibility to look after the virtualization respectively. They should be able to move throughout the virtual environment and also remote sites until the configuration and arrangement is satisfied.

4.3.6   Business Service

Business service layer provides different aspects of business controls and services like service management, identity creation and validation, authentication and access control management, service-level agreement, and renewal service management.

- *Business service management*: This block may help to manage the service orchestration, service conditions, and process management. The service manager should be able to derive a collection of desired resources and their configuration, and also placement constraints according to licensing, cost, confidentiality, etc. Process management has the authority to schedule and manage the processes. The service manager also has the responsibility to monitor the deployed services and adjust their capacity (number of VM instances).

- *Identity creation and validation*: Creation of user identity and its validation is the key responsibility of this block. When a new user comes up in the market, they need to create his/her identity and this module may identify proper validation for deployment of user application.

- *Authentication and access control management*: Authentication has the responsibility for effective governance and proper management of the authenticated process. Access control management service enables policies and rules for access control in response to a request from a client who is in need of resources, and this block is also responsible for operating system access control and network access control.

- *Service-level agreement (SLA)*: SLA management is a key aspect of business service. SLA concerns business aligned rules and policies. Distributed resources like network, storage and network are provisioned but should not be the cause of an SLA violation of any application executing with greater than predefined threshold line. Hence, the service agreement should be maintained to keep the rules of an organization.

- *Renewal service management*: This is responsible for renewal of policies, rules and access controls. Validation and updated SLAs should also be under the renewal service. This service basically is a smooth interacting medium for internet-centric places of business where both clients and CSPs could interact for their business and IT Infrastructure.

4.4   Categorization of Guest OS Virtualization Techniques

Virtualization improves the management of the system at no extra cost [12, 13]. For example, the hard drives can be separated into different partitions and there is no need to buy multiple hard drive to achieve the same goal. The principal aims of virtualization are to increase the hardware utilization to a maximum, decrease hardware costs by regrouping multiple machines virtualized into one physical machine, minimize power consumption and make things easier for security and system management. To virtualize the hardware of the physical machine, the utilization of a virtual machine monitor (VMM) is required [14-25].

There are three main techniques that can be used to virtualize a guest operating system:

- Full virtualization

- Paravirtualization

- Hardware-assisted virtualization

4.4.1   Full Virtualization

Full virtualization requires a virtualizable architecture; the hardware is fully exposed to the guest OS which runs unchanged and this ensure that this direct execution mode is efficient. In full virtualization architecture, guest operating systems are provided with all the services given by physical computing systems, including virtualized memory, virtual devices and also virtual BIOS. The full virtualization requires the hardware abstraction layer of the guest operating system to have some knowledge about the hardware. A full virtualization operating system doesn't know that it is being virtualized, which is the reason why modification is not required.

In Figure 4.5, VMM and guest operating system will run on level-0 and level-1 respectively. To run the guest operating system without any modification, a particular technique is used, which is known as binary translation.

Binary Translation: The VMM monitors the execution of guest operating systems; non-virtualizable instructions executed by a guest operating system are replaced with other instructions.

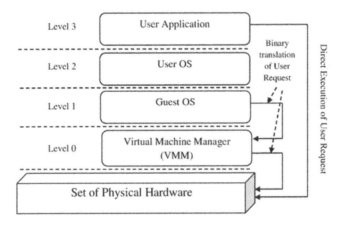

Figure 4.5: Operation performed to implement full virtualization at the kernel level.

For example, VMware EXS memory management unit full virtualization on x86 architecture. The virtualization of the MMU (memory management unit) and the fact that privileged instructions executed by a guest operating system fail silently pose some challenges.

4.4.2 Paravirtualization

Paravirtualization is a process that is used to virtualize a guest operating system. It is mainly helpful because it provides better performance than hardware-assisted or full virtualization. The reasons for adopting paravirtualization are as follows:

- Firstly, some features of the hardware can't be virtualized.

- Secondly, it is used to present users a simpler interface. Paravirtualization demands that the guest operating system be modified to run under the VMM; also, the guest operating system code must be ported for individual hardware platforms.

Paravirtualized guest operating system is capable of communicating directly with the hypervisor and for that reason, as shown in Figure 4.6, to communicate with the hypervisor or VMM, guest operating system needs the translation non-virtualizable instruction with hypercalls.

For example, Xen and Denali are based on the technique of paravirtualization.

Hypercalls: Hypercalls are a set of instructions which are able to make direct communication with the virtualization layer. Portability problems and low compatibility are shortcomings of modification of the guest operating systems.

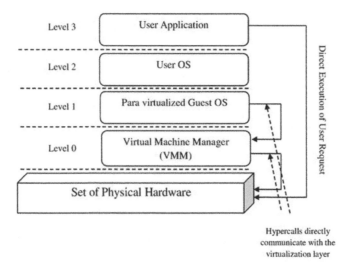

Figure 4.6: Operation performed to implement paravirtualization virtualization at the kernel level.

4.4.3   Hardware-Assisted Virtualization

Questions about the shortcomings of paravirtualization have been raised due to modification of hardware that allows the guest operating system to communicate with the hypervisor or VMM without any modifications, which may be overcome by hardware-assisted virtualization. Hardware-assisted guest operating system (level-1) is capable of communicating directly with the hypervisor (level-0) and for that reason, as shown in Figure 4.7, to communicate with the hypervisor or VMM without any paravirtualization or binary translation.

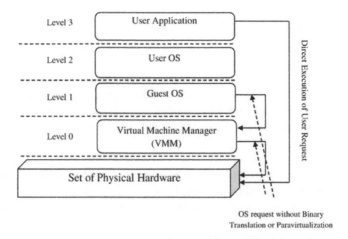

Figure 4.7: Operation performed to implement hardware-assisted virtualization at the kernel level.

4.5 Mapping Technique of Virtual Machine to Physical Machine in a Private Cloud

This section deals with a mapping approach of virtual machines onto host machines depending on the availability of the distributed resources [13]. We have defined our system as S where the set of virtual machines (V) are to be mapped onto the set of physical host machines (H); and pool of physical resources are denoted by P.

$$P = \{CPU cores, Memory, Storage, I/O, Bandwidth, Networking\} \quad (4.1)$$

According to the user needs like IT infrastructure, platform service or software usage, virtual machine instances are created by the hypervisor administrator who controls the mapping of virtual machines.

Let us consider *VS* as Virtual Machine set:

$$VS = V_1 + V_2 + \cdots + V_m = \sum V_i \quad (4.2)$$

$$V_i = \{vc, vm, vr\} \quad (4.3)$$

where

- vc = Number of CPU Cores
- vm = Main Memory
- vr = Storage Capacity
- m = Number of Virtual Machines

Now we considered HS as a Set of host machines:

$$HS = H_1 + H_2 + \cdots + H_n = \sum H_i \quad (4.4)$$

$$H_i = hc, hm, hr \quad (4.5)$$

where

- hc = Number of CPU Core
- hm = Main Memory
- hr = Storage Capacity
- n = Number of host machines.

Now we divide the host set into two subsets:

$$HS = HS_a + HS_b(a + b = n). \quad (4.6)$$

where

- HS_a = Set of physical machines having available resources to host VMs and on which VMs can be mapped.
- HS_b = Set of remaining physical machines not having enough resources to host VMs and on which VMs cannot be mapped.

Let $f : V_i \rightarrow HS_a$ be the Function which maps VM instance to the set of physical machines having enough resources to host the VM. There may be either one-to-one mapping or many-to-one mapping. In one-to-one mapping, one VM instance may be mapped onto one host machine and in many-to-one mapping, many VM instances may be mapped onto one host machine.

Function $f : V_i \rightarrow H_i$ describes the one-to-one mapping and function $f : \sum V_i \rightarrow H_i$ maps many-to-one mapping from the host set HSa based on the requirements and workload of the use.

Algorithmic Approach: Here, we are going to show an algorithmic approach [13] which leads to mapping of virtual machine onto physical machine in a private cloud.

Initial consideration:

It should be initially considered that the sufficient resources (cores, memory, and disk) are available on physical host machines on which the guest Virtual Machines are to be mapped. The amount of hardware and computing resources required by the entire guest VMs and also guest OSes mapped onto a host must not exceed the resources of the given host.

In the initial state, none of the VMs is mapped yet, therefore

$$VS = V_1, V_2 \cdots , V_m \qquad (4.7)$$

$$VS' = \varnothing \text{ and } HS' = \varnothing. \qquad (4.8)$$

Necessary conditions for mapping:

- If multiple numbers of VMs are running on the same host machine, these VMs must not interfere with each other in terms of physical resources, which means that each and every VM should run in its distinct address space.

- It should also be considered that each VM is mapped exactly once to a physical host.

- Algorithm will be successful when all the VMs will be mapped onto some physical host, i.e., $VS = \varnothing$. [All VMs have been mapped].

- The failure condition will occur when some of the VMs will not be mapped onto any physical host, i.e., $VS \neq \varnothing$. [Some of the VMs have not been mapped].

4.6 Drawbacks of Virtualization

Virtualization is an essential component of cloud computing environment [20-25], but it has some of the downsides discussed below:

- *Single point of failure*: The first and foremost drawback of virtualization is that there is a single point of failure. It is great to run multiple virtual servers in one physical server. But when the host machine on which all the virtualized applications or virtual servers run, fails, it will put all the virtual servers offline.

- *Much initial cost*: Virtualization demands powerful and high frequency machines, which lead to higher cost for initial setup. Virtualization might save money because it allows decreasing the number of physical machines, but to host enough virtual machines, the physical machine should have enough RAM and also CPU configuration, which in turn requires high initial setup costs.

- *Performance degradation*: Even if the machines on which virtualized operating systems and virtualized applications are run are powerful enough, performance issues are still possible. When multiple virtual machines are concurrently running on a particular host machine, each virtual machine may exhibit unstable and varying performance (in terms of speed of execution), which decidedly depends on the workload inflicted on the host system by other virtual machines.

- *Issues with application virtualization*: While in most cases it is not possible to predict if a particular application will act up when virtualized or not, there are also many applications which are known to experience performance degradation when virtualized. Databases are one of the most common examples of such applications. Databases require frequent disk operations and when there is a delay in reading from or writing to the disk because of virtualization, this might render the whole application useless.

KVM: Kernel-based virtual machine (KVM) is a hypervisor built right into the Linux kernel. It is similar to Xen in purpose but much simpler to get running. To start using the hypervisor, just load the appropriate KVM kernel modules and the hypervisor is up. As with Xcn's full virtualization, in order for KVM to work, you must have a processor that supports Intel's VT-x extensions or AMD's AMD-V extensions.[3] Kernel-based virtual machine (KVM) [14, 15] is a full virtualization solution for Linux. It is based upon CPU virtualization extensions (i.e., extending the set of CPU instructions with new instructions that allow writing simple virtual machine monitors). KVM is a new Linux subsystem (the kernel component of KVM is included in the mainline Linux kernel) that takes advantage of these extensions to add a virtual machine monitor (or hypervisor) capability to Linux. Using KVM, one can create and run multiple virtual machines that will appear as normal Linux processes and are integrated with the rest of the system. It works on the x86 architecture and supports hardware virtualization technologies such as Intel VT-x and AMD-V.

Xen: This is a virtual machine monitor (VMM) or hypervisor developed by the Computing Laboratory at the University of Cambridge, United Kingdom, in 2003. Since 2010, Xen has been free software, developed by the community of users and licensed under the GNU General Public License (GPLv2). It makes it possible to run many instances of an operating system or, indeed, different operating systems in parallel on a single machine (or host). Xen is the only type-1 hypervisor that is available as open source. Xen is used as the basis for a number of different commercial and open source applications, such as server virtualization, infrastructure as a service (IaaS), desktop virtualization, security applications, and embedded and hardware appliances. Xen enables users to increase server utilization, consolidate server farms, reduce complexity, and decrease total cost of ownership [14, 15].[4]

4.7 Summary

This chapter dealt with virtualization and all its aspects. Cloud computing as well as virtualization has placed itself in every field of the IT industry. Virtualization makes it easier

---

[3]https://www.linux-kvm.org/page/Management_Tools
[4]https://xenproject.org/

for cloud users to add or remove services at runtime. Virtualization incorporated some new phases to improve its capabilities. In the virtualization model, as hypervisor administrator has the control over the access to VMs and it controls the monitoring system, the hypervisor crashing or failing or attacks on hypervisor administrator may lead to the performance degradation. Dynamic mapping or runtime mapping according to the requirements of the user make the whole system slow. Each organization has their own application interface, services and policies and it is a mammoth task to maintain the heterogeneity of all organizations.

EXERCISES

1. What is virtualization? Have you seen the virtualization in your PC or laptop?

2. Define virtual memory by considering virtual memory mapping.

3. Why is there a need for virtualization in the IT industry?

4. How is virtualization related to cloud computing?

5. State some advantages of cloud computing over traditional computing.

6. Discuss the difference between cloud computing and traditional computing.

7. What is a virtual machine (VM)? How does it help in virtualization?

8. What is a virtual machine monitor (VMM)? What is its role in virtualization?

9. Draw a structure diagram of a virtual machine (VM).

10. Explain how VMM is helpful in virtualization using a schematic diagram.

11. State some advantages of virtualization.

12. What is the difference between consolidation and multi-tenancy?

13. State some prominent features that make virtualization so popular in the IT industry.

14. How can you classify VM? State some reasons for the classification.

15. Explain different types of VMs.

16. Differentiate System VM and Process VM using a schematic diagram. And provide at least two examples of each category.

17. Write down the advantages of System VM.

18. Describe the virtualization model for cloud computing and explain the functionalities of each module.

19. What are SWF and Vx32?

20. Define hypervisor. Write down the different types of hypervisors. What is HME?

21. Explain the functionalities of each module of platform service and software service.

22. What is brokering service in cloud? How is brokering service useful to the CSP and cloud user?

23. What is SLA? Why is SLA required in cloud computing?

24. Is SLA really required for cloud? Justify.

25. Write down different types of guest OS visualization techniques using a schematic diagram.

26. What is the difference between full virtualization and paravirtualization?

27. What are binary translation and hypercalls?

28. Explain the mapping technique of virtual machine onto physical machine in a private cloud.

29. What should be the initial condition for the mapping technique of virtual machine?

30. Write down the necessary conditions for the mapping technique of virtual machine.

31. Write down some drawbacks of virtualization.

32. Briefly explain some features of KVM and Xen. Illustrate their working principle.

33. What is the difference between cloud and traditional datacenters?

34. Why are APIs used in cloud services?

35. What are the different datacenters in cloud computing?

References

1. Buyya, R., Yeo, C. S., Venugopal, S., Broberg, J., & Brandic, I. (2009). Cloud computing and emerging IT platforms: Vision, hype, and reality for delivering computing as the 5th utility. *Future Generation computer systems*, 25(6), 599-616.

2. Tianfield, H. (2011, October). Cloud computing architectures. In *2011 IEEE International Conference on Systems, Man, and Cybernetics* (pp. 1394-1399). IEEE.

3. Sefton, P., & Principal, B. L. (2010). *Privacy and Data Control in the Era of Cloud Computing*. Brightline Lawyers.

4. Rowe, D. (2011). *The Impact of Cloud on Mid-size Businesses*.

5. Sarna, D. E. (2010). *Implementing and developing cloud computing applications*. CRC Press.

6. Cafaro, M., & Aloisio, G. (2011). Grids, clouds, and virtualization. In *Grids, Clouds and Virtualization* (pp. 1-21). Springer, London.

7. Pal, S., & Pattnaik, P. K. (2012). Efficient architectural framework for cloud computing. *International Journal of Cloud Computing and Services Science*, 1(2), 66.

8. Hurwitz, J. S., & Kirsch, D. (2020). *Cloud computing for dummies*. John Wiley & Sons.

9. Carrasco, J., Duran, F., & Pimentel, E. (2020). Live migration of trans-cloud applications. *Computer Standards & Interfaces*, 69, 103392.

10. Rochwerger, B., Breitgand, D., Levy, E., Galis, A., Nagin, K., Llorente, I. M., ... & Ben-Yehuda, M. (2009). The reservoir model and architecture for open federated cloud computing. *IBM Journal of Research and Development*, 53(4), 4-1.

11. Sarathy, V., Narayan, P., & Mikkilineni, R. (2010, June). Next generation cloud computing architecture: Enabling real-time dynamism for shared distributed physical infrastructure. In *2010 19th IEEE International Workshops on Enabling Technologies: Infrastructures for Collaborative Enterprises* (pp. 48-53). IEEE.

12. Pal, S., Mohanty, S., Pattnaik, P. K., & Mund, G. B. (2012). A Virtualization Model for Cloud Computing. In *the Proceedings of International Conference on Advances in Computer Science 2012*, pp. 10-16.

13. He, Z., Wang, D., Fu, B., Tan, K., Hua, B., Zhang, Z. L., & Zheng, K. (2020, July). MasQ: RDMA for Virtual Private Cloud. In *Proceedings of the Annual conference of the ACM Special Interest Group on Data Communication on the applications, technologies, architectures, and protocols for computer communication* (pp. 1-14).

14. Lublin, U., Kamay, Y., Laor, D., & Liguori, A. (2007). KVM: the Linux virtual machine monitor.

15. Le, D. N., Kumar, R., Nguyen, G. N., & Chatterjee, J. M. (2018). *Cloud Computing and Virtualization*. John Wiley & Sons.

16. Le, D., Kumar, R., Mishra, B. K., Khari, M., & Chatterjee, J. M. (2019). *Cyber Security in Parallel and Distributed Computing*. Wiley, Hoboken.

17. Seth, B., Dalal, S., Jaglan, V., Le, D. N., Mohan, S., & Srivastava, G. (2020). Integrating encryption techniques for secure data storage in the cloud. *Transactions on Emerging Telecommunications Technologies*, e4108.

18. Seth, B., Dalal, S., Le, D. N., Jaglan, V., Dahiya, N., Agrawal, A., Mayank M. S., Deo P. & Verma, K. D. (2021). Secure Cloud Data Storage System Using Hybrid Paillier-Blowfish Algorithm. *CMC-Computers Materials & Continua*, 67(1), 779-798.

19. Le, D. N., Bhatt, C. M., & Madhukar, M. (Eds.). (2019). *Security Designs for the Cloud, IoT, and Social Networking*. John Wiley & Sons.

20. Van, V. N., Long, N. Q., Nguyen, G. N., & Le, D. N. (2016). A performance analysis of openstack open-source solution for IaaS cloud computing. In *Proceedings of the Second International Conference on Computer and Communication Technologies* (pp. 141-150). Springer, New Delhi.

21. Van, V. N., Long, N. Q., & Le, D. N. (2016). Performance analysis of network virtualization in cloud computing infrastructures on openstack. In *Innovations in Computer Science and Engineering* (pp. 95-103). Springer, Singapore.

22. Hurwitz, J. S., & Kirsch, D. (2020). *Cloud computing for Dummies*. John Wiley & Sons.

23. Prokhorenko, V., & Babar, M. A. (2020). Architectural resilience in cloud, fog and edge systems: A survey. *IEEE Access*, 8, 28078-28095.

24. Shukur, H., Zeebaree, S., Zebari, R., Zeebaree, D., Ahmed, O., & Salih, A. (2020). Cloud computing virtualization of resources allocation for distributed systems. Journal of Applied Science and Technology Trends, 1(3), 98-105.

25. Utomo, A. P., Winarno, I., & Syarif, I. (2020). Towards a Resilient Server with an external VMI in the Virtualization Environment. EMITTER International Journal of Engineering Technology, 8(1), 49-66.

5

CLASSIFICATION OF VIRTUALIZATION ENVIRONMENT

SOUVIK PAL[1], DAC-NHUONG LE[2], PRASANT KUMAR PATTNAIK[3]

[1] Sister Nivedita University, Kolkata, India
[2] Haiphong University, Haiphong, Vietnam
[3] KIIT, Deemed to be University, India
 Email: souvikpal22@gmail.com, nhuongld@dhhp.edu.vn, patnaikprasant@gmail.com

Abstract
 Cloud computing is a relatively new field that is gaining more popularity day by day for ramified applications among the internet users. Virtualization plays a significant role in managing and coordinating the access from the resource pool to multiple virtual machines on which multiple heterogeneous applications are running. Various virtualization methodologies are of significant importance because they help to overcome the complex workloads, frequent application patching and updating, and multiple software architecture. Although a lot of research has been conducted on virtualization, a range of issues involved has mostly been presented in isolation from each other. Therefore, we have made an attempt to present a comprehensive survey study of different aspects of virtualization. We present our classification of virtualization methodologies and their brief explanation, based on their working principle and underlying features.
 Keywords: Virtualization, live migration, distributing pattern

5.1   Introduction

A virtualization environment that enables the configuration of systems (i.e., compute power, bandwidth and storage) as well as helps the creation of individual virtual machines, are the key features of cloud computing. Virtualization uses computer resources to imitate other computer resources or whole computers [1,2]. This chapter focuses on the classification of the virtualization environment in which we have categorized it. Also included in this chapter is the classification of virtualization environment based on the considerations such as scheduling, load distribution, energy consumption, operational strategy, VM distribution pattern, and transactional pattern.

5.2   Classification

The virtualization environment may be classified into six categories, namely scheduling-based, load distribution-based, energy-aware based, operational-based, distribution pattern-based and transactional-based, as shown in Figure 5.1, considering the host physical machines as a set of physical resources.

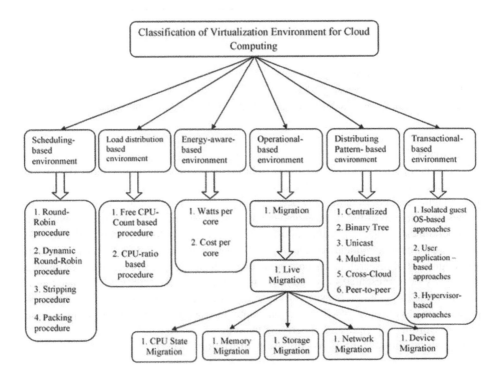

Figure 5.1: Schematic diagram of classification of virtualization environment.

$$S = \{CPU\, cores, Memory, Storage, I/O, Networking\} \qquad (5.1)$$

The pool of physical resources, denoted by P, is the sum of all sets of physical resources.

$$P = S_1 + S_2 + \cdots + S_n = \sum S_i \tag{5.2}$$

Let us consider the resource pool set P in two subsets:

$$P = S_j^1 + S_k^2 (j \neq k)(j, k \ indicates \ natural \ number) \tag{5.3}$$

Set of physical machines having available resources to host VMs + Set of the remaining physical machines not having available resources to host VMs.

5.2.1   Scheduling-Based Environment

This scheduling-based category focuses on how the virtual machines are scheduled in different scheduling algorithms by the VMM according to the request of the cloud user. Scheduling environment may be classified into the four following subcategories.

5.2.1.1   Round-Robin Policy

The round-robin scheduling process broadens the VMs across the pool of host resources as evenly as possible [1]. Eucalyptus cloud platform currently uses this as default scheduling policy. The procedure is described below.

- Step 1: For each new virtual machine, it iterates sequentially until it is able to find an available resource (physical machine that is capable of hosting virtual machines) from the resource pool P.
  - Step 1 (a): If found, then matching is done between physical machine and virtual machine.
- Step 2: For the next virtual machine, the policy iterates sequentially through resource pool P from the previous point where it left off at the last iteration and chooses the nearest host that can serve the virtual machine.
- Step 3: Now go to Step 1 and iterate the whole process until all VMs are allocated.

5.2.1.2   Dynamic Round-Robin Policy

This method is an extension of the round-robin process which includes two considerations [3]:

- *Consideration 1*: One physical machine can host multiple virtual machines. If any one of these virtual machines has finished its work and the remaining others are still working on the same physical machine, no more virtual machines will get hosted on this physical machine since it is in a "retirement" state, which means that the physical machine can be shut down when the remaining virtual machines complete their execution.

- *Consideration 2*: When a physical machine does not wait for the virtual machines to finish and goes into the "retirement" state for a long time, then it will be forcefully migrated to the other active physical machines and will shut down after the completion of the migration process.

So, this scheduling technique will consume less power than the round-robin procedure.

5.2.1.3 Stripping Policy

The stripping scheduling policy broadens the virtual machines across the pool of host resources to as many as possible [1]. For example, OpenNabula cloud platform currently uses this scheduling policy. The procedure of this sort of stripping scheduling is given below.

- Step 1: For each new virtual machine, it first discards the set S_k^2.
- Step 2: From the set S_j^1, it finds the physical machine hosting least number of virtual machines.
    - Step 2 (a): If found, then matching is done between physical machine and virtual machine.
- Step 3: Now go to Step 1 and iterate the whole process until all virtual machines are allocated.

5.2.1.4 Packing Policy

The packing policy spreads the virtual machines across the pool of host resources to as few as possible [1]. OpenNabula cloud platform currently uses this scheduling policy and implements it as a greedy policy option in Eucalyptus. The technique used is given below.

- Step 1: For each new virtual machine, it first discards the set S_k^2.
- Step 2: From the set S_j^1, it finds the physical machine hosting maximum number of virtual machines.
    - Step 2 (a): If found, then matching is done between physical machine and virtual machine.
- Step 3: Now go to Step 1 and iterate the whole process until all virtual machines are allocated.

5.2.2 Load Distribution-Based Environment

Load distribution is required when a particular host faces a huge workload, i.e., a huge number of client requests, which leads to performance degradation. Then the requests are transferred to another host or another data center to distribute the workload. In the virtualization environment, the load balancer has the responsibility to reduce the load overhead and that leads to classification of load balancing approaches considering CPU core set as Q, which is subdivided into allocated CPU core subset denoted as Q_1 and free CPU core subset denoted as Q_2 with the following:

5.2.2.1 Free CPU Count-Based Policy

This load balancing policy wants to minimize the CPU load on the hosts [1]. OpenNabula cloud platform currently uses this policy as the load-aware policy. The procedure is given below.

- Step 1: For each new VM, it first discards the set S_k^2.
- Step 2: From the set S_j^1, it finds the physical machine having maximum number of free CPU cores from set Q.
  - Step 2 (a): If found, then matching is done between physical machine and VM.
- Step 3: Now go to Step 1 and iterate the whole process until all VMs are allocated.

5.2.2.2 Radio-Based Load Balancing Policy

This is an enhanced version of count-based load balancing technique which also wants to minimize the CPU load on the hosts [1]. The procedure is given below.

- Step 1: For each new VM, it first discards the set S_k^2.
- Step 2: From the set S_j^1, it finds the physical machine having maximum ratio of Q_2 and Q_1 ($\frac{Q_2}{Q_1} > 1$) from set Q.
  - Step 2 (a): If found, then matching is done between physical machine and VM.
- Step 3: Now go to Step 1 and iterate the whole process until all VMs are allocated.

5.2.3 Energy-Aware-Based Environment

Energy is always of concern in the IT industry; that's why when virtual machines are created, ways in which less energy can be consumed in a data center have to be considered. This section deals with different energy-aware techniques which are intended to consume less energy and the policies used in each category.

5.2.3.1 Watts per Core Policy

Watts per core policy seeks out the host taking the minimum additional wattage per core, sinking overall power consumption. It is assumed that no additional power will be consumed during shut down or hibernating mode. The procedure is given below.

- Step1: For each new VM, it first discards the set S_k^2.
- Step2: From the set S_j^1, it finds the physical machine taking the minimum additional wattage per CPU core based on each physical machine's power supply.
  - Step2 (a): If found, then matching is done between physical machine and VM.
- Step3: Now go to Step 1 and iterate the whole process until all VMs are allocated.

5.2.3.2 Cost per Core Policy

The cost per core policy is an energy-aware policy and also minimizes the cost estimation by seeking the host that would capture the least additional cost per core. The principle is the same as in the watts per core policy. The procedure is given below.

- Step 1: For each new VM, it first discards the set S_k^2.
- Step 2: From the set S_j^1, it finds the physical machine taking the minimum additional cost per CPU core based on each physical machine's power supply and electricity cost.
  - Step 2 (a): If found, then matching is done between physical machine and VM.
- Step 3: Now go to Step 1 and iterate the whole process until all VMs are allocated.

5.2.4 Operational-Based Environment

The operational-based category involves virtual machine migration technique which is concerned about the transfer of the instances of the virtual machines from the local sites to the remote sites and are able to run there.

5.2.4.1 Migration

Virtual machine migration is the process of transferring a VM from one host physical machine to another host machine which is either currently running or will be running or may be booted up after placing the new VMs. Migration is initiated due to the following reasons:

1. Lack of resources in the source node or local site.

2. When remote node is running VMs on behalf of local node due to dynamic unavailability of resources.

3. For minimizing the number of host machines that are running remote sites (less energy consumption).

4. For maximizing allocation of VMs among the local machines rather than remote machines.

As shown in Figure 5.2, resource as a service (RaaS) is a physical layer consisting of a pool of physical resources, i.e., servers, networks, storage, and data center space, which provides all the resources to the VMs. Hypervisor layer is the management layer which provides overall management, such as decision-making regarding where to deploy the virtual machines, admission control, resource control, usage of accounting, etc. The implementation layer provides the hosting environment for virtual machines. Migration of a virtual machine needs the coordination in the transfer of source and destination (D) host machines and their states [5]. The main migration algorithm, migration request handler, initiate transfer handler and forced migration handler are there to handle the migration process [6].

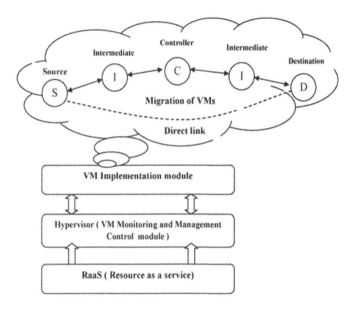

Figure 5.2: Schematic diagram of migration process.

The overall migration steps are as follows:

- Step 1: The controller and the intermediate nodes (I) send the migration request to the possible future destinations. D-nodes can be in remote sites and the request can be forwarded to another remote site depending upon resource availability.

- Step 2: The receiver may accept or reject the request depending on the account capabilities and usage of accounts.

    – Step 2 (a): If all the business rules and accounting policy permit the request, then "initiation transfer" reply message will be sent to the requesting nodes thorough I-nodes (intermediate nodes).

- Step 3: After getting the reply message, the transfer operation from the S-node to the D-node via I-nodes and VMs on the source site will be migrated to the destination sites. Here transfer initiation is done by the C-node to D-node and the transfer is verified through token [6] by the controller with the help of S-node.

In migration, monitoring is essentially needed to ensure that virtual machines obtain the capacity stipulated in the service-level agreement and get the data for accounting of the resources, which have been used by the service providers [6]. The monitoring issues may be the amount of RAM or the network bandwidth or the number of currently logged-in users.

5.2.4.2 Live Migration

In the flow of rapid usage of virtualization, the migration procedure has been enhanced due to the advantages of live migration, such as server consolidation and resource isolation [7]. Live migration of virtual machines [8,9] is a technique in which the virtual machine seems to be active and gives responses to end users during the course of the migration process. Live migration facilitates energy efficiency, online maintenance, and load balancing [10]. It is sometimes known as real-time or hot migration in the cloud computing environment. While the virtual machine is running on the source node or one host server during live migration, the virtual machine is moved to the target node or another host server without interrupting any active network connections or without any visible effect from the user's point of view. A workflow management system [4] has been described for user-deployed applications. Live migration helps to optimize the efficient utilization of available CPU resources. Different live migration algorithms are described in [12-15]. Here, a few live migration processes are presented.

- *CPU-state migration*: Migration of CPU state is concerned with process migration. While migrating the CPU state, the process control block (PCB), the number of cores, processor speed, and required process-specific memory will all transfer from the source host to the destination host.

- *Memory migration*: While concerned with the memory migration, all the pages are transferred from the source host *A* to the destination host *B*. In this memory migration, pre-copy migration [16] is involved, where all pages are iteratively copied from source host to destination host during the first round. Assume there are *n* number of rounds; and subsequent rounds up to *n* copy only those pages that got dirtied (dirty pages) during the previous transfer round (indicated by dirty bitmap). Here we have to consider that every virtual machine has some set of pages which update very frequently and this phenomenon leads to the performance degradation of the pre-copy. For every iteration, a "dirtying rate" is calculated depending upon the length of the pages and the number of pages being dirtied. Clark *et al.* [8] have bound the number of iterations of pre-copying based on the writable working set (WWS) according to the behavior of typical server workloads.

- *Storage migration*: To maintain VM migration, the system has to provide each VM with a location-independent, consistent vision of the file system which is accessible on all hosts. Each VM uses its own virtual disk, onto which the corresponding file system is mapped and transfers the contents of the virtual disk to the source machine. We depend on the storage area networks (SAN) or network attached storage (NAS) to permit us to migrate connections to the storage devices. This phenomenon allows us to migrate a disk by reconnecting to the disk on the target machine.

- *Network migration*: To locate the remote systems and communicate with a virtual machine, a virtual IP address (known to other units) has been assigned to each virtual machine. This IP address and the IP address of the currently hosting machine of the VM are distinct. Each virtual machine can have its individual unique virtual MAC address. The hypervisor maps between the virtual IP and the MAC addresses to their corresponding virtual machines. It should be noted that all the virtual machines should be in the same IP subnet. While migrating to the target node, an ARP broadcast has to be sent to the network declaring that the IP address has moved to a new MAC address (physical location), and TCP connections survive the migration.

- *Device migration*: Hypervisor makes the physical hardware virtualized and represents each VM with a standard set of virtual devices. Well-known physical hardware are completely emulated by these virtual devices in an effective way and these devices translate the VM requests to the system hardware. Device migration requires the dependency on host-specific devices as it may be difficult to migrate due to an awkward provisional state (for example, CD recording device while recording) or unavailability for migration.

5.2.5 Distribution Pattern-Based Environment

The V-machine deployment pattern helps the distribution of the virtual machine, which is made more efficient due to faster response time, minimizing communication latency, avoiding congestion and dynamic updating. The various distribution approaches are described below.

5.2.5.1 Centralized Distribution
Centralized distribution is the traditional approach. It can be implemented in a simple way so that the users and the administrators can use it easily. The virtual machine images are stored in the central NFS (network file server) and the client nodes retrieve copies of virtual machines from the central node on demand. This type of multiple point-to-point transfer creates an inconsistent situation when a large number of clients want to access a multi-terabyte file. So, client transfer should be synchronized.

5.2.5.2 Balanced Binary Tree Distribution
Balanced binary tree-based distribution is used for reducing the overhead of network congestion and allowing parallel transfers. Here, all the computing nodes are set in balanced binary tree pattern making the source node as the root node. The root node always carries the virtual machine images and distributes the virtual machine images from the parent node to child node. Newly arrived child node can easily get the data from its parent node. Thus, data and virtual machine images flow through the entire binary tree. But when a node crashes, then all the child nodes of this very node will get stopped. So, a time-out and retransmission strategy is needed to resolve the problem.

5.2.5.3 Unicast Distribution
Unicast distribution distributes the VM images in a sequential order to the destination nodes even in remote sites. But it is very time-consuming and faces network congestion.

5.2.5.4 Multicast Distribution
Multicast is an efficient way for distribution of virtual machines. In multicast, the information or data is transmitted to a required group of destination nodes in s single transmission. Since packets are sent in a group, it can minimize the CPU load but increase the packet loss probability. It works best in local area network (LAN).

5.2.5.5 Distribution Between Cross Clouds
Multicast does well in LAN, but sometimes transfer is required beyond the LAN. Consider, for example, a situation in which more than one private, physically distinguishable desktop cloud is sharing the same data and information and is using the multicast distribution method. But transferring the data is forbidden by their network policy. To overcome this type of constraint, peer-to-peer or balanced binary tree distribution mechanisms are used over the common network linking those clouds.

5.2.5.6 Peer-to-Peer Distribution
Peer-to-peer is a decentralized approach in which there is no centralized server, and every node in the system works as a server or client. Every virtual machine node may act as sender or receiver or both sender and receiver. It is possible to make multiple transfers of different files to the same node. BitTorrent protocol is an example of peer-to-peer distribution [11].

5.2.6 Transaction-Based Environment

This transaction-based category deals with different architecture-based virtualizations and deployment of different operating systems and new applications [17-25], which includes those discussed below.

5.2.6.1 Isolated Guest Operating System-Based Virtualization

In this category, host operating system runs on the hardware infrastructure. It supports multiple guest virtualized operating systems on the same physical server and it is capable of maintaining the isolation of different guest operating systems, as shown in Figure 5.3. All the operating systems use the same kernel and hardware infrastructure. The host operating system controls the guest OS.

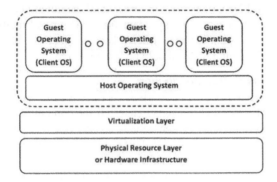

Figure 5.3: A scenario of operating system-based virtualization.

5.2.6.2 User Application-Based Virtualization

In this category, virtualization is done according to the user's on-demand requirements and is hosted on top of the host operating system, as shown in the Figure 5.4.

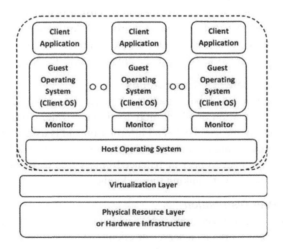

Figure 5.4: A scenario of application-based virtualization.

Upon getting a request, emulation of virtual machine containing its own guest operating system and related applications is carried out by this virtualization method so that users can get their specific on-demand service from the emulated virtual machines.

5.2.6.3 *Hypervisor-Based Virtualization Approach*

Hypervisor is a mainframe operating system which allows other operating systems to run on the same system concurrently. And its monitoring system monitors the access to virtual machines. Hypervisor is accessible when the system is booted up to regulate the allocation of hardware infrastructure to the multiple virtual machines from the resource layer. The architecture model is shown in Figure 5.5.

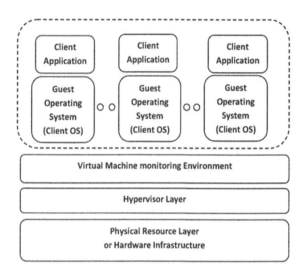

Figure 5.5: A scenario of hypervisor-based virtualization.

5.3 Summary

This chapter focused on presenting a comprehensive review study on different aspects of the virtualization procedure and the interrelationship among them. Virtualization uses computer resources to imitate other computer resources or whole computers. This chapter presented an overview of a wide range of the research work in the field of cloud computing with respect to virtualization methods, namely scheduling, load distribution, energy efficiency, and distribution pattern, and also transactional approaches which may help researchers expand these concepts in different fields of virtualization.

EXERCISES

1. State the procedure for scheduling-based virtualization environment.

2. Are round-robin scheduling and dynamic round-robin scheduling different in the case of applications? Justify your answer.

3. In what respect is packing procedure different from stripping procedure? Explain.

4. State the categories of load-balancing environment.

5. State the techniques adapted by the operational-based environment in order to transfer the data from one cloud to another. Explain.

6. Explain the migration process in cloud computing environment with a suitable schematic diagram.

7. State the activities of network migration and device migration in cloud computing environment.

8. In what way is distributed pattern-based environment helpful to virtual machines? Give at least two examples.

9. State the techniques involve in distributed pattern-based environment.

10. Why is transactional-based environment required in cloud computing environment? Explain each of the procedures with examples.

11. What are the classifications of the virtualization environment? Explain each of them.

12. What is the difference between isolated guest OS-based virtualization and hypervisor-based virtualization?

13. What are the essential things to consider before selecting a cloud computing platform?

14. What is the source of cloud computing platform databases?

15. Name some of the large cloud providers and databases.

References

1. Jansen, R., & Brenner, P. R. (2011, July). Energy efficient virtual machine allocation in the cloud. In 2011 *International Green Computing Conference and Workshops* (pp. 1-8). IEEE.

2. Pal, S., Mohanty, S., Pattnaik, P. K., & Mund, G. B. (2012). A Virtualization Model for Cloud Computing. in the *Proceedings of International Conference on Advances in Computer Science*, 2012, pp. 10 16.

3. Lin, C. C., Liu, P., & Wu, J. J. (2011, December). Energy-efficient virtual machine provision algorithms for cloud systems. In 2011 *Fourth IEEE International Conference on Utility and Cloud Computing* (pp. 81-88). IEEE.

4. Raicu, I., Zhao, Y., Foster, I. T., & Szalay, A. (2008, June). Accelerating large-scale data exploration through data diffusion. In *Proceedings of the 2008 international workshop on Data-aware distributed computing* (pp. 9-18). ACM.

5. DSP2013, D. M. T. F. (2007). *CIM System Virtualization Model White Paper*. Distributed Management Task Force.

6. Elmroth, E., & Larsson, L. (2009, August). Interfaces for placement, migration, and monitoring of virtual machines in federated clouds. In 2009 *Eighth International Conference on Grid and Cooperative Computing* (pp. 253-260). IEEE.

7. Ye, K., Jiang, X., Ye, D., & Huang, D. (2010, September). Two optimization mechanisms to improve the isolation property of server consolidation in virtualized multi-core server. In 2010 *IEEE 12th International Conference on High Performance Computing and Communications (HPCC)* (pp. 281-288). IEEE.

8. Clark, C., Fraser, K., Hand, S., Hansen, J. G., Jul, E., Limpach, C., ... & Warfield, A. (2005, May). Live migration of virtual machines. In *Proceedings of the 2nd conference on Symposium on Networked Systems Design & Implementation*-Volume 2 (pp. 273-286). USENIX Association.

9. Nelson, M., Lim, B. H., & Hutchins, G. (2005, April). Fast Transparent Migration for Virtual Machines. In *USENIX Annual technical conference, general track* (pp. 391-394).

10. Ye, K., Jiang, X., Huang, D., Chen, J., & Wang, B. (2011, July). Live migration of multiple virtual machines with resource reservation in cloud computing environments. In 2011 IEEE 4th International Conference on Cloud Computing (pp. 267-274). IEEE.

11. Schmidt, M., Fallenbeck, N., Smith, M., & Freisleben, B. (2010, February). Efficient distribution of virtual machines for cloud computing. In 2010 18th *Euromicro Conference on Parallel, Distributed and Network-based Processing* (pp. 567-574). IEEE.

12. Luo, Y., Zhang, B., Wang, X., Wang, Z., Sun, Y., & Chen, H. (2008, October). Live and incremental whole-system migration of virtual machines using block-bitmap. In 2008 *IEEE International Conference on Cluster Computing* (pp. 99-106). IEEE.

13. Liu, H., Jin, H., Liao, X., Hu, L., & Yu, C. (2009, June). Live migration of virtual machine based on full system trace and replay. In *Proceedings of the 18th ACM international symposium on High performance distributed computing* (pp. 101-110). ACM.

14. Jin, H., Deng, L., Wu, S., Shi, X., & Pan, X. (2009, August). Live virtual machine migration with adaptive, memory compression. In 2009 *IEEE International Conference on Cluster Computing and Workshops* (pp. 1-10). IEEE.

15. Hines, M. R., & Gopalan, K. (2009, March). Post-copy based live virtual machine migration using adaptive pre-paging and dynamic self-ballooning. In *Proceedings of the 2009 ACM SIGPLAN/SIGOPS international conference on Virtual execution environments* (pp. 51-60). ACM.

16. Theimer, M., Lantz, K. A., & Cheriton, D. R. (1985). Preemptable remote execution facilities for the v-system (No. STAN-CS-85-1087). STANFORD UNIV CA DEPT OF COMPUTER SCIENCE.

17. Le, D. N., Kumar, R., Nguyen, G. N., & Chatterjee, J. M. (2018). *Cloud Computing and Virtualization*. John Wiley & Sons.

18. Cao, H., Wu, S., Tian, F., & Yang, L. (2019, October). Efficient Virtualized Resources Allocation in Network Virtualization Environment: A Service Oriented Perspective. In *2019 11th International Conference on Wireless Communications and Signal Processing (WCSP)* (pp. 1-6). IEEE.

19. Elsadig Abdalla Abdalla, M. (2020). Virtualization Security Issues: Security issues arise in the virtual environment.

20. Bermejo, B., & Juiz, C. (2020). On the classification and quantification of server consolidation overheads. *Journal of Supercomputing*, 1-21.

21. Van, V. N., Long, N. Q., & Le, D. N. (2016). Performance analysis of network virtualization in cloud computing infrastructures on openstack. In *Innovations in Computer Science and Engineering* (pp. 95-103). Springer, Singapore.

22. Van, V. N., Long, N. Q., Nguyen, G. N., & Le, D. N. (2016). A performance analysis of openstack open-source solution for IaaS cloud computing. In *Proceedings of the Second International Conference on Computer and Communication Technologies* (pp. 141-150). Springer, New Delhi.

23. Seth, B., Dalal, S., Jaglan, V., Le, D. N., Mohan, S., & Srivastava, G. (2020). Integrating encryption techniques for secure data storage in the cloud. *Transactions on Emerging Telecommunications Technologies*, e4108.

24. Seth, B., Dalal, S., Le, D. N., Jaglan, V., Dahiya, N., Agrawal, A., Mayank M. S., Deo P. & Verma, K. D. (2021). Secure Cloud Data Storage System Using Hybrid Paillier-Blowfish Algorithm. *CMC-Computers Materials & Continua*, 67(1), 779-798.

25. Prokhorenko, V., & Babar, M. A. (2020). Architectural resilience in cloud, fog and edge systems: A survey. *IEEE Access*, 8, 28078-28095.

PART II

Cloud Computing Data Storage

6

AN APPROACH TO LIVE MIGRATION OF VIRTUAL MACHINES IN CLOUD COMPUTING ENVIRONMENT

DAC-NHUONG LE[1], SOUVIK PAL[2], PRASANT KUMAR PATTNAIK[3]

[1] Haiphong University, Haiphong, Vietnam
[2] Sister Nivedita University, Kolkata, India
[3] KIIT, Deemed to be University, India
 Email: nhuongld@dhhp.edu.vn, souvikpal22@gmail.com, patnaikprasant@gmail.com

Abstract

In today's enterprise environments, virtual machine migration is a cloud infrastructure capability that is increasingly being used. It is the key feature of virtualized technologies. Virtual machine live migration is basically transferring instances that include the operating system, runtime memory pages, and active CPU states from a source host to the destination host. Moreover, live migration reduces service downtime, which facilitates proactive maintenance, fault management and load balancing for the virtual machine (VM).

Keywords: Virtual machine, live migration, cloud service provider

6.1 Introduction

> Virtual machine migration means transferring a virtual machine from one host physical machine to another host machine that is either currently running or will be running or be booted up after placing the new virtual machines.
>
> While the virtual machine is running on the source node or one host server and during live migration, the virtual machine is moved to the target node or another host server without interrupting any active network connections or without any visible effect from the user's point of view. Live migration helps to optimize the efficient utilization of available CPU resources.

Virtual machines involve the virtualization technique and virtualization provides a platform for optimizing complex IT resources in a scalable manner (efficiently growing), which is ideal for delivering services [1]. In the milieu of virtual machines, migration is the process of moving a virtual machine from one storage location or host server to the other location or another host server. In migration, components like CPU, memory, networking and storage are all virtualized. Hence, while migrating the virtual machines, a set of simply movable data files is used for capturing all the states of a virtual machine. In this context, cross-cloud is a cloud which deals with different hosts within a big cloud, connected through LAN while transferring the contents. From the user's point of view, migration may lead to disruption of services from the cloud service provider (CSP) due to lack of active network connections; or workflow delay can make the user wait a long time while migration occurs. To avoid these kinds of issues, the live migration concept entered the market.

6.2 Need of Live Migration of Virtual Machine

Cloud computing is popularly and widely used mainly for application-specific services with minimal effort of both service provider and end user under the cloud computing environment umbrella, which can be organized on demand into services that can grow or shrink in real-time scenario [2,3].

Migration is needed and initiated mainly for the four reasons given below.

> The first and foremost requirement of live migration is the lack of resources in the source node or local site and when remote node is running virtual machines on behalf of local node due to dynamic unavailability of resources. Live migration is also required for minimizing the number of host machines that are running remote sites (less energy consumption) and for maximizing allocation of virtual machines among the local machines rather than remote machines.

Migration of virtual machines was previously described in Chapter 5 and the process of migration of virtual machines [3, 5] was explained.

6.3 Advantages of Live Migration

Some of the advantages of live migration are given below:

- *Less downtime*: From the customer point of view, live migration happens without any perceptible effect due to much less downtime. "Downtime" is defined as the time between stopping the virtual machine on the source node and resuming it on the destination node. In live migration, downtime is an order of magnitude of milliseconds to seconds with respect to the application and memory size.

- *Proactive maintenance*: Cloud system should take actions that are intended to cause changes, rather than just reacting to change. In case of failures, live migration facilitates proactive maintenance that helps to resolve the internal potential problem of a cloud system before the disruption of service occurs.

- *Load balancing*: A virtual machine is migrated one node to another to share the scheduled workload in order to optimize the consumption of available CPU resources.

6.4   A Design Approach to Live Migration

Live migration of a virtual machine is initiated when dynamic load-balancing is required to provide service without disruption. For example, a virtual machine, needing more CPU core, may be transferred to a machine having available CPU cycles, or sometimes taking the host machine for proactive maintenance. When client application or services are deployed on a cloud, they go through work units, the scheduler, the scalable application manager, and then a cloud host infrastructure A maintaining a workflow management system [6]. And while needed, all the VM states and memory contents are dynamically migrated to another cloud host infrastructure B as shown in Figure 6.1 [2].

The scheduler unit consists of workflow co-coordinator (controls the job flow), task manager (manages and prioritizes the task), and event service (maintains the event-driven service). Task dispatcher module transfers the task to application manager, which is able to modify itself according to the application size (scalable in nature). The client applications are executed using executor after the virtual machines are provisioned on the cloud source host A. According to the scheduling information (i.e., 1. Application priority, 2. Licensing, 3. Application dependency, 4. Architectural dependency, 5. Runtime environment, 6. Mapping dependency, 7. Mapping environment, 8. Latencies), virtual machine is dynamically provisioned according to the user application and uses physical resources from the resource pool. For load sharing or proactive maintenance or for reducing client waiting time (i.e., "zero"/no downtime), VM is dynamically migrated from the source cloud A to the target cloud B with its entire state.

In the networking context, it is required that several VMs are interrelated, with a VAN (virtual application network) being the prime link between them. A virtual infrastructure engine, such as OpenNebula [7], is able to manage the groups of interrelated virtual machines with support for VMware, KVM and Xen platforms. Virtual infrastructure engine dynamically creates the VANs and traces the MAC addresses leased in the network to the service virtual machines. The key responsibility of the service is the TCP/IP services such as NFS. DNS or NIS. As shown in Figure 6.1 [2], the two cloud hosts A and B have two different interfaces each; two distinct physical networks are there: one physical network connects the source and destination hosts using a switch and another network that establishes the connection between the hosts and the public internet. Virtual machines are able to communicate if connected via the same private VAN; otherwise, if isolated, they won't be able to connect to the network and fail to communicate.

Furthermore, in Figure 6.1, RaaS (resource as a service) [3] is a physical resource module consisting of a pool of physical resources, i.e., CPU cores, servers, networks, storage, and data center space. Hypervisor layer, which works as a virtual machine manager

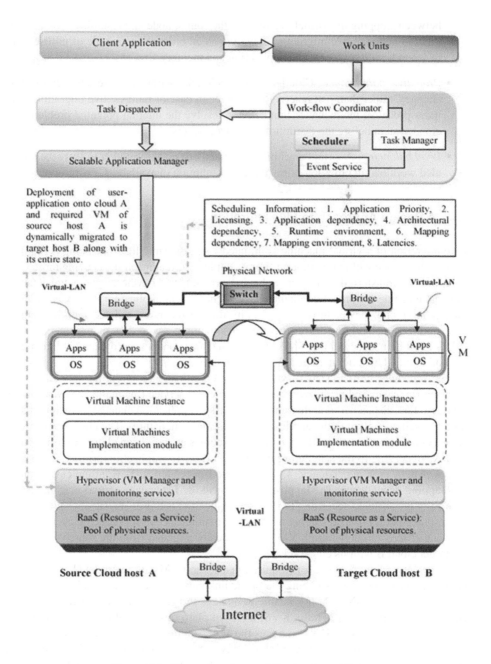

Figure 6.1: Live migration architectural workflow.

(VMM), controls the access of the guest operating system and manages the provisioning and live migration of the virtual machines. The virtual machine implementation module and virtual machine instance module provides the hosting environment for virtual machines. Nowadays, in real-time scenario, live migration of virtual machines has become the necessary feature of virtual machine manager (VMM) or hypervisor. In this chapter, we will explain our proposed cross-cloud live migration technique which will be compatible with the hybrid cloud environment. To move a virtual machine from a source node of a cloud infrastructure to the target node of another cloud infrastructure, we have to consider moving its CPU state, storage content, memory content and network connections. In Figure 6.1 a flowchart is presented in which we elaborately explain the algorithmic approach of live migration. It will help explain the live migration of virtual machines in cross-cloud environment. While live migration of virtual machines is required, it basically migrates the operating systems of one virtual machine to another virtual machine.

6.4.1 Live Migration Process

Live migration of virtual machines is the process in which virtual machine states and memory contents are transferred via the network from the source host A to the destination host B. We have already discussed that the hypervisor allows running VMs to be transferred and migrated from one server to another server [8, 9]. Le *et al.* [10] jointly explain the algorithmic steps that are executed while dynamically migrating the OS instances of a virtual machine and its memory contents. The steps are as follows:

- **Step 1**. *A virtual machine is actively running on the cloud source host A*: While running, the following attributes must be considered as the states of a virtual machine and those are:

  - The main memory size,
  - CPU details (the number of cores, processor speed),
  - A set of NICs which are attached to one or more virtual networks,
  - A set of disk images (some of the disk images need to be transferred to and from the physical machine on which the VM is running),
  - A state file or the recovery files containing the memory image of the running virtual machine and some hypervisor-specific information.

- **Step 2**. *Synchronization for resource selection on the target host B*: When a request for migration is issued from the source host to the target host, the task scheduler on the target host prioritizes the resources and selects those resources that are suitable and identical to the source host, using the scheduling information and according to information from VMs and physical source host.

- **Step 3**. *Synchronization for resource preparation on the target host B*: For the purpose of resource preparation, the disk images of the virtual machines are transferred to the target physical resource. The contextualization of the virtual machines happens during the booting process and the disk images are involved in working on a process of a given environment.

- **Step 4**: *Initialization of VMs and resource reservation on the target host B*: After the booting process, virtual machines are initialized and it has been initially verified by resource selection and resource preparation that necessary resources must be available on B. And the VMs are simply running on host A unaffected.

- **Step 5**. *Iterative copying of pages from source to target host*: After the resource reservation, all the pages are transferred from the source host A to the destination host B. In this step, pre-copy [9] migration is concerned, where all pages are iteratively copied from A to B during the first round. Assume there are n numbers of rounds; and subsequent rounds up to n copy only the pages that got dirtied (dirty pages) during the previous transfer round (indicated by dirty bitmap). Here we have to consider that every virtual machine has some set of pages which update very frequently and this phenomenon leads to the performance degradation of the pre-copy. For every iteration, a "dirtying rate" is calculated depending upon the length of the pages and the number of pages being dirtied. Le *et al.* [10] have bound the number of iterations of pre-copying based on the writable working set (WWS) according to the behavior of typical server workloads.

- **Step 6**. *Stopping the OS instances on the host A and copying*: At this phase, active instance of operating system at source host A is suspended and the following steps are carried out:

  - *Step 6(a)*. Migrating CPU state: Migration of CPU state is concerned with the context of process migration. While migrating the CPU state, the process control block (PCB), the number of cores, processor speed, and required process-specific memory all will transfer to the destination host B.

  - *Step 6(b)*. Migrating memory content: As we discussed earlier in the Step 5, pre-copy technique is used to transfer the pages of virtual machine on source host.

  - *Step 6(c)*. Migrating storage content: We depend on the storage area networks (SAN) or network attached storage (NAS) to permit us to migrate connections to the storage devices. This phenomenon allows us to migrate a disk by reconnecting to the disk on the target machine.

  - *Step 6(d)*. Migrating network traffic: To locate the remote systems and to communicate with a virtual machine, a virtual IP address (known to other units) is assigned to each virtual machine. This IP address and the IP address of the currently hosting machine of the VM are distinct. Each virtual machine can have its individual unique virtual MAC address. The hypervisor maps between the virtual IP and the MAC addresses to their corresponding virtual machines. It should be noted that all the virtual machines should be in the same IP subnet. While migrating to the target node, an ARP broadcast has to be sent to the network declaring that the IP address has moved to a new MAC address (physical location) and TCP connections survive the migration. At the end of the stage, both source and destination host A and B have a consistent suspended copy of the migrating virtual machine and the copy at A is still considered as the primary copy and is kept for proactive maintenance.

- **Step 7**. *Consignment*: After the transfer of all the VM states, OS instance and memory content, host A will get a message from the target host B saying that the host B has successfully received a consistent OS image. After getting this message, host A acknowledges the message as the commitment of the migration operation. Now the source host A may discard and release the original VM at the source host A, and the target host B will become the primary host.

- **Step 8**. *Start VM running at target host B*: Once activated, the migrated VM will start running at the destination host B.

- **Step 9**. *Post-migration activity*: The migrated virtual machine at B is now being connected to the local device divers and post-migration code is running to connect the devices to the new machine. And it advertises moved IP addresses and resumes normal operation as it has done in A.

6.5 Security Issues

In the live migration scheme, an unauthorized user may control initialization, migration and termination of a virtual machine due to inappropriate access control policy, as shown in Figure 6.2 [3, 9-20]. We will discuss the possible attacks while migrating the virtual machines from host machine to guest machine and also the possible solutions to the attacks. This will help us develop a concrete concept of live migration and its loopholes.

Figure 6.2: Schematic diagram of security issues during live migration.

6.5.1 Possible Attacks

In the live migration scheme, a lack of appropriate access policy and some certain rules regarding different kinds of security loopholes help an attacker carry out the following attacks:

- *Guest VM attack*: An attacker's virtual machine broadcasts a request to the network for an incoming migration of a virtual machine. Then the hypervisor maps between the virtual IP and the MAC addresses to the attacker VM and the IP addresses that the address has moved to a new MAC address of the attacker VM. Then the attacker easily achieves control over the requested migrating VM and can modify it.

- *False resource sharing*: An attacker's virtual machine can advertise a broadcast message, containing false information about available resources, which can influence another virtual machine to migrate to the attacker VM.

- *Denial-of-service attack*: Initiation of a large number of outgoing VMs onto a target host server by an unauthorized attacker may lead to the target server being overloaded, causing performance degradation. Meanwhile, the attacker's VM can attack the target server.

- *Hypervisor-based attack*: As the hypervisor controls all the access to VMs and monitors the environment, an attacker's VM can legitimize the target hypervisor with malicious code. VM can gain control over the destination hypervisor and other guest VMs.

6.5.2 Solutions

The live migration process has to address the following shortcomings:

- One of the emerging areas of significance is live migration between different subnet IPs. This algorithm only works within the same IP subnet. That's why this kind of future work may facilitate better live migration of virtual machines in the WAN scenario.

- In live migration, security aspects are also a considerable point in real-time application. In live migration, transmission medium security is very important. Hence, in order to make the medium secure, future work may be done by creating secure VPN, SSL, and IPSEC. A better algorithm can be used in the firewall to ensure network and perimeter security.

- To make live migration secure, client-level security is also needed. So, in the future, research work can be carried out on creating input validation, SSH and open API. This kind of work may protect from different attacks like broken authentication, SQL injection, and intrusion.

6.6 Summary

By migrating the entire state and the memory contents of one virtual machine onto another virtual machine, we facilitate rapid movement and sharing of interactive workloads. In case of failure, proactive maintenance also helps to keep the system state backup. And minimal or zero downtime also helps to make migration very fast in such a way that the user does not have to wait for a long period of time. Secure live migration continues to be a challenge in cloud computing environment.

EXERCISES

1. What is live migration of virtual machine in cloud computing environment?

2. Explain with a suitable example how live migration is related to cloud computing.

3. Why is live migration of virtual machine required?

4. State some advantage of live migration. What is downtime and proactive maintenance?

5. Explain the design process of live migration?

6. Explain the different modules of scheduler and the role of each module.

7. What kind of information is passed from the scheduler to the hypervisor?

8. Explain the basic architecture of source cloud and target cloud cloud and how they are connected to each other?

9. Write down the steps involved in the live migration process.

10. State the steps after suspension of active instances of operating system at source host.

11. What are consignment and post-migration activity in the live migration process?

12. Explain the security issues during live migration.

13. State the possible attacks during live migration.

14. Differentiate between guest virtual machine attack and hypervisor-based attack.

15. What is the drawback of live migration?

References

1. Mell, P., & Grance, T. (2011). *The NIST definition of cloud computing*.

2. Sarathy, V., Narayan, P., & Mikkilineni, R. (2010, June). Next generation cloud computing architecture: Enabling real-time dynamism for shared distributed physical infrastructure. In *2010 19th IEEE International Workshops on Enabling Technologies: Infrastructures for Collaborative Enterprises* (pp. 48-53). IEEE.

3. Pal, S., & Pattnaik, P. K. (2012). Efficient architectural framework for cloud computing. *International Journal of Cloud Computing and Services Science*, 1(2), 66.

4. "CIM System Virtualization White Paper," DMTF 2013 (Informational), Nov. 2007. [Online]. Available: http://www.dmtf.org/ standards/published documents/DSP2013 1.0.0.pdf

5. Elmroth, E., & Larsson, L. (2009, August). Interfaces for placement, migration, and monitoring of virtual machines in federated clouds. In *2009 Eighth International Conference on Grid and Cooperative Computing* (pp. 253-260). IEEE.

6. Raicu, I., Zhao, Y., Foster, I. T., & Szalay, A. (2008, June). Accelerating large-scale data exploration through data diffusion. In *Proceedings of the 2008 international workshop on Data-aware distributed computing* (pp. 9-18).

7. http://www.opennebula.org

8. VM Migration—ConVirt, http://www.convirture.com/wiki/index.php?title=VM_Migration,March 25, 2010.

9. Theimer, M. M., Lantz, K. A., & Cheriton, D. R. (1985). Preemptable remote execution facilities for the V-system. *ACM SIGOPS Operating Systems Review*, 19(5), 2-12.

10. Le, D. N., Kumar, R., Nguyen, G. N., & Chatterjee, J. M. (2018). *Cloud Computing and Virtualization*. John Wiley & Sons.

11. Gilesh, M. P., Jain, S., Madhu Kumar, S. D., Jacob, L., & Bellur, U. (2020). Opportunistic live migration of virtual machines. *Concurrency and Computation: Practice and Experience*, 32(5), e5477.

12. Liu, H., Jin, H., Xu, C. Z., & Liao, X. (2013). Performance and energy modeling for live migration of virtual machines. *Cluster computing*, 16(2), 249-264.

13. Noaki, N., Saito, T., Duolikun, D., Enokido, T., & Takizawa, M. (2020, August). Energy-Efficient Migration of Virtual Machines. In *International Conference on Network-Based Information Systems* (pp. 309-319). Springer, Cham.

14. Gupta, A., Dimri, P., & Bhatt, R. M. An Optimized Approach for Virtual Machine Live Migration in Cloud Computing Environment. In *Evolutionary Computing and Mobile Sustainable Networks* (pp. 559-568). Springer, Singapore.

15. Fernando, D., Yang, P., & Lu, H. (2020, July). SDN-based Order-aware Live Migration of Virtual Machines. In *IEEE INFOCOM 2020-IEEE Conference on Computer Communications* (pp. 1818-1827). IEEE.

16. Van, V. N., Long, N. Q., & Le, D. N. (2016). Performance analysis of network virtualization in cloud computing infrastructures on openstack. In *Innovations in Computer Science and Engineering* (pp. 95-103). Springer, Singapore.

17. Van, V. N., Long, N. Q., Nguyen, G. N., & Le, D. N. (2016). A performance analysis of openstack open-source solution for IaaS cloud computing. In *Proceedings of the Second International Conference on Computer and Communication Technologies* (pp. 141-150). Springer, New Delhi.

18. Seth, B., Dalal, S., Jaglan, V., Le, D. N., Mohan, S., & Srivastava, G. (2020). Integrating encryption techniques for secure data storage in the cloud. *Transactions on Emerging Telecommunications Technologies*, e4108.

19. Seth, B., Dalal, S., Le, D. N., Jaglan, V., Dahiya, N., Agrawal, A., Mayank M. S., Deo P. & Verma, K. D. (2021). Secure Cloud Data Storage System Using Hybrid Paillier-Blowfish Algorithm. *CMC-Computers Materials & Continua*, 67(1), 779-798.

20. Prokhorenko, V., & Babar, M. A. (2020). Architectural resilience in cloud, fog and edge systems: A survey. *IEEE Access*, 8, 28078-28095.

7

RELIABILITY ISSUES IN CLOUD COMPUTING ENVIRONMENT

DAC-NHUONG LE[1], SOUVIK PAL[2], PRASANT KUMAR PATTNAIK[3]

[1] Haiphong University, Haiphong, Vietnam
[2] Sister Nivedita University, Kolkata, India
[3] KIIT, Deemed to be University, India
 Email: nhuongld@dhhp.edu.vn, souvikpal22@gmail.com, patnaikprasant@gmail.com

Abstract

Cloud computing is a model that enables convenient access to network resources like web services, such as email, virtual servers and file transfers, over the network. Reliability of cloud services is one of the key concerns in cloud services. However, reliability of cloud services is not an easy task in large scalable environments and where there is a large amount of traffic from converged data networks. Also, converged data networks present many challenges in the cloud environment. The challenges can range from bandwidth concerns and security flaws. Hence, this study explores the reliability concerns of cloud services. It also seeks to explore the effects of convergence in cloud services. In achieving the objectives of this study, qualitative methods were used. Qualitative data was collected using an open-ended questionnaire. The data was then interpretively analyzed using the content analysis method. Based on the analysis, bandwidth, security and traffic issues were found to be the main issues.

Keywords: Cloud computing services, reliability, availability, converged data networks

7.1 Introduction

Cloud computing is the means through which IT services, from computing power to infrastructure, and collaborative personal applications can be delivered anytime [1]. IT services range from infrastructure services, such as web services, to virtualized services, such as storage [2]. In 2015, Amazon had the biggest cloud infrastructure [3].

Cloud computing has become a vital business enabler in the sphere of IT. Gartner defines cloud computing as a paradigm of computing which provides scalable IT and flexible enabled IT resources that are delivered to customers as a service of the World Wide Web. This model is vastly misunderstood but it brings value to organizations through innovation in existing business strategies. In 2017, Smith defined cloud computing as a vehicle for the next generation digital enterprise as well for agile, growing flexible solutions. Cloud computing is a term that indicates a user can have access to software, infrastructure and computing power from a remote location [2].

Cloud computing can be defined as the physical structure of a data communications network, where information is stored in enormous data centers and assessed anytime, anywhere, and from different computing devices [4]. There are different devices used for cloud computing, including servers, computers, smartphones, tablets, and WiFi devices. The cloud deployment models are: private, public, hybrid, and community. Prior to the cloud service models, organizations had to seriously consider the characteristics of cloud computing [5]. Huang and Wu [6] stated the types of cloud service models were: desktop as a service (DaaS), infrastructure as a service (IaaS), software as a service (SaaS), and platform as a service (PaaS). Furthermore, Cui *et al.* [7] stated that cloud computing allows services sharing at a large scale through the network to access pool configurable computing resources (e.g., networks, servers, storage, applications, and services). Marinescu [3] argues that cloud computing will continue to have a profound effect on individuals and organizations who are now capable of processing a large amount of data.

Huang and Wu [6] claim that cloud computing is frequently overlooked, especially given that high-performance networks characterize the foundation of cloud computing network. Some applications on the cloud, such as monitoring applications, require low latency; however, cloud networks experience a delay, caused by sending data to the cloud, and this can hinder the performance of the network, as supported by Gupta *et al.* [8].

Cloud can also be referred to as a new computing paradigm that provides scalable, on-demand, and virtualized resources for users. In this model of computing, users can access a shared pool of computing resources, delivered with minimal management efforts of users; however, there are some problems concerning cloud [9]. Adding to the concerns, Karim and Rampersad [10] maintain that public organizations are still reluctant to migrate from localized data storage to cloud computing due to reliability concerns. Data management services should be available to users in cloud computing; hence, failure to provide such services hinders the benefits of cloud computing [11]. There is much concern about the adoption of cloud computing regarding anonymity, availability, and compliance, integrity, reliability, auditability, and security; however, the focus of this research is about the reliability concerns of cloud computing in a converged network. An organization's cloud-based services should be reliable and available by resilient services; however, there is a possibility that the system could crash with no provision of their services [12]. In a cloud-computing network, applications are deployed worldwide on the clouds [13]. A redundant virtual machine has been suggested by the researchers to enhance the service reliability [14].

Currently, a number of cloud infrastructures influence service hardware; that is, those characterized by recurring failures [15]. Migrating from localized data storage to the cloud mainly focuses on issues of control, loss of data, service, and availability [12]. Zhou *et al.* [15] point out that cloud computing is an essential solution for providing resourced scalable computing via the internet; because there are a large number of computer nodes connected in data centers, the probability of a server crash is high. According to Adhikary *et al.* [16], slight attention, has been given to cloud computing to manage large amounts of data and this can add challenges in providing resources efficiently. This is because, in converged data networks, if transmission of packets is lesser than or equal to the average of available bandwidth in the cloud, then all packets of a particular link would experience the same amount of transit delay in the network link [17]. Cloud migration techniques encounter limitations in high-speed WAN infrastructures due to queuing and traffic encountered while data traverses the cloud, and that creates negative effects on the utilization of available bandwidth [18]. Some of these negative effects include application data loss that happens while data travels from nodes connected to the internet/cloud [18].

7.1.1 Research Problem Statement

Public organizations are still reluctant to migrate from localized data storage to cloud computing due to reliability concerns [10]. Cloud services should be available for users; hence, failure of availability of services hinders the benefits of cloud computing [12]. Service providers must address the issue of availability of cloud services, otherwise organizations could imminently revert to legacy or traditional systems [19].

7.1.2 Research Aim

The aim of this research is to explore how reliability concerns in cloud computing affect services in a converged data network. The research objective is to understand how the reliability concerns affect the availability of cloud computing in a converged data network.

7.1.3 Research Question

Research Question 1: How do reliability concerns affect cloud-computing services in a converged data network?
  Sub-research question:

- SRQ 1.1: What are the network convergence concerns of cloud services?

- SRQ 1.2: How do reliability concerns affect cloud computing in a converged data network?

- SRQ 1.3: How does data traffic in converged data network affect availability in cloud computing?

Method: A semi-structured questionnaire using interviews.
Objectives:

- To examine the reliability concerns that affect cloud computing services in a converged network.

- To explore how convergence affects cloud computing.

- To bring awareness to organizations about cloud computing reliability concerns.

7.2 Literature Review

This section will focus on reviewing the key research areas of the study, which are as follows: Cloud computing, cloud service models, delivery strategies, reliability elements and concerns, and trends.

Cloud computing is seen as the unit of technology that poses the next-generation computing revolution and has rapidly become the most discussed topic in technology circles [20]. The National Institute of Standards and Technology (NIST) states that: "Cloud computing is a model for enabling convenient, on-demand network access to a shared pool of configurable computing resources (e.g., networks, servers, storage, applications, and services) that can be rapidly provisioned and released with minimal management effort or service provider interaction." Cloud computing is the delivery platform that consists of services and deployment models [21]. The services range from infrastructure as a service (IaaS), platform as a service (PaaS), software as a service (SaaS), etc. IaaS uses software to emulate hardware capabilities and enable companies to grow, manage storage capabilities and bandwidth. Software as a service (SaaS) means that software is no longer procured just the once by the customer, but rather payed for when accessed. PaaS has features of SaaS; the service provider is in charge of all computing resources [22].

AlAjmi *et al.* [23] argue that higher education institutions are reluctant to relocate host services to cloud services due to reliability concerns. According to Metheny, the budget on cloud services and cloud-enabling infrastructure, such as hardware and software, will cost more than over $530 billion by 2021. According to the National Institute of Standards and Technology (NIST), cloud computing provides convenient, on-demand network access to a shared pool of configurable computing resources (e.g., networks, servers, storage, applications, and services) with minimal management effort or service provider interaction [24].

Cloud computing is composed of different infrastructures such as hardware infrastructure as computing services, routers, network switches, storage, and databases to provide a service [1]. Carey [25] argued that there is a major need to address the security, transparency and reliability of cloud computing; because these concerns compromise the benefits of cloud computing. These concerns should be addressed because user's data hosted on the cloud could be lost due to a server crashing or denial-of-service (DoS) attacks [26]. A DoS attack is defined as a network attack whose motive is to disrupt internet service such as web service, emails, etc.

Cloud computing is continuously evolving because of its multi-tenancy characteristics, which include allocation of resources, cost-effectiveness, scalability, centralization of service, virtualization and reliability. In large converged data networks, such as in cloud computing and its infrastructure, reliability is one key feature to be considered, at the design and implementation phases. When reliability is not accounted for it may lead to reduced performance of network and the service-level agreement (SLA) will be hindered. The SLA is a negotiated agreement between a customer, user and a service provider; the agreement is a legally binding contract that lays down the specific terms of service between the service provider and the customer or user [3].

Reliability of cloud computing is defined as a failure-free operation of the cloud service [16]. Zulkernine *et al.* [27] expressed that the challenges in the cloud computing environment compared to a distributed system are the surge in data traffic and users on the cloud, which introduces challenges in attaining reliability or continuity of services. Tanenbaum and van Steen [28] stated that a distributed system is a collection of independent systems that form a coherent system.

Cloud computing in high-income countries is being used as a tool to improve education, research and collaboration without having to be locally on-site to provide administration and academic services [29]. On the contrary, the authors claim that low- and middle-income countries have inadequate basic ICT infrastructure.

According to Piderit and Nyoni, challenges to cloud adoption, such as lack of security and trust issues, could ultimately affect reliability, and have hindered computing in small medium enterprises (SMEs) of the Sub-Saharan Africa region. Lack of data security on cloud is one of the key issues which is an obstacle in the adoption of cloud computing [30]. Every effort has been made to address the shortcomings of cloud computing. In the case of low latency in the enterprise converged data network, an edge cloud has been proposed to minimize low latency and data processing in the network. Computing resources like computers, routers, and storage area networks (SANs) that are interconnected using wide area network (WAN) may consist of one or more types of communication networks such as the internet and virtual networks. According to Chao [31], a cloud network can be predicted with a single packet that may be dropped while data is traversing the cloud network. A cloud network is an enterprise network that can extend to the cloud.

Narayanasamy and Pulla [18] argue that network applications such as live streaming impact the reliability of cloud computing. Singh *et al.* [17] described atomic cloud computing as a recent development. This development helps to minimize the imminent reliability issues in a converged network because it meets the requirements of quality of service (QoS). These QoS requirements include resource utilization, availability, security and reliability, which are the factors that affect the seamless operation of cloud computing.

Another effort to redress low latency and network congestion in cloud computing is the addition of load balancing mechanisms. Load balancing assists cloud service providers to perform services concurrently and minimize performance issues such as interference between data traversing the cloud [32]. It is applied to achieve user satisfaction and optimal resource allocation, thus improving system reliability. Cloud performance depicts a high variability in time; elasticity might not ramp up at the desired speed and unavailability problems exist even when 99.9 percent uptime is advertised [33]. According to Poole *et al.* [34], about 60-70% of all technology, software and services will be based on the cloud; therefore, this major change in IT delivery will require an innovative approach to interconnection that allows pervasive access to multiple clouds over direct and private connections. The scientific literature has mostly focused on scalability and accuracy of the cloud computing service; however, efforts on reliability and security concerns have not been substantially addressed. According to Raza *et al.* [35], cloud computing reliability has been affected due to various reasons such as bandwidth consumption, performance and uptime. Current trends in research and academia have concentrated on technological systems, reliability and security of cloud computing [29]. Public enterprises and SMEs must take advantage of cloud computing benefits and move away from on-site data storage. Also, cloud computing infrastructure must be maintained in order to minimize the rate of failures. Cloud computing services networks should have secure virtual data centers, and switches that are more pervasive, reliable and efficient

7.2.1   Cloud Service Models

Cloud service models are the main models for cloud computing on which computing is based. The literature distinguishes among at least three different deployment models of cloud computing. There are four models listed in Figure 7.1.

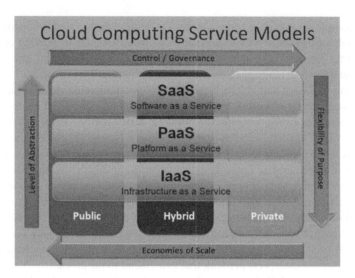

Figure 7.1: Cloud computing magnet.

- *Private cloud*: This cloud service is used for a single client; where infrastructure is, either located on or off premises, whereas public cloud is shared among several users [36]. The private cloud is widely used in higher education institutions due to their requirement of ready-to-use dedicated services [37].

- *Public cloud*: These services are provisioned for use by the public in general [24]. Public cloud has benefits such as security and improved privacy.

- *Community cloud*: This advances the concept of the private cloud to integrate multiple users with a shared environment [36]. It is further noted that the resources on the community clouds are shared in a decentralized architecture.

- *Hybrid cloud*: This cloud is built by integrating public cloud, private cloud and community cloud [38]. Martino, Cretella and Esposito [39] state that hybrid cloud uses collaboration to offer services using proprietary technologies that offer resource interoperability and portability.

7.2.2   Elements of Reliable Cloud Computing

Scalability is defined as the ability of the cloud network to add more components while the network grows without any effects [3]. A scalable data infrastructure must respond to network changes in a timely manner.

Interoperability and portability refers to the ability of a system (such as difference networks) to work with systems or use the components or subcomponents of another system [40]. Martino *et al.* [39] emphasize that interoperability and portability are both highly regarded as a prerequisite of a cloud network.

Fault tolerance refers to the ability of a system to continue to function in the event of one or more of its components failing [41]. Latiff *et al.* [42] points out that fault tolerance addresses cloud execution issues by reducing untimely failure of services.

7.2.3 Cloud Computing Gaps and Concerns

7.2.3.1 *Cloud Service Reliability*

Reliability is an important prerequisite for cloud service providers when offering specific services (e.g., enterprise data), whether through a dedicated physical connection or virtual network [43]. Enterprise data is data shared by the users of an organization from different locations/sites [44]. Reliability of a cloud service refers to the ability of a system to offer the required services at the agreed-upon time [45]. Cloud reliability has a negative impact on service providers because of business disruption and productivity loss [46]. Cloud computing has been a controversial topic in the field of information technology [47]. Reliability in cloud computing is fundamental to building a highly robust system [48]. Botta *et al.* [49] claim that the main concern of cloud computing is increasing broadband, which did not follow the evolution of storage services. According to Kaur and Kumar [38], cloud service providers can be unreliable in their response times. A cloud service is reliable if it is fault tolerant and adapts to changing situations. Another important feature of reliability raised by Ahmad *et al.* [50] is that availability of services is measured as a function of dependability and maintainability. Dependability is the system property that integrates fundamental attributes of a network, including reliability, maintainability, security, availability, privacy, and integrity.

7.2.3.2 *Security in Cloud Computing*

According to Duncan and Whittington [51], information security in cloud computing is of great concern. The security of cloud computing is still debatable, which affects the cloud reliability [52].

Vacca [53] asserts that effective cloud security must respond to all threats. The adoption of cloud computing is hindered by security concerns. According to Cheng *et al.* [54], the moment a user's information is stored on the cloud, the control is on the service provider's side. Vermaat *et al.* [55] point out that there are two categories of cloud security concerns; security concerns faced by cloud service providers and concerns faced by customers. Puthal *et al.* [20] emphasize that security on cloud computing models is different based on the service layer. Service layer is defined as an application's boundary with a layer of services that establishes a set of available operations and coordinates the application's response in each operation [56]. The security concerns for service models are briefly explain below:

- *SaaS*: In SaaS, the service providers provide the services and customers make use of SaaS to run applications on a cloud infrastructure [57]. According to Hussein and Khalid [58], the service provider has to validate that an array of users that subscribe to cloud services do not violate privacy of their counterparts.

- *PaaS*: According to Durairaj and Manimaran [59], PaaS is currently facing network-based security threats and intrusion detection issues. They further state that PaaS security threats are prevalent, and are hindering services on the cloud. Data storage and violated privilege access are also raising concerns [59].

- *IaaS*: Security concerns associated with IaaS are distributed denial-of-service attacks (DDoS), service-level agreement (SLA) attacks and domain name service (DNS) attacks [59]. DDoS is an advanced denial-of-service attack on computer networks. Hackers use DDoS attacks to disrupt availability of service by flooding the network with heavy traffic [60].

7.2.3.3 *Transparency in Cloud Computing*

With so many organizations seeing security as critical to cloud adoption, greater transparency could become a competitive differentiator for cloud vendors [61]. Ouedraogo and Islam [62] support the argument of Lins [63] that the lack of transparency in cloud computing has been acknowledged by academia as one of the most prominent security concerns. Transparency in cloud computing enables users to assess privacy-related risks for appropriate data protection. Luna *et al.* [64] claim that the economic and technological benefits of cloud computing are known, however, lack of security and transparency is still a concern. Botta *et al.* [49] support the views of Luna *et al.* [64] when they say that in the medical sector abuse of access and lack of trust in data confidentiality is predominant.

7.2.3.4 *Latency*

Latency factors refer to slow downloading speeds and response times [12]. According to Botta *et al.* [49], issues of latency can emerge when trying to transfer large amounts of data from the different interconnected devices onto the cloud. Botta *et al.* [49] further claim that there is the perception that cloud services become inadequate if the internet connection is idle. Another important performance concern raised by Schulz [65] regarding low latency is a central processing unit (CPU) for handling input/output operations. Froehlich [66] states that "The growth of public cloud computing usage in many organizations has happened so quickly that it created problems concerning throughput and latency to cloud resources accessed from the corporate office."

7.2.3.5 *Network Convergence Issues*

Network convergence is when two or more networks mix to form a single coherent network. It is important to combine a mix of networks to enable a ubiquitous cloud services. Convergence of networks and cloud computing has recently been identified as an essential component in academia and industry [67]. Internet users worldwide are now dependent on the services provided by cloud, either directly through a service provider or indirectly through their service, provider's reliance on different commercial clouds [68]. Zhou *et al.* [15] state that converged data networks pose crucial challenges to the cloud. To address these concerns, Chen *et al.* [61] suggest that scalability of the cloud needs to be improved drastically. According to Yang *et al.* [69], scalability is the ability of the network to accommodate growth.

7.2.4 Trends in Cloud Computing

The convergence of network security, where different networks such as IP, Fiber, etc., use multi-network media infrastructures, social networks and technologies, is one of the emerging areas of research and academia [70]. Multi-network media infrastructures consist of data from different client devices identified and received via multiple communication networks, and provide customized data to client devices [71].

Cook [72] states that these networks use protocols such as TCP/IP and MPLS, etc., to exchange information throughout the network. Hofmann and Rusch [73] state that Industry 4.0 and many applications must involve a mix of recent (new) technologies which in turn will give rise to technologies that emerged from Industry 4.0 technologies such as cloud computing and the internet of things (IoT). The IoT's intervention in or improvement of cloud computing has become the highlight in technology circles and its aim is to provide scalable applications and business systems [74].

7.3 Reliability Issues in Cloud Computing Research

7.3.1 Research Methodology

This study employed an inductive approach, due to data collected and qualitative data analysis, with the objective of generating theory [75]. Qualitative research method aims to answer questions about the what, how or why of a phenomenon. According to Struwig and Stead [76], there are two different research designs. These are qualitative research methods and quantitative research methods, or a mixture of both methods. Based on the aim of the study, the research strategy employed in this study is qualitative. Qualitative methods produce descriptive data, people's perceptions, and observations [77]. According to Devi [78], qualitative methods are concerned about getting quality data of a phenomenon being studied. Struwig and Stead [76] state that qualitative methods usually give answers to questions such as how, what, etc. Struwig and Stead [76] further state that researchers must understand the main issues being researched from the perception of the participants. Qualitative method is mostly used as it allows the researcher to discover an in-depth understanding of people's views and to examine a new idea, tool and experience. Qualitative research focuses on the aspects of the quality of social life and locates the study with participant's settings that provide opportunities for exploring all possible social variables. Qualitative research is a situated activity that locates the observer in the world [79]. It is the most suitable and efficient way to get the type of information required and to contend with issues of empirical situations. The qualitative research is part of the canon of evidence-based practice and is often applied in institutional contexts in which the implicit model may still be proven, rather than in social contexts. Other important features raised by Maree *et al.* [80] are that qualitative researchers are more interested in how humans arrange themselves and their settings and how populations of these settings make sense of their environments. A qualitative research method was selected because it emphasizes the meanings of experiences, and involves data collection in natural settings as opposed to affected ones [25,79]. The qualitative research method is a useful methodology where the combination of context, complexity and diversity are essential.

7.3.2 Research Strategy

Research strategy provides an outline within which research is conducted and organizing the plan for the collection and analysis of the data methodology [81]. From the qualitative research methods, the grounded theory and case study research methodologies were chosen for this research. The case study research was selected based on the aims and objectives of the study. The purpose of the study was to explore reliability in cloud computing in a converged data network. The research objective was to understand the causes of reliability concerns that affect the availability of cloud computing in a converged data network. A case study allows the researcher to study phenomenon in its real-life context [82]. According to Yazan [83], a case study is one of the most habitually used qualitative research methodologies [83].

Qualitative case study has mostly been used for technology transfer and information systems research over the past decades [33]. According to Yang *et al.* [69], qualitative methods allow the researcher to achieve quality and rigorous data analysis. Struwig and Stead [76] define rigor as the quality of data generated during the research process and it addresses issues of reliability and validity. Reliability and validity reliability define the level of an extent to which a variable is accurate, consistent and stable [84].

7.3.3 Data Collection

Due to the exploratory nature of this study, the data collection technique that was used for this research was an open-ended questionnaire [85]. It was initially proposed to use mixed methods of collecting, which were semi-structured interviews and an open-ended questionnaire.

The reason why I am adopting the semi-structured interview method is because it allows the participant to explore the related research area with a researcher asking questions [86]. The technique is flexible because the interview can be done face-to-face or telephonically anywhere without restrictions [87]. Kallio *et al.* [88] state that "Rigorous development of a qualitative semi-structured interview contributes to the subjectivity and trustworthiness of studies and makes the results more plausible." According Moser and Kalton, rigor is important for semi-structured interviews because it focuses on the experience of the participant. They further stated that a semi-structured interview allows the researcher to focus on engagement with the participant; the interviewer discovering and building upon each response. A questionnaire has also been used to collect data, because it can cover a large population easily and is considered cost-efficient [89]. McGuirk and O'Neill [90] state that a questionnaire is mostly used to gather data in a mixed method that analyzes qualitative and quantitative sources. They further claim that qualitative research method is effective when questionnaires are implemented via one-on-one and electronic media. Open-ended questions were distributed to participants to provide a comprehensive content of the research and to affirm the existing concepts [91]. The researcher has used an open-ended questionnaire to collect data for this study. The questionnaires were distributed electronically using email to different cloud service providers, and the data collected using data collection consent forms. A total number of five questionnaires were from different cloud service providers.

7.3.4 Sampling

Sampling refers to a process by which a researcher selects only a small cluster out of a large population [92]. There are two approaches used for selecting a population; namely, probability and non-probability sampling [93]. This research will employ non-probability sampling and purposive sampling. I decided to choose non-probability sampling because it allows the researcher to collect data in the area of interest [80]. It also helps the researcher avoid redundant data. According to Boddy [94], sampling in qualitative research in most cases is done using non-probability sampling and purposive sampling, and population is normally chosen based on the expert's judgement. Struwig and Stead [76] point out that by using non-random sampling and purposive sampling, the sample is certain to meet the objectives of the research. The researcher chose cloud service providers as the sampling unit of sampling for this research. A sampling unit; is defined as the element of the population that helps the researcher get relevant data for the study in order to meet the objectives of the research [76].

7.3.5 Data Analysis and Findings

Data analysis is defined as the process by which secondary data or raw data is converted into meaningful pieces of information [95]. Cunningham and Carmichael [33] emphasize that data analysis allows the researcher to make sense of the collected data from the participants' point of view, noting and identifying patterns, categories, and themes. For this research, data will be analyzed using content analysis. Content analysis attempts to generate theory and gets at the main aspect of social interactions [32]. Content analysis is a widely used method for qualitative research. Bengtsson [96] argues that when content analysis is applied in a qualitative research it emphasizes credibility of the findings. The collected data from respondents is analyzed below using the objectives of the research, which are as follows:

Reliability in cloud computing is defined by how robust a cloud computing system is able to render services over the internet without interruption and failure [97].

The reliability concern among the cloud service providers is the failure to provide cloud service to the clients. Respondent 1 pointed out that "Just with every IT infrastructure, failure is bound to happen, from the infrastructure component failure to an act of God." Similarly, Respondent 3 pointed out "Mitigating failure scenarios and responding in a manner that instills confidence in your clients when these do occur, and they will since, hardware are machines, and they break, is a key indicator to your clients whether they have invested in the correct partner."

The reliability concerns within the service providers identified are availability limitations and performance issues, which are primarily related to bandwidth problems within the cloud service providers in South Africa; to be specific, the cost of bandwidth, latency issues, and bandwidth reliability concerns are the main reliability concerns. Respondent 2 has highlighted the issues surrounding broadband issues in South Africa: "Internet connectivity is a problem in South Africa." Reliability concerns could be improved; by using updated hardware and software services, but this would need a lucrative budget. "Cloud services are elastic in terms that the underlying infrastructure is designed to scale out automatically to handle incoming requests demand and subscription. Also, cloud service infrastructure ensures that data are replicated to more than one data center for optimal performance" (Respondent 1). Similarly, Respondent 2 suggested that using the latest technology solutions could address reliability concerns: "Solutions such as Azure and AWS have autoscaling services, which cover the spikes in growth and decreases. Additionally, there are load balancers to help as well." The service providers have not identified any challenges they are currently facing.

Network convergence in communication networks refers to a network that combines storage and mobile traffic on a single network that would enable the network to transfer video, voice and data in a secure manner [98]. There are many elements that contribute to the effects of convergence in the cloud services. The main reason that causes convergence in cloud service is the accumulation of transaction data in enterprise operations, such as video, voice and data, which affects the network link utilization and slows down the speed of cloud services and data services.

This also leads to issues of traffic congestion: "Currently a large amount of data traffic between websites, ftp services as well as a heavy amount of email traffic through our VMs" (Respondent 4) and "At present any and all types of traffic are present whether running applications, mail, web, db, etc." (Respondent 3). Respondent 5 has also asserted that network traffic does affect convergence of cloud services in a converged data network. "It could slow down downloads or uploads to your cloud drive." The issue of convergence of cloud service needs to be addressed due to the scale of data which is being handled over the cloud concurrently. That it is why Respondent 4 pointed out that "A number of systems are in place that either blindly monitor traffic for data records or actively monitor the traffic in the case of compromised services and servers." Similarly, Respondent 3 has pointed out that "We have comprehensive ISP and SIEM infrastructure which constantly analyzes traffic flows and is automated to react when configured to do so. We also offer a full range of security compliance services ranging from operating system patching to CIS benchmark remediation to vulnerability scanning, etc." When the traffic is too high in the cloud, convergence is adversely affected and the customer at the receiving end will be affected [99]. Convergence affects cloud computing negatively because users lost while in transit due to heavy internet traffic cause buffers to overflow. Convergence affects cloud computing by degrading the quality of service (QoS) and network overflooding, which in turn introduces network attacks such as denial-of-service attacks.

Respondent 5 has indicated that prevention is dependent on the service provider even though they have clients using their cloud "that is monitored by the service provider." The clients must always make sure that they have a backup of their data stored on the cloud. Respondent 3 has pointed out that "All our platforms are DRaaS capable, allowing our clients to plan for and design for catastrophic failure events like a complete DC shutdown." Similarly, Respondent 1 pointed out that "It is the responsibility of the customer to ensure a disaster recovery and business continuity is built into the application." If these issues are not addressed, the cloud service provider may end up losing potential customers and this may also affect the adoption of cloud computing. To circumvent these issues, service providers must bring alternative solutions to address these, which is why Respondent 1 pointed out that "As a cloud service provider, we have clearly defined SLAs between us and our customers." Also, Respondent 2 has pointed out that "They are designed for those solutions. They sit in data centers, which have dedicated resources managing the hardware and firmware. They have their SLA in place with internet and power providers."

7.4 Findings

In this section, the main factors extracted from the data analysis section are discussed.

7.4.1 Lack of Effort to Address Reliability and Availability Issues

According to Hashemnezhad [32], there is a shortage of tools available to address the issues of reliability in cloud servers. In addition, Mahmood [100] pointed out that broadband availability remains a concern due to rising costs of mobile broadband. The number of users in the cloud is growing exponentially and web applications lead to sophisticated security risks [65]. Satyanarayanan et al. [36] state that adoption of cloudlets can circumvent bandwidth limitations in the cloud. Cloudlet is an enhanced mobility data center located on the internet with no physical state. Indhumathil et al. [101] suggest that third-party auditors must consistently audit cloud services in order to ensure reliability and transparency.

Discussion: Cloud service providers should address reliability and availability issues of cloud services. Hence, users will revert to traditional ways of storing their data, like on-site storage and hard disk drive. If users are not receiving services on the cloud at the time they are expected, this is due to high traffic caused by network convergence. Network convergence is the result of network traffic traversing cloud network simultaneously. Vermaat et al. [55] pointed out that the reliability of cloud service providers prompts very sensitive concerns. Vermaat et al. [55] also say that a converged network (video, voice and data) requires a large amount of bandwidth. The findings of the research show that the availability of the internet is still a problem in the South African context. In some areas of the country, like the Eastern Cape, broadband availability is still a problem. Accessing resources on the cloud could be a difficult mission. Botta et al. [49] emphasize that bandwidth is an issue in the cloud computing environment. Cloud service providers are not in charge of unapproved access and its recovery, absence of client organization and outsider access [102]. Ignorance in addressing reliability and availability issues may not just lead clients to return to on-site storage only, it might likewise prompt economic issues. This lack of effort to address reliability and availability will propel users to terminate their subscriptions to cloud service providers.

7.4.2 Performance Issues

Cloud computing deals with a massive amount of web-based traffic, like emails, file transfers, database and enterprise data, that affect the performance of internet massively. According to Almorsy [52], service-level agreements (SLAs) should be used to address performance and reliability concerns; he also says that the service-level agreement must be applied in case of violation. Bandwidth limitations are the result of combined traffic mix of web-based applications and file transfer protocols that consume disk storage and network in large amounts [20]. Sanaei *et al.* [103] pointed out that convergence in heterogeneous networks, such as wireless LAN, cellular technologies and physical wired networks, introduce challenges in cloud computing such as interception of data in transit and quality of service (QoS). A heterogeneous network is a network that interconnects different types of networks using different communication protocols [104, 105].

Discussion: The findings show that there are diverse applications which are running on the cloud, which negatively influences the assigned transmission capacity on every application. This decrease of transmission capacity is negative in the performance of cloud network. Performance issues in cloud services are caused when the bandwidth of the link is low; then the performance becomes degraded. Users are affected by not receiving their information stored on the cloud at the time they requested. In a given network a link bandwidth must be relatively high and delay/latency must be low. Latency is also a concern in cloud computing which adversely affects the rapid provisioning of IT services. Issues of performance in the cloud are likely to affect adoption, especially in organizations that use web-based applications.

7.4.3 Privacy Issues

The majority of respondents are familiar with the issue of cloud service being prone to failure due to hardware, software, link failure, etc.

Privacy is also any issues because user's data is being handled by different people unaware of the sensitivity of the data. According to my analysis, awareness of cloud computing reliability concerns is twofold; security awareness and location of servers. Clients are not aware of the location where their data is hosted and who has access to the data stored. According to Stergiou *et al.* [8], cloud computing is a growing and fast-paced technological concept but its unique aspects impair privacy and security. The client subscribes to company x and data is managed by another organization.

7.5 Summary

Although cloud computing is more reliable than previous technologies (grid computing, distributed computing, etc.), reliability is still a primary component to be considered in cloud computing environment. The challenge of reliability comes when the cloud service provider delivers on-demand software as a service, i.e., accessible under any network condition (slow connections). The main purpose of discussing reliability in this chapter was to highlight the failures in cloud service. From the failure characteristics in cloud we can identify the availability of cloud service when several of its components fail.

EXERCISES

1. How reliable is cloud computing?

2. How reliable is cloud computing in other areas?

3. What are the features of reliability in cloud computing?

4. Why does cloud have high reliability and availability?

5. What can be done to improve cloud computing reliability?

6. Discuss the reliability and availability of cloud computing.

7. Explain reliable cloud computing connectivity.

8. How do you ensure availability and performance of cloud applications?

9. How is high reliability achieved in cloud computing?

10. What are the advantages and challenges in terms of reliability and availability of cloud?

11. Reliability vs. availability: What's the difference?

12. How can you get high availability in cloud computing?

13. Which components play key roles in affecting cloud computing high availability and reliability?

14. Make a comparative analysis of cloud availability and reliability solutions.

15. Give the best example of availability in cloud computing.

References

1. Chopra, R. (2017). *Cloud Computing: An Introduction*. Stylus Publishing, LLC.

2. Dey, P. (2015) Cloud Computing. Available at https://bookboon.com/en/cloud-computing-ebook [20 May 2018].

3. Marinescu, D.C. (2017). Cloud Computing: Theory and Practice. Morgan Kaufmann.

4. Hartmann, S. B., Braae, L. Q. N., Pedersen, S., & Khalid, M. (2017). The Potentials of Using Cloud Computing in Schools: A Systematic Literature Review. *Turkish Online Journal of Educational Technology-TOJET*, 16(1), 190-202.

5. Bharadhwaj, R., Tripp, T.S., Shetty, R.S. & Green, J.M., Hewlett-Packard Enterprise Development LP, 2018. Cloud application deployment portability. U.S. Patent 9,882,824.

6. Huang, D., & Wu, H. (2017). Mobile cloud computing: foundations and service models. Morgan Kaufmann.

7. Cui, H., Li, Y., Liu, X., Ansari, N. & Liu, Y. (2017). Cloud service reliability modelling and optimal task scheduling. *IET Communications*, 11(2), 161-167.

8. Stergiou, C., Psannis, K.E., Kim, B.G. and Gupta, B. (2018). Secure integration of IoT and cloud computing. Future Generation Computer Systems, 78, 964-975.

9. Ghahramani, M. H., Zhou, M., & Hon, C. T. (2017). Toward cloud computing QoS architecture: Analysis of cloud systems and cloud services. *IEEE/CAA Journal of Automatica Sinica*, 4(1), 6-18.

10. Karim, F. & Rampersad, G., 2017. Cloud Computing in Education in Developing Countries. Computer and Information Science, 10(2), 87. 82.

11. Alharthi, A., Alassafi, M. O., Alzahrani, A. I., Walters, R. J., & Wills, G. B. (2017). Critical success factors for cloud migration in higher education institutions: a conceptual framework. *International Journal Intelligence. Comput. Res.(IJICR)*, 8(1), 817-825.

12. Ardagna, D., Ciavotta, M. & Passacantando, M., 2017. Generalized nash equilibria for the service provisioning problem in multi-cloud systems. IEEE Transactions on Services Computing, 10(3), 381-395.

13. Zhou, J., Cao, Z., Dong, X. & Vasilakos, A.V. 2017. Security and privacy for cloud-based IoT: Challenges. IEEE Communications Magazine, 55(1), 26-33.

14. Jhawar, R. & Piuri, V. (2017). Fault tolerance and resilience in cloud computing environments. In *Computer and Information Security Handbook* (Third Edition), 165-181.

15. Zhou, A., Wang, S., Hsu, C.H., Kim, M.H. & Wong, K. S. (2017). Virtual machine placement with (m, n)-fault tolerance in cloud data center. *Cluster Computing*, 1-13.

16. Adhikary, T., Das, A. K., Razzaque, M. A., Alrubaian, M., Hassan, M. M., & Alamri, A. (2017). Quality of service aware cloud resource provisioning for social multimedia services and applications. *Multimedia Tools and Applications*, 76(12), 14485-14509.

17. Singh, A., Gopinath, V., Sriram, B. & Kanumari, V.G., Novatium Solutions (P) Ltd. (2017). Mechanism for integrating application data with available bandwidth estimation tools for cloud computing environments. U.S. Patent 9,667,452.

18. Narayanasamy, S. & Pulla, I.R., Brocade Communications Systems Inc, (2017). Virtual machine and application movement over local area networks and a wide area network. U.S. Patent 9,781,052.

19. MacDermott, A., Shi, Q., Merabti, M. and Kifayat, K., 2015. Hosting critical infrastructure services in the cloud environment considerations. International Journal of Critical Infrastructures, 11(4), 365-381.

20. Puthal, D., Sahoo, B.P.S., Mishra, S. & Swain, S. 2015. Cloud computing features, issues, and challenges: a big picture. In *International Conference on Computational Intelligence and Networks* (CINE), 2015 (116-123). IEEE.

21. Vasudevan, R., Arun, G., Seetharam, P. and Prathipati, A.K., Oracle International Corp, 2017. Declarative and extensible model for provisioning of cloud based services. U.S. Patent 9,621,435.

22. Nilsson, V. and Dahlgren, A., 2017. A Bright Future for Cloud: A Case Study on Perceptions of Cloud Services.

23. AlAjmi, Q., Arshah, R. A., Kamaludin, A., Sadiq, A. S., & Al-Sharafi, M. A. (2017, November). A conceptual model of e-learning based on cloud computing adoption in higher education institutions. In *2017 International Conference on Electrical and Computing Technologies and Applications (ICECTA)* (pp. 1-6). IEEE.

24. Metheny, M., 2017. Federal cloud computing: The definitive guide for cloud service providers. *Syngress.*

25. Carey, M. (2017). *Qualitative Research Skills for Social Work.* London: Routledge.

26. Yu, Y., Xue, L., Au, M.H., Susilo, W., Ni, J., Zhang, Y., Vasilakos, A.V. & Shen, J. 2016. Cloud data integrity checking with an identity-based auditing mechanism from RSA. *Future Generation Computer Systems*, 62, 85-91.

27. Shafieian, S., Zulkernine, M., & Haque, A. (2014). *Cloud Computing: Challenges, Limitations and R & D Solutions.* Switzerland: Springer, 3-22.

28. Tanenbaum, AS. & Van Steen, M. 2016. *Distributed Systems Principles and Paradigms,* New York. Tanenbaum.

29. Sabi, H.M., Uzoka, F.M.E., Langmia, K. & Njeh, F.N. 2016. Conceptualizing a model for adoption of cloud computing in education. *International Journal of Information Management*, 36(2), 183-191.

30. Piderit, R. and Nyoni, T., 2016. Enhancing User Trust in Cloud Computing Applications. In *CONF-IRM* (50).

31. Chao, L. (2016). *Cloud Computing Network Theory, Practice and Development.* Danvers: Tailor & Francis

32. Hashemnezhad, H. (2015). Qualitative content analysis research: A review article. *Journal of ELT and Applied Linguistics*, 3(1).

33. Cunningham, N., & Carmichael, T. (2017, June). Sampling, interviewing and coding: Lessons from a constructivist grounded theory study. In *European Conference on Research Methodology for Business and Management Studies* (pp. 78-85). Academic Conferences International Limited.

34. Poole, C. M., Cornelius, I., Trapp, J. V., & Langton, C. M. (2012). Radiotherapy Monte Carlo simulation using cloud computing technology. *Australasian physical & Engineering Sciences in Medicine*, 35(4), 497-502.

35. Raza, M.H., Adenola, A.F., Nafarieh, A. and Robertson, W., 2015. The slow adoption of cloud computing and IT workforce. *Procedia Computer Science*, 52, 1114-1119.

36. Satyanarayanan, M., Schuster, R., Ebling, M., Fettweis, G., Flinck, H., Joshi, K. and Sabnani, K., 2015. An open ecosystem for mobile-cloud convergence. *IEEE Communications Magazine*, 53(3), 63-70.

37. Bhatia, G., Al Noutaki, I., Al Ruzeiqi, S., & Al Maskari, J. (2018, March). Design and implementation of private cloud for higher education using OpenStack. In *2018 Majan International Conference (MIC)* (pp. 1-6). IEEE.

38. Kaur, G. and Kumar, R., A. (2017). Review on Reliability Issues in Cloud Service.

39. Martino, B.D., Cretella, G. & Esposito, A. 2015. Cloud Portability and Interoperability: Issues and Current Trends.

40. Webster. M. 2018. [Online] Available at: https://www.merriam-webster.com/dictionary/phenomenon [5 June 2018]

41. Deng, S., Huang, L., Taheri, J., & Zomaya, A. Y. (2014). Computation offloading for service workflow in mobile cloud computing. *IEEE transactions on parallel and distributed systems*, 26(12), 3317-3329.

42. Latiff, M.S.A., Madni, S.H.H. & Abdullahi, M. (2018). Fault tolerance aware scheduling technique for cloud computing environment using dynamic clustering algorithm. *Neural Computing and Applications*, 29(1), 279-293

43. Han, B., Gopalakrishnan, V., Ji, L. and Lee, S., 2015. Network function virtualization: Challenges and opportunities for innovations. *IEEE Communications Magazine*, 53(2), 90-97.

44. Sarkar, Pushpak. "Chapter 4 - Enterprise Data Services". Data as a Service: A Framework for Providing Reusable Enterprise Data Services. *IEEE Computer Society Press*, 2015.

45. Li Wenhao, Yun Yang, and Dong Yuan. "Chapter 1 - Introduction". Reliability Assurance of Big Data in the Cloud: Cost-Effective Replication-Based Storage. Morgan Kaufmann Publishers, 2015.

46. Javadi, B. 2016. RELIABILITY IN CLOUD COMPUTING SYSTEMS, *6th International Conference on Cloud System & Big Data Engineering*, Sydney.

47. Rittinghouse, J. and Ransome, J. 2016. Cloud Computing: Implementation, Management, and Security. *Tailor & Francis Group*.

48. Tanveer, A. 2016. 2016. Enterprise Storage RAS augmented by native Intel Platform Storage Extensions (PSE). Stergiou, C., Psannis, K.E., Kim, B.G. and Gupta, B., 2018. Secure integration of IoT and cloud computing. Future Generation Computer Systems, 78, 964-975.

49. Botta, A., De Donato, W., Persico, V., & Pescape, A. (2016). Integration of cloud computing and internet of things: a survey. *Future generation computer systems*, 56, 684-700.

50. Ahmad, W., Hasan, O., Pervez, U., & Qadir, J. (2017). Reliability modeling and analysis of communication networks. *Journal of Network and Computer Applications*, 78, 191-215.

51. Duncan, R. A. K., & Whittington, M. (2016). Enhancing cloud security and privacy: the power and the weakness of the audit trail. *CLOUD COMPUTING* 2016.

52. Almorsy, M., Grundy, J., & Müller, I. (2016). An analysis of the cloud computing security problem. *arXiv preprint arXiv:1609.01107*.

53. Vacca, J. R. (2020). *Cloud Computing Security: Foundations and Challenges*. Taylor Francis.

54. Cheng, C. C., Cheng, F. C., Lin, P. H., Huang, W. T., & Huang, S. C. (2017). A Fastest Patchwise Histogram Construction Algorithm based on Cloud-Computing Architecture. *International Journal of Web Services Research (IJWSR)*, 14(1), 1-12.

55. Vermaat, M., Sebok, S. L., Freund, S. M., Frydenberg, M., & Campbell, J. T. (2016). *Enhanced Discovering Computers 2017*. Nelson Education.

56. Fawcett. A. (2017). Force.com Enterprise Architecture, Packt publishing.

57. Rao, R.V. & Selvamani, K., 2015. Data security challenges and its solutions in Procedia Computer.

58. Hussein, N. H., & Khalid, A. (2016). A survey of cloud computing security challenges and solutions. *International Journal of Computer Science and Information Security*, 14(1), 52.

59. Durairaj, M., & Manimaran, A. (2015). A study on security issues in cloud based e-learning. *Indian Journal of Science and Technology*, 8(8), 757-765.

60. Maciel, R., Araujo, J., Dantas, J., Melo, C., Guedes, E. & Maciel, P. 2018, April. Impact of a DDoS attack on computer systems: An approach based on an attack tree model. In *2018 Annual IEEE International Systems Conference (SysCon)*, 1-8. IEEE.

61. Chen, M., Ma, Y., Li, Y., Wu, D., Zhang, Y., & Youn, C. H. (2017). Wearable 2.0: Enabling human-cloud integration in next generation healthcare systems. *IEEE Communications Magazine*, 55(1), 54-61.

62. Ouedraogo, M. & Islam, S. 2015, June. Towards the Integration of Security Transparency in the Modelling and Design of Cloud Based Systems. In *International Conference on Advanced Information Systems Engineering* (pp. 495-506). Springer, Cham.

63. Lins, S., Grochol, P., Schneider, S. and Sunyaev, A., (2016). Dynamic certification of cloud services: Trust, but verify!. *IEEE Security & Privacy*, 14(2), 66-71.

64. Luna, J., Taha, A., Trapero, R. and Suri, N. (2017). Quantitative reasoning about cloud security using service level agreements. *IEEE Transactions on Cloud Computing*, 5(3), 457-471.

65. Schulz, G. "Chapter 8 - Data Infrastructure Services: Access and Performance." Software-Defined Data Infrastructure Essentials: Cloud, Converged, and Virtual Fundamental Server Storage I/O Tradecraft. Auerbach Publications, 2017.

66. Froehlich, A. (2018). *How Edge Computing Compares with Cloud Computing*. Networking Computing Blog.

67. Kang, H.S., Lee, J.Y., Choi, S., Kim, H., Park, J.H., Son, J.Y., Kim, B.H. & Do Noh, S., 2016. Smart manufacturing: Past research, present findings, and future directions. *International Journal of Precision Engineering and Manufacturing-Green Technology*, 3(1), 111-128.

68. Luan, T. H., Gao, L., Li, Z., Xiang, Y., Wei, G. and Sun, L. (2015). Fog computing: Focusing on mobile users at the edge. *arXiv preprint arXiv:1502.01815*.

69. Yang, Y., Pankow, J., Swan, H., Willett, J., Mitchell, S.G., Rudes, D.S. & Knight, K. 2018. Preparing for analysis: a practical guide for a critical step for procedural rigor in large-scale multisite qualitative research studies. *Quality & Quantity*, 52(2), 815-828.

70. Chang, V. & Ramachandran, M. (2016). Towards achieving data security with the cloud computing adoption framework. *IEEE Transactions on Services Computing*, 9(1), 138-151.

71. Snider, E., Chipps, T., Buxo, N., Clark, L., Dimond, R. & Winchester, J., Western Union Co. 2017. Multi-network transaction analysis. *U.S. Patent Application* 15/265,014.

72. Cook, C. I. (2018). CenturyLink Intellectual Property LLC: Multi-network access gateway. U.S. Patent 9,942,413.

73. Hofmann, E., & Rusch, M. (2017). Industry 4.0 and the current status as well as future prospects on logistics. *Computers in Industry*, 89, 23-34.

74. Parasher, Y., Kedia, D. & Singh, P. 2018. Examining Current Standards for Cloud Computing and IoT. In *Examining Cloud Computing Technologies Through the Internet of Things* (pp. 116-124). IGI Global.

75. Saunders, B., Sim, J., Kingstone, T., Baker, S., Waterfield, J., Bartlam, B., Burroughs, H. and Jinks, C., 2018. Saturation in qualitative research: exploring its conceptualization and operationalization. *Quality & Quantity*, 52(4)1893-1907.

76. Struwig, FW. & Stead, GB. 2017. Research: Planning, Designing and Reporting: Cape Town, South Africa

77. Taylor, S.J., Bogdan, R. & DeVault, M. 2015. Introduction to qualitative research methods: A guidebook and resource. John Wiley & Sons.

78. Devi, P. S. (2017). *Research methodology: a handbook for beginners*. Notion Press.

79. Alvesson, M. & Skoldberg, K. (2017). Reflexive methodology: New vistas for qualitative research. Sage.

80. Maree, K, Creswell, Ebersohn, J. W., Eloff, L., I. Ferreira, . R N, Ivankova, J. D Jansen, J., Nieuwenhuis, Pietersen & V. L. Plano-Clark. 2016. First Steps in research. Van Schaik

81. Lewis, S., (2015). Qualitative inquiry and research design: Choosing among five approaches. *Health promotion practice*, 16(4), pp.473-475.

82. Cooper. S .B. (2017). *Computability theory*. Chapman and Hall/CRC.

83. Yazan, B. (2015). The Qualitative Report Three Approaches to Case Study Methods in Education: Yin, Merriam, and Stake. *The Qualitative Report*, 20(2): 134-152

84. Isomidinova, G. & Singh, J. S. K. (2017). Determinants of financial literacy: a quantitative study among young students in Tashkent, Uzbekistan. *Electronic Journal of Business & Management*, 2(1), 61-75.

85. Kothari, A., Boyko, J.A. and Campbell-Davison, A. (2015). An exploratory analysis of the nature of informal knowledge underlying theories of planned action used for public health oriented knowledge translation. *BMC Research Notes*, 8(1), 424.

86. Hall, N., Lacey, J., Carr-Cornish, S. & Dowd, A.M. (2015). Social licence to operate: understanding how a concept has been translated into practice in energy industries. *Journal of Cleaner Production*, 86, pp.301-310.

87. Wilson, V.2016.Research methods: interviews. Evidence Based Library and Information Practice, 11(1 (S)), 47-49.

88. Kallio, H., Pietila, A. M., Johnson, M. & Kangasniemi, M. (2016). Systematic methodological review: developing a framework for a qualitative semi-structured interview guide. *Journal of advanced nursing*, 72(12), 2954-2965.

89. Moser, C.A. and Kalton, G. (2017). *Survey methods in social investigation*. Routledge.

90. McGuirk, P.M. & O'Neill, P. (2016). Using questionnaires in qualitative human geography.

91. Burg, M. A., Adorno, G., Lopez, E. D., Loerzel, V., Stein, K., Wallace, C., & Sharma, D. K. B. (2015). Current unmet needs of cancer survivors: Analysis of open-ended responses to the American Cancer Society Study of Cancer Survivors II. *Cancer*, 121(4), 623-630.

92. Betchoo, N.K., (2017). Applied Research in HRM A Qualitative Approach.

93. Schwandt, T.A. 2015. The Sage Dictionary of Qualitative Inquiry.

94. Boddy, C. R. (2016). Sample size for qualitative research. *Qualitative Market Research: An International Journal*, 19(4), 426-432.

95. Silverman, D. 2016. Qualitative Research: Sage cloud computing. *Science*, 48, 204-209.

96. Bengtsson, M. (2016). How to plan and perform a qualitative study using content analysis. *NursingPlus Open*, 2, 8-14.

97. Sharma, Y., Javadi, B., Si, W. and Sun, D., 2016. Reliability and energy efficiency in cloud computing systems: Survey and taxonomy. *Journal of Network and Computer Applications*, 74, 66-85.

98. Gordon, A. (2015). *Communications & Network Security*. New York: CRC Press.

99. Strom, N., 2015. Scalable distributed DNN training using commodity GPU cloud computing. In *Sixteenth Annual Conference of the International Speech Communication Association*.

100. Mahmood, Z. ed., 2016. Connectivity frameworks for smart devices: the internet of things from a distributed computing perspective. Springer.

101. Indhumathil, T., Aarthy, N., Devi, V. D., & Samyuktha, V. N. (2017, March). Third-party auditing for cloud service providers in multicloud environment. In *2017 Third International Conference on Science Technology Engineering & Management (ICONSTEM)* (pp. 347-352). IEEE.

102. Pattnaik, P.K., Kabat, M.R. & Pal, S. (2015). *Fundamentals of Cloud Computing*. Vikas Publishing House.

103. Sanaei, Z., Abolfazli, S., Gani, A. and Buyya, R., 2014. Heterogeneity in mobile cloud computing: taxonomy and open challenges. *IEEE Communications Surveys & Tutorials*, 16(1), 369-392.

104. Shi, C. & Philip, S.Y. 2017. Heterogeneous Information Network Analysis and Applications.Chicago: Springer

105. Seth, B., Dalal, S., Le, D. N., Jaglan, V., Dahiya, N., Agrawal, A., Mayank M. S., Deo P. & Verma, K. D. (2021). Secure Cloud Data Storage System Using Hybrid Paillier-Blowfish Algorithm. *CMC-Computers Materials & Continua*, 67(1), 779-798.

8

CLOUD DATABASE

DAC-NHUONG LE[1], SOUVIK PAL[2], PRASANT KUMAR PATTNAIK[3]

[1] Haiphong University, Haiphong, Vietnam
[2] Sister Nivedita University, Kolkata, India
[3] KIIT, Deemed to be University, India
 Email: nhuongld@dhhp.edu.vn, souvikpal22@gmail.com, patnaikprasant@gmail.com

Abstract

Cloud computing is an emerging technology that provides software and hardware re-sources to users on a pay-per-use basis; and the surge in demand for anytime anywhere access to meet the current needs of users has resulted in the concept of mobile comput-ing. Both aim to provide service to users as per their requirements; and cloud computing provides better flexibility in terms of PaaS, SaaS, and IaaS. Database handling is an im-portant consideration of the above type of computing environments. Many researchers are proposing solutions to database issues using SQL and NoSQL space suitable for the cloud computing scenario. Data in the cloud database is classified as structured and unstructured data as well as big and small data. In this research we have conducted a study of cloud databases as well as its classification in terms of ACID- and NoACID-based database trans-actions. Again our work focuses on the architectural issues of database as a service (DaaS) based on the live migration from ACID-based database to NoACID-based database and vice versa.

Keywords: ACID, database as a service, cloud databases.

8.1 Introduction

Currently, the concept of mobile computing available to the user anytime anywhere has become the focus of the market. Cloud computing and mobile computing both aim to serve users with their handheld devices according to their requirements, and PaaS, SaaS, and IaaS provide better flexibility through the cloud database. Database handling is an important consideration in compute environments [1, 2].

Database is the organization of collection of data. Informally, database is often referred to as both database management software (DBMS) and the data which it manipulates. The DBMS is responsible for maintaining both the integrity and security of stored data, and for recovering information if the system fails.

Cloud database: A stationary database is a database connected to mobile computing devices, such as mobile phones, tabs, laptops and many more, through a mobile network, and a database which is actually carried by the mobile device is called mobile database. Users of mobile database can carry out their transactions even when they are disconnected from the network by using several transactional models and applying caching techniques [3].

In this scenario, users will access traditional as well as mobile database features provided by cloud computing over lightweight portable devices through internet services as well as through traditional desktop personal computer without thinking about better CPU power and memory usage, because the large volume of data will be stored in the cloud and is processed under many database grid servers. The users can access the cloud database through web services. Because of the many technological advancements of the communication network and portable devices, a huge number of users can communicate by exchanging data continuously with the database in cloud regardless of their location.

8.2 Non-Relational Data Models

Database as a service (DaaS) is a core service of cloud computing [4-8] which provides two main database alternatives for the developers: relational cloud database and non-relational cloud database. Relational cloud database captures all the distributed relational database features like SQL-based query processing, optimization, etc. Some of the relational cloud databases are Amazon RDS and SQL Azure. Non-relational cloud database can have multiple models of data, such as key-value based, column-oriented based, document based, and graph based, to process the user queries. The available popular non-relational cloud databases are MongoDB, Amazon SimpleDB, Apache Cassandra and many others. Some non-relational reference data models are discussed below:

- *Key-value database*: The name itself signifies that it combines two entities; one is key, another is a value associated with it. Here the query speed is faster than relational database, it supports huge data storage and it has better concurrency, query, etc., and modifications of operations for data through the primary key are well supported. This category of database models is the origin of the non-relational model and can be inherited by the rest of the data models [9]. Some of the available cloud databases supporting key-value data model are Redis, MemcacheDB, VoltDB, Tokyo Cabinet, Tokyo Tyrant, and Scalaris.

- *Column-oriented database*: This database supports using a table in the data model, but not table association. The characteristics of column-oriented database are as follows:

First, data storage is by column in which data is stored separately in each column; Second, each column where the data is stored is the index of database; Third, only accessing the columns involves the queries, resulting in reduction of the I/O of system; Fourth, concurrent process queries, that is, each column is treated by one process; Fifth, there have to be the same type of data, having similar characteristics and good compression ratio. Overall, the advantage of this data model is more suitable for applying on aggregation in data warehouse [7]. Popular column-oriented databases are Cassandra, HBase, Vertica, and MonetDB.

- *Document-oriented database*: Document database and key-value database are quite similar in structure, but the value of the document database is linguistic, and is stored in the format of JSON or XML. Apart from that, the document databases can generally be a secondary index to value to facilitate the upper application, but key-value database is not able to support this [7]. MongoDB and CouchDB are the currently available popular document-oriented databases.

- *Graph database*: Graph databases are derived from the graph theory. In most cases, we notice that graph typically consists of nodes, properties and edges [9]. The most common example of graph database is Neo4j.

8.2.1 Transactions in Cloud Databases

The databases available in the cloud computing environment, or just cloud databases, are formed of any structured query able to be stored that is put up in the cloud. In the context of cloud databases, people often say different things. Someone may refer to a pay-per-use service; and another group of people may speak about a specific part of software. Cloud database as a service (DaaS) puts up databases in the cloud computing environment and provides database features, such as storage, retrieval, and data definition, on the basis of subscription over the internet. Transaction management is an important characteristic of any database system. But it can behave differently with respect to different environments. In a static environment, the ACID-based database transaction holds good as it can support all necessary transaction criteria (i.e., atomicity, consistency, isolation, and durability) [10-18]. But the scenario of transaction processing differs while on the move. Cloud computing is a distributed environment which supports location-independent transaction processing. Some details of ACID and NoAcid transactions [19] are discussed in Section 8.7.

8.2.2 Advantages of Cloud Database

Cloud databases can reduce the cost of licensing hardware and software by purchasing a database that users can use when needed and accordingly pay for it at reduced cost. Here all the resources like expensive networking equipment, servers, and IT personnel are shared so as to reduce the resource utilization cost. Maintenance of database (backing up, restoring database, managing users, upgrades and bug fixes to databases) is done by the provider of DaaS [20-24]. The user only needs to focus on the design of database and its usage. A large portion of cloud customers, are small startup companies, so a centralized database system can be a good solution to implement their database. Any vendor can employ DaaS in terms of SaaS with a popular DBMS. Furthermore, cloud database is device-independent, so it can also provide services to mobile devices; however, there are many security problems due to lack of location transparency of user information in the cloud data and accessing the user information and computing from a relational cloud database is different in comparison to the non-relational cloud database [6].

8.3   Heterogeneous Databases in DaaS

According to many researchers, traditional databases come in various forms like relational, centralized, infrastructure based, SQL based and many others. Moreover, some of the advanced databases are also developed to deal with cloud computing environment which are well known as non-relational, distributed, infrastructureless, and NoSQL databases. But as a whole, the DaaS in cloud computing environment supports multiple heterogeneous databases. Hence, the cloud database is also referred to as NoSQL database (not-only-SQL database). Here we illustrate multiple traditional databases and newly developed cloud databases in several forms [21].

8.3.1   Relational and Non-Relational Database

A relational database is one that complies with the relational rules of tables as described by Codd (i.e., relational algebra and relational calculus). The set of tables building the database are related to each other (if at all) through a primary key/foreign key structure. For example, a student table may have student ID as its primary key, at the same time a department table contains student ID as a foreign key which defines the relation between the two. In relational databases, predefined schemas and SQL queries are mainly used for storing and retrieving the information. Recently, there has been a surge of alternate technologies for huge scale analytic processing in cloud computing environment, the majority of which are not related to the relational model. For this reason, distributed file systems together with MapReduce have become strong competitors of relational database systems which would analyze large data sets, causing exploitation parallel processing. Moreover, there is a progression on using MapReduce for evaluation of relational queries. Hence, many non-relational databases are developed. Some of the important features of non-relational databases are schema free, horizontally scalable, enhanced data modeling and representation, faster computations. Non-relational databases are not fully adhering ACID transactions during write/update operations. Some of the popular non-relational DBMS are MongoDB, Cassandra, CouchDB, Amazon SimpleDB and Redis [21].

8.3.2   Centralized and Distributed Database

In a centralized database, all the data and information of an organization is stored in a single location, for instance, a mainframe computer or a server. The users can access data in remote areas via the wide area network (WAN) using the application programs which are being offered to access the data. The centralized database serves all the incoming requests to the system easily (the mainframe or the server), therefore easily becomes an issue of bottleneck. But as all the data reside in one location, it is easier for maintenance and keeping the backup of data. Moreover, it is easier for maintaining data integrity, because outdated data is no longer available in other places once data is stored in a centralized database [22].

In a distributed database, storage devices store data in different physical locations. They are not connected to a common CPU but a central DBMS control the database. The data is accessed by the user in a distributed database by accessing the WAN. It uses the replication and duplication processes to keep a distributed database up to date. Changes are identified by the replication process in the distributed database and those changes are applied to make sure that all the distributed databases look exact. This becomes a very complex and time-consuming process depending on the number of distributed databases. In the duplication process, it identifies one database as a master database and duplicates that database. This process is not as complicated as the replication process but it makes sure that all the distributed databases have the same data. Cassandra and MongoDB are two of the most popular distributed databases. The main difference between centralized and distributed databases is that the distributed databases are typically geographically separated, are separately administered, and have slower interconnection [20].

8.3.3 Structured and Unstructured Database

Different interest groups often use the labels "structured data" and "unstructured data" ambiguously; and are often lazily used to cover multiple distinct aspects of the issue. In reality, there are at least three orthogonal aspects to form the structure of the data itself, the data that is hosted by the structure of the container, and the structure of the access method used to access the data.

The definition of highly structured data according to some researchers is: Highly structured data has the content that allows the simple programmatic derivation of commonalities between different entities (e.g., rows, objects). Several data models are being developed to acquire these three main characteristics of structured database. The most prominent data model for structured database is the relational data model. But for relatively high scalability and availability issues some more advanced data models have emerged to deal with unstructured data in cloud computing environment, namely the key-value-based data model, column-based data model, document-based data model and graph-based data model. Unstructured data is typically text-heavy, but may also contain information such as dates, numbers, and facts. This results in irregularities and ambiguities that make it difficult to understand with the help of traditional computer programs as compared to the data stored in fielded form in databases [20].

8.3.4 Infrastructure-Based and Infrastructureless Databases

Traditional databases deal with infrastructure-based environment. Hence, traditional database under an infrastructure-based environment has many advantages like better data accessing speed, high bandwidth, higher energy backup, better computing units and device independence. On the other hand, it suffers from higher operational and maintenance costs. Some of the popular traditional DBMS are Microsoft SQL Server, Oracle, MySQL, and PostgreSQL. Mobile database usually operates in an infrastructureless environment. Every system acts as an individual server while communicating to each other in infrastructureless environment. A mobile computing device over a mobile network can connect mobile database in an anywhere-at-anytime fashion. It is necessary to maintain a cache to hold frequent data and transactions so that they are not lost due to connection failure. Mobile database may contain information like a list of contacts, price information, or distance travelled. Mobile databases are device-dependent. Commercially available mobile DBMS are Microsoft SQL Server Compact (SSC), IBM's DB2 Everywhere, and Oracle9i Lite [24-30].

8.3.5 SQL-Based and NoSQL-Based Databases

Structured query language (SQL) is an ANSI (American National Standards Institute) standard language for accessing and manipulating databases. All the relational DBMS are tightly coupled with SQL, hence it is also called SQL-based DBMS.

> However, due to the rapid growth of distributed systems, NoSQL-based databases have come into the picture. NoSQL database design can support several non-relational data models, namely key-value-based data model, column-based data model, document-based data model and graph-based data model. Key-value data model means a value corresponding to a Key, although the structure is simpler with higher query speed than relational database, supporting mass storage and high concurrency, query and modifying operations for data through the primary key. Column-oriented database use Table as the data model, but it does not support table association [31-35]. Column-oriented database has the following characteristics:
>
> 1. Data is stored column-wise; that is, data is stored separately in each column;
> 2. Each column consisting of data is the index of database;
> 3. Only access the columns to involve the queries resulting in reducing the I/O of system;
> 4. Concurrent process queries, that is, each column is treated by one process;
> 5. There is the same type of data, having similar characteristics and good compression ratio, are well supported.

An SQL-based database can have certain characteristics as follows:

- SQL database has a couple of sub-languages to deal with database such as data definition language, data manipulation language, data query language, and transaction control language.

- Here data can be stored in a tabular structure, i.e., set of rows and columns.

- It has maximum number of clients as it is more standardized.

- Supports all the features of relational data model.

- It is best fit for ACID transaction.

- The database focuses on schema design.

- Also, join operator is used to establish the relation between two or more tables in the database.

The SQL-based databases also suffer from many challenges like higher overhead time for data accessing in homogeneous distributed environment, and is also unable to deal with heterogeneous distributed environment.

Some of the commercial availability of SQL-based DBMS are Microsoft SQL Server, Oracle, Sybase, MySQL, and Ingress. Popular NoSQL DBMS are Cassandra, MongoDB, CouchDB, Neo4j, Redis and many others [32].

8.4   Study of a Document-Oriented Cloud Database - MongoDB

MongoDB[1] is a schemaless document-based database developed by 10gen and an open source community [31]. The name MongoDB originated from the word "humongous." The database written in C++ is intended to be scalable and fast. In addition to its document-oriented database features, MongoDB can be stored and distributed in large binary files like images and videos. Different techniques used by MongoDB are given below.

8.4.1   Data Model

MongoDB, which uses binary encoded JSON-like objects, stores documents as BSON (binary JSON) objects [31]. BSON supports objects which are nested in structure with objects which are embedded and arrays like JSON does. MongoDB supports modifications of attributes which are in place, so if the application is a single attribute, then only this attribute is sent back to the database. The primary key is the ID field held by each document. The developer can create an index for each queryable field in a document to enable fast queries. MongoDB also supports indexing over embedded objects and arrays. A special feature for arrays is created, which is called "multikeys": This feature allows using an array as index, which could be used for many things; for example, containing tags for a document. With the help of such an index, documents can be searched by their associated tags. MongoDB supports organization of the documents, so-called "collections." Each collection may contain any kind of document, but queries and indexes can only be made against one collection. Since MongoDB has made the current restriction of 40 indexes per collection, for the better performance of queries against smaller collections it is advisable to use each type of document as a collection. MongoDB relations can be modeled by using embedded objects and arrays. Therefore, the data model has to be in the form of a tree. If data model is unable to be transformed into a tree, there are two options: denormalization of the data model or client side joins. The first option would imply the replication of the document inside the database. This solution should only be used when very frequent updates are not needed by the replicated documents. The second option is to use client side joins for all relations which cannot be put into the form of a tree. This requires more work in the layer of application and this increases the network traffic within the database.

> JSON: JSON stands for JavaScript Object Notation. JSON is a lightweight text-data interchange format. Basically JSON syntax is used for exchanging and storing the text information. It is completely language independent. It is very easy and fast to parse the documents.

8.4.2   Replication

MongoDB does not provide optimistic replication (it does not use MVCC (multi-version concurrency control)) and is required to have only one master node with the capabilities of writing at a time. The implementation of replication in MongoDB is with the use of a log file on the master node containing all high-level writing operations performed on the database. During the replication process, the slaves ask the master for all the operations for writing since their last synchronization and performance of the operations from the log on

---

[1] https://www.mongodb.com

their own local database. There is repetition of performance of all the operations in the log, for performing the replication without endangering the consistance of the slave database even if the slave, after failure, is not sure about its local database state [32, 33]. MongoDB supports the following replication setups:

- *Master-Slave*: One master with capabilities of writing and a transaction log, which is asynchronously forwarded to the slave.

- *Replica Pairs*: Configuration of replica pairs is supported by MangoDB, which is basically a master-slave configuration, but with the extension that the paired nodes can negotiate between themselves which one the master is. On the failure of current master of the pair, the current slave becomes the new master. On the failure of the connection of network between the pair, they ask an arbiter server. The node which reaches the arbiter first becomes the master. The paired nodes know if the other node is down or if they are only disconnected with the help of an arbiter node.

- *Limited Master-Master*: A restricted master-master setup is also supported by MongoDB. In this configuration only insert and delete of the write operations is allowed. This is because any updates would compromise the integrity of the database's existing documents, due to the lack of a distributed lock manager or a multi-version concurrency mechanism.

> MVCC: MVCC or MVC stands for multi-version concurrency control. It is a concurrency control method which is used by database management systems. It is an advance technique which is used to improve the performance of the database in multi-user environment, and provides concurrent access to the database which helps to implement transactional memory.

8.4.3 Sharding

MongoDB supports sharding automatically, which is currently in an alpha stage and consequently has some limitations. A MongoDB cluster consists of three components: shard nodes, configuration servers and routing services, which are called mongos in MongoDB terminology. Figure 8.1 shows an overview of a MongoDB cluster. Storing the actual data is done by shard nodes. Either one node or a replication pair of shards composes each shard. In upcoming versions of MongoDB, for better redundancy, each shard may consist of more than two nodes and read performance. The config servers store the metadata and routing information of the MongoDB cluster and are accessed from the shard nodes and routing services [31].

In mongos, the tasks are performed by the routing process as per the requests of the clients. Depending on the type of operation the necessary shard nodes are sent requests by the mongos and merge the results before returning them to the client. Mongos themselves are stateless and therefore can be run in parallel. The documents in a MongoDB cluster are partitioned by their owning collection and by a user specified shard key. A shard key in MongoDB is similar to an index and can contain multiple fields.

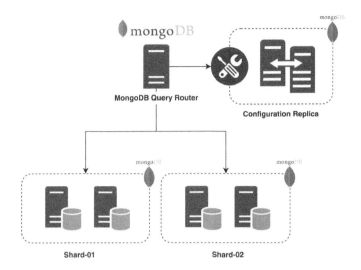

Figure 8.1: An overview of a MongoDB cluster.

This shard key is used in partitioning the whole collection into shards. Assigned documents ordered by this key are stored by each shard. The documents are organized into chunks inside a shard. Each chunk containing an ordered set of documents starts from one shard key and ends with a specific shard key. A chunk is split if it gets too big. MongoDB uses chunks for the automatic rebalancing of the shards. Some of its contained chunks are migrated to other shards if the size of one shard is too big. When new nodes are added or removed, then chunks are also used to redistribute the data. A record for each chunk in the cluster is stored by the config servers, which consist of the start and end key of the chunk and its assigned shard. The mongos use this information to decide which shard nodes are needed for which requests. On the basis of the type of the operation either only one chard or nearly all shards need to be consulted to fulfill a request. For example, if the user id is also the shard key, it can find a simple query to search for a document with a specific id to be routed only to the shard that stores this document. But with the usage of a shard key queries that cannot be restricted need to be sent to each shard node of the cluster [34, 35].

8.4.4   Architecture

C++ is implemented by MongoDB and consists of two types of services: the databases core MongoDB and the routing and auto-sharding service mongos. Memory-mapped files are used by MongoDB for storage, which lets the operating system's virtual memory manager make the decision concerning which parts of the database will be stored in memory and which ones only on the disk. This is why when the data is written to the hard disk it cannot be controlled by MongoDB. The motivation for using the memory mapped files is to instrument as much of the available memory as possible to boost the performance. In some cases the need for a separate cache layer on the client side might be eliminated. But there is currently an alternative storage engine for MongoDB in development, which allows MongoDB to take control over the timing of read and write operations. MongoDB stores indexes as B+Trees like in most other databases.

8.4.5 Consistency

There is no version concurrency control and no transaction management in MongoDB. So, if a client reads a document and writes a modified version back to the databases and if another client also happens to write a new version of the same document, then between the read and write operation the first client will be chosen. Only eventual consistency is provided by MongoDB, so an old version of a document is read by process even if another process has already performed an update operation on it.

8.4.6 Failure Handling

A transaction log is not used by MongoDB to ensure the newly written data is durable or not and because of the usage of memory mapped files lazy writes are performed. Some data might be lost if a MongoDB node crashes. Because of interruption of writes during a crash or hardware failure, there may be corruption in some of the database files. If a crashed node comes back online, it will require that maintenance utilities of MongoDB are used for searching for corrupted database files to fix them. If there is a crash of a single shard node and it is part of a replication pair, then the complete workload of that shard will be overtaken by the other member of the pair until the broken node is back online or replaced. If all nodes of a shard fail, then the cluster on data in this shard will be unable to perform operations. If one of the config servers fail, the MongoDB cluster will not be able to perform any kind of split or migrate operations on the data chunks until the lost config server is back online or replaced.

8.5 CAP Theorem for Cloud Database Transaction

Dr. Eric Brewer proposed the CAP theorem that is widely adopted today by large web companies, such as Amazon, as well as the cloud database community [27]. The acronym CAP stands for Consistency, Availability and Partition Tolerance, as shown in Figure 8.2.

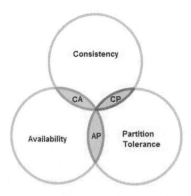

Figure 8.2: CAP theorem.

Consistency means that after execution of an operation a system is in a consistent state. A distributed system is typically considered to be in a state of consistency if after an operation is updated of some writer, all readers see his updates in some shared data source.

(Nevertheless there are several alternatives to this strict notion of consistency, as we will see below.)

Availability and especially high availability means that a system is designed and implemented in such a way to allow the continuation of operation (i.e., allowance of read and write operations) if, for example, nodes in a cluster crash or some hardware or software parts are down due to upgrades.

Partition tolerance is understood as the ability to continue the operation of the system when the network partitions are present. This occurs if two or more "islands" of network nodes arise which (temporarily or permanently) cannot be connected to each other. Some people also understand partition tolerance as the system being able to cope with the dynamic addition and removal of nodes (e.g., for maintenance purposes, removed and again added nodes are considered an own network partition in this notion) [8].

Brewer also states that one can at most choose from two of these three characteristics in a shared-data system. As cloud computing environment supports shared-data system it also follows the CAP theorem. According to the CAP theorem and different concerns of cloud database, a cloud database is preliminarily classified as follows:

- *Based on consistency and availability (CA)*: Here part of the database is not concerned about the partition tolerance and the replication approach is mainly used to ensure data consistency and availability [8]. Systems concerned with consistency and availability are the traditional relational databases Vertica (column-oriented), Aster Data (relational), Greenplum (relational) and so on.

- *Based on consistency and partition tolerance (CP)*: Under this category of database systems data is stored in the distributed nodes. Though the consistency of these data are also ensured, but the support is not good enough for the availability [9]. Bigtable (column-oriented), Hypertable (column-oriented), HBase (column-oriented), MongoDB (document), Terrastore (document), Redis (key-value), Scalaris (key-value) , MemcacheDB (key-value), Berkeley DB (key-value) are the main CP systems.

- *Based on availability and partition tolerance (AP)*: The availability and partition tolerance are ensured by these systems primarily by the consistency achieved [9]. Some of the available AP systems are Voldemort (key-value), Tokyo Cabinet (key-value), KAI (key-value), CouchDB (document-oriented), SimpleDB (document-oriented) and many more.

8.6 Issues in Live Migration of Databases in Cloud

Live migration [10] in cloud database allows a server administrator to move the running virtual machine or database transactions between different CDS nodes without disconnecting the client. Many times migration of database transaction suffers from some of the factors that affect cost, such as system downtime, service interruption due to aborted transactions of user database (UDB), and migration overhead. But live migration of database transactions may provide low overhead migration and minimize overall system downtime [13]. In addition, some other benefits of live migration over traditional migration are energy conservation, load balancing, and online maintenance [11].

Traditional migration techniques developed for UDB migration in the cloud computing environment [12] are as follows:

- *Stop and Copy*: The simplest way of migrating UDB is Stop and Copy [12]. Initially the source CDS node is stopped to serve the UDB and the data is copied to destination CDS node and the UDB transactions are restarted at destination CDS node. There are also some limitations in this approach such as the increased downtime of overall system (due to the stopping of source CDS node) with the increase of UDB size. Apart from that, the entire database cache is lost due to the restarting of the transaction at destination node so that the post migration overhead time is greatly increased to warm up the cache. Hence, this approach is not well suited for live migration due to these weaknesses.

- *On-Demand Migration*: The reduction of downtime period of source CDS node may occur by using the on-demand migration approach [11], where there is migration of minimal data of the UDB to the destination node to avoid the disruption of services. The corresponding transaction starts executing once the UDB comes online at destination node. However, the only problem is that if the transaction requires the data that has not been migrated to the destination, then an expensive cache miss occurs. The post migration overhead will increase with the increase in warm-up time for caching the data at destination, due to which the on-demand migration approach also is not fit for live migration.

8.7 Cloud Database Classification Based on Transaction Processing

This section deals with a classification of cloud databases in terms of database transaction among many classifications [20, 30]. A transaction is a unit of program execution that can be accessed and which possibly updates various data items. Here we classify the cloud database in two ways: ACID-based cloud database and NoACID-based cloud database.

All the database storage systems in cloud apply the CAP theory [6], which stands for Consistency, Availability, and Partition Tolerance. Consistency means all clients always have the same view of the data; availability means each client can always read and write; and partition tolerance means despite physical network partitions, the system works well. For all of the database storage, only two of those characteristics could be taken. Existing ACID-based cloud database takes consistency and availability but it can't be applied to partition tolerance. So the NoACID-based cloud database takes partition tolerance by giving up either consistency or availability. To make it work, relational database can be given up and only things that it needs for each function can be taken.

8.7.1 ACID-Based Cloud Database

The traditional DBMSs come under ACID-based cloud databases. Commercially available DBMS under ACID-based cloud database are Amazon Relational Database System (RDS), Microsoft SQL, Azure Supporting SQL Server, and Amazon Machine Image, which support (MySQL, Oracle, PostgreSQL, Sybase and so. Moreover, these databases are best suited for write-intensive database applications like OLTP (online transaction processing).

8.7.1.1 Characteristics of ACID-Based Cloud Database
Some of the basic characteristics in this category of databases are discussed below;

- *ACID transaction*: ACID-based cloud databases are the strong followers of ACID transactions in order to retain and protect the consistency of the database system.

- *Relational data model*: To store and retrieve data from the data store these databases only use relational data model. Data can be stored here in the form of tables (i.e., combination of rows and columns).

- *Query language*: During transaction processing a user can interact with the database only by using the structured query language (SQL).

- *Constraints allowed*: One method of implementing business rules in the database is provided by constraints. Constraint functionality is implemented by SQL in the form of primary key constraint, foreign key constraint, unique key and so on.

- *Normalization*: This encompasses a set of procedures designed to eliminate simple domains (non-atomic values) and the redundancy (duplication) of data, which in turn prevents data manipulation anomalies and loss of data integrity.

- *Joins and triggers allowed*: Joins are used to relate information in different tables. Rows from two or more tables are retrieved by a join condition, which is a part of the SQL query. The SQL WHERE clause of select, update, delete statements uses an SQL join condition. Whereas a database trigger is procedural code that automatically executes in response to certain events on a particular table or view in a database. The trigger is mostly used for the maintenance of the integrity of the information on the database. For example, when there is a new record (representing a new worker) and it is added to the employee's table, new records are also created in the tables of the taxes, vacations and salaries.

- *Schema required*: Insertion of data can occur in an ACID-based database after defining a database schema.

- *Maturity*: Data is more mature and is standardized as it has been used by a large number of users or clients for a long time.

8.7.1.2   *Challenges of ACID-Based Cloud Database*

The database system faces several challenges, which are described below:

- *Database replication*: This deals with the case that is most available in a cloud computing environment.

- *Bottleneck problem*: In RDBMS, atomicity, consistency and isolation are usually implemented using a central lock manager. A central lock manager would be the bottleneck for a distributed system because all database nodes would need to contact the lock manager for every operation.

- *Low performance*: It is very time-consuming and costly to accomplish serializability during concurrent execution in an ACID-based database transaction.

8.7.2   NoACID-Based Cloud Database

The advanced distributed DBMSs come under the NoACID-based cloud databases. Commercially available DBMSs under NoACID-based cloud databases are Amazon SimpleDB, Apache Cassandra, 10gen MongoDB, CouchDB, Redis and several others. Moreover, these databases are best suited for both read- and write-intensive database applications like OLTP (online transaction processing) and OLAP (online analytical processing).

8.7.2.1   Characteristics of NoAcid-Based Cloud Database

NoACID-based cloud databases have the following characteristics:

- *BASE transaction*: According to Brewer, the BASE transactions [6] relax the ACID properties which are consistent and isolated in favor of availability, graceful degradation, and performance. The BASE properties are summarized by Ippolito in the following way: an application works all the time basically (basically available), consistency is not needed all the time (soft-state) but it will eventually be in some known-state state (eventual consistency).

- *Multiple data models*: NoACID-based cloud databases are not restricted for use only in the single data model as ACID-based cloud databases usually are. They may use several data models like key-value-based, column-oriented, document-oriented, and graph-based data models for storing and retrieval of data from the data store.

- *Query language*: Users can interact with the NoACID-based cloud databases in various forms such as using MapReduce functions, JSON scripts, GQL and CQL queries and so on.

- *Replication*: Replication in the case of distributed cloud databases means that a data item is stored on more than one node. This is very useful for increasing the reading performance of the database, because it allows a load balancer to distribute all read operations over many machines. It also has an advantage of making the cluster robust against failures of single nodes. If there is a failure in one machine, then there is at least another one with the same data which can replace the lost node.

- *Sharding*: The term sharding is derived from the noun "shard," which means that the data inside a database is split into many shards that can be distributed over many nodes. The data partitioning can, for example, be done with a consistent hash function that is applied to the primary key of the data items for determination of the associated shard.

8.7.2.2   Challenges of NoACID-Based Cloud Database

- *Maturity*: Since NoACID-based cloud databases only emerged a few years back, they have a small set of users and clients. However, due to its popularity in the current scenario, it is in the process of being standardized as many projects and researches are continuing on with this field.

- *No Joins and triggers*: NoACID-based cloud databases lose the concept of association data through joins and imposing some sort of validation and restriction to access the data through triggers.

A comparison of ACID and NoACID-based cloud databases is given in Table 8.1.

8.8   Commercially Available Cloud Database Platform

In cloud computing, database as a service is another platform which can deliver several distinct cloud databases. Many database service providers are available that are currently offering DaaS in public cloud environments. Some of the popular database services providers are Amazon, Microsoft, Google and more [6].

Table 8.1: A comparison of ACID-based and NoACID-based cloud databases.

Characteristics	ACID-based Cloud database	NoACID-based Cloud Database
Transaction property	Strictly follow ACID transactions	Follow BASE transactions
Data models	Relational model	Key-value based data models, Column-oriented data models, Document-oriented data models, Graph-based data models
Query language	SQL Queries	MapReduce functions, JSON scripts, GQL, CQL queries and so on
Constraints	Allowed	Not allowed
Normalization	Allowed	Not allowed
Joins and Triggers	Allowed	Not allowed
Database schema	Required	Not required
Maturity	Well mature and standardized	Still in a process to standardized
Database Replication	Not supported	Supported very well
Performance during concurrent execution	Expensive and more time consuming	Cheap and less time consuming
Sharding	Not supported	Supported very well
Scalability	Low	High
OLAP support	Not supported	Supported
OLTP Support	Supported	Supported
Storage	Limited	High
Location independent	May be	Yes
Device independent	May be	Yes
Availability	not very well	Highly available
Data accuracy in database	Always preserve	May not be always
Commercial DBMSs	Amazon RDS, Microsoft SQL Azure, Amazon Machine Image should be supports DBMSs (i.e., MySQL, Oracle, PostgreSQL, Sybase and so on.)	Amazon SimpleDB, Apache Cassandra, 10gen MongoDB, CouchDB, Redis Neo4j and several others.

8.8.1   Amazon Web Services

Amazon was the first company to provide cloud services under the name Amazon Web Services (AWS) to external customers in 2006, and is constantly expanding their service portfolio. A Xen-based cloud computing service called Elastic Compute Cloud forms the core of AWS (EC2). Currently, two structured database services are offered by Amazon: Amazon SimpleDB, a non-relational data store which is distributed, and Amazon Relational Database Service (RDS), which is a fully-featured relational database. The SimpleDB API can be used with the help of a REST- or SOAP-based transport. Response messages are given in XML. There are only four management domains (`-CreateDomain`, `-DeleteDomain`, `-ListDomains`, `-DomainMetadata`) and five data management operations (`-PutAttributes`, `-BatchPutAttributes`, `-DeleteAttributes`,

`-GetAttributes, -Select`). The API of RDS is twofold: The first part is an API for database instance management. It allows the creation and deletion of instances as well as for scaling of CPU, memory and storage resources, which are provided to a DB instance. Its availability is with SOAP or a proprietary HTTP-based transport. The second part of the API is provided with the interface to the data and is an ordinary MySQL socket interface. Thus, the access of data can be accomplished with both the MySQL tools and the ODBC/JDBC drivers for MySQL [6].

8.8.2   Microsoft Windows Azure

Windows Azure is the cloud computing platform which is provided by Microsoft. Two structured database services are offered by Microsoft: The Azure Table Service conceptually matches with the Amazon SimpleDB, whereas the counterpart of Amazon RDS is formed by the SQL Azure. The Azure Table Service can be used with HTTP-based and RESTful API, and it can either be used directly, or through ADO.NET data services. The API is used for SQL Azure and is a Tabular Data Stream (TDS) interface. Thus, the established access mechanisms like ADO.NET and ODBC/JDBC work and no modifications are needed [6].

8.8.3   Google App Engine

The foundation of Google App Engine (GAE) is fundamentally different from the infrastructures of other clouds, like, for example, Amazon's infrastructure. This is because GAE does not provide bare VMs, but an application framework consisting of various services to build web applications. That's why GAE is commonly called Platform as a Service (PaaS), whereas Infrastructure as a Service (IaaS) is provided by the other cloud operators like Amazon and Microsoft. Since GAE in general is targeted to scalable distributed applications, there is no relational SQL-based database service in GAE. DataStore is the sole database service of GAE. Currently, a GAE API is provided for Java and one for Python. GAE cannot use other languages [6].

8.9   Summary

Database as a service is one of the cloud computing services that encompasses numerous database features like relational/non-relational, centralized/distributed, structured/unstructured, infrastrucure-based/infrastructureless, and SQL-based/NoSQL-based, which can be made available on a subscription basis adhering to a pay-per-use policy. In subsequent sections of the book we will take up features like cost, storage, security, data accessing speed for both traditional distributed database and mobile database for an intensive study.

EXERCISES

1. What is meant by cloud database?

2. Are there any differences between mobile database and cloud database? If yes, what are they?

3. Who are the main database providers of DaaS? Explain them.

4. What are the differences between relational and non-relational cloud databases?

5. What are the non-relational reference data models? Explain.

6. What are the differences between column-oriented and document-oriented databases?

7. What are the advantages of cloud database?

8. What is meant by SQL-based and NoSQL-based database?

9. What are the differences between centralized and distributed databases?

10. Classify the database in DaaS according to advance database.

11. What is structured database?

12. What is unstructured database?

13. What are the differences between structured and unstructured databases?

14. What are the differences between SQL-based and NoSQL-based databases?

15. What is meant by infrastructure-based and infrastructureless database?

16. What are the differences between infrastructure-based and infrastructureless databases?

17. What is MongoDB?

18. Briefly describe the data model of MongoDB?

19. What is replication? How is it implemented in MongoDB?

20. What are JSON and MVCC?

21. What are the different replication setups for MongoDB?

22. What are the components of a MongoDB cluster?

23. How do Mongos perform the requested task of the clients?

24. What is meant by sharding? How is it implemented in MongoDB?

25. Briefly explain the architecture of MongoDB?

26. What is meant by consistency in MongoDB?

27. How does MongoDB handle the failure in database?

28. Briefly explain the CAP theorem?

29. What is the live migration of database in cloud computing?

30. What are the benefits of live migration over traditional migration in cloud computing?

31. What are the traditional migration techniques developed for UDB migration in the cloud computing environment?

32. Classify cloud database transaction processing.

33. What is meant by ACID-based cloud database? What are the characteristics of ACID-based cloud database?

34. What are the challenges of ACID-based cloud database?

35. What is meant by NoAcid cloud database?

36. What are the characteristics of NoAcid cloud database?

37. What are the challenges of NoAcid cloud database?

38. Compare ACID-based and NoACID cloud database?

39. What are the available cloud database platforms?

40. What is meant by demand migration?

41. What are the characteristics of SQL-based cloud database?

42. Give examples of at least two cloud database platforms.

43. If you store your data in the cloud, what about its integrity?

44. What is the type of storage account used in your current project?

References

1. Madria, S. K., & Bhowdrick, S. S. (2001). Mobile data management. *IEEE Potentials*, 20(4), 11-15.

2. Buyya, R., Yeo, C. S., & Venugopal, S. (2008, September). Market-oriented cloud computing: Vision, hype, and reality for delivering it services as computing utilities. In 2008 *10th IEEE International Conference on High Performance Computing and Communications* (pp. 5-13). Ieee.

3. Mell, P., & Grance, T. (2011). The NIST definition of cloud computing., NIST Special Publication 800-145.

4. Panda, P. K., Swain, S., & Pattnaik, P. K. (2011). Review of some transaction models used in mobile databases. *International Journal of Instrumentation, Control & Automation (IJICA)*, 1(1), 99-104.

5. Sharma, S. D., & Kasana, D. R. (2010). Mobile database system: Role of mobility on the query processing. *International Journal of Computer Science and Information Security*, Vol. 7(3), pp.211-216, 2010.

6. Mateljan, V., Cisic, D., & Ogrizovic, D. (2010, May). Cloud database-as-a-service (DaaS)-ROI. In The 33rd *International Convention MIPRO* (pp. 1185-1188). IEEE.

7. Cattell, R. (2010). *Relational Databases, Object Databases, Key-Value Stores, Document Stores, and Extensible Record Stores: A Comparison*.

8. Pasayat, S. K., Pati, S. P., & Pattnaik, P. K. (2013, March). Classification and Live Migration of Data-Intensive Cloud Computing Environment. In *International Conference on Intelligent Interactive Technologies and Multimedia* (pp. 316-324). Springer, Berlin, Heidelberg.

9. Han, J., Haihong, E., Le, G., & Du, J. (2011, October). Survey on NoSQL database. In 2011 6th *international conference on pervasive computing and applications* (pp. 363-366). IEEE.

10. Khan, M. S., Qamar, N., Khan, M. A., Masood, F., Sohaib, M., Khan, N., ... & Ahmed, S. A. (2012). Mobile multimedia storage: A mobile cloud computing application and analysis. *International Journal of Computer Science and Telecommunications*, 3(3), 68-71.

11. Dash, S. K., Mohapatra, S., & Pattnaik, P. K. (2010). A survey on applications of wireless sensor network using cloud computing. *International Journal of Computer Science & Emerging Technologies*, 1(4), 50-55.

12. Ye, K., Jiang, X., Huang, D., Chen, J., & Wang, B. (2011, July). Live migration of multiple virtual machines with resource reservation in cloud computing environments. In 2011 *IEEE 4th International Conference on Cloud Computing* (pp. 267-274). IEEE.

13. Ye, K., Jiang, X., Huang, D., Chen, J., & Wang, B. (2011, July). Live migration of multiple virtual machines with resource reservation in cloud computing environments. In 2011 *IEEE 4th International Conference on Cloud Computing* (pp. 267-274). IEEE.

14. Das, S., Nishimura, S., Agrawal, D., & El Abbadi, A. (2010). Live database migration for elasticity in a multitenant database for cloud platforms. *CS, UCSB, Santa Barbara, CA, USA, Tech. Rep*, 9, 2010.

15. Barker, S., Chi, Y., Moon, H. J., Hacigümüş, H., & Shenoy, P. (2012, March). Cut me some slack: Latency-aware live migration for databases. In *Proceedings of the 15th international conference on extending database technology* (pp. 432-443). ACM.

16. Elmore, A. J., Das, S., Agrawal, D., & El Abbadi, A. (2011, June). Zephyr: live migration in shared nothing databases for elastic cloud platforms. In *Proceedings of the 2011 ACM SIGMOD International Conference on Management of data* (pp. 301-312). ACM.

17. Pal, S., & Pattnaik, P. K. (2012). Efficient architectural framework for cloud computing. *International Journal of Cloud Computing and Services Science*, 1(2), 66.

18. Mateljan, V., Cisic, D., & Ogrizovic, D. (2010, May). Cloud database-as-a-service (DaaS)-ROI. In The 33rd *International Convention MIPRO* (pp. 1185-1188). IEEE.

19. Wei, Z., Pierre, G., & Chi, C. H. (2009, August). Scalable transactions for web applications in the cloud. In European Conference on Parallel Processing (pp. 442-453). Springer, Berlin, Heidelberg.

20. Chohan, N., Bunch, C., Krintz, C., & Nomura, Y. (2011, July). Database-agnostic transaction support for cloud infrastructures. In 2011 *IEEE 4th International Conference on Cloud Computing* (pp. 692-699). IEEE.

21. Mukherjee, A., Datta, J., Jorapur, R., Singhvi, R., Haloi, S., & Akram, W. (2012, December). Shared disk big data analytics with apache hadoop. In 2012 *19th International Conference on High Performance Computing* (pp. 1-6). IEEE.

22. Jain, A., & Mahajan, N. (2017). *Introduction to Database as a Service*. In The Cloud DBA-Oracle (pp. 11-22). Apress, Berkeley, CA.

23. Dijcks, J. P. (2012). Oracle: Big data for the enterprise. Oracle white paper, 16.

24. Mao, H., Zhang, Z., Zhao, B., Xiao, L., & Ruan, L. (2011, October). Towards deploying elastic Hadoop in the cloud. In 2011 *International Conference on Cyber-Enabled Distributed Computing and Knowledge Discovery* (pp. 476-482). IEEE.

25. Lombardo, S., Di Nitto, E., & Ardagna, D. (2012, September). Issues in handling complex data structures with nosql databases. In 2012 14th *International Symposium on Symbolic and Numeric Algorithms for Scientific Computing* (pp. 443-448). IEEE.

26. Silberschatz, A., Korth, H. F., & Sudarshan, S. (2000). *Database system concepts*. New York: McGraw-Hill. Fourth edition, pp:564-586.

27. Zhong, J., & Zhou, W. (1998, September). A web-based design for the mobile transaction management of a distributed database system. In *Proceedings Technology of Object-Oriented Languages. TOOLS 27* (Cat. No. 98EX224) (pp. 372-380). IEEE.

28. Gilbert, S., & Lynch, N. (2012). Perspectives on the CAP Theorem. *Computer*, 45(2), 30-36.

29. Bhat, U., & Jadhav, S. (2010). Moving towards non-relational databases. *International Journal of Computer Applications*, 1(13), 40-46.

30. Bunch, C., Chohan, N., Krintz, C., Chohan, J., Kupferman, J., Lakhina, P., ... & Nomura, Y. (2010, July). An evaluation of distributed datastores using the AppScale cloud platform. In *2010 IEEE 3rd International Conference on Cloud Computing* (pp. 305-312). IEEE.

31. Burtica, R., Mocanu, E. M., Andreica, M. I., & Ţăpuş, N. (2012, March). Practical application and evaluation of no-SQL databases in Cloud Computing. In *2012 IEEE International Systems Conference SysCon 2012* (pp. 1-6). IEEE.

32. KChodorow, K. (2013). *MongoDB: the definitive guide: powerful and scalable data storage.* O'Reilly Media, Inc.

33. Tiwari, S. (2011). *Professional NoSQL.* John Wiley & Sons.

34. Le, D. N., Kumar, R., Nguyen, G. N., & Chatterjee, J. M. (2018). Cloud computing and virtualization. John Wiley & Sons.

35. Le, D. N., Bhatt, C. M., & Madhukar, M. (Eds.). (2019). *Security Designs for the Cloud, IoT, and Social Networking.* John Wiley & Sons.

9

CLOUD-BASED DATA STORAGE

Dac-Nhuong Le[1], Souvik Pal[2], Prasant Kumar Pattnaik[3]

[1] Haiphong University, Haiphong, Vietnam
[2] Sister Nivedita University, Kolkata, India
[3] KIIT, Deemed to be University, India
Email: nhuongld@dhhp.edu.vn, souvikpal22@gmail.com, patnaikprasant@gmail.com

Abstract

Hadoop is a distributed programming model infrastructure researched and developed by the Apache Foundation. The users can develop the distributed data applications although they do not know the lower distributed layer so that the users can make full use of the power of the cluster to perform the high-speed computing and storage. The core technologies of Hadoop are MapReduce and the Hadoop Distributed File System (HDFS). HDFS provides the huge storage ability while MapReduce provides the client the computing ability of Big Data. Since HDFS and MapReduce have become open source, their low cost and high processing performance helped them to be adopted by many enterprises and organizations. With the popularity of Hadoop, there are more tools and technologies which are developed on the basis of the Hadoop framework.

Keywords: Hadoop, MapReduce, data storage

9.1 Relevant Hadoop Tools

Today, Hadoop has developed a collection of many projects. Although the core technologies are HDFS and MapReduce, Chukwa, Hive, HBase, Pig, and ZooKeeper and other sub-projects under Hadoop will soon be realized as indispensable. They provide the complementary services and higher level service on the core layer [1-3].

1. MapReduce[1] is a programming model used for the parallel computation of large-scale data sets into small input blocks. The concepts of mapping and reducing functions are a reference to the functional programming languages. The programmers who are not acquainted with distributed parallel programming model can also run their programs on the distributed system.

2. Hadoop Distributed File System (HDFS)[2] is a distributed file system. Because it is highly fault-tolerant, it can be deployed on low-cost hardware. By providing high throughput access to the data of the applications, it is suitable for applications which contain large data sets.

3. Chukwa[3] is a data collection system which is used for data monitoring and analysis. Chukwa is built on the architecture of HDFS and MapReduce. Chukwa system stores the data by HDFS and relies on the MapReduce to manage the data. Chukwa system is a flexible and powerful tool to display, monitor, and analyze the data.

4. Hive[4] was originally designed and developed by Facebook. It is a data warehouse based on the Hadoop framework which provides large data sets searching, special querying, and analysis. Hive is a structured data mechanism that supports the SQL query languages like RDBMS query language to help those users who are familiar with SQL queries. This kind of query language is called HiveQL. In fact, the conventional MapReduce programmers can query data on the mapping or reducing procedure by using HiveQL. The Hive compiler compiles the HiveQL into a MapReduce task.

5. HBase[5] is a distributed and open source NoSQL database. As mentioned in detail in Chapter 2, the concept of Hadoop originally originated with Google; therefore, HBase shares the common data model. Because the forms of HBase are loose and the users can define various sections, HBase is usually used for Big Data.

6. Pig[6] is a platform which was designed for the analysis and assessment of Big Data. The important advantage of its structure is that it can manage the highly parallel test that is based on parallel computing. Currently, the base layer of Pig is composed of a complier. When the complier is running, it will produce some program sequences of MapReduce.

7. ZooKeeper[7] is an open source allocation service for distributed applications. It is used to provide users' configuration management, synchronization, naming service and grouping. It can minimize the coordination tasks for the conveyed applications.

[1] https://hadoop.apache.org/docs/r1.2.1/mapred_tutorial.html
[2] https://hadoop.apache.org/docs/r1.2.1/hdfs_design.html
[3] https://chukwa.apache.org/
[4] https://hive.apache.org/
[5] https://hbase.apache.org/
[6] https://pig.apache.org/
[7] https://zookeeper.apache.org/

These are all the related tools with Hadoop, but here we will only concentrate on HDFS, MapReduce, and HBase, which are the core technologies of Hadoop.

9.2   Hadoop Distributed File System (HDFS)

9.2.1   HDFS Architecture

Hadoop Distributed File System (HDFS) [4, 5] is a distributed file system which is suitable for running on the commodity hardware. There are many common characteristics in the existing distributed file systems but the differences between them are also obvious. HDFS is a highly fault-tolerant system and uses the parts of the POSIX confinement to provide high throughput access to the data so that it is reasonable to appropriate the Big Data. HDFS is the master/slave structure. The Name node is the master node, while the Data node is the slave node. Documents are stored as data blocks in the Data node. The default size of a data block is 64M and it cannot be changed. If the files are less than a block data size, HDFS will not take up the entire block storage space. The Name node and the Data node normally run as Java programs in the Linux operating system.

In Figure 9.1 the Name node is the manager of the HDFS that is responsible for the management of the namespace in the file procedure. It will put all the files and folders metadata into a file system tree which maintains all of the metadata of the file directories. In the meantime, Name node also saves the corresponding relations between each file and the location of the data block. Data node is the place to store the real data in the system. However, all data is not stored in the hard drives but will be collected when the system starts to find the resource data server of the required documents.

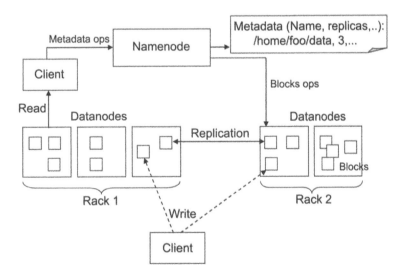

Figure 9.1: Hadoop distributed file system architecture.

The Secondary Name node is a backup node for the Name node. If there is only one Name node in the Hadoop cluster environment, the Name node will obviously become the weakest point of the process in the HDFS. Once the failure of the Name node occurs, it will affect the whole operation of the system. This is the reason why Hadoop designed the

Secondary Name node as the alternative backup. The Secondary Name node usually runs on a separate PC and keeps correspondence at certain time intervals to keep a snapshot of the file system metadata with the Name node so that it can recover the data immediately in case some error happens.

The Data node is the place where the real data is saved and handles most of the fault-tolerant mechanism. The files in HDFS are commonly divided into multiple data blocks stored in the form of redundancy backup in the Data node. The Data node reports the data storage lists to the Name node regularly so that the user can obtain the data by directly accessing the Data node.

The client is the HDFS user. They can read and write the data through calling the API provided by HDFS. At the same time, within the read and write process, the client first needs to obtain the metadata information from the Name node, and afterward the client can perform the corresponding read and write operations.

9.2.2 Data Read Process in HDFS

The data reading system in HDFS is not troublesome. It is similar to the programming logic which has created the object, i.e., called the method, and performs the execution. This section will introduce the read process of the HDFS [6-9].

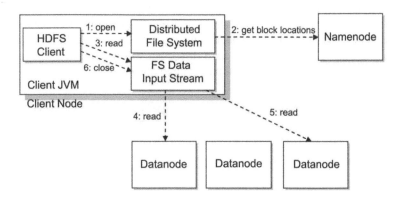

Figure 9.2: Hadoop distributed file system reading process.

According to Figure 9.2, there are six steps when the HDFS has the read process:

- The client will generate an Distributed File System object of the HDFS class library and uses the open() interface to open a file.

- Distributed File System sends the reading request to the Name node by using the Remote Procedure Call Protocol to obtain the vicinity address of the data block. After figuring and sorting the distance between the client and the Data node, the Name node will return the location information of the data block to the Distributed File System.

- After the Distributed File System has already received the distances and address of the data block, it will generate a FS Data Input Stream object instance to the client. At the same time, the FS Data Input Stream also encapsulates a DFS Input Stream object which is accountable for saving the address of the Data node and the storing data blocks.

- When everything is ready, the client will call the `read()` method.

- After receiving the call method, the encapsulated DFS Input Stream of FS Data Input Stream will choose the nearest Data node to read and return the data to the client.

- When all the data has been read successfully, the DFS Input Stream will be in charge of closing the link between the client and the Data node.

While the DFS Input Stream is reading the data from the Data node, it is hard to avoid the failure that may be triggered by network disconnection or node errors. When this happens, DFS Input Stream will give up the failure Data node and select the nearest Data node. In the later reading process, the disfunctioning Data node will not be received anymore. It is found that HDFS isolates the index and data reading to the Name node and Data node. The Name node is in charge of the light file index functions while the heavy data reading is accomplished by several distributed Data nodes. This kind of platform can be easily adapted to the multiple user access and huge data reading.

9.2.3 Data Write Process in HDFS

The data write process in HDFS is the opposite process of the read process but the write process is more complex. This section will briefly introduce the write process in HDFS. The structure of the HDFS read process is similar to the write process [10-12]. It includes the following seven steps:

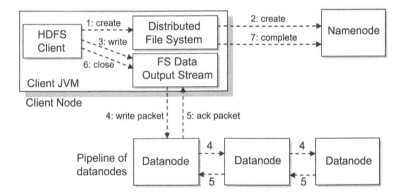

Figure 9.3: Hadoop distributed file system write process.

1. The client generates a Distributed File System object of the HDFS class library and uses the `create()` interface to open a file.

2. Distributed File System sends the write request to the Name node by using the Remote Procedure Call Protocol (RPC). The Name node will check if there is a duplicate file name in it. After that, the client with writing authority can create the comparing records in the namespace. If an error happens, the Name node will return the IO Exception to the client.

3. After the Distributed File System has received the successful return message from the Name node, it will generate a FS Data Output Stream object to the client. In the

FS Data Output Stream, there is an encapsulated DFS Output Stream object which is responsible for the write process. The client calls the `write()` method and sends the data to the FS Data Input Stream. The DFS Output Stream will put the data into a data queue which is read by the Data Streamer. Before the real writing, the Data Streamer needs to ask for some blocks and the suitable address from the Data node to store the data.

4. For each data block, the Name node will assign several Data nodes to store the data block. For example, if one block requires being stored in three Data nodes. Data Streamer will write the data block at the first Data node, then the first Data node will pass the data block to the second Data node, and the second one passes to the third one. Finally, it will finish the write data in the Data node chain.

5. After every Data node has been written, Data node will report to the Data Streamer. Step 4 and Step 5 will be repeated until all the data has been written effectively.

6. When all the data has been written, then the client will call the `close()` method of FS Data Input Stream to close the writing operation.

7. Finally, the Name node will be informed by the Distributed File System that all the write processes have been completed.

   In the process of data writing, if one Data node makes an error and causes writing failure, all the links between the Data Streamer and the Data node will be closed. At the same time, the failure node will be deleted from the Data node chain. The Name node will notice the failure by the returned packages and will assign a new Data node to continue the processing. As long as one Data node is written successfully, the writing operation will regard the process as completed.

9.2.4 Authority Management of HDFS

The HDFS shares a similar authority method to POSIX. Each file or directory has a proprietor and a group. The authority permissions for the files or the directories are different from the owner, users in the same group, and other users. On the one hand, for the files, users are required to have both read and write authority, i.e., the $-r$ authority to read and the $-w$ authority to write. On the other hand, for the directories, users need the $-r$ authority to list the listing content and $-w$ authority to create or delete. Unlike the POSIX system, there is no sticky, setgid or setuid of directories because there is no concept of executable files in HDFS [13-15].

9.2.5 Limitations of HDFS

The HDFS as the open source implementation of GFS is an excellent distributed file system and has many advantages. HDFS was intended to run on the cheap commodity hardware not on expensive machines. This means that the possibilities of node failure are rather high. To offer a full consideration to the design of HDFS, we may find that HDFS no longer has only advantages but also limitations for managing with some particular issues. These limitations are mainly displayed in the following characteristics:

1. *High access latency*: HDFS does not fit for requests which should be applied in a short time. The HDFS was intended for the Big Data storage and it is mainly used

for its high throughput abilities. This will result in excessive latency instead. Because HDFS has only one single Master system, all the file requests need to be processed via the Master. At the point where there are a huge number of requests, deferral is inevitable. At present, there are some additional projects to address this quandary, such as HBAse, which uses the Upper Data Management project to manage the data.

2. *Poor small files performance*: HDFS needs to use the Name node to manage the metadata of the file system to respond to the client and return the locations so that the limitation of a file size is determined by the Name node. In general, each file, folder, and block needs to occupy the 150 bytes' space. In other words, if there are 1,000,000 files and each file occupies one block, it will take 300MB space. Based on the current technology, it is possible to manage millions of files. However, when the files extend to billions, the work pressures on the Name node are heavier and the time it takes to retrieve data is unacceptable.

3. *Unsupported multiple clients write permissions*: In HDFS, one file simply has one writer because multiple clients' writer permissions will not be supported yet. The write operations must be added at the end of the file now, not at any positions of the file, by using the Append strategy. We believe that, with the endeavors of the developers of HDFS, HDFS will become more effective and can meet more needs of the users.

While the volume of the Big Data expands, so do the relationships and the complexity underneath the data. In an early phase of centralized data information systems, the emphasis is on finding the best characteristic values to symbolize each observation. This is similar to using a large number of data fields, such as income, age, gender, education background, etc., to characterize each individual. This type of feature inherently regards each individual as an unbiased entity without considering their social connections, which is likely one of the predominant factors of human society. Our companion circles may be formed based on long-established hobbies or people are connected by natural connections. Such social connections traditionally exist in our day-by-day activities, but are also very popular in the world of the internet. For example, social network sites, such as Facebook or Twitter, are probably characterized by social functions like friend-connections and followers (in Twitter). The relationships between individuals innately complicate the whole data representation and any reasoning procedure on the data. In the sample-feature representation, individuals are considered similar if they share equivalent feature values, whereas within the sample-feature-relationship representation, two individuals can be connected together (through their social connections) even though they share nothing in like manner in the feature domains at all. In a dynamic world, the aspects used to represent the social ties and the individuals used to symbolize our connections may additionally evolve with respect to spatial, temporal, and other factors. Such an intricacy is becoming part of the reality for Big Data applications, where the key is to take the complex (many-to-many, nonlinear) data relationships, along with the advancing changes, into consideration, to detect valuable patterns from Big Data collections.

9.3 Data Mining Challenges with Big Data

For an intelligent learning database system to handle Big Data, the essential key is to scale up to the specifically large volume of data and provide treatments for the characteristics featured by the aforementioned HACE theorem. A conceptual view of the Big Data processing framework includes three tiers from inside out, with issues on data accessing and computing (Tier I), data privacy and domain knowledge (Tier II), and Big Data mining algorithms (Tier III). The difficulties at Tier I focus on arithmetic computing procedures and data accessing. Since Big Data are often stored at different locations and data volumes may consistently grow, an effective computing platform will need to take distributed large-scale data storage into consideration for computing. For instance, typical data mining algorithms require all data to be stacked into the main memory; this, however, is becoming a clear technical barrier for Big Data because moving data across different locations is expensive (e.g., subject to intensive network communication and other IO costs), even if we do have a super large main memory to hold all data for computing. The difficulties at Tier II center around semantics and domain knowledge for different Big Data applications. Such information can provide additional benefits to the mining process, as well as add technical barriers to the Big Data access (Tier I) and mining algorithms (Tier III) [16, 17].

For instance, depending on different domain applications, the data privacy and knowledge sharing mechanisms between data producers and data consumers can be significantly specific. Sharing sensor network data for applications like water quality monitoring may not be a problem, whereas releasing and sharing cell phone users' location information is now clearly unacceptable for the majority, if not all, applications. In addition to the above privacy problems, the application domains can also provide additional information to benefit or guide Big Data mining algorithm designs. For instance, in market basket transactions data, each transaction is considered independent and the discovered knowledge is typically represented by finding highly correlated items, possibly with respect to different temporal and/or spatial confinements. In a social network, on the other hand, users are linked and share dependency structures. The knowledge is then represented by user communities, leaders in each group, and social influence modeling, and so on. Therefore, understanding semantics and application knowledge is important for both low-level data access and for high-level mining algorithm designs. At Tier III, the data mining challenges concentrate on algorithm designs in tackling the difficulties raised by the Big Data volumes, distributed data distributions, and by complex and dynamic data characteristics. The circle at Tier III contains three stages. First, sparse, heterogeneous, uncertain, incomplete, and multisource data are preprocessed by data fusion techniques. Second, complex and dynamic data are mined after preprocessing. Third, the global knowledge obtained by local learning and model fusion is tested and relevant information is feedback to the preprocessing stage. Then, the model and parameters are adjusted according to the feedback. In the whole process, information sharing is not only a promise of smooth development of each stage, but also a purpose of Big Data processing.

In the following, the author has elaborated challenges with respect to the three tier framework in

a. Tier I: Big Data Mining Platform.

b. Tier II: Big Data Semantics and Application Knowledge.

c. Tier III: Big Data Mining Algorithms.

To tackle the Big Data challenges and "seize the opportunities afforded by the new, data-driven resolution," the US National Science Foundation (NSF), under President Obama Administration's Big Data initiative, announced the Big Data solicitation in 2012. Such a federal initiative has resulted in a number of winning projects to investigate the foundations for Big Data management (led by the University of Washington), analytical approaches for genomics-based massive data computation (led by Brown University), large-scale machine learning techniques for high-dimensional data sets that may be as large as 500,000 dimensions (led by Carnegie Mellon University), social analytics for large-scale scientific literatures (led by Rutgers University), and several others. These projects seek to develop methods, algorithms, frameworks, and research infrastructures that allow us to bring the massive amounts of data down to a human manageable and interpretable scale. Institutions in other countries, such as the National Natural Science Foundation of China (NSFC), are also catching up with national grants on Big Data research [18, 19].

Meanwhile, since 2009, the authors have taken the lead in the following national projects that all involve Big Data components: they broadly studied the big data domain in context of the data mining field and proposed a 3-tier paradigm to cover all the computation fields derived from IT technology known as HACE.

The authors have reviewed all the domains in general, including the whole field as research initiatives. But we have to limit ourselves to the following domain as a research proposal.

Our proposed research agenda includes the following points:

1. Analysis of MapReduce technology using Hadoop by applying various huge data set like Cloud cluster dataset, Facebook database, etc.

2. Comparing and evaluating other platforms, like Pig 2004, and evaluating the performance of their methods, in a thesis published by Google [2] to introduce MapReduce. At the time of Google publishing the thesis, the greatest achievement of MapReduce was that it could rewrite Google's index file system. Until now, MapReduce has been widely used in log analysis, data sorting, and specific data searching. According to Google, implementing Hadoop in the programming framework of MapReduce renders it an open source framework. MapReduce is the core technology of Hadoop. It provides a parallel computing model for the Big Data and supports a set of programming interfaces for the developers.

9.4 MapReduce

9.4.1 MapReduce Architecture

MapReduce is a standard functional programming model. This kind of model has been used in the early programming languages such as Lisp. The core concept of the computation model is that it can pass on the function as the parameter to another function. Through multiple connections of functions, the data processing can turn into a series of function executions. MapReduce has two stages of processing. The first one is Map and the other one is Reduce. The reason why MapReduce is popular is that it is very simple, easy to implement, and offers strong expansibility [16, 20]. MapReduce is suitable for processing the Big Data it is given so that it can be processed by the multiple hosts at the same time to gain a faster speed. The MapReduce operation architecture includes the following three basic components:

1. Client: Every job of the Client might be packaged into a JAR file which is stored in HDFS and the client submits the path to the Job Tracker.

2. Job Tracker: This is a master service which is responsible for coordinating all the jobs that are executed on MapReduce. When the software is on, the Job Tracker is starting

to receive the jobs and monitor them. The functions of MapReduce include designing the job execution plan, assigning the jobs to the Task Tracker, monitoring the tasks, and redistributing the failed tasks.

3. Task Tracker: This is a slave service which runs on the different nodes. It is accountable for executing the jobs which are assigned by the Job Tracker. The Task Tracker receives the tasks through actively communicating with the Job Tracker.

9.4.2 MapReduce Procedure

The MapReduce procedure is complex and smart. Usually, MapReduce and HDFS are running in the same group of nodes. This means that the storage nodes and computing nodes are working together. This kind of design allows the framework to schedule the tasks rapidly so that the entire cluster will be used efficiently. In brief, the process of MapReduce can be divided into the following six steps shown in Figure 9.4 and described below [21]:

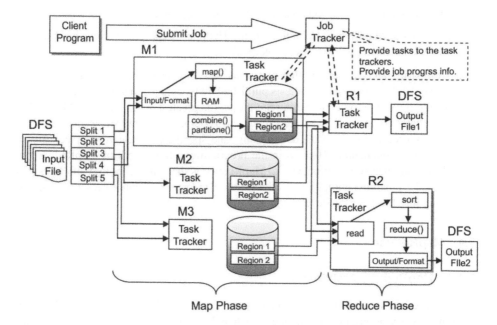

Figure 9.4: MapReduce procedure.

1. *Job submission*: When the user writes a program to create a new Job Client, the Job Client will send their quest to Job Tracker to obtain a new Job ID. Then, the Job Client will check if the input and output directories are correct. After this check, Job Client will store the related resources which contain the configuration files, the number of the input data fragmentations, and Mapped/Reducer JAR files to HDFS. In particular, the JAR files will be stored as multiple backups. After all the preparations have been completed, the Job Client will submit a job request to the Job Tracker.

2. *Job initialization*: As the master node of the system, Job Tracker will receive several Job Client requests so Job Tracker implements a queue mechanism to deal with these

problems. All the requests will be in a queue that is managed by the job scheduler. When the Job Tracker starts to initialize, its job is to create a Job in Progress instance to represent the job. The Job Tracker needs to retrieve the input data from HDFS and to decide on the number of the Map tasks. The Reduce tasks and the Task In Progress are determined by the parameters in the configuration files.

3. *Task allocation*: The task allocation mechanism in MapReduce drives the whole process. Before the task allocation, the Task Tracker which is responsible for Map tasks and Reduce tasks has already been launched. The Task Tracker will send the heartbeat message to the Job Tracker to ask if there are any tasks that can be done any time. When the Job Tracker job queue is not empty, the Task Tracker will receive the tasks to do. Due to the lack of the Task Tracker computing capability, the tasks that can be done on the Task Tracker are also limited. Each Task Tracker has two fixed task slots which correspond to the Map tasks and Reduce tasks. During the tasks allocation, the Job Tracker will use the Map task slot first. Once the Map task slot is empty, it will be assigned to the next Map task. After the Map task slot is full, then the Reduce task slot revives the tasks to do.

4. *Map Tasks execution*: After the Map Task Tracker has received the Map tasks, there is a series of operations to finish the tasks. Firstly, the Map Task Tracker will create a Task In Progress object to schedule and monitor the tasks. Secondly, the Map Task Tracker will take out and copy the JAR files and the related parameter configuration files from HDFS to the local working directory. Finally, when all the preparations have been completed, the Task Tracker will create a new Task Runner to run the Map task. The Task Runner will launch a separate JVM and will start the Map Task inside to execute the `map()` function in case the abnormal Map Task affects how the normal Task Tracker works. During the process, the Map Task will communicate with Task Tracker to report the task progress until all the tasks are completed. At that time, all the computing results will be stored in the local disk.

5. *Reduce Tasks execution*: When the part of the Map Tasks is completed, the Job Tracker will follow a similar mechanism to allocate the tasks to the Reduce Task Tracker. Similar to the process of Map tasks, the Reduce Task Tracker will also execute the `reduce()` function in the separate JVM. At the same time, the Reduce Task will download the results data files from the Map Task Tracker. Until now, the real Reduce process has not started yet. Only when all the Map tasks have been completed, the Job Tracker will inform the Reduce Task Tracker to start to work. Similarly, the Reduce Task will communicate with the Task Tracker about the progress until the tasks are finished.

6. *Job completion*: At each Reduce execution stage, every Reduce Task will send the result to the temporary files in HDFS. When all the Reduce Tasks are competed, all these temporary files will be combined into a final output file. After the Job Tracker has received the completion message, it will set the state to show that jobs are done. After that, the Job Client will receive the completion message, then notify the user and display the necessary information.

9.4.3 Limitations of MapReduce

Although MapReduce is popular all over the world, most people still have realized its limits. Following are the four main limitations of MapReduce:

1. *The bottleneck of Job Tracker*: As previously mentioned, the Job Tracker should be responsible for job allocation, management, and scheduling. In addition, it should also communicate with all the nodes to know the processing status. It is obvious that the Job Tracker, which is unique to MapReduce, takes too many tasks. If the number of clusters and the jobs submitted increase rapidly, it will cause network bandwidth consumption. As a result, the Job Tracker will reach bottleneck and this is the core risk of MapReduce.

2. *The Task Tracker*: Because the jobs allocation information is too simple, the Task Tracker might assign a few tasks that need more sources or need a long execution time to the same node. In this situation, it will cause node failure or slow down the processing speed.

3. *Jobs delay*: Before the MapReduce starts to work, the Task Tracker will report its own resources and operation situation. According to the report, the Job Tracker will assign the jobs and then the Task Tracker starts to run. As a consequence, the communication delay may make the Job Tracker wait too long so that the jobs cannot be completed in time.

4. *Inflexible framework*: Although MapReduce currently allows the users to define their own functions for different processing stages, the MapReduce framework still limits the programming model and the resources allocation.

9.5   Next Generation of MapReduce: YARN

In this big data world, massive data storage and faster processing is a big challenge. Hadoop is the solution to this challenge. Hadoop is an open source software framework for storing and processing big data in a distributed fashion on large clusters (thousands of machines) of commodity (low cost) hardware. Hadoop has two core components; HDFS and MapReduce. The Hadoop distributed file system (HDFS) stores massive data in commodity machines in a distributed manner. MapReduce is a distributed data processing framework to work with this massive data [20-25].

MapReduce framework is designed to process only batch data processing. It is not fit to process real-time data. Today's market demands big data with stream data processing (faster than real time). However, MapReduce fails to provide a solution to this problem. YARN (next generation MapReduce) is the answer. YARN provides a solution to process batch, interactive, real-time and stream data as per demand. A classic example, like MapReduce, is a Windows operating system with only Notepad; and YARN is a Windows operating system with Microsoft Office, with applications to watch movies, listen to music, etc.

Apache YARN (yet another resource negotiator) is Hadoop's cluster resource management system. YARN was introduced in Hadoop 2.0 to improve the MapReduce implementation, but it is general enough to support other distributed computing paradigms as well.

The YARN platform provides APIs for requesting and working with cluster resources (memory, CPU, disk/network I/O), but these APIs are not typically used directly by user code. Instead, users write to higher-level APIs provided by distributed computing frameworks (MapReduce, Tez, Impala, Storm, Spark, etc.), which themselves are built on YARN and hide the resource management details from the user. This process is illustrated in Figure 9.5.

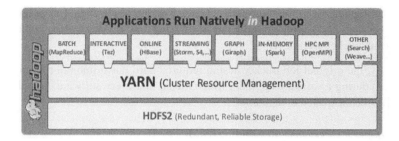

Figure 9.5: Applications run natively in Hadoop.

There is a further layer of applications built on the frameworks shown in Figure 9.5. Pig, Hive and Crunch are all examples of processing frameworks that run on MapReduce or Spark or Tez (depends on the versions), and don't interact with YARN directly.

9.5.1 YARN Compared to MapReduce 1.0 (MRv1)

The distributed implementation of MapReduce in the original version of Hadoop (version 1 and earlier) is sometimes referred to as "MapReduce 1(MRv1)" to distinguish it from "MapReduce 2(MRv2)," the implementation that uses YARN (in Hadoop 2 and later).

In MRv1, there are two types of daemons (background processes) that control the job execution process: a job tracker and one or more task trackers. The jobtracker coordinates all the jobs run on the system by scheduling tasks to run on task trackers. Task trackers run tasks and send progress reports to the job tracker, which keeps a record of the overall progress of each job. If a task fails, the job tracker can reschedule it on a different task tracker.

In MRv1, the job tracker takes care of both job scheduling (matching tasks with task trackers) and task progress monitoring (keeping track of tasks, restarting failed or slow tasks, and doing task bookkeeping, such as maintaining counter totals). By contrast, in YARN these responsibilities are split into separate entities: the resource manager and an application master (one for each MapReduce job).

Limitations of the MapReduce 1 framework are:

1. The job tracker has two primary responsibilities: i) managing the cluster resources and ii) scheduling all user jobs. As the cluster size and the number of jobs at Facebook grew, the scalability limitations of this design became clear. The job tracker could not handle its dual responsibilities adequately. At peak load, cluster utilization would drop precipitously due to scheduling overhead.

2. Another limitation of the Hadoop MapReduce 1 framework is its pull-based scheduling model. Task trackers provide a heartbeat status to the job tracker in order to get tasks to run. Since the heartbeat is periodic, there is always a predefined delay when scheduling tasks for any job. For small jobs this delay was problematic.

3. Static slot allocation: Hadoop MapReduce is also constrained by its static slot-based resource management model. Rather than using a true resource management system, a MapReduce cluster is divided into a fixed number of map and reduce slots based on a static configuration; therefore, slots are wasted anytime the cluster workload does not fit the static configuration (e.g., suppose the number of MapReduce tasks

are configured 10 in the cluster but cluster workload is 6, then 4 slots are wasted). Furthermore, the slot-based model makes it hard for non-MapReduce applications to be scheduled appropriately.

4. Finally, the original job tracker design required hard downtime (all running jobs are killed) during a software upgrade, which meant that every software upgrade resulted in significant wasted computation.

9.5.2 YARN and MapReduce 2.0 (MRv2)

The simplest way to understand the difference between Hadoop 1.x and Hadoop 2.x is that the architecture went from being a single use system that only handled batch jobs to a multi-purpose (multi-tenancy) system that could not only run the batch jobs that Hadoop 1.x did but also more interactive, online, streaming jobs as well.

In Hadoop 1.x, everything that was submitted to cluster only for batch processing. In Hadoop 2.x (YARN), there can be any type of processing like interactive, real-time, online, streaming and even batch processing. It's important to realize that the old and new MapReduce APIs are not the same thing as the MapReduce 1 and MapReduce 2 implementations. MRv1 and MRv2 are two different frameworks with two different implementations. The APIs are user-facing client-side features and determine how you write MapReduce programs, whereas the implementations are just different ways of running MapReduce programs. All four combinations are supported: both the old and new MapReduce APIs run on both MRv1 and MRv2 (see Figure 9.6).

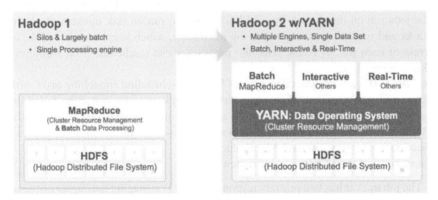

Figure 9.6: Hadoop 1 verus Hadoop 2 w/YARN.

9.5.3 YARN Architecture

Compared with the old MapReduce architecture, it is easy to see that YARN is more structured and simple. This section will introduce the YARN architecture.

According to Figure 9.7, there are four core components of the YARN Architecture:

1. *Resource Manager*: According to the different functions of the Resource Manager, designers have divided it into two lower level components: The Scheduler and the Application Manager. On the one hand, the Scheduler assigns the resource to the different running applications based on the cluster size, queues, and resource constraints.

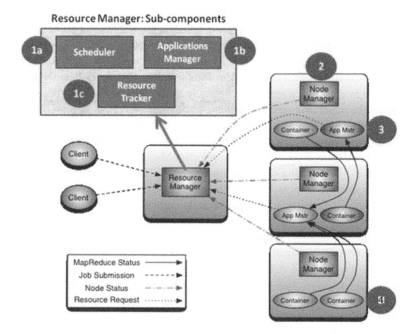

Figure 9.7: YARN architecture.

The Scheduler is only responsible for the resources allocation but is not responsible for monitoring the application implementation and task failure. On the other hand, the Application Manager is in charge of receiving jobs and redistributing the containers for the failure objects.

- *1(a) Scheduler*: The Scheduler is purely a scheduler in the sense that it only performs scheduling jobs based on resource status (memory, CPU, disk/network I/O), not monitoring or tracking the status of a job, i.e., it doesn't attempt to provide fault-tolerance (failure of resources affects job execution fatally) for resources. We shifted that to become a primary responsibility of the ApplicationMaster instance. It optimizes for cluster utilization (keeps all resources in use all the time). The Scheduler is pluggable and allows for different algorithms. There are currently two types of schedulers; one is Capacity Scheduler and another is Fair Scheduler. Capacity Scheduler is used by default. I will cover YARN schedulers in detail later on.

- *1(b) Applications Manager*: The Applications Manager is responsible for maintaining a collection of submitted applications. Also, a cache of completed applications is kept so as to serve users' requests via web UI or command line long after the applications in question are completed.

- *1(c) Resource Tracker*: The Resource Tracker contains settings such as the maximum number of ApplicationMaster retries, how often to check that containers are still alive, and how long to wait until a NodeManager is considered dead. ResourceManager works together with the per-node NodeManagers and the per-application ApplicationMasters.

2. *Node Manager*: The Node Manager is the per-machine slave (same as per-node agent) and long-running deamon in DataNode, which is responsible for launching the applications' containers, monitoring resource usage (memory, CPU, disk/network I/O) of individual containers, tracking node health and reporting the same to the Resource-Manager. NodeManager takes instructions from the ResourceManager and manages resources available on a single machine. On startup, this component registers with the ResourceManager and sends information about the resources available on the nodes. Subsequent NodeManager-ResourceManager communication is to provide updates on container statuses – new containers running on the node, completed containers, etc. Requests are accepted from ApplicationMasters to start new containers, or to stop running others. It also maintains a pool of threads to prepare and launch containers as quickly as possible. Every NodeManager in a YARN cluster periodically sends a heartbeat request to the ResourceManager – by default, one heartbeat per second. Heartbeats carry information about the NodeManagers running containers and the resources available for new containers, so each heartbeat is a potential scheduling opportunity for an application to run a container.

3. *Application Master*: The Application Master cooperates with the NodeManager to put tasks in the suitable containers to run the tasks and monitor the tasks. When the container has errors, the ApplicationMaster will apply for another resource from the Scheduler to continue the process. Every application has its own instance of an ApplicationMaster which runs for the duration of the application. However, it's completely feasible to implement an ApplicationMaster to manage a set of applications (e.g., ApplicationMaster for Pig or Hive to manage a set of MapReduce jobs). An application (via the ApplicationMaster) can request resources to satisfy its resource needs with highly specific requirements, as depicted in the Figure 9.8.

4. *Container*: A container is an abstract notion in YARN platform. It represents a collection of physical resources which could mean CPU cores and disk along with RAM. When an application is about to get submitted into the YARN platform, the YARN client allocates a container from the ResourceManager, where its ApplicationMaster will run. ApplicationMaster itself runs on an individual container. After the ApplicationMaster gets started, it should request more containers for ResourceManager to deploy the tasks and to actually start the application (e.g., MapReduce, Pig, Hive, HBase, Tez, Storm, etc., are applications). A MapReduce job has a specific (built in) ApplicationMaster (called MRAppMaster), which runs on a specific container, called container 0, and each mapper and reducer runs on its own container to be accurate. The ApplicationMaster allocates these containers for the mappers and reducers as it sees fit. To execute the actual map or reduce task, YARN will run a JVM within the container. In YARN an application (via the ApplicationMaster) can ask for containers spanning any number of memory (RAM) chunks, and can ask for a varied number of container types (CPU and disk) also. The ApplicationMaster, usually asks for specific hosts/racks with specified container capabilities. For example, the ApplicationMaster can request containers for ResourceManager's scheduler with appropriate resource requirements, inclusive of specific machines. They can also request multiple containers on each machine. All resource requests are subject to capacity constraints for the application, its queue, etc. The ApplicationMaster is responsible for computing the resource requirements of the application, e.g., input splits for MapReduce applications, and translating them into the protocol understood by the Scheduler. The pro-

tocol understood by the scheduler is `<priority,(host,="" rack,="" *)`
`,="" memory,=""#containers="">`.

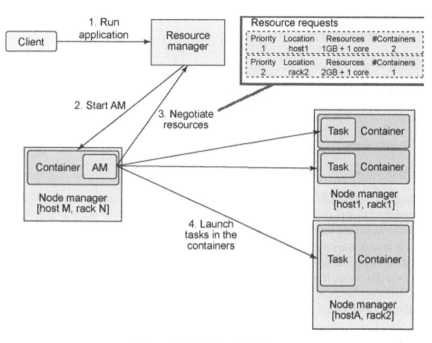

Figure 9.8: ApplicationMaster.

9.5.4   Advantages of YARN

Compared to MapReduce, there are many advantages of the YARN framework. The four main advantages of YARN compared to MapReduce are:

1. YARN greatly enhances the scalability and availability of the cluster by distributing the tasks to the Job Tracker. The ResourceManager and ApplicationMaster greatly relieve the bottleneck of the Job Tracker and the safety problems in MapReduce.

2. In YARN, the ApplicationMaster is a customized component. That means that the users can write their own program based on the programming model. This makes YARN more flexible and suitable for wide use.

3. YARN, on the one hand, supports the program to have a specific checkpoint. It can ensure that the ApplicationMaster can reboot immediately based on the status which was stored on HDFS. On the other hand, it uses ZooKeeper on the ResourceManager to implement the failover.

4. When the ResourceManager receives errors, the backup ResourceManager will reboot quickly. These two measures improve the availability of YARN. The cluster has the same containers as the Reduce and Map pools in MapReduce. Once there is a request for resources, the Scheduler will assign the available resources in the cluster to the tasks and regard the resource type. It will increase the utilization of the cluster resources, and is still considered as the best choice.

9.6   Classification of Data Mining Systems

The data mining system can be classified according to the following criteria:

1. Database Technology

2. Statistics

3. Machine Learning

4. Information Science

5. Visualization

6. Other Disciplines

One thing we should note is that the scaling of total data size can automatically scale the number of mappers, but it doesn't scale the number of reducers accordingly. Therefore, in order to make the learning experience of one experiment consistent with another experiment, it is necessary to make sure the execution time of each reduce task is the same in both of the experiments. An easy strategy is to make the number of reducers proportional to the total data size. If we use 6 reducers for 1GB's data (the input size for map), then we use 12 reducers for 2GB's data; initially we tested our approach on KB data in the form of textual data (sentences).

9.6.1   Classification According to Kind of Databases Mined

We can classify the data mining system according to the kinds of databases mined. Database framework can be classified according to different criteria such as data models, types of data and many others; and the data mining process will be classified accordingly. For example, if we classify the database according to data model then we may have a object-relational, transactional, relational, or data warehouse mining system.

9.6.2   Classification According to Kind of Knowledge Mined

We can classify the data mining system as per sort of knowledge mined. Data mining systems are classified on the basis of functionalities such as:

1. Characterization

2. Discrimination

3. Association and Correlation Analysis

4. Classification

5. Prediction

6. Clustering

7. Outlier Analysis

8. Evolution Analysis

9.6.3 Classification According to Kind of Techniques Utilized

We can classify the data mining system according to types of techniques used. We can describe these strategies according to the degree of user interaction involved or the methods of analysis employed.

9.6.4 Classification According to the Applications Adapted

We can classify data mining systems according to the application adapted. These applications are as follows:

1. Finance

2. Telecommunications

3. DNA

4. Stock Markets

5. Email

Major Issues in Data Mining:

- *Mining different types of information in databases*: The needs of different clients is not the same. And different clients may be in interested in different types of knowledge. Thus, it is necessary for data mining to cover a broad range of knowledge discovery tasks.

- I*nteractive mining of knowledge at various levels of abstraction*: The data mining process should be interactive in order to allow end users to focus on searching for patterns, and offering and refining data mining requests based on returned results.

- *Consolidation of background information*: To guide the discovery method and to express the discovered patterns, background information can be used. Background information may be used to express the discovered patterns that are not user-friendly in concise terms but at multiple levels of abstraction.

- *Data mining query languages and ad-hoc data mining*: Data mining query language allows the user to describe ad-hoc mining tasks incorporated with a data warehouse query language and streamlined for efficient and flexible data mining.

- *Presentation and visualization of data mining results*: Once the patterns are found, they need to be expressed in high-level languages with visual representations. These representations should be easily understandable by the users.

- *Handling noisy or incomplete data*: Data cleaning approaches are required that can handle noise and incomplete objects even when mining the data regularities. If data cleaning approaches are not present then the accuracy of the learned patterns will be poor.

- *Pattern evaluation*: This refers to an intriguing problem. The patterns discovered should be fascinating because they either represent common knowledge or lack oddity.

- *Efficiency and scalability of data mining algorithms*: In order to effectively extract the information from the large amount of data in databases, the data mining algorithm needs to be efficient and scalable.

- *Parallel, distributed, and incremental mining algorithms*: Variables, such as large size of databases, broad distribution of data, and complexity of data mining methods, propel the development of distributed and parallel data mining algorithms. These algorithms divide the data into partitions which are further processed in parallel. Then the results from the partitions are merged. The incremental algorithms update databases without having to mine the data again from scratch [22].

9.7 Summary

The relationship between individuals inherently complicates the entire data representation process and any reasoning process on the information. In the sample-feature representation, individuals are respected the same if they share similar feature values; while in the sample-feature-relationship representation, two individuals can be linked together (through their social connections) even though they might share nothing in common in the feature domains at all. In a dynamic world, the features used to represent the individuals and the social ties used to represent our connections may also evolve with respect to temporal, spatial, and other factors. Such confusion is becoming part of the reality for Big Data applications, where the key is to change the complex (many-to-many, nonlinear) data relationships, along with the evolving changes, into thought, to find useful patterns from Big Data collections.

This chapter presented a brief introduction to the core technology of the MapReduce distributed programming model, which allows users to develop their own applications without having to understand the bottom layer of MapReduce. Because of the advantages of Hadoop, the users can easily manage the computer resources and build their own distributed data processing platform.

Above all, the convenience that Hadoop has brought to Big Data processing is obvious. It also should be pointed out that although Google published the first study on the distributed file system in 2003, the history of Hadoop is only 10 years old. With the advancement of computer science and internet technology, Hadoop has rapidly solved key problems and been widely used in real life. In spite of this, there are still some problems that need to be faced due to the rapid changes and ever-increasing demand of analysis. To solve these problems, internet providers such as Google have also introduced the newer technologies. It is predictable that with the key problems being solved, Big Data processing based on Hadoop will have wider application prospects.

EXERCISES

1. Where is your data located in the cloud?

2. What if there's a data breach?

3. How big is the cloud? Will you run out of space?

4. Who has access to our data in the cloud?

5. What are your procedures for suspected security violations?

6. How do you protect access to GUIs and APIs?

7. What are your procedures for suspected security violations?

8. What level of technical support is included in your standard SLA?

9. What are your security measures for protecting your data centers and other facilities?

10. What are your terms when it comes to ownership of data? How about any metadata generated while using your service/platform/application?

11. Do you have a disaster recovery plan? How often do you test it? In the case of a data center disaster, where do you backup your data?

12. Who has access to your data in the cloud? What is your company policy for ensuring only authorized employees can access your data?

13. Where do your servers physically reside? Are there any legal ramifications regarding your data privacy you should know about before having your data stored in that location?

14. Which specific data transmissions do you encrypt?

15. What role does your company play in the protection of our data (if any) and what is your company's role in protecting our data and mitigating security incidents?

References

1. Sammer, E. (2012). Hadoop operations. " O'Reilly Media, Inc.".

2. Condie, T., Conway, N., Alvaro, P., Hellerstein, J. M., Elmeleegy, K., & Sears, R. (2010, April). MapReduce online. In Nsdi (Vol. 10, No. 4, p. 20).

3. Dean, J., & Ghemawat, S. (2010). MapReduce: a flexible data processing tool. Communications of the ACM, 53(1), 72-77.

4. Shvachko, K., Kuang, H., Radia, S., 7 & Chansler, R. (2010, May). The hadoop distributed file system. In *2010 IEEE 26th symposium on mass storage systems and technologies (MSST)* (pp. 1-10). Ieee.

5. Borthakur, D. (2007). The hadoop distributed file system: Architecture and design. Hadoop Project Website, 11(2007), 21.

6. Nathanael, R., Widodo, S., Abe, H.,& Kato, K. (2020, August). HDRF: Hadoop data reduction framework for hadoop distributed file system. In Proceedings of the 11th ACM SIGOPS Asia-Pacific Workshop on Systems (pp. 122-129).

7. Veeraiah, D., & Rao, J. N. (2020, February). An Efficient Data Duplication System based on Hadoop Distributed File System. In 2020 International Conference on Inventive Computation Technologies (ICICT) (pp. 197-200). IEEE.

8. Elkawkagy, M., & Elbeh, H. (2020). High Performance Hadoop Distributed File System. International Journal of Networked and Distributed Computing, 8(3), 119-123.

9. Le, D. N., Kumar, R., Nguyen, G. N., & Chatterjee, J. M. (2018). Cloud computing and virtualization. John Wiley & Sons.

10. Le, D. N., Bhatt, C. M., & Madhukar, M. (Eds.). (2019). *Security Designs for the Cloud, IoT, and Social Networking*. John Wiley & Sons.

11. Newberry, E., & Zhang, B. (2019, September). On the Power of In-Network Caching in the Hadoop Distributed File System. In Proceedings of the 6th ACM Conference on Information-Centric Networking (pp. 89-99).

12. Asim, M., McKinnel, D. R., Dehghantanha, A., Parizi, R. M., Hammoudeh, M., & Epiphaniou, G. (2019). Big data forensics: Hadoop distributed file systems as a case study. In *Handbook of Big Data and IoT Security* (pp. 179-210). Springer, Cham.

13. Chattaraj, D., Bhagat, S., & Sarma, M. (2020). Storage Service Reliability and Availability Predictions of Hadoop Distributed File System. In *Reliability, Safety and Hazard Assessment for Risk-Based Technologies* (pp. 617-626). Springer, Singapore.

14. Hussein, O. (2019, December). Identification of Threats and Vulnerabilities in Public Cloud-Based Apache Hadoop Distributed File System. In 2019 15th International Computer Engineering Conference (ICENCO) (pp. 44-49). IEEE.

15. Elkawkagy, M., & Elbeh, H. (2020). High Performance Hadoop Distributed File System. International Journal of Networked and Distributed Computing, 8(3), 119-123.

16. Almansouri, H. T., & Masmoudi, Y. (2019, April). Hadoop Distributed File System for Big data analysis. In 2019 4th World Conference on Complex Systems (WCCS) (pp. 1-5). IEEE.

17. Veeraiah, D., & Rao, J. N. (2020, February). An Efficient Data Duplication System based on Hadoop Distributed File System. In *2020 International Conference on Inventive Computation Technologies (ICICT)* (pp. 197-200). IEEE.

18. Adnan, A., Tahir, Z., & Asis, M. A. (2019, July). Performance Evaluation of Single Board Computer for Hadoop Distributed File System (HDFS). In 2019 International Conference on Information and Communications Technology (ICOIACT) (pp. 624-627). IEEE.

19. Soe, N. K., Yee, T. T., & Htoon, E. C. Resource-based Data Placement Strategy for Hadoop Distributed File System.

20. Nathanael, R., Widodo, S., Abe, H., & Kato, K. (2020, August). HDRF: Hadoop data reduction framework for hadoop distributed file system. In *Proceedings of the 11th ACM SIGOPS Asia-Pacific Workshop on Systems* (pp. 122-129).

21. He, B., Fang, W., Luo, Q., Govindaraju, N. K., & Wang, T. (2008, October). Mars: a MapReduce framework on graphics processors. In *Proceedings of the 17th international conference on Parallel Architectures and Compilation Techniques* (pp. 260-269).

22. Le, D. N., Kumar, R., Mishra, B. K., Chatterjee, J. M., & Khari, M. (Eds.). (2019). *Cyber Security in Parallel and Distributed Computing: Concepts, Techniques, Applications and Case Studies*. John Wiley & Sons.

23. Seth, B., Dalal, S., Le, D. N., Jaglan, V., Dahiya, N., Agrawal, A., ... & Verma, K. D. (2021). Secure Cloud Data Storage System Using Hybrid Paillier-Blowfish Algorithm. CMC-Computers Materials & Continua, 67(1), 779-798.

24. Seth, B., Dalal, S., Jaglan, V., Le, D. N., Mohan, S., & Srivastava, G. (2020). Integrating encryption techniques for secure data storage in the cloud. *Transactions on Emerging Telecommunications Technologies*, e4108.

25. Le, D. N., Seth, B., & Dalal, S. (2018). A hybrid approach of secret sharing with fragmentation and encryption in cloud environment for securing outsourced medical database: a revolutionary approach. *Journal of Cyber Security and Mobility*, 379-408.

10

AUDITING CONCEPT IN CLOUD COMPUTING

DAC-NHUONG LE[1], SOUVIK PAL[2], PRASANT KUMAR PATTNAIK[3]

[1] Haiphong University, Haiphong, Vietnam
[2] Sister Nivedita University, Kolkata, India
[3] KIIT, Deemed to be University, India
 Email: nhuongld@dhhp.edu.vn, souvikpal22@gmail.com, patnaikprasant@gmail.com

Abstract
Cloud computing is an emerging field in the era of the internet where information and physical resources can be provided to cloud users according to their needs on a pay-as-you-go basis. Security and privacy are major concerns in the cloud computing environment. To address these issues all physical resources, such as computing resources, sensitive user data, and processes, are managed by a third-party service provider. Auditing in a cloud computing environment paves the way for the cloud service provider to make performance and security data readily available to the cloud user. Hence, to maintain data confidentiality, privacy, integrity, and availability, auditing is introduced within third-party service providers. This chapter studies various issues in auditing that have been encountered in practice and also proposes a framework that helps the designer to incorporate auditing aspects in a cloud computing environment.

Keywords: Auditing, auditing service, cloud computing environment

10.1 Introduction

A cloud computing environment (CCE) itself is an infrastructure or framework that consists of a pool of physical computing resources, i.e., a set of hardware, processors, memory, storage, networks and bandwidth, which can be organized on demand into services that can grow or shrink in real-time scenarios [1, 2]. In the early days of cloud, different organizations managed their computing resources on their own and hesitated to disclose their raw data to others. They had to bear extra costs for supporting and maintaining all the resources. This concept was going to be highly expensive due to extra overhead costs. Hence, to lessen this burden, a third-party service provider was introduced. In this concept, all the physical resources, including computing resources, sensitive user data and processes are managed by the third-party provider. The concerned organizations have to provide all the data to the provider and those data are easily accessible by anyone within the third-party provider or another user or other organizations related to the third-party provider or even any customer of the organization itself. Therefore, to maintain the privacy of sensitive data and resources, an auditing concept has been introduced within the third-party provider for maintaining data privacy and performing a data integrity check.

10.2 Data Security in Cloud Computing Environment

When discussing security aspects of cloud computing, data security becomes the most significant issue at all levels of services, such as resource as a service (RaaS) [2], infrastructure as a service (IaaS), platform as a service (PaaS) and software as a service (SaaS). Cloud service providers (CSPs) have to look after all aspects of customer data security, including the customer data itself as well as metadata about that data and monitoring of that data. In this context, we have to consider aspects of data security such as data in transit (during transmission), data at rest (during storage), data provenance (data integrity with computational accuracy), and data remanence (residual representation of data being nominally erased or removed) [3-14]. At the network level, CSPs provide monitoring, collecting and protecting firewall, intrusion prevention system and router data flow. At the host level, service providers should be integrating system log files and at the application level, they should also be gathering application log data, including authorization and authentication information. So, data security is the most important concern in the recent cloud scenario.

10.2.1 Characteristics of a Secure Cloud Computing Environment

While making a cloud secure, public clouds are more sensitive to new attacks, threats and vulnerabilities than the private cloud. If we look at the network level of security, we have to ensure the confidentiality and integrity of the data transmitted to and from the public cloud provider. We have to ensure proper access control of authorization, authentication and auditing of the physical and virtual resources used by the public cloud provider. The availability of the internet-facing resources in a public cloud being used by the organization also needs to be ensured. At the host level of security, virtualization security threats, like system configuration change, weak access control of the hypervisor [2], and faulty provisioning of resources, the proper use of instances of virtual machines are to be considered for making cloud secure. The integrity and availability of the hypervisor should be guaranteed because a vulnerable hypervisor could expose all user domains to malicious insiders. We have to maintain security controls applicable to platform level (PaaS) applications where user authentication, account management, endpoint security measures including antivirus, and browser with the latest patches, should be authorized. However, data security becomes more important when customers' raw data is managed and customized by the third-party cloud service provider. While accessing those data, cloud providers should be concerned with their security.

10.2.2   Need for Auditing in Cloud Computing Environment

In a Swift cloud computing audit, a web server, application server, and database server are needed in every phase of cloud infrastructure in order to maintain data confidentiality, privacy, integrity and availability. In the recent scenario, data is being stored, transferred and processed outside the company or organization. The raw data is not physically controlled by the organization and shared computing environments are also making it public. These kinds of loopholes need more security and privacy. In respect to data access, no controls have been implemented to restrict data modification and no logging events, such as access, transmission, or modification of data, have been monitored. Limited capabilities for change control and provider feasibility are also the drawbacks of cloud infrastructure. One more thing; all the physical and logical accesses are managed and maintained by the cloud service provider (CSP). So, auditing is highly required to maintain the privacy of the sensitive data, restricted access of computing and physical resources and for integrity check [15-17].

10.2.3   Auditing Background Within Third-Party Service Provider

Several security issues have arisen due to the rapid surge in the use of the internet throughout the world, such as handling web attacks [3], data access control [4], enhancing dynamic allocation strategies [5], and controlling sensitive information flow [6]. According to *Information Systems Control and Audit*, IT auditing can be defined as a process of aggregating and evaluating evidence to decide whether a computing information system safeguards resources, maintains data integrity, secures sensitive user data, attains organizational objectives effectively and consumes physical and computing resources efficiently. Audibility also enables accountability (retrospectively). It allows taking an action to be reviewed against a predetermined policy. Wang *et al.* [12] have described an auditing system in which an auditor is able to audit without knowing the user's data contents. They explained the batch auditing protocols where multiple auditing jobs of different users are concurrently performed by a third-party auditor.

10.3   Cloud Auditing Outsourcing Life Cycle Phases

When organizations have outsourced all their sensitive data, processes and computing resources to a third-party vendor for handling and maintenance of those data and resources, it goes through the different phases [10] given below:

- *Phase 1: Selecting the appropriate third-party vendor*: When an organization wants to deploy its application or wants to rent the physical resources or needs an independent platform where heterogeneous applications can be executed, it needs to select the proper vendor to handle all the requirements.

- *Phase 2*: *Define strategy*: The service provider/vendor should be transparent in defining its business strategy and risk management philosophy. This kind of decision strategy will enable the service provider to meet the baseline requirements of its consumers.

- *Phase 3*: *Define policies and workflow*: Having defined its strategy and customer requirement, the service provider needs to translate these requirements into policies applicable to industry standards. In this phase, providers need to determine the configuration settings, flow control, platforms and to maintain the workflow.

- *Phase 4*: *Establishing business case*: Driven by the strategy and policies of the service provider, the business case is established and different concerns related to privacy, security and availability should be in the business protocol.

- *Phase 5*: *Due diligence of the third-party vendor*: An act with a firm standard of care should be established within the third-party service provider. Due diligence is a process concerned with issues like the compatibility audit, marketing audit, financial audit, management audit, legal audit, and information systems audit. The technological direction of both the third-party service provider and the concerned organization should the directly aligned.

- *Phase 6*: *Validating agreement protocol and establishing relationships*: A service-level agreement (SLA) protocol and escrow service are established between both vendor and the organization so that both can meet in a standardized platform. Both should know the responsible authorities with their functionalities.

- *Phase 7*: *Dynamic monitoring*: In this phase of the life cycle, a dynamic monitoring service is enabled and dynamically monitors whether the vendor can continue the stable operations and provide services or not. In the meantime, auditors are actively maintaining the privacy of the sensitive data and computing resources and preparing an independent auditor's report.

- *Phase 8*: *Closing the relationship*: In the last phase of the cycle, data is transferred and unused data are cleaned up. An acknowledgment message is also transferred from the user and even related organization end. And then the concerned vendor will be getting ready for the next transaction.

10.4 Auditing Classification

Auditing is a process which can be implemented in different phases when an organization is renting the cloud infrastructure from the cloud service providers or is going to deploy its application onto a cloud. There are different aspects [11] where auditing is concerned (see Figure 10.1):

1. *Auditing for regulation or compliance*: A set of rules and principles are designed to govern or control the conduct for auditing. Compliance is concerned with legal issues, social activities, marketing strategies, and co-operative conduct. In every aspects of compliance, auditing is highly needed for maintenance of governing conduct. Auditing for regulations and compliance is also needed to restrict increasing complexity to comply with standards and to maintain the agreement for privacy laws.

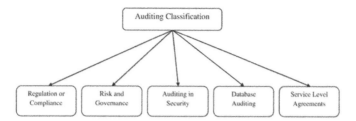

Figure 10.1: Auditing classification.

2. *Auditing for risk and governance*: Governance is exceedingly concerned with the performance measurement and its strategies and risk management and its proper administration is also an important issue of an IT landscape. The different management laws and policies, priorities and resources are needed for the processes and alignment of customs are the basic functionalities of this category.

3. *Auditing for security*: Security issues are the concern of auditing. In the administration of security, everyone should know the responsibilities of each designation. Technical auditing is also concerned with security issues. Physical resources are also in need of auditing for its priority, availability and cost complexity.

4. *Database auditing*: Database auditing is related with observing a cloud database so that database auditors and administrators can take care of the actions like accesses, modifications, and updating issues of the database users. Database auditing is mainly query-based auditing. Queries are presented to the auditor one at a time; the auditor checks if answering the query combined with past answers reveals the secret or forbidden information.

5. *Service-level agreement (SLA) auditing*: In the business service provider (BSP) layer [2], SLAs are concerned with business-oriented agreement and laws. So, at every level of an agreement, auditing is highly required to maintain proper use of laws and terms and conditions.

10.5   Auditing Service

Auditing service consists of a policy database, strategy rules engine, event processor, query manager having two modules like Query access manager and Query rules manager, and an audit control module consisting of an audit manager, audit trails, audit alerts, and rules engine [18-20].

The policy database is the repository of information on security policies that provide management direction and support for information security according to the business requirements and relevant laws, policies, and regulations. The strategy rules engine defines the strategic plan on the implementation of security policy, asset management, communications and operational management, information systems acquisition and development and maintenance, and business continuity management. The event processor is the most important module in auditing service. The event processor is associated with the dynamic change in the user events and related to the log server. The log server consists of consumer logs having details of cloud subscribers like user ID, usage time, etc., service broker logs containing broker ID and broker details, and service hosting logs having virtual machine ID, datacenter ID, resource usage, storage details, etc. The event processor maintaining all the log tables from the log server, also has the authority to set the priority of the events and process activities. The query access manager manages and controls the access of the query processing unit in an authorized way and the query rules manager sets the rules for query processing. These two modules directly interact with the database server for query processing. While processing the database query, a query audit is needed. The audit manager manages the overall auditing process, whereas audit trails have the responsibility of tracing unauthorized queries, and an audit alert alerts the manager in case of unauthorized query access. Therefore, a set of auditing rules and query access policies are made by the rules engine (see Figure 10.2).

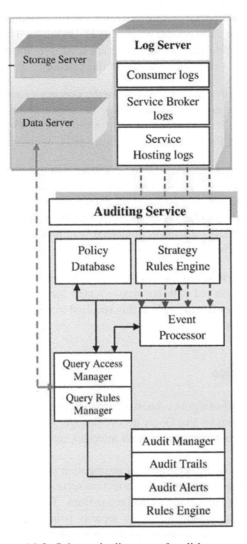

Figure 10.2: Schematic diagram of auditing concept.

10.5.1   How Third-Party Service Provider is Enabling Auditing Service

Consider a cloud data storage and database service involving four different entities: Cloud user, hosting machine in cloud service provider (CSP), cloud database server (CDS) and third-party auditing service (TPAS), as shown in Figure 10.3.

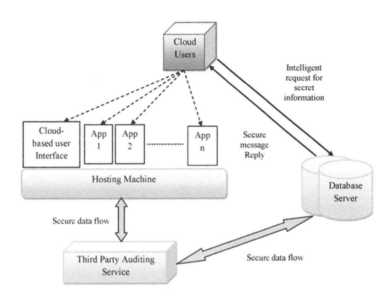

Figure 10.3: Cloud auditing service.

The cloud user has a huge amount of data files which are to be stored in the cloud. The cloud user interacts with hosting machine in CSP through cloud-based user interface and deploys various applications. The cloud users may also dynamically communicate with CDS for storing and maintenance of their data files [19,20].

While deploying their various applications onto the host machine, the users may rely on TPAS in assuring the confidentiality, availability and integrity of their outsourced data to preserve the privacy of their own data. TPAS is quite expert and capable of maintaining the privacy of user data and can be trusted as it may review the cloud database storage reliability in support of the cloud user upon request. An unauthorized user can put a set of intelligent queries to the database server, none of which are forbidden. So, an unauthorized user, combining the set of replies, may access the secret information which is forbidden. Hence, TPAS has the responsibility to maintain the privacy of user data.

10.5.2   Auditing Process Analysis

Both Ateniese and his colleagues and Juels and Kaliski have proposed proof of retrievability (POR) and provable data possession (PDP) auditing schemes [21, 22]. These schemes enable the cloud storage system to produce proof of a client's data without retrieving data from the system. These models demonstrate the minimum use of I/O cycles between the client and server. However, POR methods aren't suitable for third-party auditing schemes because the file is divided into blocks of data, and each block of data is encrypted [21].

During the auditing process, the client or verifier should explicitly mention the position of the block for verification; this technique is applicable only to static cloud data.

Another method involves the privacy-preserving public auditing of stored data proposed by Cong Wang and his colleagues, who also advised the use of a TPA to efficiently and simultaneously perform data audits for multiple users [23].

Privacy as a service was put forth by Kui Ren and his colleagues, who proposed a security protocol that provides security and privacy feedback for the client when storing and retrieving data [24]. Data protection as a service brings data security and privacy and deals with the evidence of privacy for data owners in the presence of potential threats [25].

Chang Liu and his colleagues formally studied and proposed a scheme that supports authorized auditing and fine-grained update requests [26]. Kan Yang and Xiaohua Jia also discussed a third-party storage auditing service that guards data privacy; the auditor mixes cryptography modules with the bilinearity property of bilinear pairing [27]. Yang and Jia extended their work by implementing a random Oracle model for batch auditing for multiple owners and multiple clouds without any third-party cloud auditing [28].

Table 10.1 compares recent auditing algorithms and services, with various functions, techniques, and programming libraries.

Table 10.1: Auditing algorithms and services.

Function	Technique	Service type	Cloud service	Programming library
Proofs of retrievability[6]	Prior to archiving a file, the auditor computes and stores a hash value	Verify	No	No
Homomorphic encryption[10]	Local file can be deleted, provided its metadata is locally saved	Verify	No	No
Homomorphic linear authenticator with random masking technique[2]	Third party; allows batch auditing of remote data	Privacy-preserving public auditing	No	Yes
Boneh–Lynn–Shacham signature and Merkle hash tree[5]	Fine-grained dynamic data updates	Verifiable fine-grained dynamic data operations	Yes	No
Homomorphic authenticator[15]	Performs multiple auditing tasks simultaneously; data dynamics for remote data integrity	Verifiable dynamic data operations	No	Yes
Homomorphic message authentication code (MAC; Li Chen et al.)[26]	Auditing of shared data	Privacy preserving	No	Yes
Bilinear map (Boyang Wang et al.)[24]	Batch auditing for multiword and multicloud	Privacy preserving	No	Yes
Homomorphic authenticable ring signatures[8]	Signature maker on each block in shared data is kept private from a third-party auditor	Privacy preserving	No	Yes
Homomorphic MAC (Cong Wang et al.)[27]	Auditing of shared data	Integrity	No	Yes
Homomorphic authenticable proxy (Boyang Wang et al.)[28]	Batch auditing for the shared data	Integrity	No	Yes
Multicloud[29]	Signature maker on each block in shared data is kept private from third-party auditor	Privacy preserving	No	No

MACs, signatures, and tags are the foundations of auditing algorithms. However, they also contribute to storage overhead. For example, MAC-based solutions must store the MACs for each block of data, whereas homomorphic linear authenticators have much less storage overhead because the tags for a linear combination of multiple messages can be homomorphically unified to form a single tag [29].

BLS-based auditing algorithms have an edge over MAC and homomorphic methods because they, with the help of a homomorphic linear authenticator, support public auditing and data dynamics. Furthermore, BLS's signature size is much shorter than the RSA-based homomorphic algorithms [30]. The POR and PDP methods are also built with BLS signature schemes using verifiable homomorphic linear authenticators; however, these algorithms can't maintain the auditing process's privacy [21, 31]. POR methods are used to aggregate proof of small authenticator values; hence, public irretrievability is achieved only for static data [32]. Dan Boneh and his colleagues propose dynamic provable data possession as the extension of POR methods [33]. Moreover, Qian Wang and his colleagues uncover POR's and PDP's security shortcomings through a proposed verification protocol with public auditability for dynamic data support [30].

In homomorphic authentication (HA) schemes, the client must pay extra attention to store the data blocks or file tags apart from the file itself. Another shortfall of homomorphic authentication is the uniquely generated tags, which aren't repeated at all. Eventually, these random values (tag index values) will run out. Furthermore, the tag indexed value is directly proportional to the file size; hence, CPU processing will be greater for the larger files (files are usually represented as a combination of sectors) [31]. However, malleability is often undesirable because it allows an adversary to form a ciphertext in another ciphertext, which decrypts the plaintext. However, homomorphic authentication tags have recently been shown to help achieve non-malleability by combining linear blocks of data so that adversaries can't produce valid signatures [29].

On the other hand, communication costs are directly proportional to the number of parties involved in the auditing process, apart from the size of the data transferred between them. In most cases, only two parties are involved; hence, signature tag size is crucial to communication cost. Communication costs are less with BLS-based algorithms because they use smaller signature tags [25].

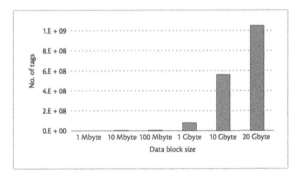

Figure 10.4: Transaction between cloud server and auditor: generation of security tags between TPA and cloud storage during auditing.

Computational complexity during TPA-based auditing is based on three entities: the auditor, the server, and the client who owns the data. For the lowest computational complexity and storage overhead, the algorithm should divide the file to be audited into a combination of blocks or sectors [25]. However, finding a design that integrates uniform allocation methods and auditing schemes for data storage services is challenging in cloud computing. Therefore, the proposed schemes can't provide data privacy because the TPA doesn't retrieve data using a data generator key algorithm. The drawbacks of auditing systems with respect to MACs are that security bits are only 180 bits or 20 bytes, and 1-Gbyte data blocks will have 53,687,091 tags and the same number of network transactions between the client and the server. Figure 10.4 shows the number of tags for different data sizes.

10.5.3 Privacy and Integrity

Remote verification (integrity) of data would allow third-party verification apart from the users themselves [21, 30, 31]. Provable data possession allows a client machine to verify remote data without downloading it [31] is a technique that employs the probabilistic possession of a random dataset from the remote server with the help of homomorphic linear authenticators. However, to achieve deterministic verification, the client must access the complete data block. Qian Wang and his colleagues extended the work on proof of storage for data dynamics by using tree datatypes for block-tag authentication [30]. They achieved public auditability for dynamic data operations and blockless verification. Previous work showed that if the server has a corrupted file, then the verifying phase of the cloud-auditing algorithm would detect this misbehavior with a probability of $O(1)$ [21, 30, 31].

Furthermore, these integrity schemes have faced difficulties when verifying small data updates [30]. One of the most well-known techniques for data integrity is the ranked Merkle hash tree, extended for the cloud-auditing scheme [24], which is a technique that maintains data integrity based on the signature scheme [34] and provides authorized auditing (which avoids a malicious user posing as a TPA). This scheme is similar to the binary tree, wherein each node N will have a maximum of two child nodes. Each node is represented as $\{H, rN\}$, where H is the hash value and rN is the rank of the node. A leaf node LN contains the message or data block m_i, and its H value is calculated as $H(m_i), rLN$. This tag generation scheme s uses the following equation:

$$\sigma = \left(H(m_i) \prod_{j=1}^{s_i} u_j m_{ij} \right) \tag{10.1}$$

file blocks of sector s. Segment F is divided into m_{ij}, where i is the block length and j is the set of sectors s.

An important feature of this scheme is that during the challenge phase, the TPA should receive an authentication tag from the cloud client for auditing; an adversary can't challenge TPA without this authentication tag. Furthermore, data auditing protocols, especially those designed for integrity, are unable to protect data privacy against the TPA [21, 30, 31, 35]. It has already been reported that a TPA might obtain the data information by recovering the data blocks from the data proof phase of the auditing process [36-40].

All these proposed protocols have missed the importance of data privacy. Hence, new privacy-preserving protocols are critical for maintaining data integrity and privacy [35]. For example, Cong Wang and his colleagues have used a public key-based homomorphic linear authenticator [23] that empowers the TPA to perform auditing without downloading the data; hence, the proposed algorithm reduces the communication overhead compared to general auditing techniques. Furthermore, it also random masks the auditing process to prevent the TPA from learning about the data. However, some cloud service features have become issues for cloud data; for instance, multitenancy, which means that the cloud platform (VM concepts) is shared and used by various geographically distributed users. Hence, the data dynamic feature should be equipped with auditing algorithms.

Cong Wang and his colleagues also implemented an authenticator for each block of data [35]; cloud users should attach metadata during the auditing process's setup. In response, the server will encapsulate the corresponding auxiliary authentication information during the audit phase and calculate the aggregated authenticators s as follows:

$$\sigma = \prod_{i \in I} \sigma_i^{vi} \tag{10.2}$$

For each element $i \in I$, the TPA chooses a random value v_i. Then, it transmits the proof of correctness to the TPA as $\{m, s, R\}$, where m is the combination of the sampled blocks specified during the challenge phase and R is the random element belonging to the multiplicative cyclic group. Then, the TPA calculates the following as the verification equation:

$$R \cdot e(\sigma^\gamma, g) = \left[\left(\prod_{i=s_i}^{S_c} H(W_i v_i) \right)^\gamma \cdot \mu^\mu, v \right] \tag{10.3}$$

where H is a secure map-to-point hash function, W_i is the name of the e, and $is_1, ..., s_c$ is the set of challenge elements. The public parameters are $\{v, g, e(u, v)\}$. Boyang Wang and his colleagues proposed a privacy-preserving protocol for shared data in the cloud environment [37]. They utilized ring-based signatures to construct a homomorphic authenticator. With such an approach, the TPA can't determine the block's signer. Batch auditing for the shared data is also achieved with the help of bi-linear maps; auditing shared data for different users is a single auditing job assigned to a TPA.

Ring-based signing includes public keys, $(pk_1, .., pk_d) = (w_1, .., w_d)$, for all d users, and a block of data with its identifier, $m \in Z_p$ and id, respectively. The ring signature s of the block is given by the following equation:

$$\sigma_s = \left(\frac{\beta}{\varphi \left(\prod_{i \neq s} \omega_\sigma \right)} \right)^{\frac{1}{x_s}} \in G \tag{10.4}$$

To produce ring signature for s users, we need to have computable isomorphism φ, a_i and x_i randomly picked prime ordered Z_p, and public key ω_i and private key s_k, for identifier $i \in [1, d]$. The verifier first computes challenge β as follows:

$$\beta = H_1(id)g_1^m \in G_1 \tag{10.5}$$

where $H_1\{0, 1\}^* \in G_1$ is a public map to point to the hash function. G_1 is the cyclic group of order g_1.

Yang and Jia suggested using the bilinearity property of bilinear pairing during the proof phase of auditing [28]. However, the auditor can still check the proof's correctness without having to decrypt the proof. Furthermore, this is the first proposal to have batch auditing on multiclouds and multiowners along with data dynamics. In this scheme, the key generation algorithm is a combination of a secret public key $(skt–pkt)$ and a hash secret key $(skh, kl) \in S$, such that there exists a different hash key for each server. Each data component is denoted as Mkl, where M is the data component owned by owner O_k, and maintained by server S_l. W_{kl}, i is the data block of owner k and server l, and i represents the data block of m_i. J is the sector number and is represented as $j \in [1, s]$. For each sector, data tags are calculated as

$$u_j = g_l^{X_j} \in G_l \tag{10.6}$$

To generate the batch proof, after receiving a challenge, each server (site) generates a tag proof as follows

$$TP_l = \prod_{k \in O_{chal}} \prod_{i \in Q_{kl}} t_{kl,i}^{Vkl,i} \tag{10.7}$$

where Q is the challenge set of data blocks and k is the owner of the data block for which the server generates the O_{chal}. The challenge phase takes information, such as a set of owners and a set of cloud servers. This information is used to generate a random number Vkl, i for each chosen data block, as tag tkl, i.

It has been proven that cryptography isn't a suitable solution for cloud privacy [38]. The abovementioned studies have done tremendous work on data dynamics and batching auditing; yet, many obstacles to maintaining data privacy remain. Most of the proposed auditing techniques are built on the assumption that TPAs are trustworthy, which is an unscientific assumption that might lead to privacy issues. TPAs will possess data that might be encrypted or random masked during the proofing phase of the auditing process. Thus, during this crucial phase of auditing, researchers must very carefully utilize cryptographic systems to secure the data from the TPAs. With random masking, TPA can't retrieve the data using linear equations [35]. Hence, we can conclude that randomization of data blocks and tags is the most suitable technique for preventing data leakage during auditing's proofing phase β.

Another layer of information can also be implemented to protect data privacy: encrypting the data before passing it to the cloud owner. The auditing process consists of the exchange of cryptographic keys between the servers and a TPA. A typical challenge sent to the server consists of the position of the data block and a random value stored in some variable. According to Minqi Zhou and his coleagues [39], this variable can be static or private to the customer C_1, and preserved at the server S_1. Because of multitenancy, the private area is shared with the other customers of S_1. Adversaries could benefit from this multitenancy and exploit the preserved data.

10.5.4 Cloud-Auditing Architecture Analysis

The research we've discussed thus far never mentions auditing architecture. The rapidly increasing use of cloud service applications and services on devices has led CSPs to evolve their technological approach to dynamic requirements. Cloud computing, which is elastic in nature, can fulfill these dynamic requirements by providing a suitable architecture for the services chosen by the client. Cloud architecture isn't monolithic; it can contain several modules stored in different machines in the cloud architecture. These machines, or nodes, have dedicated tasks, some of which are dynamic, and each act according to the demand presented. Furthermore, most of the nodes must be programmed to provide services according to the CSPs' service offerings. The cloud architecture will vary according to the services offered. Provisioning the services is a major contribution of the cloud.

CSPs usually provide clients with dynamic resource allocation such that the CSP doesn't over- or underprovide resources. Numerous CSPs are commercially available; thus, the first questions clients should ask before opting for CSP services (such as information as a service, platform as a service, and software as a service) are whether the CSP provides elasticity of services, will meet the agreed service level of the agreement, and has the required architecture to run the desired services. An architecture for auditing should also be provided, where all the modules responsible for the auditing process are programmed and assigned a duty for their role in the process. The cloud service architecture is the cloud's backbone; a group of components or modules that work together to achieve certain tasks. This group of modules is loosely coupled together to achieve elasticity and varies with the CSPs' service offerings. To gain the faith of cloud users, CSPs must have flexible services.

There are many avenues for future research in this particular area of cloud computing. For instance, unified data storage space allocation according to users' requirements and facility reservations could reduce the cost and time involved in the auditing process. Haar wavelet matrix operations have only addition, and many of its elements are zero. By compressing data before transferring it to the client, data integrity is maintained and costs decrease. Furthermore, clients or end users can schedule auditing based on data usage. If the most recently used data is scheduled for later use, it will be less of a burden on the server hosting the data. This will also benefit data with multiple owners.

Another potential research area involves giving cloud providers responsibility for maintaining client files' metadata. Client metadata can be placed in the blocks that are protected by software-based memory locks. Hence, this process can be used for data dynamics. Furthermore, it can reduce communication costs and computation for carrying secured tags between the TPA and the server. This process is also helpful for avoiding data retrieval from the tags by the TPA because it resides only in the cloud.

Studying the framework of an interaction-based system using a graphical dynamic system would also be useful. Because the communication path between the TPA and the server can't be predicted, data integrity and privacy remain secure.

From the data auditing perspective, the technical challenges of auditing services can be addressed by employing a separate architecture for auditing purposes. Data stored on the cloud comes from devices with different backhaul networks, such as 2G, 3G, LTE, and 4G. These architectures have different network delivery systems and must be synchronized to provide seamless connections. Apart from these differences, heterogeneous data also exists; although this data runs only on IP networks, it contains different types, such as audio, video, image, or text message. Hence, the data also has different provisioning requirements that must be harmonized to provide rational knowledge to the cloud client.

The core network of cloud architecture attempts to differentiate between victims and intruders with random early detection (RED) and weighted RED. Hence, when auditing is scheduled, these routers must be able to differentiate between valid traffic and intruders. Thus, another potential area for research is the introduction of explicit congestion notification (ECN), so that the application-level quality of service (QoS) can be met. Most of the techniques applied in service-level agreement (SLA) verification analyze QoS metrics at the domain gateways to discover abnormal activities. The SLA verifier agent can be used to recognize machine/end-users with an ECN echo notification; it can further probe the traffic for the packet transmission rate. RED always monitors the average queue size of the network edge router to avoid the threshold limits.

10.6 Summary

The auditing technique has different issues that occur during implementation. Identity federation of audit logs from distributed sources across multiple domains creates a problem for proper auditing. Architecture and protocols for data storage and retrieval of secure distributed audit logs are also loopholes of this framework because heterogeneous architectural platform is problematic for implementation. Compliance analysis of the federated audit logs for SLAs and regulation is also a considerable issue for auditing.

EXERCISES

1. What is the auditing concept?

2. Why is auditing required cloud infrastructure?

3. What is the role of audit in cloud computing?

4. How can data be made secure in cloud computing environment?

5. What are the aspects of data security?

6. Explain the characteristics of cloud which make it secure.

7. Explain how a third-party service provider can create the auditing background.

8. What are the steps involved in auditing outsourcing life cycle? Briefly explain them.

9. State different aspects of auditing. Classify them.

10. Explain the auditing service with a schematic diagram. And also describe the functionalities of each module.

11. How does the TPAS enable the auditing service?

12. Briefly describe:

    (a) Regulation/Compliance

    (b) Risk and Governance

    (c) SLA auditing

13. Why is there a need for auditing in cloud computing? Classify the types of auditing used in cloud architecture.

14. What are some audit objectives in cloud computing?

15. What should be on your cloud audit checklist?

References

1. Sarathy, V., Narayan, P., & Mikkilineni, R. (2010, June). Next generation cloud computing architecture: Enabling real-time dynamism for shared distributed physical infrastructure. In 2010 *19th IEEE International Workshops on Enabling Technologies: Infrastructures for Collaborative Enterprises* (pp. 48-53). IEEE.

2. Pal, S., & Pattnaik, P. K. (2012). Efficient architectural framework for cloud computing. *International Journal of Cloud Computing and Services Science*, 1(2), 66.

3. Jensen, M., Gruschka, N., Herkenhoner, R., & Luttenberger, N. (2007, November). Soa and web services: New technologies, new standards-new attacks. In *Fifth European Conference on Web Services (ECOWS'07)* (pp. 35-44). IEEE.

4. Sundareswaran, S., Squicciarini, A., Lin, D., & Huang, S. (2011, July). Promoting distributed accountability in the cloud. In 2011 *IEEE 4th International Conference on Cloud Computing* (pp. 113-120). IEEE.

5. Hu, R., Dou, W., Liu, X. F., & Liu, J. (2011, December). WSRank: a method for web service ranking in cloud environment. In 2011 *IEEE Ninth International Conference on Dependable, Autonomic and Secure Computing* (pp. 585-592). IEEE.

6. She, W., Yen, I. L., Thuraisingham, B., & Huang, S. Y. (2011, July). Rule-based run-time information flow control in service cloud. In 2011 *IEEE International Conference on Web Services* (pp. 524-531). IEEE.

7. http://www.zhen.org/zen20/2008/06/03/defining-saas-paas-iaas-etc/

8. Buyya, R., Yeo, C. S., & Venugopal, S. (2008, September). Market-oriented cloud computing: Vision, hype, and reality for delivering it services as computing utilities. In 2008 10th IEEE *International Conference on High Performance Computing and Communications* (pp. 5-13). Ieee.

9. Jianfeng Yang *et al.*, *Cloud Computing Research and Security Issues*, IEEE 978-1-4244-5392-4

10. Heather Paquetle, Tom Humbert (2011). *Cloud Computing-An Internal Audit Perspective*, March 10, 2011

11. Yang, K., & Jia, X. (2012). Data storage auditing service in cloud computing: challenges, methods and opportunities. *World Wide Web*, 15(4), 409-428.

12. Wang, C., Wang, Q., Ren, K., & Lou, W. (2010, March). Privacy-preserving public auditing for data storage security in cloud computing. In 2010 *proceedings ieee infocom* (pp. 1-9). Ieee.

13. Dash, S. K., Mohapatra, S., & Pattnaik, P. K. (2010). A survey on applications of wireless sensor network using cloud computing. *International Journal of Computer Science & Emerging Technologies*, 1(4), 50-55.

14. Mather, T., Kumaraswamy, S., & Latif, S. (2009). *Cloud security and privacy: an enterprise perspective on risks and compliance*. O'Reilly Media, Inc.

15. Buyya, R., Yeo, C. S., Venugopal, S., Broberg, J., & Brandic, I. (2009). Cloud computing and emerging IT platforms: Vision, hype, and reality for delivering computing as the 5th utility. *Future Generation computer systems*, 25(6), 599-616.

16. Le, D. N., Kumar, R., Nguyen, G. N., & Chatterjee, J. M. (2018). Cloud computing and virtualization. John Wiley & Sons.

17. Le, D. N., Bhatt, C. M., & Madhukar, M. (Eds.). (2019). *Security Designs for the Cloud, IoT, and Social Networking*. John Wiley & Sons.

18. Rabaninejad, R., Ahmadian, M., Asaar, M. R., & reza Aref, M. (2019). A lightweight auditing service for shared data with secure user revocation in cloud storage. IEEE Transactions on Services Computing.

19. Tian, H., Nan, F., Chang, C. C., Huang, Y., Lu, J., & Du, Y. (2019). Privacy-preserving public auditing for secure data storage in fog-to-cloud computing. Journal of Network and Computer Applications, 127, 59-69.

20. Alrabea, A. (2020). A Modified Boneh-Lynn-Shacham Signing Dynamic Auditing In Cloud Computing. Journal of King Saud University-Computer and Information Sciences.

21. Ateniese, G., Burns, R., Curtmola, R., Herring, J., Kissner, L., Peterson, Z., & Song, D. (2007, October). Provable data possession at untrusted stores. In *Proceedings of the 14th ACM conference on Computer and communications security* (pp. 598-609).

22. Juels, A., & Kaliski Jr, B. S. (2007, October). PORs: Proofs of retrievability for large files. In *Proceedings of the 14th ACM conference on Computer and communications security* (pp. 584-597).

23. Wang, C., Wang, Q., Ren, K., & Lou, W. (2010, March). Privacy-preserving public auditing for data storage security in cloud computing. In *2010 proceedings ieee infocom* (pp. 1-9). Ieee.

24. Ren, K., Wang, C., & Wang, Q. (2012). Security challenges for the public cloud. *IEEE Internet Computing*, 16(1), 69-73.

25. Ateniese, G., Kamara, S., & Katz, J. (2009, December). Proofs of storage from homomorphic identification protocols. In *International conference on the theory and application of cryptology and information security* (pp. 319-333). Springer, Berlin, Heidelberg.

26. Liu, C., Chen, J., Yang, L. T., Zhang, X., Yang, C., Ranjan, R., & Kotagiri, R. (2013). Authorized public auditing of dynamic big data storage on cloud with efficient verifiable fine-grained updates. *IEEE Transactions on Parallel and Distributed Systems*, 25(9), 2234-2244.

27. Yang, K., & Jia, X. (2014). *Security for Cloud Storage Systems*. Springer.

28. Yang, K., & Jia, X. (2012). An efficient and secure dynamic auditing protocol for data storage in cloud computing. *IEEE Transactions on Parallel and Distributed Systems*, 24(9), 1717-1726.

29. Wang, B., Li, B., & Li, H. (2014). Oruta: Privacy-preserving public auditing for shared data in the cloud. *IEEE Transactions on Cloud Computing*, 2(1), 43-56.

30. Wang, Q., Wang, C., Ren, K., Lou, W., & Li, J. (2010). Enabling public auditability and data dynamics for storage security in cloud computing. *IEEE Transactions on Parallel and Distributed Systems*, 22(5), 847-859.

31. Silva, L. A. B., Costa, C., & Oliveira, J. L. (2013). A common API for delivering services over multi-vendor cloud resources. *Journal of Systems and Software*, 86(9), 2309-2317.

32. Boneh, D., Lynn, B., & Shacham, H. (2001, December). Short signatures from the Weil pairing. In *International Conference on the Theory and Application of Cryptology and Information Security* (pp. 514-532). Springer, Berlin, Heidelberg.

33. Boneh, D., Gentry, C., Lynn, B., & Shacham, H. (2003). A survey of two signature aggregation techniques.

34. Merkle, Ralph C. "A certified digital signature." In *Conference on the Theory and Application of Cryptology*, pp. 218-238. Springer, New York, NY, 1989.

35. Wang, C., Chow, S. S., Wang, Q., Ren, K., & Lou, W. (2011). Privacy-preserving public auditing for secure cloud storage. *IEEE Transactions on Computers*, 62(2), 362-375.

36. Zissis, D., & Lekkas, D. (2012). Addressing cloud computing security issues. *Future Generation computer systems*, 28(3), 583-592.

37. Wang, B., Li, B., & Li, H. (2012, June). Knox: privacy-preserving auditing for shared data with large groups in the cloud. In *International Conference on Applied Cryptography and Network Security* (pp. 507-525). Springer, Berlin, Heidelberg.

38. Van Dijk, M., & Juels, A. (2010). On the impossibility of cryptography alone for privacy-preserving cloud computing. *HotSec*, 10, 1-8.

39. Sheikh, M. S., Liang, J., & Wang, W. (2020). Security and Privacy in Vehicular Ad Hoc Network and Vehicle Cloud Computing: A Survey. *Wireless Communications and Mobile Computing*, 2020.

40. Kolhar, M., Abu-Alhaj, M. M., & Abd El-atty, S. M. (2017). Cloud data auditing techniques with a focus on privacy and security. *IEEE Security & Privacy*, 15(1), 42-51.

Cloud Computing Implementation, Security and Application

11

SECURITY PARADIGMS IN CLOUD COMPUTING

PRASANT KUMAR PATTNAIK[1], DAC-NHUONG LE[2], SOUVIK PAL[3]

[1] KIIT, Deemed to be University, India
[2] Haiphong University, Haiphong, Vietnam
[3] Sister Nivedita University, Kolkata, India
Email: patnaikprasant@gmail.com, nhuongld@dhhp.edu.vn, souvikpal22@gmail.com

Abstract

The chief apprehension concerning cloud environments is the security provided in multitenant and isolated systems in order to make customers more comfortable with the concept. In cloud computing, access control and security are the two main parameters where researchers may work at their fullest. There has been a survey of works reported that classify security threats in cloud based on the nature of the service delivery models of a cloud computing system. In accordance with security and privacy, various types of security breaches or techniques may occur, which have been classified in this chapter. Security at different levels is necessary in order to ensure proper implementation of cloud computing environment such as server access security, internet access security, database access security, data privacy security, and program access security.

Keywords: Cloud computing, database access security, server access security, data privacy security

11.1 Security Paradigms and Issues

Cloud computing is dependent upon a paradigm shift with reflective implications on computing issues. A paradigm shift in cloud computing is the basic pillar of change in the traditional computing and there are various issues related to data security and privacy [1, 2]. There are multiple elements concerned with these issues which we will discuss below.

1. *User data is controlled by third-party service*: In the current scenario, the control is relinquished to the third-party services; so different security and privacy issues are concerned like unauthorized access, data access control, data corruption, enhancing dynamic allocation strategies, controlling sensitive information flow, etc. As far as third-party service is concerned, users keep all their sensitive data in the database and storage service of the third party. So, the third party has the responsibility to maintain the security and privacy of the data and that's why third party has to enable auditing service. According to *Information Systems Control and Audit*, IT auditing can be defined as a process of aggregating and evaluating evidence to decide whether a computing information system safeguards resources, maintains data integrity and secures sensitive user data, attains organizational objectives effectively and consumes physical and computing resources efficiently.

2. *How third party is enabling auditing service*: We are considering cloud data storage and database service involving four different entities, as shown in Figure 11.1: The cloud user, hosting machine in cloud service provider (CSP), cloud database server (CDS) and third-party auditing service (TPAS). The cloud user has a huge amount of data files which are to be stored in the cloud. The cloud users interact with hosting machine in CSP through cloud-based user interface and deploy various applications. They may also dynamically communicate with CDS for storing and maintenance of their data files.

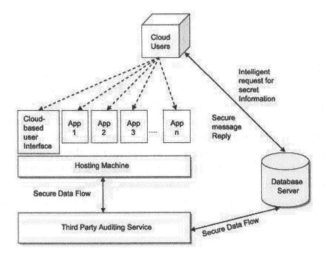

Figure 11.1: Third-party enabling auditing services.

While deploying their various applications onto the host machine, the users may rely on TPAS in assuring the confidentiality, availability, and integrity of their outsourced data to preserve the privacy of their own data. TPAS is quite expert and capable at maintaining the privacy of user data and can be trusted as it may review the cloud database storage reliability in support of the cloud user upon request. An unauthorized user can put a set of intelligent queries to the database server, of which none of the queries are forbidden. So, the unauthorized user, combining the set of replies, may get the secret information which is forbidden. Hence, TPAS has the responsibility to maintain the privacy of user data.

3. *The data is stored on various sites which are administered by multiple organizations*: Cloud services are provided by different service providers and the providers maintain the physical resources, such as processors, memory, and storage at their respective places. As a result, the user data has been stored on multiple sites, which are controlled by several organizations. Hence, the so-called "problem of many hands" would arise because of the authority or ability of individuals to work out and control the management over the collection, use, sharing, and disclosure of their personal data by others. Unlimited and ubiquitous data usage, data sharing and pool of data storage among the organizations would become a problem in the complex organization of cloud services. It is quite difficult to determine who will take the responsibility if something unwanted happens to data storage. In respect to data access, no controls have been implemented to restrict data modification and no logging events, such as access, transmission, or modification of data, have been monitored.

4. *How data can be safe in cloud computing environment*: There is a serious concern about the ethics of cloud computing. For data-usage and data-storage, there is a need for some rules and regulations which are to be maintained and governed by the service providers. The term "governance" deals with the manner in which something is regulated or governed, the system or criteria of regulations, and the way it is managed. These serious issues should be taken into account, and explicit attention should be given by the governmental organizations. In the recent scenario, data is being stored, transferred, and processed outside the company or organization. The raw data is not physically controlled by the organization and shared computing environments are also making it public. These kinds of loopholes need more security and privacy. Limited capabilities for change control and provider feasibility are also the drawbacks of cloud infrastructure. Governance is exceedingly concerned with the performance measurement and its strategies and risk management, and its proper administration is also an important issue of an IT landscape. Different management laws and policies, priorities and resources are needed for the processes; alignment of customs are the basic functionalities of governing organizations.

Accountability is another component regarding privacy and security issues. Adequate information is required regarding how data is managed by the cloud providers so that they can maintain logging events like data access, data transmission or data modification. That's why the governing organizations are enforcing the rules and regulations that account for access to the records.

11.2 Cloud Security Challenges

Different aspects of the emerging technology of cloud computing have faced many challenges, some of which are given below.

1. *Security and Privacy*: Security and protection of data is a significant challenge to distributed computing. Security and protection issues can be vanquished by utilizing security applications, security equipment, and encryption.

2. *Portability*: This is an extra challenge to distributed computing because applications need to effortlessly be relocated, starting with one cloud supplier then onto the next. There ought not be vendor lock-in. However, this has yet to be made possible on the grounds that each of the cloud suppliers utilize different standard dialects for their stages.

3. *Interoperability*: Applications on one stage must have the capacity to join administrations from another stage. It is made conceivable by means of web administrations. Moreover, composing such web administrations is extremely intricate.

4. *Reliability and Availability*: It is key for cloud frameworks to be predictable and vigorous. However, currently organizations are fundamentally lacking when it comes to administration provided by an outsider or third party.

5. *Authentication*: Cloud administration suppliers request clients to store their record data in the cloud, cloud administration suppliers have the privilege of passing on this data. This presents a security issue concerning the client's data. Numerous SLAs have been determined to protect the defenseless data; in any case, it is difficult for clients to ensure that the right standards are upheld.

6. *Trust*: Trust is not a new topic explored in software engineering, as there are differing sides to a range of issues, including security and the right of section control in PC systems, unwavering quality in circulated frameworks, special frameworks, and strategies for decision-making. This changed by and large by the Trusted Computer System Evaluation Criteria (TCSEC) of the late 70s and updated in the early 80s. This theory proposed utilizing a trusted third party inside a cloud domain by empowering trust and utilizing cryptography to confirm the uprightness, privacy and genuineness of information and correspondence, while endeavoring to address exact security vulnerabilities.

7. *Confidentiality and Privacy*: Confidentiality alludes to just approved gatherings or frameworks having the rite of passage to ensure information. Because of the increased number of gadgets, gatherings, and apps in the cloud, the risk of information arrangement increases, resulting in an increase in the number of purposes of admittance. Incorrectly assigning information to the cloud results in an increase in the danger of information trade-off, as it becomes less difficult to get the data to a greater number of gatherings.

8. *Integrity*: A key component of data security is honesty. Honesty implies that benefits can be tweaked just by approved gatherings or in approved ways and alludes to information, programming and the equipment. A distributed computing supporter is trusted to safeguard information trustworthiness and precision. Programming integrity alludes to guarding programming from unapproved change, erasure, robbery or manufacture. Cancellation, creation or alteration can be deliberate or accidental.

11.3   Cloud Economics

Cloud computing users can avoid capital expenditure (CapEx) on hardware, software and service, and pay a service provider only for what they use of the service (Figure 11.2) [5, 6].

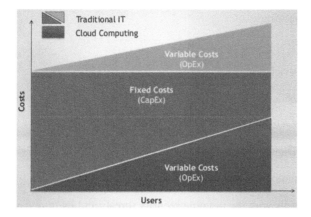

Figure 11.2: Cloud computing economics.

Consumption is billed depending on use, such as the resources consumed for applications or subscriptions like time-based ones with little or no upfront cost. Other profits of this time-sharing style approach are low batteries to process, low management overhead, shared and reusable infrastructure and costs and immediate random access to a broad choice of applications. Cloud users are generally able to terminate the contract at any time, which helps them avoid return on risk and uncertainty. And the applications and services are often covered by service-level agreements (SLA) with financial penalties. According to Nicholas Carr, the strategic significance of IT is diminishing as it is becoming standardized and cheaper. He argues that the cloud computing paradigm shift is analogous to the displacement of electricity generators by electricity grids early in the 20th century.

11.4   Security of Big Data in Cloud

Traditionally, statistics were saved on users' personal computers, so data owners didn't have to be concerned about their data; but now, in the cutting-edge generation of cloud computing, where large amounts of data are stored in unknown far-flung locations, several security issues must be addressed. Cloud computing is a way to dynamically enhance capabilities and abilities while spending little money on infrastructures, technologies, and software licencing. Despite the numerous benefits, customers are less likely to use the Cloud for private documents. The most important reason for this is security. According to a company survey conducted by IDC (International Data Corporation), safety is the most important project, followed by availability and overall performance. The Cloud Security Alliance (CSA) Top Threats Working Group compiled their final report *The Notorious Nine: Cloud Computing Top Threats in 2013* using the survey findings and their experience. The poll methodology confirmed that the threat list reflected the industry's most pressing issues [7, 8].

Experts identified the following nine key threats to cloud security in the most recent version of this report (as per Cloud Security Alliance data).

- Data Breaches

- Data Loss

- Account Hijacking

- Insecure APIs

- Denial of Service

- Malicious Insiders

- Abuse and Nefarious Use

- Insufficient Due Diligence

- Shared Technology Issues

This section deals with the top nine security threats and its implications in cloud environment.

11.4.1   The Biggest Risk: Data Breach

It's every CIO's greatest nightmare: critical internal data from the company leaks into the hands of competitors. While this scenario has kept executives awake at night long before computing, cloud computing opens up significant new attack avenues. Researchers from the University of North Carolina, the University of Wisconsin, and the RSA Corporation published a paper in November 2012 describing how a virtual machine could extract private cryptographic keys used in other virtual machines on the same physical server using side channel timing information. In many cases, however, an attacker would not need to go to such lengths. A weakness in one client's application could facilitate an attack if a multitenant cloud service database is not correctly built [9, 10].

Implications: Unfortunately, while both data loss and data leakage are important threats to cloud computing, the procedures you take to address one might increase the other. You can encrypt your data to lessen the impact of a data breach, but if you lose your encryption key, you'll also lose your data. On the other hand, you may choose to preserve offline backups of your data to mitigate the impact of a catastrophic data loss, but this raises your risk of data breaches.

11.4.2   Data Loss

The possibility of permanently losing one's data is alarming for both individuals and corporations. Just ask Mat Honan, a *Wired* magazine writer, who had his Apple, Gmail, and Twitter accounts hacked in the summer of 2012. The hackers utilized that access to delete all of Mat's personal information from those accounts, including all of Mat's baby photos of his 18-month-old daughter.

Data saved in the cloud can, of course, be lost for a variety of causes other than hostile attackers. Unless the cloud service provider takes proper backup mechanisms, any inadvertent deletion by the provider, or worse, a physical disaster such as a fire or earthquake, could result in the irreversible loss of customers' data. Furthermore, the responsibility for preventing data loss does not lie primarily on the shoulders of the provider. If a client encrypts data before uploading it to the cloud but loses the encryption key, the data is also lost [11, 12].

Implications: Data destruction and corruption of personal data are considered kinds of data breaches under the new EU data protection standards, and would require proper notifications. In addition, many compliance regulations mandate that audit reports or other evidence be kept on file. If this information is stored on the cloud, its loss could affect the organization's compliance status.

11.4.3   Account or Service Traffic Hijacking

Theft of an account or a service is nothing new. Phishing, fraud, and exploiting software flaws are still effective attack strategies. Because credentials and passwords are frequently reused, the impact of such assaults is amplified. Cloud computing introduces a new threat to the scene. If an attacker gets their hands on your credentials, they can listen in on your conversations and transactions, modify data, send false information, and lead your clients to malicious websites. The attacker may use your account or service instances as a new foundation. They may then use the strength of your reputation to launch additional attacks. Amazon had a cross-site scripting (XSS) flaw in April 2010 that allowed attackers to steal credentials from the site [13, 14].

Implications: Account and service hijacking, which is frequently done with stolen credentials, is still a major concern. Assailants can typically get access to vital sections of deployed cloud computing systems using stolen credentials, compromising the confidentiality, integrity, and availability of those services. To limit the harm (and potential litigation) caused by a breach, organizations should be aware of these tactics as well as typical defense in-depth protection strategies. Organizations should try to prevent users and services from exchanging account credentials, and implement robust two-factor authentication procedures whenever possible.

11.4.4   Insecure Interfaces and APIs

Customers use a set of software interfaces or APIs provided by cloud computing providers to administer and communicate with cloud services. These interfaces are used for provisioning, management, orchestration, and monitoring. The security and availability of generic cloud services are inextricably linked to the security of these fundamental APIs. These interfaces must be designed to guard against both inadvertent and intentional attempts to evade rules, from authentication and access control to encryption and activity monitoring. Furthermore, companies and third parties frequently build on these interfaces to provide customers with value-added services. This not only adds to the complexity of the new layered API, but it also raises the possibility of enterprises being forced to hand up their credentials to third parties in order to enable their agency [15, 16].

Implications: While most providers seek to integrate security into their service models, it is vital for users of those services to understand the security risks associated with cloud service usage, management, orchestration, and monitoring. Organizations that rely on a shoddy collection of interfaces and APIs suffer a slew of security risks, including confidentiality, integrity, availability, and accountability.

11.4.5   Denial of Service

Denial-of-service attacks, simply described, are attempts to prohibit customers of a cloud service from accessing their data or apps. The attacker (or attackers, in the case of distributed denial-of-service (DDoS) attacks) causes an intolerable system slowdown by forcing the victim cloud service to consume excessive amounts of finite system resources such as processor power, memory, disc space, or network bandwidth. This leaves all legitimate service users confused and angry as to why the service isn't responding.

While DDoS attacks tend to elicit a lot of terror and media attention (especially when perpetrators are motivated by political "hactivism"), they are far from the sole type of DoS attack. Asymmetric application-level DoS attacks exploit flaws in web servers, databases, and other cloud services, allowing a malevolent individual to take down an application with a single, incredibly small attack payload – sometimes less than 100 bytes long [17, 18].

Implications: A denial-of-service assault is similar to getting stuck in rush-hour traffic: there's no way to get to your destination, and there's nothing you can do about it but sit and wait. As a customer, service disruptions not only annoy you, but they also make you wonder if shifting your essential data to the cloud to save money on infrastructure was really worth it. Worse, because cloud providers generally charge clients depending on the number of compute cycles and disc space they use, an attacker may not be able to entirely disable your service, but they may be able to cause it to take so much processing time that it becomes too expensive to maintain.

11.4.6   Malicious Insiders

The security industry has discussed the threat of malevolent insiders. While the magnitude of the threat is debatable, the notion that the insider threat is a serious issue is not.

An insider threat is defined by CERN as follows: "A malicious insider threat to an organization is a current or former employee, contractor, or other business partner who has or had authorized access to an organization's network, system, or data and intentionally exceeded or misused that access in a manner that negatively affected the confidentiality, integrity, or availability of the organization's information or information systems." [19, 20]

Implications: In an inadequately configured cloud scenario, a malicious insider, such as a system administrator, can gain access to potentially sensitive information. As the hostile insider progresses from IaaS to PaaS and SaaS, he or she gains access to increasingly key systems and, eventually, data. Systems that rely only on the cloud service provider (CSP) for security are particularly vulnerable in this situation. Even if encryption is used, the system is still vulnerable to a malicious insider attack if the keys are not kept with the customer and are only available when data is used.

11.4.7   Abuse of Cloud Users

One of the biggest advantages of cloud computing is that it gives even tiny businesses access to massive amounts of processing power. Purchasing and maintaining tens of thousands of servers would be prohibitively expensive for most businesses, but renting time on tens of thousands of servers from a cloud computing provider is far more cheap. Not everyone, however, wants to put this power to good use. An attacker may take years to crack an encryption key using his own constrained technology, but he may be able to do so in minutes utilizing a network of cloud servers. He may also utilize the cloud server cluster to launch a DDoS assault, deliver malware, or distribute pirated software [21, 22].

Implications: This threat is more of a concern for cloud service providers than for cloud users, but it has a number of serious consequences for them. How will you know when someone is misusing your service? What do you mean when you say "abuse"? How are you going to keep them from doing it again?

11.4.8 Inadequate Due Diligence

Cloud computing has sparked a gold rush, with many businesses rushing to capitalize on the promise of cost savings, operational improvements, and increased security. While these are achievable goals for organizations with the resources to properly implement cloud technology, far too many businesses go into the cloud without fully comprehending the project's scope.

Organizations are taking on unknown levels of risk in ways they may not even understand, but that are a far cry from their current risks, without a complete understanding of the CSP environment, applications or services being pushed to the cloud, and operational responsibilities such as incident response, encryption, and security monitoring [23, 24].

Implications: An organization that rushes to implement cloud technologies faces a slew of problems. By creating misaligned expectations between the CSP and the client, contractual concerns develop around responsibilities on liability, response, or transparency. Pushing apps to the cloud that rely on "internal" network-level security measures might be risky if those controls go away or don't meet the customer's expectations. When designers and architects who are unfamiliar with cloud technologies develop applications that will be pushed to the cloud, they may encounter unknown operational and architectural challenges.

The bottom line for businesses and organizations considering adopting a cloud technology model is that they must have adequate resources and conduct substantial internal and CSP due diligence to understand the dangers they are taking on by doing so.

11.4.9 Vulnerabilities in Shared Technology

By sharing infrastructure, platforms, and applications, cloud service providers may scale their offerings. The threat of shared vulnerabilities exists in all delivery models, whether it's the underlying components that make up this infrastructure (e.g., CPU caches, GPUs, etc.) that weren't designed to offer strong isolation properties for a multi-tenant architecture (IaaS), re-deployable platforms (PaaS), or multi-customer applications (SaaS). Whether the service type is IaaS, PaaS, or SaaS, a defensive in-depth strategy is required, which should cover computing, storage, network, application and user security enforcement, and monitoring. The point is that a single vulnerability or misconfiguration can result in a cloud provider's entire cloud being compromised [25, 26].

Implications: In an SaaS context, a compromise of an essential piece of shared technology like the hypervisor, a shared platform component, or an application exposes more than just the affected customer; it exposes the entire system to the risk of compromise and breach. This flaw is hazardous since it has the potential to affect an entire cloud at the same time.

11.5 Security as a Service in Cloud

In the security-as-a-service model, the objective is to provide security as one of the cloud services. In this model the security is provided from the cloud in place of on-premise implementation. This helps enhance the capability of existing on-premise solutions by working with them in a hybrid manner. Intrusion Management is a method for intrusion detection, intrusion prevention and giving alerts for intrusion attempts. In physical environments, intrusion management mechanisms have already matured. However, due to the growth of cloud computing, virtualization, and multi-tenant resource sharing, there are several new targets for intrusion. The intrusion risk also increases due to the complexity of the system. There are many issues related to intrusion detection and prevention in a cloud environment, and even in a traditional environment with intrusion management service to be delivered as a service from the cloud. The primary purpose of intrusion management is to monitor the clients' organization infrastructure at important points to find malicious activity intended at interruption, interception, modification of data, applications, and systems. The objective is also to respond in such a way to block the intrusion, reduce it, or continue normal operations in the event of attack. An effective intrusion service should combine a prevention, detection and response management mechanism for control and reporting. It should have interface to the rest of the security architecture. Delivering these capabilities from the cloud often requires various administrative associations, raised user rights, and an end-to-end transactional access between hosted elements. There is also a need for central control and reporting of all incidents [27, 28].

The easiest way to implement security as a service (SECaaS) is directly forwarding the traffic to the cloud-based intrusion detection services. This can be done by transparently forwarding traffic from clients' network firewall or proxy that supports forwarding to an upstream proxy. Intrusion detection is a combination of inspection of network traffic using various methods, detection of signatures, and other anomaly-based algorithms. According to guidelines in CSA implementation guidance, the main functional areas covered for intrusion management are:

1. Intrusion detection through:

    (a) Inspection of network traffic, behavioral analysis, and analysis of traffic flow,

    (b) OS, virtualization layer, and events at host process,

    (c) Events at application layer, and

    (d) Techniques of correlation and other capabilities at distributed and cloud level.

2. Intrusion response using various mechanisms like automatic, manual, or hybrid.

3. Intrusion management service infrastructure, including:

    (a) Detection and response architectures,

    (b) Intrusion management service components,

    (c) Application, process, and data requirements, and

    (d) Regulatory and compliance issues for data privacy.

Intrusion detection as a service (IDSaaS) focuses on security at the infrastructure level of a public cloud. The intrusion detection technology provided is elastic, portable, and fully controllable. A prototype of IDSaaS is also described. The implementation of the prototype is done through Amazon Web Services.

In signature-based intrusion detection system (IDS), the focus is on the signature-based IDSaaS, a privacy-preserving intrusion detection mechanism designed. The process of signature matching hides specific content of network packets. It uses a fingerprint-based comparison.

Mullti-level IDS and log management is based on the behavior of the client for applying IDS effectively to cloud computing systems. The system uses different levels of security strength for users based on the degree of anomaly. The proposed method provides a way of decreasing the size of IDS rule set and management of user logs.

The goal of a distributed, collaborative, and data-driven intrusion detection and prevention (DCDIDP) system is to provide a holistic intrusion detection and prevention system (IDPS) for all cloud service providers. The scheme proposes collaboration among peers in a distributed manner at different architectural levels to respond to attacks. A DCDIDP framework is presented with three logical layers at global and software levels: network, host, and global. The various challenges have been identified in realizing the framework. Cloud computing architecture-based IDS gives a classification of specific and traditional attacks on the cloud computing environment according to their origin and their category. The existing cloud computing architecture-based intrusion detection systems (IDS) discussed, have their strengths and weaknesses. A new architecture has been proposed by correcting some weaknesses and integrating certain new concepts.

A software defined network (SDN)-based intrusion prevention system (IPS) was presented. It is a full life-cycle solution including detection and prevention in the cloud. A new IDPS architecture is proposed based on Snort-based IDS and Open vSwitch (OVS). There are some differences between the SDN-based IPS solution with the traditional IPS approach for both mechanism analysis and evaluation.

Evaluation of SECaaS

Several experiments have been conducted to evaluate the effectiveness of our proof-of-concept prototype of SECaaS in public cloud [29, 30]. The following criteria have been considered for the purpose of evaluation:

- *Reliability*: The service will be provided in the form of multiple web servers running in the cloud environment. The redundancy of servers will lead to high reliability and high availability to the clients. The proof of concept (POC) was tested in the form of two web servers to provide uninterrupted SECaaS services to the clients.

- *Effectiveness*: To make the service more effective, the core module handles multiple functionalities like intrusion detection, prevention, response, reporting, and logging.

- *Performance*: The performance was tested by comparing the average time taken by on-premise intrusion management W.r.t. SECaaS mechanism. The testing was done by running the SECaaS under various cloud environments. The overall overhead also depends on the traffic in public cloud, but it does not increase by more than 20-25%, which is fairly good given the advantages it offers over legacy systems.

- *Flexibility*: The solution can work with existing legacy systems as well. The POC implementation uses Snort but in actual systems the IDPS from multiple vendors can actually be used to run on VMs. It can provide more flexibility to customers to choose varying functionalities of security as per their need.

- *Control*: The client can access the service from various devices, viz. desktops and handheld mobile devices, etc. A central portal is provided through which all the policies can be easily administered.

- *Privacy and Security*: The SECaaS filters all doubtful inbound traffic before entering clients' organization. This filtering is done based on the policies defined. This ensures the privacy and security of users' data.

- *Cost of ownership*: The cost of ownership is borne by the cloud security service provider. The client does not invest in anything in the on-premise solution. The client will have to pay only on the basis of the pay-per-use model. Since SECaaS is available as cloud service it is only charged to the customer in the form of operating expense (OPEX) model.

11.6 Summary

The definition of big data, statistics authentication and their authorization with various procedures that ease the transfer of records has been analyzed especially in regard to authentication parameters. These methods have been categorized according to single- and multi-tier authentication. This authentication may use virtual certificate, HMAC or OTP on registered devices.

An SECaaS, in the form of a framework is discussed. It enables the cloud service provider to provide intrusion management security functionality as a cloud service in public cloud. SECaaS is compatible with prominent cloud features, including portability, elasticity, and pay-per-use service. The approach was implemented as a collection of VMs in public cloud to work in the cloud model. This solution can also work along with existing on-premise platform-based implementations in a hybrid manner to enhance their security capabilities. With SECaaS, users can detect and prevent any intrusions and secure their protected resources.

In the future, system availability, reliability and performance can be enhanced by creating replicas of core VM to distribute the heavy load of traffic and prevent single point of failure. Additional functionalities related to intrusion management can be added to make it more effective and efficient.

EXERCISES

1. What are the four areas of cloud security?

2. What are the cloud application security issues?

3. What are the five possible cloud security issues?

4. Which specific data transmissions do you encrypt?

5. Where do our servers physically reside?

6. Who has access to our data in the cloud?

7. What are your procedures for suspected security violations?

8. How do you protect access to GUIs and APIs?

9. What are your terms when it comes to ownership of data?

10. What are your security measures for protecting your data centers?

References

1. Behl, A., & Behl, K. (2012, July). Security paradigms for cloud computing. In *2012 Fourth International Conference on Computational Intelligence, Communication Systems and Networks* (pp. 200-205). IEEE.

2. Ogiela, L., & Ogiela, M. R. (2020). Cognitive security paradigm for cloud computing applications. *Concurrency and Computation: Practice and Experience*, 32(8), e5316.

3. Parikh, S., Dave, D., Patel, R., & Doshi, N. (2019). Security and privacy issues in cloud, fog and edge computing. *Procedia Computer Science*, 160, 734-739.

4. Arivazhagan, C., & Natarajan, V. (2020, July). A Survey on Fog computing paradigms, Challenges and Opportunities in IoT. In 2020 International Conference on Communication and Signal Processing (ICCSP) (pp. 0385-0389). IEEE.

5. Le, D. N., Bhatt, C. M., & Madhukar, M. (Eds.). (2019). *Security Designs for the Cloud, IoT, and Social Networking*. John Wiley & Sons.

6. Wang, Z., Wang, N., Su, X., & Ge, S. (2020). An empirical study on business analytics affordances enhancing the management of cloud computing data security. *International Journal of Information Management*, 50, 387-394.

7. Butt, U. A., Mehmood, M., Shah, S. B. H., Amin, R., Shaukat, M. W., Raza, S. M., ... & Piran, M. (2020). A Review of Machine Learning Algorithms for Cloud Computing Security. Electronics, 9(9), 1379.

8. Tabrizchi, H., & Rafsanjani, M. K. (2020). A survey on security challenges in cloud computing: issues, threats, and solutions. The Journal of Supercomputing, 1-40.

9. Li, Y., Xu, H. L. G., Xiang, T., Huang, X., & Lu, R. (2020). Towards Secure and Privacy-Preserving Distributed Deep Learning in Fog-Cloud Computing. IEEE Internet of Things Journal.

10. Mishra, S., Sharma, S. K., & Alowaidi, M. A. (2020). Analysis of security issues of cloud-based web applications. Journal of Ambient Intelligence and Humanized Computing, 1-12.

11. Le, D. N., Kumar, R., Nguyen, G. N., & Chatterjee, J. M. (2018). *Cloud Computing and virtualization*. John Wiley & Sons.

12. Shawish, A., & Salama, M. (2014). Cloud computing: paradigms and technologies. In *Inter-cooperative collective intelligence: Techniques and applications* (pp. 39-67). Springer, Berlin, Heidelberg.

13. Rong, C., Nguyen, S. T., & Jaatun, M. G. (2013). Beyond lightning: A survey on security challenges in cloud computing. *Computers & Electrical Engineering*, 39(1), 47-54.

14. Sen, J. (2015). Security and privacy issues in cloud computing. In *Cloud Technology: Concepts, Methodologies, Tools, and Applications* (pp. 1585-1630). IGI Global.

15. Zhang, J., Chen, B., Zhao, Y., Cheng, X., & Hu, F. (2018). Data security and privacy-preserving in edge computing paradigm: Survey and open issues. IEEE Access, 6, 18209-18237.

16. Sarvabhatla, M., Konda, S., Vorugunti, C. S., & Babu, M. N. (2017, November). A dynamic and energy efficient greedy scheduling algorithm for cloud data centers. In *2017 IEEE International Conference on Cloud Computing in Emerging Markets (CCEM)* (pp. 47-52). IEEE.

17. Tsai, J. L., & Lo, N. W. (2015). A privacy-aware authentication scheme for distributed mobile cloud computing services. *IEEE Systems Journal*, 9(3), 805-815.

18. Singh, A., & Chatterjee, K. (2017). Cloud security issues and challenges: A survey. *Journal of Network and Computer Applications*, 79, 88-115.

19. Bansal, M., & Upadhyaya, A. (2018). Three-level GIS data security: Conjointly cryptography and digital watermarking. In *Cyber Security* (pp. 241-247). Springer, Singapore.

20. Priya, K., & Gunavathi, I. (2015, April). Ensure cloud storage correctness based on public auditing mechanism. In 2015 International Conference on Communications and Signal Processing (ICCSP) (pp. 1468-1472). IEEE.

21. Zegers, W., Chang, S. Y., Park, Y., & Gao, J. (2015, March). A lightweight encryption and secure protocol for smartphone cloud. In 2015 *IEEE Symposium on Service-Oriented System Engineering* (pp. 259-266). IEEE.

22. Al-Jaberi, M. F., & Zainal, A. (2014, August). Data integrity and privacy model in cloud computing. In *2014 International Symposium on Biometrics and Security Technologies (ISBAST)* (pp. 280-284). IEEE.

23. Doe, N. P., & Suganya, V. (2014, January). Secure service to prevent data breaches in cloud. In *2014 International Conference on Computer Communication and Informatics* (pp. 1-6). IEEE.

24. Srividya, R., & Ramesh, B. (2019). Implementation of AES using biometric. *International Journal of Electrical and Computer Engineering*, 9(5), 4266.

25. Sreenivas, V., Narasimham, C., Subrahmanyam, K., & Yellamma, P. (2013, July). Performance evaluation of encryption techniques and uploading of encrypted data in cloud. In *2013 Fourth International Conference on Computing, Communications and Networking Technologies (IC-CCNT)* (pp. 1-6). IEEE.

26. Nguyen, T. C., Shen, W., Lei, Z., Xu, W., Yuan, W., & Song, C. (2013, June). A probabilistic integrity checking approach for dynamic data in untrusted cloud storage. In *2013 IEEE/ACIS 12th International Conference on Computer and Information Science (ICIS)* (pp. 179-183). IEEE.

27. Le, D. N., Kumar, R., Nguyen, G. N., & Chatterjee, J. M. (2018). Cloud computing and virtualization. John Wiley & Sons.

28. Le, D. N., Bhatt, C. M., & Madhukar, M. (Eds.). (2019). *Security Designs for the Cloud, IoT, and Social Networking*. John Wiley & Sons.

29. Seth, B., Dalal, S., Jaglan, V., Le, D. N., Mohan, S., & Srivastava, G. (2020). Integrating encryption techniques for secure data storage in the cloud. *Transactions on Emerging Telecommunications Technologies*, e4108.

30. Le, D. N., Seth, B., & Dalal, S. (2018). A hybrid approach of secret sharing with fragmentation and encryption in cloud environment for securing outsourced medical database: a revolutionary approach. *Journal of Cyber Security and Mobility*, 379-408.

12

PRIVACY PRESERVATION ISSUES IN CLOUD COMPUTING

Prasant Kumar Pattnaik[1], Dac-Nhuong Le[2], Souvik Pal[3]

[1] KIIT, Deemed to be University, India
[2] Haiphong University, Haiphong, Vietnam
[3] Sister Nivedita University, Kolkata, India
 Email: patnaikprasant@gmail.com, nhuongld@dhhp.edu.vn, souvikpal22@gmail.com

Abstract
Privacy means that a person is free from all interference. Privacy control is the administrative, technical, and physical safeguards employed within agencies to protect and ensure the proper handling of personally identifiable information or prevent activities that create privacy risk. Privacy breaches may create a lot of trouble for cloud users.

The American Institute of Certified Public Accountants (AICPA) and Canadian Institute of Charted Accountants (CICA) define privacy as "the right and obligation of individuals and organizations with respect to the collection, use, retention, and disclosure of personal information."

Keywords: Encryption, storage security, privacy and security

12.1   Privacy Issues in Cloud Storage

Considering privacy risks in the context of cloud is very important as privacy threats differ according to the type of cloud scenario. Some of those privacy risks concern lack of user control, lack of training and expertise, unauthorized secondary usage, complexity of regulatory compliance, addressing transporter data flow restrictions, litigation, legal uncertainty, compelled disclosure to the government, data security and disclosure of breaches, data accessibility, location of data, and transfer and retention.

Possible solutions to privacy problems based on different methods

Cloud Computing is presently one of the hottest topics in information technology (IT). Since the outsourcing of all essential data is available with a third party, there is always a concern about the cloud service provider's trustworthiness. Due to data privacy issues, it is essential for users to encrypt their sensitive data before storing them on the cloud. Yet, there exist some shortcomings in the scenario of traditional encryption. When a secret key owner wants to look for some data that are stored in the cloud storage, he may need to download all encrypted data from the cloud server, and then decrypt and search them. If the encrypted data are huge or the client is a mobile user, then it will be very inefficient and is not convenient. Otherwise he must send his key to the cloud server, which performs the decryption and search procedures. The cloud server obtaining the secret key can cause serious trouble; therefore, many models exist to ensure the integrity of data files.

The Provable Data Possession (PDP) model ensures the possession of data files in untrusted storage. It uses a RSA-based homomorphic linear authenticator for auditing outsourced data, but this model leaks the data to external auditors and hence is not provably privacy preserving. Juels and Kaliski [1] describe a Proof of Retrievability (POR) model, where spot-checking and error-correcting codes are used in order to ensure the possession and retrievability. But this approach works only with encrypted data. Improved versions of POR protocols have been proposed which guaranteed private auditability and one which makes use of BLS signatures. But these approaches were not privacy-preserving. Then the TPA-based approach came along to keep online storage honest. This scheme only works for encrypted files which requires the auditor to manage state, and suffers from bound usage, which potentially puts the burdens on online users when the keyed hashes are used up [2-7].

Thus, to provide secure cloud storage supporting privacy preservation, many methodologies, frameworks and protocols have been proposed. This chapter examines those existing methodologies that guarantee privacy in cloud storage by categorizing it into four types by which privacy in cloud storage is achieved and analyzes the existing methodologies which are best suited to deal with privacy issues.

12.1.1   Encryption Methods

There are approaches that make use of encryption techniques to achieve privacy in cloud computing. Hao *et al.* [8] proposed the design of privacy-preserving cloud storage framework to solve privacy security problems, which consists of the design of data organization structure, the generation and management of keys, the interaction between participants and the handling of change of user's access rights; and also supports the dynamic operations of data. It uses an interactive protocol and an extirpation-based key derivation algorithm. It ensures data confidentiality, solves ineffectiveness of key derivation, reduces the burden of encryption and decryption, is able to manage numerous keys, saves owners storage space, reduces runtime overheads of the system, gives excellent privacy security and can apply to multiple users, data owners and service providers. But it needs to have techniques to reduce the owner's encryption burden and to work on ciphertext.

A method for improving user privacy with secret key recovery in cloud storage that allows users to encrypt their files in the cloud storage has been proposed in [7]. A secret sharing algorithm to key recovery mechanism is used. AES-128 uses a 128-bit key length to encrypt user files. The key recovery scheme is trusted in part because no one has the full information about the encryption key except the user himself. The compression algorithm used here is ZIP. The user's privacy is protected and it decreases the risk of encryption key loss. However, it puts a big computation burden on users. There are also concerns about its transforming speed. Renewing a user's key is a challenge here; users can't search words and there is dispersal of information. Hao *et al.* provide a privacy-preserving cloud storage framework supporting ciphertext retrieval to solve problems while operating on encrypted data and reduce the data owner's workload by managing data and supporting data sharing. Interaction protocol, a key derivation algorithm, a combination of symmetric and asymmetric encryption, and a Bloom filter are used here. It can operate on encrypted data, reduce data owner's workload on managing the data and storage space, reduce communication, computation and storage overhead. It can manage numerous keys and is efficient, safe, and economic. But it supports only owner-write-user-read and lacks a technique that supports ciphertext-based computing.

A study was conducted on controllable privacy-preserving search functionalities which include revocable delegated search and un-decryptable delegated search that are based on symmetric predicate encryption in the cloud storage [9]. Thus, the owner of cloud can easily control lifetime and search privileges of data, which is suitable for delegation-based business applications. But it cannot support complex access control and search privileges. A method is discussed that uses discretion algorithm [10] for preserving privacy through data control in a cloud computing architecture, which provides a security solution that requires more than user authentication and digital certificate. Here, the SP can directly use data without any key and it is more flexible and safe to protect individuals' privacy. But the use of encryption limits data usage and needs communication and compatibility with heterogeneous host.

The main problem in using an encryption-based technique is that it limits the data usage and puts an additional burden on the user. The access control mechanisms are available which will overcome the burden of the above methods.

12.1.2 Access Control Mechanisms

The access control mechanisms that provide privacy are discussed in papers [9] and [11]. A privacy-preserving access authenticated access control scheme for securing data in clouds that verifies the authenticity of the user without knowing the user's identity before storing information has been introduced in [11]. Here, only valid users are able to decrypt the stored information. This prevents reply attack, and achieves authenticity and privacy. It is decentralized and robust, which allows multiple read and write, distributed access control, and user identity protection. But according to [9], the access policy for each record stored in the cloud should be known and should be based on the assumption that the cloud administrator is honest, but it does not support complex access control.

12.1.3 Query Integrity/Keyword Searches

There are approaches that make use of queries and keyword search schemes to check the privacy in cloud and papers [12,13] that discuss those schemes. Wang *et al.* [12] proposed an efficient privacy-preserving keyword search scheme in cloud computing that allows a service provider to participate in partial decipherment and enables them to search the keywords on encrypted files. It makes use of an efficient privacy-preserving keyword search scheme (EPPKS). It provides protection of user data privacy, query privacy, and supports keyword search on encrypted data. It is found efficient, practical and provably and semantically secure. But the computation on encrypted data was a challenge. A privacy-preserving approach for data outsourcing in cloud environment which makes use of fragmentation and heuristic algorithm was used by Tang *et al.* [13]. It proves to be efficient and effective but confidentiality is not achieved.

12.1.4 Auditability Schemes

Auditing reduces risks for customers as well as provides incentives to providers to improve their services [14]. Auditability falls under two categories concerning the available schemes in auditability: private auditability and public auditability. Even though schemes with private auditability can attain higher scheme efficiency, public auditability permits anyone, not just the client (data owner), to deal with the cloud server for correctness of data storage while keeping no private information. Moreover, clients are able to pass on the evaluation of the service performance to an independent third-party auditor (TPA), without giving their computation resources. So we can denote the types of auditing protocols as Data Owner Auditing and Third-Party Auditing.

According to [15], the data auditing methods can be classified into three categories: Message authentication code (MAC)-based methods, RSA-based homomorphic methods, and Boneh–Lynn–Shacham (BLS) signature-based homomorphic methods. The challenging issues of data storage auditing include dynamic auditing, collaborative auditing, and batch auditing. The following three performance criteria need to be met when it comes to designing auditing protocols: low storage overhead, low communication cost and low computational complexity. The following papers compare the schemes available in public auditability. The papers in [16-22] are some works related to public auditability in cloud. However, even though the papers in [16-19] are not provably privacy-preserving, they led to the development of efficient privacy-preserving methodologies in papers [20-22].

12.1.4.1 Remote Data Possession at Untrusted Host

A study [16] has been proposed with the goal of remote data possession checking schemes. This paper proposes an efficient remote data possession checking (RDPC) scheme which is efficient in terms of computation and communication; it allows verification without the need for the challenger to compare against the original data; it uses only small challenges and responses, and users need to store only two secret keys and several random numbers. Finally, a challenge updating method is proposed based on Euler's theorem.

12.1.4.2 Public Verifiability for Storage Security

The research by Nguyen *et al.* [17] studied the problem of ensuring the integrity of data storage in cloud. To ensure the correctness of data they allowed a third-party auditor to work on behalf of the cloud consumer to check the integrity of the stored data in the cloud. This scheme ensures that the storage at the client side is minimal, which will be helpful for thin clients.

12.1.4.3 Remote Data Checking Using Provable Data Possession

A study by Ateniese *et al.* [19] introduces a model for provable data possession which can be used for remote data checking. By having a sampling random set of blocks from the server, this model produces probabilistic proofs of possession which will significantly reduce I/O costs. In order to minimize network communication the challenge/response protocol transmits a small and constant amount of data. The model incorporates some mechanisms for mitigating arbitrary amounts of data corruption and it is robust. It offers two efficient secure PDP schemes and the overhead at the server is low. To add robustness to any remote data checking scheme based on spot-checking, it proposes a generic transformation.

12.1.4.4 Privacy-Preserving Data Integrity Checking

A privacy-preserving remote data integrity checking protocol with data dynamics and public verifiability [20] makes use of a remote data integrity checking (RDIC) protocol. The protocol provides public verifiability without the help of a third-party auditor. It doesn't leak any privacy information to third party, which provides good performance without the support of the trusted third party and provides a method for independent arbitration of data retention contracts. But it gives unnecessary computation and communication cost.

12.1.4.5 Privacy-Preserving Public Auditability for Storage Security

The problem of ensuring the integrity of the data storage in cloud computing has been analyzed in studies [18]. It allows a third-party auditor to confirm the integrity of dynamic data stored in the cloud. This scheme achieves both public auditability and dynamic data operations. Vasudevan *et al.* [21] propose privacy-preserving public auditing for secure cloud storage. The protocol design to achieve the security and performance guarantees like public auditability, storage correctness, preserving privacy, batch auditing, and is lightweight. The method is found to be scalable and efficient, which provides a completely outsourced solution to integrity checking, and thus saves auditing time. It relies on third-party auditors and has the use of expensive modular exponentiation operations, which lead to storage overhead on server and extra communication cost. Zhu *et.al* [14] propose an efficient audit service outsourcing for data integrity in clouds. It is based upon the creation of an interactive PDP protocol to inhibit the dishonesty of prover (soundness property) and verified data leakage (zero-knowledge property). It describes the periodic verification used for improving the performance of audit services. Here, the approach adopts a way of sampling verification. The scheme not only prevents the deception and forgery of cloud storage providers, but also prevents the leakage of outsourced data in the process of verification. It supports an adaptive parameter selection. The system shows only lower computation cost as well as less extra storage, and the scheme is less complex due to fragment structure. It achieves audit without downloading, verification correctness, privacy preservation, and high performance [22-27].

12.2 Privacy and Security

The fundamental factor defining the success of any new computing technology is the level of security it provides [28-30]. Is the data residing in the cloud secure enough to avoid any sort of security breach or is it more secure to store the data away from cloud in our own personal computers or hard drives? At least we can access our hard drives and systems whenever we wish to, but cloud servers could potentially reside anywhere in the world and any sort of internet breakdown can deny us access to the data stored in the cloud. The cloud service providers insist that their servers and the data stored in them is sufficiently protected from any sort of invasion and theft. Such companies argue that the data on their servers is inherently more secure than data residing on a myriad of personal computers and laptops. However, since it is also a part of cloud architecture, the client data will be distributed over these individual computers regardless of where the base repository of data is ultimately located. There have been instances when their security has been invaded and the whole system has been down for hours. At least half a dozen security breaches occurred last year, bringing out the fundamental limitations of the security model of major cloud service providers (CSPs). With respect to cloud computing environment, privacy is defined as "the ability of an entity to control what information it reveals about itself to the cloud/cloud SP, and the ability to control who can access that information." Piderit and Nyoni discuss the standards for collection, maintenance and disclosure of personality identifiable information in [30]. Information requiring privacy and the various privacy challenges need specific steps to be taken in order to ensure privacy in the cloud, as discussed in [31, 32]. In the case of a public-cloud computing scenario, there are multiple security issues that need to be addressed in comparison to a private-cloud computing scenario. A public cloud acts as a host to a number of virtual machines, virtual machine monitors, and supporting middleware [33], etc. The security of the cloud depends on the behavior of these objects as well as on the interactions between them. Moreover, in a public cloud enabling a shared multi-tenant environment, as the number of users increase, security risks become more intensified and diverse. It is necessary to identify the attack surfaces which are prone to security attacks and mechanisms ensuring successful client-side and server-side protection [34]. Because of the multifarious security issues in a public cloud, adopting a private cloud solution is more secure with an option to move to a public cloud in the future if needed [35]. The emergence of cloud computing is significantly due to mashup. A mashup is an application that combines data or functionality from multiple web sources and creates new services using them. As these involve usage of multiple subapplications or elements towards a specific application, the security challenges are diverse and intense. Based on this idea, various security architectures, such as a secure component model addressing the problem of securing mashup applications and an entropy-based security framework for cloud-oriented service mashups, have been proposed in [36-66]. Also, privacy needs to be maintained as there is a high chance of an eavesdropper being able to sneak in.

12.2.1 Performance Unpredictability, Latency and Reliability

It has been observed that virtual machines can share CPUs and main memory in a much better way in comparison to the network and disk I/O. Different EC2 instances vary more in their I/O performance than main memory performance [37]. One of the ways to improve I/O performance is to improve architecture and operating systems to efficiently virtualize interrupts and I/O channels. Another possibility is to make use of flash memory, which is a type of semiconductor memory that preserves information even when powered off, and since it has no moving parts, it is much faster to access and uses comparatively less energy. Flash memory can sustain many more I/O operations than disks, so multiple virtual machines with a large number of I/O operations would coexist better on the same physical computer [37]. Latency [38, 39] has always been an issue in cloud computing with data expected to flow around different clouds. The other factors that add to the latency are: encryption and decryption of the data when it moves around unreliable and public networks, congestion, packet loss, and windowing. Congestion adds to the latency when the traffic flow through the network is high and there are many requests (could be of same priority) that need to be executed at the same time. Windowing is another message passing technique whereby the receiver has to send a message to the sender that it has received the earlier sent packet and hence this additional traffic adds to the network latency. Moreover, the performance of the system is also a factor that should be taken into account. Sometimes the cloud service providers run short of capacity either by allowing access to too many virtual machines or reaching upper throughput thresholds on their internet links because of high demand arising from the customer community. This affects the system performance and adds to the latency of the system.

12.2.2 Portability and Interoperability

Organizations may need to change cloud providers and there have been cases when companies are unable to move their data and applications to another cloud platform that they would prefer over the existing one. Such a scenario is termed a "lock-in" and refers to the challenges faced by a cloud customer trying to migrate from one cloud provider to another. More often, it has been seen that changing a cloud provider involves multiple risks and may lead to system breakdown if not executed properly. The nature of lock-in and associated issues are very much dependent on the cloud type being used [40]. For SaaS vendor lock-ins, an application is used by the customer provided by the cloud provider. While migrating between the cloud providers, there may be instances when the data to be moved does not really fit the data format as required in the new application. This will require expending extra effort to make sure that the data is arranged in a format that matches the new application, ensuring no data loss in the process. Additional steps such as performing regular data extraction and backups to a format that is usable even without the SaaS application, understanding how the application has been developed and monitored, and the major interfaces and their integration between the platforms, need to be taken care of.

PaaS lock-in can be observed in cases where the language used to develop an application on a platform is not supported on the platform to be migrated to. It is more visible at API level as different providers offer different APIs. PaaS lock-in can be avoided if the following points are considered and addressed:

▪ Cloud offering with an open architecture and standard syntax should be supported.

▪ Understand the application components and modules specific to the PaaS provider and how the basic services like monitoring, logging, etc., are performed.

▪ Understand the control functions specific to the cloud provider and their counterparts on an open platform.

▪ IaaS lock-in depends on the infrastructure services being used.

The most obvious form of IaaS lock-in can be observed in the form of data lock-in. With more and more data pushed to the cloud, data lock-in increases unless the cloud provider ensures data portability. Understanding how the virtual machine images are maintained and eliminating any provider specific dependency for a virtual machine environment will serve at the time of transition from one IaaS platform to other.

Identifying the hardware dependencies will minimize the issues at the time of migration. In order to avoid these lock-ins, the customer should be clear of the choices available in the market and the extent to which they match up to its business, operational and technical requirements. Also, some companies use different cloud platforms for different applications based on their requirements and the services provided by the cloud service providers (CSPs). In some cases, different cloud platforms are used for a particular application or different cloud platforms have to interact with each other for completing a particular task. The internal infrastructure of the organization is needed to maintain a balance to handle the interoperability between different cloud platforms [41]. The risk of outsourced services going out of control is high in a hybrid, public and private cloud environment. All data has to be encrypted for proper security, and key management becomes a difficult task in such situations [42]. The users actually have no idea of where their information is stored [43]. Normally, a user's data is stored in a shared environment, along with other user's data. The issue of inter-security handling becomes important in such cases. A cloud security management model is discussed in [42] to serve as a standard for designing cloud security management tools. The model uses four interoperating layers for managing the cloud security. Thus, we see that although the buzz of cloud computing prevails everywhere because of the multi-fold features and facilities provided by it, there are still issues that need to be solved in order to reach the landmarks set by it.

12.2.3 Data Breach Through Fiber-Optic Networks

It has been noticed that the security risks for the data in transit has increased over the last few years. Data transitioning is quite normal nowadays and it may include multiple data centers and other cloud deployment models such as public or private cloud. Security of the data leaving one data center to another data center is a major concern as it has recently been breached quite a number of times. This data transfer is done over a network of fiber-optic cables which were considered to be a safe mode of data transfer, until recently, when an illegal fiber eavesdropping device in Telco Verizon's optical network placed at a mutual fund company was discovered by US security forces [44]. There are devices that can tap the data flow without even disturbing it and access fiber through which data is being transferred. They are generally laid underground and hence it is difficult to access these fiber-optic cables. And hence it becomes quite important to ensure data security over the transitioning networks.

12.2.4 Data Storage over IP Networks

Online data storage is becoming quite popular nowadays and it has been observed that a majority of enterprise storage will be networked in the coming years, as it allows enterprises to maintain huge chunks of data without setting up the required architecture. Although there are many advantages of having online data storage, there are security threats that could cause data leakage or data unavailability at crucial hours. Such issues are observed more frequently in the case of dynamic data that keeps flowing within the cloud in comparison to static data. Depending upon the various levels of operations and storage provided, these networked devices are categorized into SAN (storage area network) and NAS (network-attached storage), and since these storage networks reside on various servers, there are multiple threats associated with them. Various threat zones that may affect and cause the vulnerability of a storage network have been discussed in [45]. Besides these, from a mobile cloud computing (MCC) perspective, unlike cloud computing there are several additional challenges that need to be addressed to enable MCC to reach its maximum potential:

- *Network accessibility*: The internet has been a major contributing factor in the evolution of cloud computing, and without having the network (internet) access it would not be possible to access the mobile cloud, limiting the available applications that can be used.

- *Data latency*: Data transfer in a wireless network is not as continuous and consistent as it is in the case of a dedicated wired LAN. And this inconsistency is largely responsible for longer time intervals for data transfer at times. Also, the distance from the source adds up to the longer time intervals observed in the case of data transfer and other network-related activities because of an increase in the number of intermediate network components.

- *Dynamic network monitoring and scalability*: Applications running on mobile devices in a mobile cloud computing platform should be intelligent enough to adapt to the varying network capacities and also these should be accessible through different platforms without suffering any data loss. Sometimes, while working on a smartphone a user may need to move on to a feature phone, and when he accesses the application through a smartphone; he should not encounter any data loss.

- *Confidentiality of mobile cloud-based data sharing*: The confidential data on mobile phones using cloud-based mobile device support might become public due to better access control and identity management. Cloud computing involves virtualization, and hence the need for user authentication and control across the clouds is high. The existing solutions are not able to handle the case of multiple clouds. Since data belonging to multiple users may be stored in a single hypervisor, specific segmentation measures are needed to overcome the potential weaknesses and flaws in the hypervisor platform. Security challenges in a mobile cloud computing environment are slightly different as compared to the abovementioned network-related challenges. With applications lying in a cloud, it is possible for the hackers to corrupt an application and gain access to a mobile device while accessing that application. In order to avoid these, strong virus-scanning and malware protection software need to be installed to avoid any type of virus/malware in the mobile system. Besides, by embedding device identity protection, like allowing access to the authorized user based on some form of identity check feature, unauthorized access can be blocked. Two types of services, have been defined in [46], namely (i) critical security service, and (ii) normal security service. The resource in a cloud has to be properly partitioned according to different user's requests. The maximal system rewards and system service overheads are considered for the security service. Hence, we see that although mobile cloud computing is still in its nascent state, there are various security issues, that plague cloud computing and its derivatives.

12.2.5 Data Storage and Security in Cloud

Many cloud service providers provide storage as a form of service. They take the data from the users and store them in large data centers, hence providing users a means of storage. In spite of claims by the cloud service providers about the safety of the data stored in the cloud, there have been cases where the data stored in these clouds have been modified or lost due to some security breach or some human error. Attack vectors in a cloud storage platform have been discussed in [47], along with how the same platform is exploited to hide files with unlimited storage. In [47], the authors have studied the storage mechanism of Dropbox (a file storage solution in the cloud) and carried out three types of attacks, viz. hash value manipulation attack, stolen host id attack, and direct download attack. Once the host id is known, the attacker can upload and link arbitrary files to the victim's Dropbox account. Various cloud service providers adopt different technologies to safeguard the data stored in their cloud. But the question is: Is the data stored in these clouds really secure? The virtualized nature of cloud storage makes the traditional mechanisms unsuitable for handling the security issues [23]. These service providers use different encryption techniques, such as public key encryption and private key encryption to secure the data stored in the cloud. A similar technique providing data storage security, utilizing the homomorphic token with distributed verification of erasure-coded data, has been discussed in [48]. Trust-based methods are useful in establishing relationships in a distributed environment. A domain-based trust model has been proposed in [49] to handle security and interoperability in cross clouds. Every domain has a special agent for trust management. It proposes different trust mechanisms for users and service providers.

The following aspects of data security should be taken care of while moving into a cloud:

1. Data in Transit

2. Data at Rest

3. Data Lineage

4. Data Remanence

5. Data Provenance

In the case of data in transit, the biggest risk is associated with the encryption technology being used, whether it is up-to-date with current security threats and makes use of a protocol that provides confidentiality as well as integrity to the data in transit. Simply going for an encryption technology does not serve the purpose. In addition to using an encryption-decryption algorithm for secure data transfer, data can be broken into packets and then transferred through disjoint paths to the receiver. It reduces the chances of all the packets being captured by an adversary. And the data cannot be known until all the packets are coupled together in a particular manner. A similar approach has been discussed in [50, 51]. Managing data at rest in an IaaS scenario is more feasible in comparison to managing the same over an SaaS and PaaS platform because of restricted rights over the data. In an SaaS and PaaS platform, data is generally commingled with other users' data. There have been cases wherein even after implementing data tagging to prevent unauthorized access, it was possible to access data through exploitation of application vulnerability [25]. The main issue with data at rest in the cloud is loss of control, even a non-authorized user/party may have access to the data (it is not supposed to access) in a shared environment. However, nowadays, storage devices with in-built encryption techniques are available which are resilient to unauthorized access to a certain extent. Even in such a case, nothing can be done in the case where encryption and decryption keys are accessible to the malicious user. A lockbox approach wherein the actual keys are stored in a lockbox and there is a separate key to access that lockbox is useful in the abovementioned case. In such a scenario, a user will be provided a key to access the lockbox based on the identity management technique corresponding to the COI (community of interest) he belongs to. Whenever the user wants to access the data, he needs to acquire the COI key to the lockbox and then the user gets appropriate access to the relevant data [9]. Homomorphic encryption techniques, which are capable of processing the encrypted data and then bringing back the data into its original form, are also providing better means to secure the data at rest. A simple technique for securing data at rest in a cloud computing environment has been mentioned in [52]. This technique makes use of public encryption technique.

Tracing the data path is known as data lineage and it is important for auditing purposes in the cloud. Providing data lineage is a challenging task in a cloud computing environment and more so in a public cloud. Since the data flow is no longer linear in a virtualized environment within the cloud, it complicates the process of mapping the data flow to ensure integrity of the data. Proving data provenance is yet another challenging task in a cloud computing environment.

Data provenance refers to maintaining the integrity of the data, ensuring that it is computationally correct. Taxonomy of provenance techniques and various data provenance techniques have been discussed in [53]. Another major issue that is mostly neglected is of data remanence. It refers to the data left out in the case of data transfer or data removal. It causes minimal security threats in private cloud computing offerings; however, severe security issues may emerge in the case of public cloud offerings as a result of data remanence [54, 55].

Various cases of cloud security breach came into light in the recent past. Cloud-based email marketing services company, Epsilon, suffered a data breach, due to which a large proportion of its customers, including J.P. Morgan Chase, Citibank, Barclays Bank, hotel chains such as Marriott and Hilton, and big retailers such as Best Buy and Walgreens, were affected heavily and a huge chunk of customer data was exposed to the hackers, which included customer email ids and bank account details [56].

A similar incident happened with Amazon causing the disruption of its EC2 services. Popular sites, like Quora, Foursquare, and Reddit, were the main sufferers [57]. The above-mentioned events show the vulnerability of the cloud services.

Another important aspect is that the known and popular domains have been used to launch malicious software or hack into companies' secure databases. A similar issue happened with Amazon's S3 platform and the hackers were able to launch corrupted codes using a trusted domain [58]. Hence, the question that now arises is who is to be provided the "trusted" tag. It was established that Amazon was prone to side-channel attacks, and a malicious virtual machine, occupying the same server as the target, could easily gain access to the confidential data [59]. The question is: Should any such security policy be in place for these trusted users as well? An incident related to the data loss occurred sometime back, with the online storage service provider MediaMax (also known as The Linkup), when due to system administration error, active customer data was deleted, leading to huge data loss [60]. The service-level agreement (SLA) with the cloud service providers should contain all the points that may cause data loss due to either some human or system generated error. Hence, it must be ensured that redundant copies of the user data should be stored in order to handle any sort of adverse situation leading to data loss.

Virtualization in general increases the security of a cloud environment. With virtualization, a single machine can be divided into many virtual machines, thus providing better data isolation and safety against denial-of-service attacks [61-68]. The VMs (virtual machines) provide a security testbed for execution of untested code from untrusted users. A hierarchical reputation system has been proposed in the study in [61] for managing trust in a cloud environment.

12.3   Threats to Security in Cloud Computing

The chief concern in cloud is to provide security around multi-tenancy and isolation en-viorments, giving customers more assurance besides the "trust us" idea of clouds [62]. There has been a survey of studies reported, which classify security threats in cloud based on the nature of the service delivery models of a cloud computing system [63]. However, security requires a holistic approach. A service delivery model is one of many aspects that need to be considered for a comprehensive survey on cloud security. Security at different levels, such as the network, host, and application levels, is necessary to keep the cloud up and running continuously and the same has been discussed in [64] for Amazon EC2 cloud. In accordance with these different levels, various types of security breaches may occur, which have been classified in this section.

12.3.1   Basic Security

Web 2.0, a key technology towards enabling the use of software as a service (SaaS), re-lieves the users of tasks like maintenance and installation of software. It has been widely used by people all around the world. As the user community using Web 2.0 is increasing by leaps and bounds, the security has become more important than ever for such an envi-ronment [65-67]. SQL injection attacks are ones in which a malicious code is inserted into a standard SQL code. Thus, the attackers gain unauthorized access to a database and are able to access sensitive information [68]. Sometimes the hacker's input data is misunder-stood by the website as the user data and allows it to be accessed by the SQL server, and this lets the attacker gain insight into the functioning of the website and make changes in it. Various techniques, like avoiding the usage of dynamically generated SQL in the code, using filtering techniques to sanitize the user input, etc., are used to check the SQL injec-tion attacks. A proxy-based architecture towards preventing SQL injection attacks which dynamically detects and extracts users' inputs for suspected SQL control sequences, has been proposed in [69].

Cross-site scripting (XSS) attacks, which inject malicious scripts into web contents, have become quite popular since the inception of Web 2.0. There are two methods for injecting the malicious code into the webpage displayed to the user: Stored XSS and Re-flected XSS. In a Stored XSS, the malicious code is permanently stored in a resource man-aged by the web application and the actual attack is carried out when the victim requests a dynamic page that is constructed from the contents of this resource [70]. However, in the case of a Reflected XSS, the attack script is not permanently stored; in fact, it is immedi-ately reflected back to the user [70]. Based on the type of services provided, a website can be classified as static or dynamic. Static websites do not suffer from the security threats which the dynamic websites do because of their dynamism in providing multi-fold services to the users. As a result, these dynamic websites get victimized by XSS attacks. It has been observed quite often that amidst working on the internet or surfing, some webpages or popups open up with the request to be clicked away to view the content contained in them. More often, either unknowingly (about the possible hazards) or out of curiosity, users click on these hazardous links and thus the intruding third party gets control over the user's pri-vate information or hacks their accounts after having known the information available to them. Various techniques, like active content filtering, content-based data leakage preven-tion technology, and web application vulnerability detection technology, have already been proposed to prevent XSS attacks [71]. These technologies adopt various methodologies to detect security flaws and fix them. A blueprint-based approach that minimizes the dependency on web browsers towards identifying untrusted content over the network has been proposed in [72].

Another class of attacks, quite popular in SaaS, are called man-in-the-middle attacks (MITM). In such attacks, an entity tries to intrude in an ongoing conversation between a sender and a client to inject false information and to have knowledge of the important data transferred between them. Various tools implementing strong encryption technologies, like Dsniff, Cain, Ettercap, Wsniff, Airjack, etc., have been developed in order to provide a safeguard against them. A detailed study towards preventing man-in-the-middle attacks has been presented in [73].

A few important points, like evaluating SaaS security, separate endpoint and server security processes, and evaluating virtualization at the endpoint, have been mentioned by Eric Ogren in an article at Security.com to tackle traditional security flaws [74]. Hence, security at different levels is necessary in order to ensure proper implementation of cloud computing environment such as server access security, internet access security, database access security, data privacy security, and program access security. In addition, we need to ensure data security at network layer, and data security at physical and application layer to maintain a secure cloud.

12.3.2 Network-Level Security

Networks are classified into different types, such as shared and non-shared, public or private, small area or large area networks, and each of them have a number of security threats to deal with. While considering the network-level security, it is important to distinguish between public and private clouds. There is less vulnerability in a private cloud in comparison to public cloud. Almost all the organizations have got a private network in place and hence the network topology for a private cloud gets defined. And in most of the cases, the security practices implemented (in the organization's private network) apply to the private cloud too. However, in the case of a public cloud implementation, network topology might need to be changed in order to implement the security features, and the following points need to be addressed as part of public cloud implementation:

- Confidentiality and integrity of the data in transit needs to be ensured while adopting a public cloud architecture.

- Ensuring proper access controls within the cloud:

  - Migrating to a cloud exposes the resources to the internet, and the data which has been hosted over a private network till now, becomes accessible over the internet. This also increases the chances of data leakage or a security breach which should be taken care of.

  - It may happen that the security policies implemented inside the cloud are not up to date and as a result other parties within the cloud are able to access data belonging to some other customer.

- The trusted encryption schemes and tokenization models need to be changed to enhance the security in a public cloud.

We can now see the reasons why organizations are not moving their sensitive data to public clouds and instead relying on private cloud. In addition to the concerns mentioned above, issues associated with network-level security consist of DNS attacks, Sniffer attacks, issue of reused IP address, denial-of-service (DoS) and distributed denial-of-service attacks (DDoS), etc. [75].

12.3.2.1 DNS Attacks

A domain name server (DNS) performs the translation of a domain name to an IP address since the domain names are much easier to remember. Hence, the DNS servers are needed. But there are cases when having called the server by name, the user has been routed to some other malicious cloud instead of the one he asked for, and hence using an IP address is not always feasible. Although using DNS security measures, like domain name system security extensions (DNSSEC), reduces the effects of DNS threats, there are still cases when these security measures prove to be inadequate, such as when the path between a sender and a receiver gets rerouted through some malicious connection. It is possible that even after all the DNS security measures are taken, the route selected between the sender and receiver causes security problems [76].

12.3.2.2 Sniffer Attacks

These types of attacks are launched by applications which can capture packets flowing in a network, and if the data that is being transferred through these packets is not encrypted, it can be read. There is a chance that vital information flowing across the network can be traced or captured. A sniffer program, through the NIC (network interface card), ensures that the data/traffic linked to other systems on the network also gets recorded. This can be achieved by placing the NIC in promiscuous mode, which allows it to track all data, flowing on the same network. A malicious sniffing detection platform based on ARP (address resolution protocol) and RTT (round-trip time) can be used to detect a sniffing system running on a network [77].

12.3.2.3 Issue of Reused IP Addresses

Each node of a network is provided an IP address and the number of IP addresses that can be assigned is limited. A large number of cases related to reused IP-address issues have been observed lately. When a particular user moves out of a network, then the IP address associated with him (earlier) is assigned to a new user. This sometimes risks the security of the new user as there is a certain time lag between the change of an IP address in DNS and the clearing of that address in DNS caches [25]. Hence, we can say that sometimes though the old IP address is being assigned to a new user, the chances of accessing the data by some other user are still not negligible, as the address still exists in the DNS cache and the data belonging to a particular user may become accessible to some other user violating the privacy of the earlier user.

12.3.2.4 BGP Prefix Hijacking

Prefix hijacking is a type of network attack in which a wrong announcement related to the IP addresses associated with an autonomous system (AS) is made. Hence, malicious parties get access to the untraceable IP addresses. On the internet, IP space is associated in blocks and remains under the control of ASs. An autonomous system can broadcast information of an IP contained in its regime to all its neighbors. These ASs communicate using the border gateway protocol (BGP) model. Sometimes, due to some error, a faulty AS may broadcast incorrectly about the IPs associated with it. In such a case, the actual traffic gets routed to some IP other than the intended one. Hence, data is leaked or reaches some other unintended destination. A security system for autonomous systems has been explained in [78].

12.3.3 Application-Level Security

Application-level security refers to the use of software and hardware resources to provide security to applications such that the attackers are not able to get control over these applications and make undesirable changes to their format. Nowadays, attacks are launched disguised as a trusted user, and the system considering them as a trusted user, allows full access to the attacking party and gets victimized. The reason behind this is that the outdated network-level security policies allow only the authorized users to access the specific IP address. Because of technological advancements, these security policies have become obsolete as there have been instances when the system's security has been breached, having accessed the system in the disguise of a trusted user. With the recent technological advancements, it is quite possible to imitate a trusted user and corrupt entire data without being noticed.

Hence, it is essential to install a higher level of security checks to minimize these risks. The traditional methods to deal with increased security issues have been to develop a task-oriented ASIC device which can handle a specific task, providing greater levels of security with high performance [79]. But with application-level threats being dynamic and adaptable to the security checks in place, these closed systems have been observed to be slow in comparison to the open-ended systems. The capabilities of a closed system as well as the adaptability of an open-ended system have been incorporated to develop the security platforms based on Check Point Open Performance Architecture using Quad Core Intel Xeon Processors [79]. Even in the virtual environment, companies like VMware are using Intel Virtualization Technology for better performance and security base. It has been observed that websites are most often secured at the network level and have strong security measures but there may be security loopholes at the application level which may allow information access to unauthorized users. The threats to application level security include XSS attacks, cookie poisoning, hidden field manipulation, SQL injection attacks, DoS attacks, backdoor and debug options, CAPTCHA breaking, etc., resulting from the unauthorized usage of the applications.

12.3.3.1 Security Concerns with the Hypervisor

Cloud computing rests mainly on the concept of virtualization. In a virtualized world, hypervisor is defined as a controller popularly known as virtual machine manager (VMM) that allows multiple operating systems to be run on a system at a time, providing the resources to each operating system such that they do not interfere with each other.

As the number of operating systems running on a hardware unit increases, the security issues concerned with those new operating systems also need to be considered. Because multiple operating systems run on a single hardware platform, it is not possible to keep track of all such systems and hence maintaining the security of the operating systems is difficult. It may happen that a guest system tries to run a malicious code on the host system and bring the system down or take full control of the system and block access to other guest operating systems [80].

It cannot be denied that there are risks associated with sharing the same physical infrastructure between a set of multiple users, even one being malicious can cause threats to the others using the same infrastructure [81], and hence security with respect to hypervisor is of great concern as all the guest systems are controlled by it. If a hacker is able to get control over the hypervisor, he can make changes to any of the guest operating systems and get control over all the data passing through the hypervisor. Various types of attacks can be launched by targeting different components of the hypervisor [82]. Based on the understanding of how the various components in the hypervisor architecture behave, an advanced cloud protection system can be developed by monitoring the activities of the guest VMs (virtual machines) and intercommunication among the various infrastructure components [83, 84].

12.3.3.2 Denial-of-Service Attacks

A denial-of-service (DoS) attack is an attempt to make the services assigned to the authorized users unavailable. In such an attack, the server providing the service is flooded by a large number of requests and hence the service becomes unavailable to the authorized user. Sometimes, when we try to access a site we see that due to overloading of the server with the requests to access the site, we are unable to access the site and observe an error. This happens when the number of requests that can be handled by a server exceeds its capacity. The occurrence of a DoS attack increases bandwidth consumption besides causing congestion, making certain parts of the clouds inaccessible to the users. Using an intrusion detection system (IDS) is the most popular method of defense against this type of attack [85]. A defense federation is used in [31] for guarding against such attacks. Each cloud is loaded with separate IDSs. The different intrusion detection systems work on the basis of information exchange. In case a specific cloud is under attack, the cooperative IDS alerts the whole system. A decision on trustworthiness of a cloud is taken by voting, and the overall system performance is not hampered.

12.3.3.3 Cookie Poisoning

Cookie poisoning involves changing or modifying the contents of a cookie to have an unauthorized access to an application or to a web page. Cookies basically contain the user's identity-related credentials and once these cookies are accessible, the content of these cookies can be forged to impersonate an authorized user. This can be avoided either by performing regular cookie cleanup or implementing an encryption scheme for the cookie data [71].

12.3.3.4 Hidden Field Manipulation

While accessing a web page, there are certain fields that are hidden and contain the page's related information, which is basically used by developers. However, these fields are highly prone to attacks by hackers as they can be modified easily and posted on the web page. This may result in severe security violations [86].

12.3.3.5 Backdoor and Debug Options

A common practice by the developers is to enable the debug option while publishing a website. This enables them to make developmental changes in the code and get them implemented on the website. Since these debug options facilitate backend entry to the developers, and sometimes these debug options are left enabled unnoticed, this may provide an easy entry to a hacker onto the website that lets him make changes at the website level [87].

12.3.3.6 Distributed Denial-of-Service Attacks

Distributed denial of service (DDoS) may be called an advanced version of DoS in terms of denying the important services running on a server by flooding the destination server with large numbers of packets such that the target server is not able to handle it. Unlike the DoS attack, in DDoS the attack is relayed from different dynamic networks which have already been compromised. The attackers have the power to control the flow of information by allowing some information to be available at certain times. Thus, the amount and type of information available for public usage is clearly under the control of the attacker [87].

The DDoS attack is run by three functional units: a Master, a Slave, and a Victim. The Master is the launcher of the attacks causing DDoS, the Slave is the network which acts like a launch pad for the Master. It provides the platform to the Master to launch the attack on the Victim. Hence, it is also called a co-ordinated attack. Basically a DDoS attack is operational in two stages: the first one being the intrusion phase where the Master tries to compromise less important machines to support in flooding the more important one. The next one is installing DDoS tools and attacking the Victim server or machine. Hence, a DDoS attack results in making the service unavailable to the authorized user similar to the way it is done in a DoS attack but different in the way it is launched. A similar case of a DDoS attack was experienced with CNN news channel's website, leaving most of its users unable to access the site for a period of three hours [88]. In general, the approaches used to fight the DDoS attack involve extensive modification of the underlying network. These modifications often become costly for the users. A swarm-based logic for guarding against the DDoS attack was proposed in [87]. This logic provides a transparent transport layer, through which the common protocols, such as HTTP, SMTP, etc., can easily pass. The use of IDS in the virtual machine is proposed in [16] to protect the cloud from DDoS attacks. A Snort-like intrusion detection mechanism is loaded onto the virtual machine for sniffing all traffic, either incoming or outgoing. Another method commonly used to guard against DDoS is to have intrusion detection systems on all the physical machines which contain the user's virtual machines [89]. This scheme has been shown to perform reasonably well in a Eucalyptus [90] cloud.

12.3.3.7 CAPTCHA Breaking

CAPTCHAs (Completely Automated Public Turing test to tell Computers and Humans Apart) were developed in order to prevent the use of internet resources by bots or computers. They are used to prevent spam and overexploitation of network resources by bots. Even multiple website registrations, dictionary attacks, etc., by an automated program are prevented using a CAPTCHA. But recently, it has been found that the spammers are able to break the CAPTCHA [91] provided by the Hotmail and Gmail service providers. They make use of the audio system able to read the CAPTCHA characters for the visually impaired users and use speech-to-text conversion software to defeat the test. In yet another instant of CAPTCHA breaking, it was found that the net users are provided some form of motivation towards solving these CAPTCHAs by the automated systems, and thus CAPTCHA breaking takes place. Integration of multiple authentication techniques along with CAPTCHA identification (as adopted by companies like Facebook, Google, etc.) may be a suitable option against CAPTCHA breaking. Various techniques, such as implementing letter overlap, variable fonts of the letters used to design a CAPTCHA, increasing the string length and using a perturbative background, can be used to avoid CAPTCHA breaking [92].

A safe CAPTCHA design framework based on the problems of multiple moving object recognition in complex background has been presented in [93]. Single-frame zero-knowledge CAPTCHA design principles have been proposed, which will be able to resist any attack method of static optical character recognition (OCR). Such a design to create CAPTCHAs will be resistant to attack methods launched by intercepting pictures to identify or intercept each video frame to recognize the CAPTCHA separately.

12.3.3.8 Dictionary Attack

Data security in a cloud computing environment can be compromised by carrying out a dictionary or brute force attack. In a dictionary attack, the intruder makes use of all the possible word combinations which could have been successfully used to decrypt the data residing in/flowing over the network. They can be avoided by making use of a challenge-response system as explained in [94]. In this protocol, the client is presented a challenge whenever it tries to access a network. It is then required to compute the response to the same and reply back to the server in order to be able to access the network. Response computation is a time-consuming process, thus preventing users from being able to launch brute force or dictionary attacks in a short period of time, and hence ensuring security against the same.

12.3.3.9 *Google Hacking*

Google has emerged as the best option for finding details regarding anything on the internet. Google hacking refers to using Google search engine to find sensitive information that a hacker can use to his benefit while hacking a user's account. Generally, hackers try to discover the security loopholes by probing Google about the system they wish to hack. After having gathered the necessary information, they carry out the hacking of the concerned system. In some cases, a hacker is not sure of the target. Instead he tries to discover the target, using Google, based on loopholes in systems he wishes to hack. The hacker then searches all the possible systems with such a loophole and finds those having the loopholes he wishes to exploit. A Google hacking event was observed recently when login details of various Gmail users were stolen by a group of hackers [95]. These have been some of the security threats that can be launched at the application level and cause system downtime,disabling the application access even to the authorized users. In order to avoid these threats, application security should be assessed at the various levels of the three service delivery models in cloud: IaaS, PaaS and SaaS. In the case of an IaaS delivery model, cloud providers are mostly not concerned with the security policies applied by the customer and the application's management. The whole application runs on the customer's server on the cloud provider's infrastructure and is managed by them, and hence they are for securing the application. The following points should be taken care of while designing the application:

- Standard security measures must be implemented to safeguard against the common vulnerabilities associated with the web.

- Custom implementation of authorization and authentication schemes should not be implemented unless they are tested properly.

- Backup policies such as continuous data protection (CDP) should be implemented in order to avoid issues with data recovery in case of a sudden attack [96].

Additionally, they should be aware if the virtual network infrastructure used by the cloud provider is secured and the various security procedures implemented to ensure the same [25]. Security challenges for IaaS cloud computing and multiple levels of security as operational in Amazon EC2 cloud have been discussed in [64]. It discusses identity/access management and multifactor authentication techniques in Amazon Web Service (AWS) cloud. PaaS service providers are responsible for maintaining the security of the platform an application is built upon and the following aspects should be considered to assess the security policy of the service provider:

- How the different applications on PaaS platform are isolated from each other and whether the data belonging to one customer is inaccessible to any other customer or not (in the case of public cloud).

▪ Does the service provider keep checking and updating its security policies at regular intervals and ensure that the new security policies are implemented?

The abovementioned concerns apply to an SaaS scenario as well, as the security control lies with the provider instead of the customer.

12.4 Security Issues in Cloud Deployment Models

Each of the three ways in which cloud services can be deployed has its own advantages and limitations. And from the security perspective, all three have certain areas that need to be addressed with a specific strategy to avoid them.

12.4.1 Security Issues in a Public Cloud

In a public cloud, there exist many customers on a shared platform and infrastructure security is provided by the service provider. A few of the key security issues in a public cloud include:

1. Confidentiality, integrity, and availability are required to protect data throughout its life cycle. Data must be protected during the various stages of creation, sharing, archiving, processing, etc. However, situations become more complicated in the case of a public cloud where we do not have any control over the service provider's security practices [97].

2. In the case of a public cloud, the same infrastructure is shared between multiple tenants and the chances of data leakage between these tenants are very high. However, most of the service providers run a multitenant infrastructure. Proper investigations at the time of choosing the service provider must be done in order to avoid any such risk [97, 98].

3. In the case where a cloud service provider uses a third-party vendor to provide its cloud services,the service-level agreements they have between them should be ensured, as well as the contingency plans in case of the breakdown of the third-party system.

4. Proper SLAs defining the security requirements such as what level of encryption data should undergo, when it is sent over the internet, and what are the penalties in case the service provider fails to do so. Although data is stored outside the confines of the client organization in a public cloud, we cannot deny the possibility of an insider attack originating from the service provider's end.

Moving the data to a cloud computing environment expands the circle of insiders to the service provider's staff and subcontractors [34]. An access control policy based on the inputs from the client and provider to prevent insider attacks has been proposed in [99]. Policy enforcement implemented at the nodes and the data centers can prevent a system administrator from carrying out any malicious action. The three major steps to achieve this are: defining a policy, propagating the policy by means of a secure policy propagation module, and enforcing it through a policy enforcement module.

12.4.2   Security Issues in a Private Cloud

A private cloud model enables the customer to have total control over the network and provides the flexibility to the customer to implement any traditional network perimeter security practice. Although the security architecture is more reliable in a private cloud, there are still issues/risks that need to be considered:

1. Virtualization techniques are quite popular in private clouds. In such a scenario, risks to the hypervisor should be carefully analyzed. There have been instances when a guest operating system has been able to run processes on other guest VMs or host. In a virtual environment it is possible for virtual machines to communicate with all the VMs, including the ones they are not supposed to. To ensure that they only communicate with the ones which they are supposed to, proper authentication and encryption techniques, such as IPsec (IP-level security), should be implemented [100].

2. The host operating system should be free from any sort of malware threat and monitored to avoid any such risk [101]. In addition, guest virtual machines should not be able to communicate with the host operating system directly. There should be dedicated physical interfaces for communicating with the host.

3. In a private cloud, users are facilitated with an option to be able to manage portions of the cloud, and access to the infrastructure is provided through a web interface or an HTTP endpoint. There are two ways of implementing a web interface, either by writing a whole application stack or by using a standard applicative stack, to develop the web interface using common languages such as Java, PHP, Python, etc. As part of the screening process, Eucalyptus web interface has been found to have a bug, allowing any user to perform internal port scanning or HTTP requests through the management node, which it should not be allowed to do. In a nutshell, interfaces need to be properly developed and standard web application security techniques need to be deployed to protect the diverse HTTP requests being performed [102].

4. While we talk of standard internet security, we also need to have a security policy in place to safeguard the system from the attacks originating within the organization. This vital point is left out on most occasions, with internet security mainly being stressed. Proper security guidelines across the various departments should exist and control should be implemented as per the requirements [101].

Thus, we see that although private clouds are considered safer in comparison to public clouds, they still have multiple issues which if unattended may lead to major security loopholes as discussed earlier. The hybrid cloud model is a combination of both public and private cloud and hence the security issues discussed with respect to both are applicable in the case of hybrid cloud. A trust model of cloud security in terms of social security has been discussed in [103]. Social insecurity has been classified as a multiple stakeholder problem, open space security problem, and mission critical data handling problem. All these issues have been considered while proposing a cloud trust model, also known as "security aware cloud." Two additional layers of trust, the internal trust layer and contracted trust layer, have been proposed to enhance security in a cloud computing environment.

12.5 Ensuring Security Against Various Types of Attacks

In order to secure cloud against various security threats such as SQL injection, cross-site scripting (XSS), DoS and DDoS attacks, Google hacking, and forced hacking, different cloud service providers adopt different techniques. A few standard techniques to detect the abovementioned attacks include avoiding the use of dynamically generated SQL in the code, finding the meta-structures used in the code, validating all user entered parameters, and disallowance and removal of unwanted data and characters, etc. A comparative analysis of some of the currently existing security schemes are presented in Table 12.1. A generic security framework needs to be worked out for an optimized cost performance ratio. The main criterion to be fulfilled by the generic security framework is to interface with any type of cloud environment, and to be able to handle and detect predefined as well as customized security policies. A similar approach is being used by Symantec MessageLabs Web Security cloud that blocks the security threats originating from the internet and filters the data before they reach the network. Web security cloud's security architecture rests on two components:

- *Multilayer security*: In order to ensure data security and block possible malware, it consists of multilayer security and hence it has a strong security platform.

- *URL filtering*: It has been observed that attacks are launched through various web pages and internet sites and hence filtering the web pages ensures that no such harmful or threat-carrying web pages are accessible. Also, content from undesirable sites can be blocked. With its adaptable technology, it provides security even in highly conflicting environments and ensures protection against new and converging malware threats.

The security model of Amazon Web Services, one of the biggest cloud service providers on the market, makes use of multi-factor authentication technique, ensuring enhanced control over AWS account settings and the management of AWS services and resources for which the account is subscribed. If customers opt for multi-factor authentication (MFA), they have to provide a 6-digit code in addition to their username and password before access is granted to AWS account or services. This single-use code can be received on mobile devices every time they try to login into their AWS account. Such a technique is called multi-factor authentication because two factors are checked before access is granted [64, 104].

A Google hacking database identifies the various types of information such as login passwords, pages containing logon portals, session usage information, etc. Various software solutions, such as a web vulnerability scanner, can be used to detect the possibility of a Google hack. In order to prevent a Google hack, users need to ensure that only information that does not affect them should be shared with Google. This would prevent sharing of any sensitive information that may result in adverse conditions.

The symptoms of a DoS or DDoS attack are: system speed gets reduced and programs run very slowly, large number of connection requests from a large number of users, and less available resources. Although, when launched in full strength, DDoS attacks are very harmful as they exhaust all the network resources, a careful monitoring of the network can still help in keeping these attacks in control [105]. An approach based on game theory against bandwidth-consuming DoS and DDoS attacks has been proposed in [106]. The authors have modeled the interaction between the attacker and the user as a two player non-zero-sum game in two attack scenarios: a) single attacking node for DoS and b) multiple attacking nodes for DDoS attack. Based on these two scenarios, the user is supposed to determine firewall settings to block unauthorized requests while allowing the authorized ones [106].

In the case of IP spoofing, an attacker tries to spoof authorized users by creating the impression that the packets are coming from reliable sources. Thus, the attacker takes control over the client's data or system showing himself/herself as the trusted party. Spoofing attacks can be checked by using encryption techniques and performing user authentication based on key exchange. Techniques like IPSec do help in mitigating the risks of spoofing. By enabling encryption for sessions and performing filtering for incoming and outgoing packets, spoofing attacks can be reduced.

Table 12.1: Comparative analysis of strengths and limitations of some of the existing security schemes.

Security Scheme	Suggested Approach	Strengths	Limitations
Data Storage security [48]	Uses homomorphic token with distributed verification of erasure-coded data towards ensuring data storage security and locating the server being attacked.	1. Supports dynamic operations on data blocks such as: update, delete and append without data corruption and loss. 2. Efficient against data modification and server colluding attacks as well as against byzantine failures.	The security in case of dynamic data storage has been considered. However, the issues with fine-grained data error location remain to be addressed.
User identity safety in cloud computing	Uses active bundles scheme, whereby predicates are compared over encrypted data and multiparty computing.	Does not need trusted third party (TTP) for the verification or approval of user identity. Thus the user's identity is not disclosed. The TTP remains free and could be used for other purposes such as decryption.	Active bundle may not be executed at all at the host of the requested service. It would leave the system vulnerable. The identity remains a secret and the user is not granted permission to his requests.
Trust model for interoperability and security in cross cloud [81]	1. Separate domains for providers and users, each with a special trust agent. 2. Different trust strategies for service providers and customers. 3. Time and transaction factors are taken into account for trust assignment.	1. Helps the customers to avoid malicious suppliers. 2. Helps the providers to avoid cooperating/serving malicious users.	Security in a very large scale cross cloud environment is an active issue. This present scheme is able to handle only a limited number of security threats in a fairly small environment.
Virtualized defence and reputation based trust management	1. Uses a hierarchy of DHT-based overlay networks, with specific tasks to be performed by each layer. 2. Lowest layer deals with reputation aggregation and probing colluders. The highest layer deals with various attacks.	Extensive use of virtualization for securing clouds.	The proposed model is in its early developmental stage and needs further simulations to verify the performance.
Secure virtualization [83]	1. Idea of an Advanced Cloud Protection system (ACPS) to ensure the security of guest virtual machines and of distributed computing middleware is proposed. 2. Behaviour of cloud components can be monitored by logging and periodic checking of executable system files.	A virtualized network is prone to different types of security attacks that can be launched by a guest VM. An ACPS system monitors the guest VM without being noticed and hence any suspicious activity can be blocked and system's security system notified.	System performance gets marginally degraded and a small performance penalty is encountered. This acts as a limitation towards the acceptance of an ACPS system.
Safe, virtual network in cloud environment [81]	Cloud Providers have been suggested to obscure the internal structure of their services and placement policy in the cloud and also to focus on side-channel risks in order to reduce the chances of information leakage.	Ensures the identification of adversary or the attacking party and helping us find a far off place for an attacking party from its target and hence ensuring a more secure environment for the other VMs.	If the adversary gets to know the location of the other VMs, it may try to attack them. This may harm the other VMs in between.

12.6   Survey of Privacy Preservation Using Fuzzy Set and Genetic Algorithm

Privacy preservation in association rules is already present in various fields. In recent years, many methods have been designed for it. Many studies have been done to find the privacy preservation policy from a quantitative database using the concepts of fuzzy logic. Here, we have selected some popular studies, each of which are discussed below.

12.6.1   Fuzzy-Based Approach for Privacy-Preserving Publication of Data

This section mainly concentrates on privacy preservation, and is useful for both numerical and categorical attributes. Here, the authors have pointed out numerous problems with k-anonymity and have proposed techniques to counter them or avoid them. Data privacy is the most acclaimed problem when publishing individual data. It ensures individual data publishing without disclosing sensitive data. The most popular approach is k-anonymity, where data is transformed to equivalence classes, each class having a set of k-records that are indistinguishable from each other; l-diversity and t-closeness are such techniques to name a few. All these techniques increase computational effort to practically infeasible levels, though they increase privacy. A few techniques account for too much information loss, while achieving privacy.

In this section, we propose a novel, holistic approach for achieving maximum privacy with no information loss and minimum overheads (as only the necessary tuples are transformed). It addresses the data privacy problem using a fuzzy set approach, a total paradigm shift and a new perspective of looking at the privacy problem in data publishing. This practically feasible method also allows for personalized privacy preservation, and is useful for both numerical and categorical attributes.

A brief look at this method consists of an overview of fuzzy sets, a description of the fuzzy-based privacy-preserving model. The proposed privacy-preserving model primarily has two objectives: preserving privacy while revealing useful information for i) numerical attributes, and ii) categorical (non-numerical) attributes.

(i) Identifier Attributes (A^i): These attributes uniquely identify the individual associated with the tuple, as anonymization requires that the data be disassociated with the identifiers. One specific example is the name attribute.

(ii) Sensitive Attributes (A^s): These attributes should not be disclosed to the public or may be disclosed after disassociating their value with an individual's other information.

(ii) Quasi Identifier (A^{qi}): These values may be published, but it so happens that with a combination of these attributes an individual may get identified. For instance, age and zip code might disclose the identity.

$$A^i = \{Name\} \tag{12.1}$$

$$A^s = \{Income, Disease\} \tag{12.2}$$

$$A^{qi} = \{Age, zipcode, gender\} \tag{12.3}$$

12.6.1.1 *Fuzzy-Based Approach for Privacy Preservation of Numerical Attributes*

In the equation (12.1), $A^i = \{Name\}$, as income is a sensitive attribute and is numerical, Rule1 is applied for transforming its values. L is the linguistic term set. Suppose the linguistic term set for the variable income $L(A^s = income)$ is: $\{High, Medium, Low\}$ with membership functions defined as below. The minimum and maximum values of income according to the business organization are min and max respectively and a1, a2, a3 are the midpoints of each fuzzy set and k is the number of fuzzy sets.

The k fuzzy sets will have ranges of:

$$\{min - a2\}, \{a1 - a3\}, \{a(i-1) - a(i+1)\}, ..., \{a(k-1) - max\} \qquad (12.4)$$

12.6.1.2 *Taxonomy-Based Privacy-Preserving Transformation for Categorical Attributes*

For categorical attributes like disease, the following taxonomy tree is taken.

- 0.0 Disease

- 1.0 Respiratory Problem

    – 1.1 Flu

    – 1.2 Pneumonia

    – 1.3 Bronchitis

- 2.0 Digestive problem

    – 2.1 Gastric Ulcer

    – 2.2 Dyspepsia

    – 2.3 Gastritis

The representation for this taxonomy tree is shown in Figure 12.1.

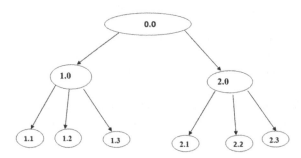

Figure 12.1: Taxonomy tree for disease.

12.6.2 Privacy-Preserving Fuzzy Association Rules Hiding in Quantitative Data

Here, a method is proposed to hide the fuzzy association rule, in which the fuzzified data is mined using a modified Apriori algorithm in order to extract rules and identify sensitive rules. Hiding association rules are associated with binary items without giving importance to their quantity. However, many transactions in real-world applications have quantitative values. For example, for a diabetes patient the quantity of the attribute sugar in blood is more important than the presence or absence of sugar. The basic idea in quantitative data mining is to map the categorical attribute values into corresponding binary attribute values. Some work has been done to discover fuzzy association rules from quantitative data using fuzzy set concepts.

An association rule is defined as an implication $X \rightarrow Y$, where both X and Y are defined as sets of attributes (interchangeably called items). Here, X is called as the body (LHS) of the rule and Y is called as the head (RHS) of the rule. It is interpreted as follows: "for a specified fraction of the existing transactions, a particular value of an attribute set X determines the value of attribute set Y as another particular value under a certain confidence." For instance, an association rule in a supermarket basket data may be stated as, "In 20% of the transactions, 75% of the people buying butter also buy milk in the same transaction"; 20% and 75% represent the support and the confidence, respectively. The significance of an association rule is measured by its support and confidence. Simply, support is the percentage of transactions that contain both X and Y, while confidence is the ratio of the support of $X \cup Y$ to the support of X.

Fuzzy association rule hiding algorithm first finds the useful fuzzy association rules in quantitative data using fuzzy set concepts and then hide them using privacy-preserving technique. Mining fuzzy association rules is the discovery of association rules using fuzzy concepts such that the quantitative attributes can be handled properly.

Let $I = \{i_1, i_2, ..., i_m\}$ be the complete item set where each $i_j (1 \leq j \leq m)$ is a quantitative attribute. Given a database $D = \{t_1, t_2, .., t_n\}$ with attributes I and the fuzzy sets associated with attributes in I, they want to find out some interesting useful association rules.

Let $X = \{x_1, x_2, .., x_p\}$ and $Y = \{y_1, y_2, .., y_q\}$ be two large item sets. Then, the fuzzy association rule is given as follows:

$$A \rightarrow B \tag{12.5}$$

where

- $A = \{f_1, f_2, .., f_p\}$

- $B = \{g_1, g_2, .., g_q\}$

- $f_i \in \{The\ fuzzy\ regions\ related\ to\ attribute\ x_i\}$

- $g_j \in \{The\ fuzzy\ regions\ related\ to\ attribute\ y_j\}$

X and Y are subsets of I and are disjoint, which means that they share no common attributes. A and B contain the fuzzy sets associated with the corresponding attributes in X and Y. Here, A is called as the body or Left Hand Side (L.H.S.) of the rule and B is called as the head or Right Hand Side (R.H.S.) of the rule. The significance of an association rule is measured by its support and confidence. Support is defined as the percentage of transactions that contain both A and B, while confidence is defined as the ratio of the support of $A \rightarrow B$ to the support of A. In other words, the support of a rule measures the significance of the correlation between itemsets, while the confidence of a rule measures the degree of the correlation between itemsets. If a rule is useful/interesting, it should have support larger than or equal to minimum support value and confidence larger than or equal to minimum confidence value.

Fuzzy association rule mining finds an interesting association among a large set of data items. Many organizations are acquiring interest in mining the fuzzy association rules from their databases. The discovery of the interesting association relationship among a huge amount of data can help in many decision-making processes. Besides, the association rule hiding is essential to hide sensitive fuzzy association rules. The association rule hiding technique is broadly classified into two categories: a distortion-based technique and a blocking-based technique.

12.6.3 A Rough Computing-Based Performance Evaluation Approach for Educational Institutions

In this subsection, the authors use two processes: pre-processing and post-processing. In pre-processing they use a rough set on fuzzy approximations with ordering rules and rough set data reduction to reduce the dataset dimensionality and fuzzification to mine fuzzified association rules.

12.6.3.1 Rough Set on Fuzzy Approximation Space

Indiscernibility relation, an equivalence relation, is the basic viewpoint of rough sets. But in many real-life situations, the equivalence relation does not depict the need accurately. Therefore, it is necessary to make the relations less stringent by excluding one or more requirement of the equivalence relation. A fuzzy proximity relation is more generalized than an equivalence relation defined over the universe U and is more suitable due to its non-transitivity property. The membership function has been adjusted in such a manner that their values must lie within and the function must also be symmetric. The fuzzy proximity relation identifies the almost indiscernibility among the objects. This result induces the α-equivalence classes. They obtain qualitative or categorical classes by imposing order relation on this classification. Moreover, the attribute reduction, an important aspect of the rough set theory, is done on the ordered information system. This can minimize the set of attributes and make the object classification satisfy the full set of attributes. In practical applications it can be observed that the reduced attributes can remove the superfluous attributes with respect to a specific classification generated by attributes $B \subset A$ and give the decision maker simple and easy information. If the set of attributes is dependent, using the dependency properties of the attributes, they find all possible minimal subsets of attributes which have the same number of elementary sets without loss of the classification power of the reduced information system. The fuzzy proximity relation identifies the almost indiscernibility among the objects. The problem of privacy-preserving data mining deals with two conflicting issues:

1. The data from which the rules are generated, are usually presented in the form of an information system which consists of attributes and objects. It is observed that the attribute values are either symbolic or quantitative. But many of the attributes may not be relevant while studying the information system. Therefore, the attribute reduction becomes an important aspect for handling large databases efficiently, by eliminating superfluous or redundant data. Though privacy-preserving fuzzy association rules hide the quantitative data.

2. It is observed that in the information system, the quantitative attribute values are almost similar, hence it is very difficult to eliminate these attributes from the information system. Therefore, efforts have been made to convert the quantitative attribute values to symbolic values by using a fuzzy proximity relation.

In addition, the ordering rules are introduced to get the ordered symbolic information system. Further on, rough set techniques are used to eliminate the superfluous attributes. Finally, the fuzzy association rules can be obtained from the ordered information system and sensitive rules can be hidden using genetic algorithm techniques. There are two processes, which are a pre-process and post-process, to mine fuzzified association rules and to hide sensitive rules. In the pre-process, we use a rough set on fuzzy approximations with ordering rules and rough set data reduction to reduce the dataset dimensionality and fuzzification to mine fuzzified association rules. In the post-process, we use GA to hide sensitive fuzzy association rules.

12.6.3.2 Why Rough Set?

The limitation of this approach is that it maps all the values in the scale 0-1. Real-time data contains uncertainties. In many real-life applications it is observed that the attribute values are not exactly identical but almost identical. Keeping this in mind, rough sets defined on fuzzy approximation spaces extend the concept of rough sets on knowledge bases.

An ordered information system is defined as OIS $a = \{I, \{\prec a : a \in A\}\}$, where I is a standard information system and $\prec a$ is an order relation on attribute $a \in A$.

12.6.4 A New Method for Preserving Privacy in Quantitative Association Rules Using Genetic Algorithm

In this subsection, the authors use genetic algorithm to ensure security of the database and keep the utility and certainty of the mined rules at the highest level. The sensitive rules are hidden by decreasing the support value of the right hand side (RHS) of the rule.

A genetic algorithm (GA) uses genetics as its model of problem solving. It is a search technique to find approximate solutions to optimization and search problems. The GA method is used for moving from one population of "chromosomes" (e.g., strings of "bits" representing candidate solutions to a problem) to a new population. In terms of the GA, the dataset is called a population and the transaction is called a chromosome. Moreover, a GA is an evolutionary and metaheuristic technique used to solve complex problems. Therefore, a GA is used to hide restrictive patterns, $X \rightarrow Y$, by decreasing the support of Y or by increasing the support of X. Furthermore, it often requires a "fitness function." Hence, the fitness function assigns a value to each transaction (chromosome) in the database (population). Additionally, the fitness of the transaction depends on how well that transaction solves the problem at hand. The fitness is calculated using the fitness function.

12.6.4.1 Why Are We Using a Genetic Algorithm in Privacy Preservation?

Privacy preservation is an extremely complex domain and needs to be standardized. Such standardization in PPDM refers to a NP-hard problem. Therefore, a genetic algorithm is used to provide the optimal solution to the hard problem. Such optimality of the solution depends on the complexity of the fitness function. The possible strength of the fitness function ensures a desirable level of the optimal solution to modify the dataset in such a way that the utility of modified dataset should be maintained in order to extract useful information and rules. Therefore, a genetic algorithm approach is used to solve this optimization problem.

12.6.4.2 Flowchart of Genetic Algorithm

In a quantitative database, if a critical rule $X \rightarrow Y$ needs to be hidden, its confidence value is decreased to a value smaller than the minimum confidence value. One way of decreasing confidence value is decreasing the support value of an item Y at RHS, and the other way is increasing the support value of item X at LHS. Our approach decreases confidence value of a rule, by decreasing the support value of the item. If the difference between the value of item in RHS and LHS is greater than 0.5 and RHS value is greater than LHS value then the RHS value is replaced with a value obtained by subtracting this difference from 0.5. Similarly, if LHS value is greater than RHS value then the LHS value is replaced with a value obtained by subtracting this difference from 0.5 [101-110].

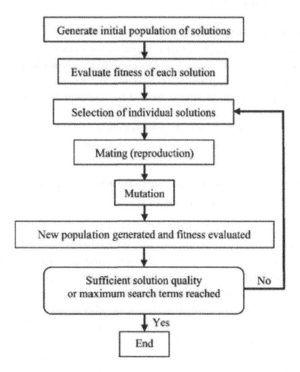

Figure 12.2: Flowchart of genetic algorithm.

12.6.5   Privacy Preserving in Association Rules Using a Genetic Algorithm

The objective of privacy preserving using genetic algorithm is described in this study. Genetic algorithm is used to counter the side effects of lost rules and ghost rules. This work has a partial resemblance to the work. However, the difference is that we define our own fitness strategy. The question arises, "Why are we using a GA in PPDM?" The answer to such a question is that PPDM is an extremely complex domain and needs to be standardized. Such standardization in PPDM refers to a NP-hard problem. Therefore, a GA is used to provide the optimal solution to the hard problem. Such optimality of the solution depends on the complexity of the fitness function. The possible strength of the fitness function ensures a desirable level of the optimal solution. GA is a method for moving from one population of "chromosomes" (e.g., strings of "bits" representing candidate solutions to a problem) to a new population. In terms of the genetic algorithm, the dataset is called a population and the transaction is called a chromosome. Moreover, a genetic algorithm is an evolutionary and metaheuristic technique used to solve complex problems. Therefore, a genetic algorithm is used to hide restrictive patterns, $X \rightarrow Y$, by decreasing the support of Y or by increasing the support of X. Furthermore, it often requires a "fitness function." Hence, the fitness function assigns a value to each transaction (chromosome) in the database (population). Additionally, the fitness of the transaction depends on how well that transaction solves the problem at hand. The fitness is calculated with the help of fitness equations. In the next generation, the sensitivity of the rule is checked by comparing the confidence and support of the rule to the user-specified threshold. If the sensitivity of the rule is below the specified threshold, it means that the rule is hidden. Subsequently, the modified dataset is compared to the original dataset to achieve the lost rule and ghost rule side effects.

12.7 Summary

In this chapter, different privacy preservation attributes discussed in this chapter, such as lack of user control, lack of training and expertise, unauthorized secondary usage, complexity of regulatory compliance, addressing transporter data flow restrictions, litigation, legal uncertainty, compelled disclosure to the government, data security and disclosure of breaches, data accessibility, location of data, and transfer and retention, have to be ensured through different protocols. In the later part of this chapter, a survey of privacy preservation using fuzzy set and genetic algorithm was discussed. Different methods, like a fuzzy-based approach for privacy-preserving publication of data, privacy-preserving fuzzy association rules hiding in quantitative data, a rough computing-based performance evaluation approach for educational institutions, and privacy preserving in association rules using a genetic algorithm, were discussed.

EXERCISES

1. What is the primary security consideration in a cloud environment?

2. Which of the following security-related questions should you ask before using cloud services?

3. What is network security in cloud computing?

4. How does the fuzzy-based approach for privacy-preserving publication of data work?

5. What are the various data centers deployed for cloud computing?

6. Do you know the security laws that are implemented to secure data in the cloud?

7. How do you secure your data while transferring it to the cloud?

8. How does cloud provide automation and transparency in performance?

9. What level of technical support is included in your standard SLA?

10. What are your procedures for suspected security violations?

References

1. Juels, A., & Kaliski Jr, B. S. (2007, October). PORs: Proofs of retrievability for large files. In *Proceedings of the 14th ACM conference on Computer and communications security* (pp. 584-597).

2. Liu, X., Zhang, Y., Wang, B., & Yan, J. (2012). Mona: Secure multi-owner data sharing for dynamic groups in the cloud. *IEEE transactions on Parallel and Distributed Systems*, 24(6), 1182-1191.

3. Grzonkowski, S., & Corcoran, P. M. (2011). Sharing cloud services: user authentication for social enhancement of home networking. *IEEE Transactions on Consumer Electronics*, 57(3), 1424-1432.

4. Nabeel, M., Shang, N., & Bertino, E. (2012). Privacy preserving policy-based content sharing in public clouds. *IEEE Transactions on Knowledge and Data Engineering*, 25(11), 2602-2614.

5. Wang, C., Wang, Q., Ren, K., Cao, N., & Lou, W. (2011). Toward secure and dependable storage services in cloud computing. *IEEE Transactions on Services Computing*, 5(2), 220-232.

6. Sundareswaran, S., Squicciarini, A., & Lin, D. (2012). Ensuring distributed accountability for data sharing in the cloud. *IEEE Transactions on Dependable and Secure Computing*, 9(4), 556-568.

7. Sánchez, R., Almenares, F., Arias, P., Diaz-Sanchez, D., & Marin, A. (2012). Enhancing privacy and dynamic federation in IdM for consumer cloud computing. *IEEE Transactions on Consumer Electronics*, 58(1), 95-103.

8. Hao, Z., Zhong, S., & Yu, N. (2011). A privacy-preserving remote data integrity checking protocol with data dynamics and public verifiability. *IEEE Transactions on Knowledge and Data Engineering*, 23(9), 1432-1437.

9. Xiao, Y., Lin, C., Jiang, Y., Chu, X., & Liu, F. (2010, December). An efficient privacy-preserving publish-subscribe service scheme for cloud computing. In *2010 IEEE Global Telecommunications Conference GLOBECOM 2010* (pp. 1-5). IEEE.

10. Lien, I. T., Lin, Y. H., Shieh, J. R., & Wu, J. L. (2013). A novel privacy preserving location-based service protocol with secret circular shift for k-nn search. *IEEE Transactions on Information Forensics and Security*, 8(6), 863-873.

11. Li, W., Xue, K., Xue, Y., & Hong, J. (2015). TMACS: A robust and verifiable threshold multi-authority access control system in public cloud storage. *IEEE Transactions on Parallel and Distributed Systems*, 27(5), 1484-1496.

12. Wang, C., Chow, S. S., Wang, Q., Ren, K., & Lou, W. (2011). Privacy-preserving public auditing for secure cloud storage. *IEEE Transactions on Computers*, 62(2), 362-375.

13. Tang, Y., Lee, P. P., Lui, J. C., & Perlman, R. (2012). Secure overlay cloud storage with access control and assured deletion. *IEEE Transactions on Dependable and Secure Computing*, 9(6), 903-916.

14. Zhu, Y., Hu, H., Ahn, G. J., Huang, D., & Wang, S. (2012, March). Towards temporal access control in cloud computing. In *2012 Proceedings IEEE INFOCOM* (pp. 2576-2580). IEEE.

15. Ruj, S., Stojmenovic, M., & Nayak, A. (2013). Decentralized access control with anonymous authentication of data stored in clouds. *IEEE Transactions on Parallel and Distributed Systems*, 25(2), 384-394.

16. Van, V. N., Long, N. Q., Nguyen, G. N., & Le, D. N. (2016). A performance analysis of openstack open-source solution for IaaS cloud computing. In *Proceedings of the Second International Conference on Computer and Communication Technologies* (pp. 141-150). Springer, New Delhi.

17. Nguyen, H. H. C., Le, D. N., Van Son Le, & Nguyen, T. T. (2015, February). A New Technical Solution for Resource Allocation in Heterogeneous Distributed Platforms. In *ICADIWT* (pp. 184-194).

18. Van, V. N., Long, N. Q., & Le, D. N. (2016). Performance analysis of network virtualization in cloud computing infrastructures on openstack. In *Innovations in Computer Science and Engineering* (pp. 95-103). Springer, Singapore.

19. Ateniese, G., Kamara, S., & Katz, J. (2009, December). Proofs of storage from homomorphic identification protocols. In *International conference on the theory and application of cryptology and information security* (pp. 319-333). Springer, Berlin, Heidelberg.

20. Le, D. N., Kumar, R., Mishra, B. K., Chatterjee, J. M., & Khari, M. (Eds.). (2019). *Cyber Security in Parallel and Distributed Computing: Concepts, Techniques, Applications and Case Studies*. John Wiley & Sons.

21. Vasudevan, R., Arun, G., Seetharam, P. and Prathipati, A.K., Oracle International Corp, 2017. Declarative and extensible model for provisioning of cloud based services. U.S. Patent 9,621,435.

22. Nilsson, V. and Dahlgren, A., 2017. A Bright Future for Cloud: A Case Study on Perceptions of Cloud Services.

23. AlAjmi, Q., Arshah, R. A., Kamaludin, A., Sadiq, A. S., & Al-Sharafi, M. A. (2017, November). A conceptual model of e-learning based on cloud computing adoption in higher education institutions. In *2017 International Conference on Electrical and Computing Technologies and Applications (ICECTA)* (pp. 1-6). IEEE.

24. Metheny, M., 2017. Federal cloud computing: The definitive guide for cloud service providers. *Syngress*.

25. Carey, M. (2017). *Qualitative Research Skills for Social Work*. London: Routledge.

26. Yu, Y., Xue, L., Au, M.H., Susilo, W., Ni, J., Zhang, Y., Vasilakos, A.V. & Shen, J. 2016. Cloud data integrity checking with an identity-based auditing mechanism from RSA. *Future Generation Computer Systems*, 62, 85-91.

27. Shafieian, S., Zulkernine, M., & Haque, A. (2014). *Cloud Computing: Challenges, Limitations and R & D Solutions*. Switzerland: Springer, 3-22.

28. Tanenbaum, AS. & Van Steen, M. 2016. *Distributed Systems Principles and Paradigms*, New York. Tanenbaum.

29. Sabi, H.M., Uzoka, F.M.E., Langmia, K. & Njeh, F.N. 2016. Conceptualizing a model for adoption of cloud computing in education. *International Journal of Information Management*, 36(2), 183-191.

30. Piderit, R. and Nyoni, T., 2016. Enhancing User Trust in Cloud Computing Applications. In *CONF-IRM* (50).

31. Chao, L. (2016). *Cloud Computing Network Theory, Practice and Development*. Danvers: Tailor & Francis

32. Hashemnezhad, H. (2015). Qualitative content analysis research: A review article. *Journal of ELT and Applied Linguistics*, 3(1).

33. Cunningham, N., & Carmichael, T. (2017, June). Sampling, interviewing and coding: Lessons from a constructivist grounded theory study. In *European Conference on Research Methodology for Business and Management Studies* (pp. 78-85). Academic Conferences International Limited.

34. Poole, C. M., Cornelius, I., Trapp, J. V., & Langton, C. M. (2012). Radiotherapy Monte Carlo simulation using cloud computing technology. *Australasian physical & Engineering Sciences in Medicine*, 35(4), 497-502.

35. Raza, M.H., Adenola, A.F., Nafarieh, A. and Robertson, W., 2015. The slow adoption of cloud computing and IT workforce. *Procedia Computer Science*, 52, 1114-1119.

36. Satyanarayanan, M., Schuster, R., Ebling, M., Fettweis, G., Flinck, H., Joshi, K. and Sabnani, K., 2015. An open ecosystem for mobile-cloud convergence. *IEEE Communications Magazine*, 53(3), 63-70.

37. Bhatia, G., Al Noutaki, I., Al Ruzeiqi, S., & Al Maskari, J. (2018, March). Design and implementation of private cloud for higher education using OpenStack. In *2018 Majan International Conference (MIC)* (pp. 1-6). IEEE.

38. Kaur, G. and Kumar, R., A. (2017). Review on Reliability Issues in Cloud Service.

39. Martino, B.D., Cretella, G. & Esposito, A. 2015. Cloud Portability and Interoperability: Issues and Current Trends.

40. Webster. M. 2018. [Online] Available at: https://www.merriam-webster.com/dictionary/phenomenon [5 June 2018]

41. Deng, S., Huang, L., Taheri, J., & Zomaya, A. Y. (2014). Computation offloading for service workflow in mobile cloud computing. *IEEE transactions on parallel and distributed systems*, 26(12), 3317-3329.

42. Latiff, M.S.A., Madni, S.H.H. & Abdullahi, M. (2018). Fault tolerance aware scheduling technique for cloud computing environment using dynamic clustering algorithm. *Neural Computing and Applications*, 29(1), 279-293

43. Han, B., Gopalakrishnan, V., Ji, L. and Lee, S., 2015. Network function virtualization: Challenges and opportunities for innovations. *IEEE Communications Magazine*, 53(2), 90-97.

44. Sarkar, Pushpak. "Chapter 4 - Enterprise Data Services". Data as a Service: A Framework for Providing Reusable Enterprise Data Services. *IEEE Computer Society Press*, 2015.

45. Li Wenhao, Yun Yang, and Dong Yuan. "Chapter 1 - Introduction". Reliability Assurance of Big Data in the Cloud: Cost-Effective Replication-Based Storage. Morgan Kaufmann Publishers, 2015.

46. Javadi, B. 2016. RELIABILITY IN CLOUD COMPUTING SYSTEMS, *6th International Conference on Cloud System & Big Data Engineering*, Sydney.

47. Rittinghouse, J. and Ransome, J. 2016. Cloud Computing: Implementation, Management, and Security. *Tailor & Francis Group*.

48. Tanveer, A. 2016. 2016. Enterprise Storage RAS augmented by native Intel Platform Storage Extensions (PSE). Stergiou, C., Psannis, K.E., Kim, B.G. and Gupta, B., 2018. Secure integration of IoT and cloud computing. Future Generation Computer Systems, 78, 964-975.

49. Botta, A., De Donato, W., Persico, V., & Pescape, A. (2016). Integration of cloud computing and internet of things: a survey. *Future generation computer systems*, 56, 684-700.

50. Ahmad, W., Hasan, O., Pervez, U., & Qadir, J. (2017). Reliability modeling and analysis of communication networks. *Journal of Network and Computer Applications*, 78, 191-215.

51. Duncan, R. A. K., & Whittington, M. (2016). Enhancing cloud security and privacy: the power and the weakness of the audit trail. *CLOUD COMPUTING* 2016.

52. Almorsy, M., Grundy, J., & Müller, I. (2016). An analysis of the cloud computing security problem. *arXiv preprint arXiv:1609.01107*.

53. Vacca, J. R. (2020). *Cloud Computing Security: Foundations and Challenges*. Taylor Francis.

54. Cheng, C. C., Cheng, F. C., Lin, P. H., Huang, W. T., & Huang, S. C. (2017). A Fastest Patchwise Histogram Construction Algorithm based on Cloud-Computing Architecture. *International Journal of Web Services Research (IJWSR)*, 14(1), 1-12.

55. Fawcett. A. (2017). Force.com Enterprise Architecture, Packt publishing.

56. Vermaat, M., Sebok, S. L., Freund, S. M., Frydenberg, M., & Campbell, J. T. (2016). *Enhanced Discovering Computers 2017*. Nelson Education.

57. Rao, R.V. & Selvamani, K., 2015. Data security challenges and its solutions in Procedia Computer.

58. Hussein, N. H., & Khalid, A. (2016). A survey of cloud computing security challenges and solutions. *International Journal of Computer Science and Information Security*, 14(1), 52.

59. Durairaj, M., & Manimaran, A. (2015). A study on security issues in cloud based e-learning. *Indian Journal of Science and Technology*, 8(8), 757-765.

60. Maciel, R., Araujo, J., Dantas, J., Melo, C., Guedes, E. & Maciel, P. 2018, April. Impact of a DDoS attack on computer systems: An approach based on an attack tree model. In *2018 Annual IEEE International Systems Conference (SysCon)*, 1-8. IEEE.

61. Chen, M., Ma, Y., Li, Y., Wu, D., Zhang, Y., & Youn, C. H. (2017). Wearable 2.0: Enabling human-cloud integration in next generation healthcare systems. *IEEE Communications Magazine*, 55(1), 54-61.

62. Ouedraogo, M. & Islam, S. 2015, June. Towards the Integration of Security Transparency in the Modelling and Design of Cloud Based Systems. In *International Conference on Advanced Information Systems Engineering* (pp. 495-506). Springer, Cham.

63. Lins, S., Grochol, P., Schneider, S. and Sunyaev, A., (2016). Dynamic certification of cloud services: Trust, but verify!. *IEEE Security & Privacy*, 14(2), 66-71.

64. Luna, J., Taha, A., Trapero, R. and Suri, N. (2017). Quantitative reasoning about cloud security using service level agreements. *IEEE Transactions on Cloud Computing*, 5(3), 457-471.

65. Schulz, Greg. "Chapter 8 - Data Infrastructure Services: Access and Performance". Software-Defined Data Infrastructure Essentials: Cloud, Converged, and Virtual Fundamental Server Storage I/O Tradecraft. Auerbach Publications, 2017

66. Froehlich, A. (2018). *How Edge Computing Compares with Cloud Computing*. Networking Computing Blog.

67. Kang, H.S., Lee, J.Y., Choi, S., Kim, H., Park, J.H., Son, J.Y., Kim, B.H. & Do Noh, S., 2016. Smart manufacturing: Past research, present findings, and future directions. *International Journal of Precision Engineering and Manufacturing-Green Technology*, 3(1), 111-128.

68. Luan, T. H., Gao, L., Li, Z., Xiang, Y., Wei, G. and Sun, L. (2015). Fog computing: Focusing on mobile users at the edge. *arXiv preprint arXiv:1502.01815*.

69. Yang, Y., Pankow, J., Swan, H., Willett, J., Mitchell, S.G., Rudes, D.S. & Knight, K. 2018. Preparing for analysis: a practical guide for a critical step for procedural rigor in large-scale multisite qualitative research studies. *Quality & Quantity*, 52(2), 815-828.

70. Chang, V. & Ramachandran, M. (2016). Towards achieving data security with the cloud computing adoption framework. *IEEE Transactions on Services Computing*, 9(1), 138-151.

71. Snider, E., Chipps, T., Buxo, N., Clark, L., Dimond, R. & Winchester, J., Western Union Co. 2017. Multi-network transaction analysis. *U.S. Patent Application* 15/265,014.

72. Cook, C. I. (2018). CenturyLink Intellectual Property LLC: Multi-network access gateway. U.S. Patent 9,942,413.

73. Hofmann, E., & Rusch, M. (2017). Industry 4.0 and the current status as well as future prospects on logistics. *Computers in Industry*, 89, 23-34.

74. Parasher, Y., Kedia, D. & Singh, P. 2018. Examining Current Standards for Cloud Computing and IoT. In *Examining Cloud Computing Technologies Through the Internet of Things* (pp. 116-124). IGI Global.

75. Saunders, B., Sim, J., Kingstone, T., Baker, S., Waterfield, J., Bartlam, B., Burroughs, H. and Jinks, C., 2018. Saturation in qualitative research: exploring its conceptualization and operationalization. *Quality & Quantity*, 52(4)1893-1907.

76. Struwig, FW. & Stead, GB. 2017. Research: Planning, Designing and Reporting: Cape Town, South Africa

77. Taylor, S.J., Bogdan, R. & DeVault, M. 2015. Introduction to qualitative research methods: A guidebook and resource. John Wiley & Sons.

78. Devi, P. S. (2017). *Research methodology: a handbook for beginners*. Notion Press.

79. Alvesson, M. & Skoldberg, K. (2017). Reflexive methodology: New vistas for qualitative research. Sage.

80. Maree, K, Creswell, Ebersohn, J. W., Eloff, L., I. Ferreira, . R N, Ivankova, J. D Jansen, J., Nieuwenhuis, Pietersen & V. L. Plano-Clark. 2016. First Steps in research. Van Schaik

81. Lewis, S., (2015). Qualitative inquiry and research design: Choosing among five approaches. *Health promotion practice*, 16(4), pp.473-475.

82. Cooper. S .B. (2017). *Computability theory*. Chapman and Hall/CRC.

83. Yazan, B. (2015). The Qualitative Report Three Approaches to Case Study Methods in Education: Yin, Merriam, and Stake. *The Qualitative Report*, 20(2): 134-152

84. Isomidinova, G. & Singh, J. S. K. (2017). Determinants of financial literacy: a quantitative study among young students in Tashkent, Uzbekistan. *Electronic Journal of Business & Management*, 2(1), 61-75.

85. Kothari, A., Boyko, J.A. and Campbell-Davison, A. (2015). An exploratory analysis of the nature of informal knowledge underlying theories of planned action used for public health oriented knowledge translation. *BMC Research Notes*, 8(1), 424.

86. Hall, N., Lacey, J., Carr-Cornish, S. & Dowd, A.M. (2015). Social licence to operate: understanding how a concept has been translated into practice in energy industries. *Journal of Cleaner Production*, 86, pp.301-310.

87. Wilson, V.2016.Research methods: interviews. Evidence Based Library and Information Practice, 11(1 (S)), 47-49.

88. Kallio, H., Pietila, A. M., Johnson, M. & Kangasniemi, M. (2016). Systematic methodological review: developing a framework for a qualitative semi-structured interview guide. *Journal of advanced nursing*, 72(12), 2954-2965.

89. Moser, C.A. and Kalton, G. (2017). *Survey methods in social investigation*. Routledge.

90. McGuirk, P.M. & O'Neill, P. (2016). Using questionnaires in qualitative human geography.

91. Burg, M. A., Adorno, G., Lopez, E. D., Loerzel, V., Stein, K., Wallace, C., & Sharma, D. K. B. (2015). Current unmet needs of cancer survivors: Analysis of open-ended responses to the American Cancer Society Study of Cancer Survivors II. *Cancer*, 121(4), 623-630.

92. Betchoo, N.K., (2017). Applied Research in HRM A Qualitative Approach.

93. Schwandt, T.A. 2015. The Sage Dictionary of Qualitative Inquiry.

94. Boddy, C. R. (2016). Sample size for qualitative research. *Qualitative Market Research: An International Journal*, 19(4), 426-432.

95. Silverman, D. 2016. Qualitative Research: Sage cloud computing. *Science*, 48, 204-209.

96. Bengtsson, M. (2016). How to plan and perform a qualitative study using content analysis. *NursingPlus Open*, 2, 8-14.

97. Sharma, Y., Javadi, B., Si, W. and Sun, D., 2016. Reliability and energy efficiency in cloud computing systems: Survey and taxonomy. *Journal of Network and Computer Applications*, 74, 66-85.

98. Gordon, A. (2015). *Communications & Network Security*. New York: CRC Press.

99. Strom, N., 2015. Scalable distributed DNN training using commodity GPU cloud computing. In *Sixteenth Annual Conference of the International Speech Communication Association*.

100. Mahmood, Z. ed., 2016. Connectivity frameworks for smart devices: the internet of things from a distributed computing perspective. Springer.

101. Indhumathil, T., Aarthy, N., Devi, V. D., & Samyuktha, V. N. (2017, March). Third-party auditing for cloud service providers in multicloud environment. In *2017 Third International Conference on Science Technology Engineering & Management (ICONSTEM)* (pp. 347-352). IEEE.

102. Pattnaik, P.K., Kabat, M.R. & Pal, S. (2015). *Fundamentals of Cloud Computing*. Vikas Publishing House.

103. Sanaei, Z., Abolfazli, S., Gani, A. and Buyya, R., 2014. Heterogeneity in mobile cloud computing: taxonomy and open challenges. *IEEE Communications Surveys & Tutorials*, 16(1), 369-392.

104. Shi, C. & Philip, S.Y. 2017. Heterogeneous Information Network Analysis and Applications.Chicago: Springer

105. Seth, B., Dalal, S., Le, D. N., Jaglan, V., Dahiya, N., Agrawal, A., Mayank M. S., Deo P. & Verma, K. D. (2021). Secure Cloud Data Storage System Using Hybrid Paillier-Blowfish Algorithm. *CMC-Computers Materials & Continua*, 67(1), 779-798.

106. Le, D. N., Seth, B., & Dalal, S. (2018). A hybrid approach of secret sharing with fragmentation and encryption in cloud environment for securing outsourced medical database: a revolutionary approach. *Journal of Cyber Security and Mobility*, 379-408.

107. Le, D. N., Kumar, R., Nguyen, G. N., & Chatterjee, J. M. (2018). *Cloud Computing and Virtualization*. John Wiley & Sons.

108. Le, D. N., Bhatt, C., & Madhukar, M. (Eds.). (2019). *Security Designs for the Cloud, IoT, and Social Networking*. John Wiley & Sons.

109. Seth, B., Dalal, S., Jaglan, V., Le, D. N., Mohan, S., & Srivastava, G. (2020). Integrating encryption techniques for secure data storage in the cloud. *Transactions on Emerging Telecommunications Technologies*, e4108.

110. Seth, B., Dalal, S., Le, D. N., Jaglan, V., Dahiya, N., Agrawal, A., ... & Verma, K. D. (2021). Secure cloud data storage system using hybrid Paillier–Blowfish algorithm. *CMC-Computer Materials & Continua*, 67(1), 779-798.

13

APPLICATIONS OF WIRELESS SENSOR NETWORK IN CLOUD

Prasant Kumar Pattnaik[1], Dac-Nhuong Le[2], Souvik Pal[3]

[1] KIIT, Deemed to be University, India
[2] Haiphong University, Haiphong, Vietnam
[3] Sister Nivedita University, Kolkata, India
Email: patnaikprasant@gmail.com, nhuongld@dhhp.edu.vn, souvikpal22@gmail.com

Abstract

The popularity of cloud computing is increasing day by day in distributed computing environment. There is a growing trend of using cloud environments for storage and data processing needs. Furthermore, wireless sensor networks, which are seen as being one of the most essential technologies for the 21st century, distribute spatially connected node that automatically forms a network to transmit and receive data among themselves, which are popularly known as sensor network. For security and easy access of data, cloud computing is widely used in distributed/mobile computing environment. This is possible due to miniaturization of communication technology. Many researchers have cited different types of technology in this context. But the application scenarios are of important consideration when designing a specific protocol for sensor network with reference to cloud computing.

Keywords: Cloud computing, wireless sensor network, routing protocol, distributed computing

13.1   Introduction

In this chapter, we will survey some typical applications of sensor network using cloud computing as backbone. Since cloud computing provides plenty of application, platforms and infrastructure over the internet, it may be combined with sensor network in the application areas such as environmental monitoring, weather forecasting, transportation, business, healthcare, military application, etc. Various wireless sensor networks (WSNs) can be deployed for different applications under one roof and is seen as a single virtual WSN entity through the novelty of cloud computing infrastructure.

The communication among sensor nodes using the internet is often a challenge. It makes a lot of sense to integrate sensor networks with the internet [1]. At the same time, the data in the sensor network should be available at any time and at any place. It is possibly a difficult issue to assign an address to a large number of sensor nodes; so sensor node may not establish connection with the internet exclusively. Cloud computing strategy can help business organizations conduct their core business activities with less hassle and greater efficiency. Companies can maximize the use of their existing hardware to plan for and serve specific peaks in usage. Thousands of virtual machines and applications can be managed more easily using a cloud-like environment. Businesses can also save on power costs as they reduce the number of servers required.

13.2   Architectural Issues of Combining Cloud Computing and Wireless Sensor Networks

Figure 13.1 consists of WSNs (i.e., WSN1, WSN2, and WSN3), cloud infrastructure, and the clients. Clients seek services from the system. A WSN consists of physical wireless sensor nodes to sense different applications like transport monitoring, weather forecasting, military applications, etc.

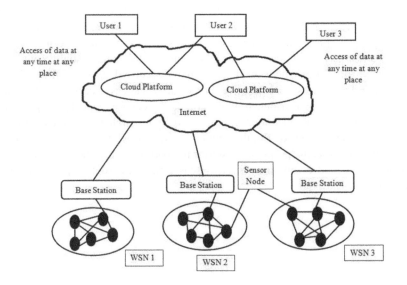

Figure 13.1: Combination of cloud computing and wireless sensor networks.

Each sensor node is programmed with the required application. Sensor node also consists of operating system components and network management components. On each sensor node, an application program senses the application and sends it back to the cloud storage gateqy directly through a base station or through multi-hop routing to other nodes. Routing protocol plays a vital role in managing the network topology and accommodating the network dynamics. Cloud provides on-demand service and storage resources to the clients. It provides access to these resources through the internet and comes in handy when there is a sudden requirement for resources [2, 3].

13.3 Sensor Network Overview

A wireless sensor network (WSN) consists of spatially distributed autonomous sensors to cooperatively monitor physical or environmental conditions such as temperature, sound, vibration, pressure, motion or pollutants [4, 5]. The development of wireless sensor networks was motivated by military applications such as battlefield surveillance. They are now used in many industrial and civilian application areas, including industrial process monitoring and control, machine health monitoring [6], environment and habitat monitoring, healthcare applications, home automation, and traffic control [4, 7]. Each node in a sensor network is typically equipped with a radio transceiver or other wireless communications device, a small microcontroller, and an energy source, usually a battery. The size of sensor node may vary from shoebox down to a grain of dust. The cost of sensor nodes is also varies from hundreds of dollars to a few pennies, depending on the size of the sensor network and the complexity required of individual sensor nodes [4]. Size and cost constraints on sensor nodes result in corresponding constraints on resources such as energy, memory, computational speed, and bandwidth [4].

A sensor network is a computer network composed of a large number of sensor nodes [8]. The sensor nodes that are densely deployed inside the phenomenon, deploy randomly and have cooperative capabilities. Usually these devices are small and inexpensive, so that they can be produced and deployed in large numbers, and so their resources in terms of energy, memory, computational speed and bandwidth are severely constrained. There are different sensors such as pressure, accelerometer, camera, thermal, microphone, etc. They monitor conditions at different locations, such as temperature, humidity, vehicular movement, lightning condition, pressure, soil makeup, noise levels, the presence or absence of certain kinds of objects, mechanical stress levels on attached objects; and the current characteristics such as speed, direction and size of an object. Normally these sensor nodes consist of components for: sensing, processing, and communicating [9]. The development of sensor networks requires technologies from three different research areas: sensing, communication, and computing (including hardware, software, and algorithms). Thus, combined and separate advancements in each of these areas have driven research in sensor networks. Examples of early sensor networks include the radar networks used in air traffic control; and the national power grid, with its many sensors, can be viewed as one large sensor network. These systems were developed with specialized computers and communication capabilities before the term sensor networks came into vogue.

13.3.1 Terminology

Following are the important terms which are used widely in sensor network:

1. Sensor: A transducer that converts a physical phenomenon such as heat, light, sound or motion into electrical or other signal that may be further manipulated by other apparatus.

2. Sensor node: A basic unit in a sensor network, with processor, memory, wireless modem and power supply.

3. Network topology: A connectivity graph where nodes are sensor nodes and edges are communication links.

4. Routing: The process of determining a network path from a source node to its destination.

5. Resource: This includes sensors, communication links, processors and memory and node energy.

6. Data storage: The runtime system support for sensor network application. Storage may be local to the node where the data is generated, load balanced across a network, or anchored at a few points.

13.3.2   Routing Protocols in WSNs

Routing protocols in WSNs are broadly divided into two categories: network structure based and protocol operation based. Network structure-based routing protocols are further divided into flat-based routing, hierarchical-based routing, and location-based routing. Protocol operation-based routing protocols are further divided into multipath based, query based, QoS based, coherent based, and negotiation based.

In flat-based routing, all nodes are typically assigned equal roles or functionality sensor nodes collaborate together to perform the sensing task. Due to the large number of such nodes, it is not feasible to assign a global identifier to each node. The examples of flat-based routing protocols are: SPIN [10, 11], Directed Diffusion [12], Rumor Routing [13], MCFA [14], GBR [15], IDSQ and CADR [16], Cougar [17], ACQUIRE [18], Energy-Aware Routing [19], etc.

In hierarchical-based or cluster-based routing, nodes will play different roles in the network. In a hierarchical architecture, higher energy nodes can be used to process and send the information while low energy nodes can be used to perform the sensing in the proximity of the target. This means that creation of clusters and assigning special tasks to cluster heads can greatly contribute to overall system scalability, lifetime, and energy efficiency. Hierarchical routing is an efficient way to lower energy consumption within a cluster and by performing data aggregation and fusion in order to decrease the number of transmitted messages to the BS. Hierarchical routing is mainly two-layer routing where one layer is used to select cluster heads and the other layer is used for routing. The examples of hierarchical-based routing protocols are: LEACH [20], PEGASIS [21], TEEN [22], APTEEN [23], MECN [24], SMECN [25], SOP [26], Sensor Aggregate Routing [27], VGA[28], HPAR [29], TTDD [30], etc.

In location-based routing, the position of the sensor nodes are exploited to route data in the network. In this kind of routing, sensor nodes are addressed by means of their locations. The distance between neighboring nodes can be estimated on the basis of incoming signal strengths. Relative coordinates of neighboring nodes can be obtained by exchanging such information between neighbors [37-39]. Alternatively, the location of nodes may be available directly by communicating with a satellite, using GPS (global positioning system), if nodes are equipped with a small, low power GPS receiver [40]. The examples of location-based routing protocols are: GAF [31], GEAR [32], GPSR [33], MFR, DIR, GEDIR [34], GOAFR [35], SPAN [36], etc.

In multipath routing, communication among nodes uses multiple paths to enhance the network performance instead of single path. In query-based routing, the destination nodes propagate a query for data from a node through the network and a node having this data sends the data which matches the query back to the node, which initiates the query. Usually these queries are described in natural language, or in high-level query languages. In QoS-based routing protocols, the network has to balance between energy consumption and data quality. The network has to satisfy certain QoS metrics, e.g., delay, energy, bandwidth, etc., for delivering data to the BS. In coherent routing, the data is forwarded to aggregators after minimum processing. The minimum processing typically includes tasks like time stamping, duplicate suppression, etc. In negotiation-based routing, protocols use high-level data descriptors in order to eliminate redundant data transmissions through negotiation. Communication decisions are also taken based on the resources that are available to them.

13.4   Application Scenarios

Combining WSNs with cloud makes it easy to share and analyze real-time sensor data on-the-fly. It also gives an advantage of providing sensor data or sensor event as a service over the internet. The terms Sensing as a Service (SaaS) and Sensor Event as a Service (SEaaS) were coined to describe the process of making the sensor data and event of interest available to the clients, respectively, over the cloud infrastructure [37-41].

Merging of two technologies makes sense for a large number of applications. Some applications of sensor network using cloud computing are explained below.

13.4.1   Military Use

Sensor networks are used in the military for monitoring friendly forces, equipment and ammunition, battlefield surveillance, reconnaissance of opposing forces, targeting, battle damage assessment; and nuclear, biological and chemical attack detection reconnaissance, etc. [43].

The data collected from these applications are of greatest importance and need top-level security which may not be provided using normal internet connectivity for security reason. Cloud computing may be one of the solutions for this problem by providing a secure infrastructure exclusively for military application, which will be used only for defense purposes.

13.4.2   Weather Forecasting

Weather forecasting is an application to predict the state of the atmosphere for a future time and a given location. Weather monitoring and forecasting system typically includes data collection, data assimilation, numerical weather prediction, and numerical presentation [41].

Each weather station is equipped with sensors to sense the following parameters: wind speed/direction, relative humidity, temperature (air, water and soil), barometric pressure, precipitation, soil moisture, ambient light (visibility), sky cover and solar radiation. The data collected from these sensors is huge in size and is difficult to maintain using the traditional database approaches. After collecting the data, assimilation process is done. The complicated equations that govern how the state of the atmosphere changes (weather forecast) with time require supercomputers to solve them.

13.4.3 Healthcare

Sensor networks are also widely used in the healthcare area. In some modern hospitals, sensor networks are constructed to monitor patient physiological data, to control the drug administration track, and monitor patients and doctors inside a hospital.

In the above scenario, the data collected from the patients are very sensitive and should be maintained properly as collected data are required by the doctors for their future diagnoses. In a traditional approach the database containing a patient's history is maintained in the local nursing home. So, reputed doctors who are specially invited from abroad to handle critical cases cannot analyze the patient's disease frequently. They will only make a diagnosis when they visit the particular nursing home. This problem may be solved by forming a cloud where the critical data of the patients can be maintained and authorized doctors sitting abroad can analyze the data and give proper treatment.

13.4.4 Transport Monitoring

A transport monitoring system includes basic management systems like traffic signal control, navigation, automatic number-plate recognition, toll collection, emergency vehicle notification, dynamic traffic lights, etc. [42-45].

In transport monitoring system, sensors are used to detect vehicles and control traffic lights. Video cameras are also used to monitor road segments with heavy traffic and the videos are sent to human operators at central locations. Sensors with embedded networking capability can be deployed at every road intersection to detect and count vehicle traffic and estimate its speed. The sensors will communicate with neighboring nodes to eventually develop a global traffic picture which can be queried by users to generate control signals. Data available from sensors is acquired and transmitted for central fusion and processing. This data can be used in a wide variety of applications. Some of the applications are vehicle classification, parking guidance and information system, collision avoidance systems, electronic toll gates and automatic road enforcement.

In the above scenarios, the applications require both storage of data and huge computational cycles. They also require analysis and prediction of data to generate events. Access to this data is limited in both cases. Integrating these WSN applications with the cloud computing infrastructure will ease the management of storage and computational resources. It also improves the application data over the internet through the web.

13.5 Summary

The communication among sensor nodes using the internet is a challenging task since sensor nodes contain limited bandwidth, memory, and small-size batteries. The issues of storage capacity may be overcome by the widely used cloud computing technique. In this chapter, we have discussed some issues of cloud computing and sensor network. To develop a new protocol in sensor network, specific application-oriented scenarios are an important consideration. With this in mind, we have discussed some applications of a sensor network using cloud computing.

EXERCISES

1. What is the relation between the WSN and cloud?

2. How is a radio transceiver used in WSN?

3. How are network topologies responsible for data communication?

4. Provide some names of flat-based routing protocols.

5. Provide some names of location-based routing protocols.

6. Provide some names of the application senarios that combine wireless sensor networks with cloud.

7. Please explain LEACH and PEGASIS routing protocols.

8. What is sensor-cloud security?

9. What is the senario for integration of wireless sensor networks with cloud computing?

10. Why should wireless sensor network be integrated with cloud environment?

References

1. C. Ulmer, L. Alkalai and S. Yalamanchili, Wireless distributed sensor networks for in-situ exploration of mars, Work in progress for NASA Technical Report. Available in: http://users.ece.gatech.edu/

2. P. Mell and T. Grance, "Draft nist working definition of cloud computing - v15," 21. Aug 2005, 2009.

3. M. Armbrust, A. Fox, R. Griffith, A. Joseph, R. Katz, A. Konwinski, G. Lee, D. Patterson, A. Rabkin, and I. Stoica, "Above the clouds: A Berkeley view of cloud computing," EECS Department, University of California, Berkeley, Tech. Rep. UCB/EECS-2009-28, 2009.

4. Romer, Kay; Friedemann Mattern (December 2004), "The Design Space of Wireless Sensor Networks", IEEE Wireless Communications 11 (6): 54–61, doi:10.1109/MWC.2004.1368897, http://www.vs.inf.ethz.ch/publ/papers/wsn-designspace.pdf

5. Thomas Haenselmann (2006-04-05). Sensornetworks. GFDL Wireless Sensor Network textbook. http://pi4.informatik.uni-mannheim.de/haensel/sn_book. Retrieved 2006-08-29.

6. Tiwari, Ankit et. al, Energy-efficient wireless sensor network design and implementation for condition-based maintenance, ACM Transactions on Sensor Networks (TOSN), http:// portal.acm.org/citation.cfm?id=1210670

7. Hadim, Salem; Nader Mohamed (2006), "Middleware Challenges and Approaches for Wireless Sensor Networks", IEEE Distributed Systems Online 7 (3): 1, doi:10.1109/MDSO.2006.19, http://doi.ieeecomputersociety.org/10.1109/MDSO.2006.19 art. no. 0603-o3001.

8. http://en.wikipedia.org/wiki/Sensor_Networks

9. Akyildiz, I.F., W. Su, Y. Sankarasubramaniam, E. Cayirci, "A Survey on Sensor Networks", IEEE Communications Magazine, August, 102-114(2002).

10. W. Heinzelman, J. Kulik, and H. Balakrishnan, "Adaptive Protocols for Information Dissemination in Wireless Sensor Networks," Proc. 5th ACM/IEEE Mobicom Conference (MobiCom '99), Seattle, WA, August, 1999. pp. 174-85.

11. J. Kulik, W. R. Heinzelman, and H. Balakrishnan, "Negotiation-based protocols for disseminating information in wireless sensor networks," Wireless Networks, Volume: 8, pp. 169-185, 2002.

12. C. Intanagonwiwat, R. Govindan, and D. Estrin, "Directed diffusion: a scalable and robust communication paradigm for sensor networks," Proceedings of ACM MobiCom '00, Boston, MA, 2000, pp. 56-67.

13. D. Braginsky and D. Estrin, Rumor Routing Algorithm for Sensor Networks," in the Proceedings of the First Workshop on Sensor Networks and Applications (WSNA), Atlanta, GA, October 2002.

14. F. Ye, A. Chen, S. Liu, L. Zhang, A scalable solution to minimum cost forwarding in large sensor networks", Proceedings of the tenth International Conference on Computer Communications and Networks (ICCCN), pp. 304-309, 2001.

15. C. Schurgers and M.B. Srivastava, Energy efficient routing in wireless sensor networks", in the MILCOM Proceedings on Communications for Network-Centric Operations: Creating the Information Force, McLean, VA, 2001.

16. M. Chu, H. Haussecker, and F. Zhao, Scalable Information-Driven Sensor Querying and Routing for ad hoc Heterogeneous Sensor Networks," The International Journal of High Performance Computing Applications, Vol. 16, No. 3, August 2002.

17. Y. Yao and J. Gehrke, The cougar approach to in-network query processing in sensor networks", in SIGMOD Record, September 2002.

18. N. Sadagopan et al., The ACQUIRE mechanism for efficient querying in sensor networks, in the Proceedings of the First International Workshop on Sensor Network Protocol and Applications, Anchorage, Alaska, May 2003.

19. R. C. Shah and J. Rabaey, Energy Aware Routing for Low Energy Ad Hoc Sensor Networks", IEEE Wireless Communications and Networking Conference (WCNC), March 17-21, 2002, Orlando, FL.

20. W. Heinzelman, A. Chandrakasan and H. Balakrishnan, "Energy-Efficient Communication Protocol for Wireless Microsensor Networks," Proceedings of the 33rd Hawaii International Conference on System Sciences (HICSS '00), January 2000.

21. S. Lindsey, C. Raghavendra, PEGASIS: Power-Efficient Gathering in Sensor Information Systems", IEEE Aerospace Conference Proceedings, 2002, Vol. 3, 9-16 pp. 1125-1130.

22. A. Manjeshwar and D. P. Agarwal, "TEEN: a routing protocol for enhanced efficiency in wireless sensor networks," In 1st International Workshop on Parallel and Distributed Computing Issues in Wireless Networks and Mobile Computing, April 2001.

23. A. Manjeshwar and D. P. Agarwal, "APTEEN: A hybrid protocol for efficient routing and comprehensive information retrieval in wireless sensor networks," Parallel and Distributed Processing Symposium., Proceedings International, IPDPS 2002, pp. 195-202.

24. V. Rodoplu and T. H. Meng, Minimum Energy Mobile Wireless Networks", IEEE Journal Selected Areas in Communications, vol. 17, no. 8, Aug. 1999, pp. 133344.

25. L. Li, and J. Y. Halpern, Minimum-Energy Mobile Wireless Networks Revisited," IEEE International Conference on Communications (ICC) 2001. Vol. 1, pp. 278-283.

26. L. Subramanian and R. H. Katz, An Architecture for Building Self Configurable Systems", in the Proceedings of IEEE/ACM Workshop on Mobile Ad Hoc Networking and Computing, Boston, MA, August 2000.

27. Q. Fang, F. Zhao, and L. Guibas, Lightweight Sensing and Communication Protocols for Target Enumeration and Aggregation", Proceedings of the 4th ACM international symposium on Mobile ad hoc networking and computing (MOBIHOC), 2003, pp. 165-176.

28. Jamal N. Al-Karaki, Raza Ul-Mustafa, Ahmed E. Kamal, "Data Aggregation in Wireless Sensor Networks - Exact and Approximate Algorithms'", Proceedings of IEEE Workshop on High Performance Switching and Routing (HPSR) 2004, April 18-21, 2004, Phoenix, Arizona, USA.

29. Q. Li and J. Aslam and D. Rus, Hierarchical Power-aware Routing in Sensor Networks", In Proceedings of the DIMACS Workshop on Pervasive Networking, May, 2001.

30. F. Ye, H. Luo, J. Cheng, S. Lu, L. Zhang, A Two-tier data dissemination model for large-scale wireless sensor networks", proceedings of ACM/IEEE MOBICOM, 2002.

31. Y. Xu, J. Heidemann, D. Estrin, Geography-informed Energy Conservation for Ad-hoc Routing," In Proceedings of the Seventh Annual ACM/IEEE International Conference on Mobile Computing and Networking 2001, pp. 70-84.

32. T. Yu, D. Estrin, and R. Govindan, Geographical and Energy-Aware Routing: A Recursive Data Dissemination Protocol for Wireless Sensor Networks", UCLA Computer Science Department Technical Report, UCLA-CSD TR-01-0023, May 2001.

33. B. Karp and H. T. Kung, GPSR: Greedy perimeter stateless routing for wireless sensor networks", in the Proceedings of the 6th Annual ACM/IEEE International Conference on Mobile Computing and Networking (MobiCom '00), Boston, MA, August 2000.

34. I. Stojmenovic and X. Lin. GEDIR: Loop-Free Location Based Routing in Wireless Networks", In International Conference on Parallel and Distributed Computing and Systems, Boston, MA, USA, Nov. 3-6, 1999.

35. F. Kuhn, R. Wattenhofer, A. Zollinger, Worst-Case optimal and average-case efficient geometric ad-hoc routing", Proceedings of the 4th ACM International Conference on Mobile Computing and Networking, Pages: 267-278, 2003.

36. B. Chen, K. Jamieson, H. Balakrishnan, R. Morris, SPAN: an energy-efficient coordination algorithm for topology maintenance in ad hoc wireless networks", Wireless Networks, Vol. 8, No. 5, Page(s): 481-494, September 2002.

37. N. Bulusu, J. Heidemann, D. Estrin, GPS-less low cost outdoor localization for very small devices", Technical report 00-729, Computer science department, University of Southern California, Apr. 2000.

38. A. Savvides, C-C Han, aind M. Srivastava, Dynamic ne-grained localization in Ad-Hoc networks of sensors," Proceedings of the Seventh ACM Annual International Conference on Mobile Computing and Networking (MobiCom), July 2001. pp. 166-179.

39. S. Capkun, M. Hamdi, J. Hubaux,"GPS-free positioning in mobile ad-hoc networks", Proceedings of the 34th Annual Hawaii International Conference on System Sciences, 2001 pp. 3481-3490.

40. Y. Xu, J. Heidemann, D. Estrin, Geography-informed Energy Conservation for Ad-hoc Routing," In Proceedings of the Seventh Annual ACM/IEEE International Conference on Mobile Computing and Networking 2001, pp. 70-84.

41. http://en.wikipedia.org/wiki/Weather_forecasting

42. Sanjit Kumar Dash, Subasish Mohapatra, Prasant Kumar Pattnaik, "A Survey on Application of Wireless Sensor Network Using Cloud Computing", International Journal of Computer Science & Engineering Technologies (IJCSET), (E-ISSN:2044-6004), Volume 1, Issue 4, December 2010, pp 50-55.

43. Seth, B., Dalal, S., Le, D. N., Jaglan, V., Dahiya, N., Agrawal, A., Mayank M. S., Deo P. & Verma, K. D. (2021). Secure Cloud Data Storage System Using Hybrid Paillier-Blowfish Algorithm. *CMC-Computers Materials & Continua*, 67(1), 779-798.

44. Le, D. N., Seth, B., & Dalal, S. (2018). A hybrid approach of secret sharing with fragmentation and encryption in cloud environment for securing outsourced medical database: a revolutionary approach. *Journal of Cyber Security and Mobility*, 379-408.

45. Le, D. N., Bhatt, C. M., & Madhukar, M. (Eds.). (2019). *Security Designs for the Cloud, IoT, and Social Networking*. John Wiley & Sons.

14

APPLICATIONS OF MOBILE CLOUD COMPUTING

Prasant Kumar Pattnaik[1], Dac-Nhuong Le[2], Souvik Pal[3]

[1] KIIT, Deemed to be University, India
[2] Haiphong University, Haiphong, Vietnam
[3] Sister Nivedita University, Kolkata, India
 Email: patnaikprasant@gmail.com, nhuongld@dhhp.edu.vn, souvikpal22@gmail.com

Abstract

Mobile cloud computing is a combination of mobile computing, cloud computing, and wireless networks that work together to deliver plentiful computational resources to mobile customers, network operators, and cloud computing providers. Rich mobile applications are supposed to be able to run on a variety of mobile devices thanks to mobile cloud computing. Data processing and storage take place outside of mobile devices under this technology. This chapter mainly deals with the characteristics, advantages, and applications of mobile cloud applications.

Keywords: Mobile cloud computing, mobile commerce, mobile heathcare, mobile learning, mobile gaming

14.1   What is Mobile Cloud Computing?

Mobile devices allow users to run powerful applications that take advantage of the growing availability of built-in sensing and better data exchange capabilities of mobile devices. As a result, mobile applications seamlessly integrate with real-time data streams and Web 2.0 applications, such as mashups, open collaboration, social networking and mobile commerce. The mobile execution platform is being used for more and more tasks, e.g., for playing games; capturing, editing, annotating and uploading video; handling finances; managing personal health, micro payments, ticket purchase, interacting with ubiquitous computing infrastructures. Even if mobile device hardware and mobile networks continue to evolve and to improve, mobile devices will always be resource-poor, less secure, with unstable connectivity, and with less energy since they are powered by battery. Resource poverty is a major obstacle for many applications. Therefore, computation on mobile devices will always involve a compromise [1].

Mobile devices can be seen as entry points and interface of cloud online services. Recently, there has been a discussion about what cloud computing really means. Rodero-Merino *et al.* [2] studied more than 20 definitions using the main characteristics associated with cloud computing. The cloud computing paradigm is often confused about its capabilities, described in general terms that include almost any kind of outsourcing of hosting and computing resources. According to the NIST, cloud computing is a model for enabling convenient, on-demand network access to computing resources that can be rapidly provisioned and released with minimal management effort [3].

The combination of cloud computing, wireless communication infrastructure, portable computing devices, location-based services, mobile web, etc., has laid the foundation for a novel computing model, called mobile cloud computing, which allows users an online access to unlimited computing power and storage space. Taking the cloud computing features in the mobile domain, we define:

"Mobile Cloud Computing (MCC) is a model for transparent elastic augmentation of mobile device capabilities via ubiquitous wireless access to cloud storage and computing resources, with context-aware dynamic adjusting of offloading in respect to change in operating conditions, while preserving available sensing and interactivity capabilities of mobile devices."

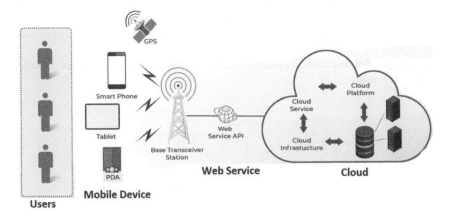

Figure 14.1: Mobile cloud computing.

In mobile cloud computing, the customer can access the data anytime and from anywhere very easily. It offers many business opportunities for the mobile network operator along with cloud providers. The goal of mobile cloud computing (MCC) is to allow the access of cloud from a mobile phone by providing an excellent experience to the customers and to promote it. MCC is economical and it saves time too. It is economical because the platforms are based on the pay-as-you-go principle.

14.2   The Architecture of Mobile Cloud Computing

Mobile cloud computing works on an computational augmentation approach which is executed remotely rather than executing on the device. With the help of computational augmentation, the mobile device can use the computational resources of varied cloud-based resources. Mobile cloud computing consists of four types of cloud-based resources, which are: Distant immobile clouds, proximate immobile computing entities, proximate mobile computing entities, and hybrid cloud [4-6]. Big companies such as Amazon are in the distant immobile cloud group whereas small-scale organizations are members of proximate immobile computing entities.

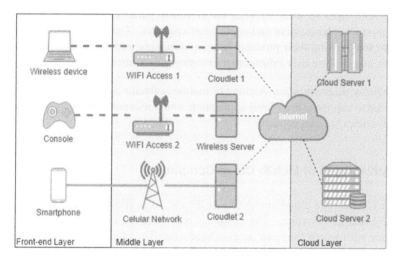

Figure 14.2: The architecture of mobile cloud computing.

14.3   Characteristics of Mobile Cloud Computing

Following are the reasons which remove all doubt as to why we choose mobile cloud computing [7, 8].

- *Rapid Development*: Cloud companies are developing mobile applications which are helping customers on a daily basis. These applications come up with upgrades which continuously improve the performance of the applications. The fact that companies are improving their applications regularly has led to there being a rapid development in mobile cloud computing.

- *Flexibility*: The applications built have greater reach and flexibility. There are a variety of development approaches and devices supported by mobile cloud computing. In mobile cloud computing, the customer can select the services which are required for their business, which makes it more flexible.

- *Security*: Mobile cloud computing is reliable and backs up all the data in the cloud and keeps it secure. That backup can be retrieved anytime in a secure manner. These applications are protected by a password so that if the mobile is lost or stolen the cloud does not face any risk. From one phone to another the process is very easy and no data is lost.

Mobile cloud computing can support:

- *Hosting Services*: As leverage, mobile cloud computing clients surrender a certain amount of control in the operating system for the promise of fewer configuration issues. It is one of the best ways to leverage the cloud.

- *Functionality Outsourcing*: Tasks such as video indexing and speech recognition offshore to the cloud living leave intensive tasks to be executed on the phone itself.

- *Web Analytics*: In web analytics the company gathers information and analyzes it for product enhancement and application upgrades. The company continuously puts effort into making their products better and making mobile applications that capture, store, and analyze user information to improve user interface.

- *Hardware Augmentation*: A clone of mobile software is created which is further enhanced to support a high-level application which was not previously possible because of its computational capacity.

14.4 Advantages of Mobile Cloud Computing

- *Flexible*: Mobile cloud computing is flexible as it allows accessing data from anywhere and at any time. The customer only requires an internet connection and a device with which they can access cloud data. The cloud computing application introduced by a company is used in multiple platforms such as Android, IOS, and many more. The cloud can easily access and modify data regardless of the platform.

- *Economical*: Mobile cloud computing eliminates the cost of hardware and is one of the most cost-efficient methods to use and maintain. The upfront costs of mobile cloud computing is much less and the customer has to pay only for what they have used.

- *Backup and Recovery*: The data stored with the help of mobile cloud application can be backed up easily and retrieved when needed. Cloud disaster recovery is a plan which consists of storing and maintaining copies of data at several places while keeping a high quality of security measures.

To execute mobile application there is a need for several factors, which are the availability of the local resource, user requirement, service-level agreement, and faster network availability. This execution highly depends on the context [9, 10].

Remote storage is a part of mobile cloud computing in which the data can be stored and retrieved with the help of a mobile phone. Mobile phone storage gets completely used up if there is data stored on it. So, by removing data stored on the mobile phone and uploading it in the cloud, the storage space in the phone can be used for another purpose. Data being remotely stored in the cloud ensures that the desired information is in the right place and can be retrieved anytime, assuming the availability of reliable connectivity. Cloud storage is not only virtually expands but also enhances data safety.

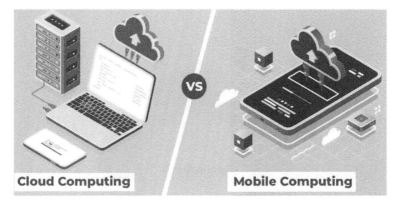

Figure 14.3: The difference between cloud computing and mobile computing.

How is cloud computing different from mobile computing? The basic similarity that exists between these two is that they use wireless systems for transmitting their data.

- With cloud computing deployed, it bridges the affordability gap that exists between the client's local/closed networks and their private data storage as well as backup systems. On the other hand, mobile computing allows many functions, such as accessibility of the internet using browsers and several supporting applications. All these functions are supported by a core operating system and have the ability to perform an exchange between different data types.

- Cloud computing is all about designing the latest technologies and services that will allow wireless or wired data sharing to take place across distributed networks. Whereas, mobile computing refers to the development of new hardware along with interfaces.

- With cloud computing, businesses get the ability to access services and functionalities that were unavailable using wired connections. The mobile cloud operates by making the services functionality available using different mobile network operators.

- In cloud computing, it is assumed that there is a joint entry point allowing the users to store and manage their files while using the entire range of advanced computing resources. On the other hand, mobile computing emphasizes smart connectivity more than focusing on virtual hosting and hosting of resources.

The Mobile Cloud market was valued at $30.71 billion in 2019. It is predicted that the market will reach $118.70 billion by the year 2025. During the forecasted period, i.e., 2020-2025, this market will witness a compound annual growth rate (CAGR) of 25.28%.

14.5   Mobile Cloud Applications

Mobile cloud applications try to reduce the resource requirement and consumption of an application while maintaining peak performance. The application requires much less space and provides maximum availability. The mobile applications come up with new updates which continuously provide better services to the customers. The main aim of the company is to enable maximum flexibility and deliver a rich user experience to the end user [11-15].

Figure 14.4: Mobile cloud applications.

14.5.1   Mobile Commerce

Mobile commerce (m-commerce) is a business model for commerce using mobile devices. The m-commerce applications generally fulfill some tasks that require mobility (e.g., mobile transactions and payments, mobile messaging, and mobile ticketing). The m-commerce applications can be classified into a few classes, including finance, advertising, and shopping [16, 17].

The m-commerce applications have to face various challenges (e.g., low network bandwidth, high complexity of mobile device configurations, and security). Therefore, they are integrated into cloud computing environment to address these issues. Shamshirband *et al.* propose a 3G E-commerce platform based on cloud computing. This paradigm combines the advantages of both third-generation (3G) network and cloud computing to increase data processing speed and security level based on public key infrastructure (PKI). The PKI mechanism uses an encryption-based access control and an over-encryption to ensure privacy of user's access to the outsourced data. A 4PL-AVE trading platform utilizes cloud computing technology to enhance the security for users and improve customer satisfaction, customer intimacy, and cost competitiveness [18, 19].

14.5.2 Mobile Learning

Mobile learning (m-learning) is designed based on electronic learning (e-learning) and mobility. However, traditional m-learning applications have limitations in terms of high cost of devices and network, low network transmission rate, and limited educational resources [20]. Cloud-based m-learning applications are introduced to solve these limitations. For example, utilizing a cloud with large storage capacity and powerful processing ability, the applications provide learners with much richer services in terms of data (information) size, faster processing speed, and longer battery life.

Zhao and Okamoto [21] discuss the benefits of combining m-learning and cloud computing to enhance the communication quality between students and teachers. In this case, a smartphone software based on the open source Java ME GUI framework and Jabber for clients is used. Through a website built on Google Apps Engine, students communicate with their teachers at anytime. Also, the teachers can obtain information about a student's knowledge level of the course and can answer students' questions in a timely manner. In addition, a contextual m-learning system based on mobile interaction in augmented reality environment platform [22] shows that a cloud-based m-learning system helps learners access learning resources remotely.

Another example of mobile cloud computing applications in learning is Cornucopia, which was implemented for the research of undergraduate genetics students; and Plantations Pathfinder, which was designed to supply information and provide a collaboration space for visitors when they visit gardens [23]. The purpose of the deployment of these applications is to help the students enhance their understanding about the appropriate design of MCC in supporting field experiences. In [24], an education tool was developed based on cloud computing to create a course about image/video processing. Through mobile phones, learners can understand and compare different algorithms used in mobile applications (e.g., deblurring, denoising, face detection, and image enhancement).

14.5.3 Mobile Healthcare

The purpose of applying mobile cloud computing in medical applications is to minimize the limitations of traditional medical treatment (e.g., small physical storage, security and privacy, and medical errors [25, 26]). Mobile healthcare (m-healthcare) provides mobile users with convenient help to access resources (e.g., patient health records) easily and efficiently. Besides, m-healthcare offers hospitals and healthcare organizations a variety of on-demand services on clouds rather than owning standalone applications on local servers.

There are a few schemes of mobile cloud computing applications in healthcare. For example, the authors in [27] present five main mobile healthcare applications in a pervasive environment.

- Comprehensive health monitoring services enable patients to be monitored at anytime and anywhere through broadband wireless communications.

- Intelligent emergency management system can manage and coordinate the fleet of emergency vehicles effectively and on time when receiving calls from accidents or incidents.

- HealthAware mobile devices detect pulse rate, blood pressure, and level of alcohol to alert healthcare emergency systems.

- Pervasive access to healthcare information allows patients or healthcare providers to access current and past medical information.

- Pervasive lifestyle incentive management can be used to pay healthcare expenses and manage other related charges automatically.

Similarly, the authors in [28] propose HealthCloud, a prototype implementation of m-healthcare information management system based on cloud computing and a mobile client running Android operating system (OS). This prototype presents three services utilizing Amazon's S3 cloud storage service to manage patient health records and medical images.

- Seamless connection to cloud storage allows users to retrieve, modify, and upload medical contents (e.g., medical images, patient health records, and biosignals) utilizing web services and a set of available APIs called Representational State Transfer.

- Patient health record management system displays the information regarding patients' status, related biosignals, and image contents through application's interface.

- Image viewing support allows the mobile users to decode the large image files at different resolution levels given different network availability and quality.

A practical telemedicine homecare management system [29] has been implemented in Taiwan to monitor participants, especially for patients with hypertension and diabetes. The system monitors 300 participants and stores more than 4736 records of blood pressure and sugar measurement data on the cloud. When a participant performs blood glucose/pressure measurement via specialized equipment, the equipment can send the measured parameters to the system automatically. Also, the participant can send parameters by SMS via their mobile devices. After that, the cloud will gather and analyze the information about the participant and return the results. The development of mobile healthcare clearly is a tremendous help to the participants. However, the information to be collected and managed related to personal health is sensitive. Therefore, solutions are proposed in [30, 31] to protect the participant's health information, thereby, increasing the privacy of the services. Although [32] uses peer-to-peer paradigm to federate clouds to address security issue, data protection, and ownership, the model in [33] provides security as a service on the cloud to protect mobile applications. Therefore, mobile health application providers and users will not have to worry about the security issue because it is ensured by the security vendor.

14.5.4 Mobile Gaming

Mobile games (m-games) are a potential market for generating revenues for service providers. M-games can completely offload a game engine requiring large computing resources (e.g., graphic rendering) to the server in the cloud, and gamers only interact with the screen interface on their devices.

Liu and Li [34] demonstrated that offloading (multimedia code) can save energy for mobile devices, thereby increasing game playing time on mobile devices. Cuervo *et al.* proposed MAUI, a system that enables fine-grained energy-aware offloading of mobile codes to a cloud [35]. Also, a number of experiments have been conducted to evaluate the energy used for game applications with 3G network and WiFi network. It is found that instead of offloading all codes to the cloud for processing, MAUI partitions the application codes at a runtime based on the costs of network communication and CPU on the mobile device to maximize energy savings given network connectivity. The results demonstrate that MAUI not only helps energy reduction significantly for mobile devices (i.e., MAUI saves 27% of energy usage for the video game and 45% for chess), but also improves the performance of mobile applications (i.e., the game's refresh rate increases from 6 to 13 frames per second).

Prasad *et al.* [36] presented a new cloud-based m-game using a rendering adaptation technique to dynamically adjust the game rendering parameters according to communication constraints and gamers' demands. The rendering adaptation technique is mainly based on the idea of reducing the number of objects in the display list, because not all objects in the display list created by the game engine are necessary for playing the game, and scale the complexity of rendering operations. The objective is to maximize the user experience given the communications and computing costs.

14.5.5 Mobile Social Network

Mobile social networking (MSN) [37, 38] is social networking where individuals with similar interests converse and connect with one another through their mobile phone and/or tablet. Much like web-based social networking, mobile social networking occurs in virtual communities.

Many web-based social networking sites, such as Facebook and Twitter, have created mobile applications to give their users instant and real-time access from anywhere they have access to the internet. Additionally, native mobile social networks have been created to allow communities to be built around mobile functionality.

More and more, the line between the mobile app and the mobile web is being blurred as mobile apps use existing social networks to create native communities and promote discovery, and web-based social networks take advantage of mobile features and accessibility.

As mobile web evolved from proprietary mobile technologies and networks, to full mobile access to the internet, the distinction changed to the following:

1. Web-based social networks being extended for mobile access through mobile browsers and smartphone apps.

2. Native mobile social networks with dedicated focus on mobile use such as mobile communication, location-based services, and augmented reality.

While mobile- and web-based social networking systems often work symbiotically to spread content, increase accessibility, and connect users, consumers are increasingly focusing on native apps compared to web browsers.

The rise of the digital age has made social media a lasting trend. Facebook, which is still the leader of social networks, was initially web-based and then extended towards access via mobile browsers and smartphone apps. Compared with Twitter, Instagram, and Pinterest, Facebook continues to dominate the social media world. As of the fourth quarter of 2015, 823 million Facebook users accessed the social network exclusively through mobile devices, surpassing the 526 million users in the previous year. In 2016, Instagram started out being mobile and later developed into web-based platforms as well. In 2016, there were practically 1.6 billion active users around the world. Moreover, in the United States, a study of social media audiences determined that according to the percentage of users, the most popular mobile social network spent a total of 230 billion minutes on Facebook in 2014, 80% higher than Instagram. Until January 2016, 52% of users in North America accessed social media through mobile devices when the global mobile social penetration rate was 27% [38]. A 2017 report showed that around 1 billion users visited Facebook via mobile devices during that year, with the US market playing a significant role with nearly 80% of Facebook users using mobile devices to access their accounts. Facebook mobile advertising revenue accounted for 10 billion dollars, which translates into 74% of total revenue. It shows that by 2021, more than 98% of the Facebook users worldwide will access the service via their mobile phones.

14.5.6 Multimedia Sharing

By seeing the name we can easily understand this helps in sharing of data from one mobile devices to another mobile devices. Mobile users can share all types of data. Again, here MCC helps in sharing all types of data and security [39].

Furthermore, it is not just textual content that can be shared, annotated or discussed, but also any multimedia content such as pictures, videos, or even presentation slides. Moreover, this content can also benefit from semantic web technologies [40].

14.6 Summary

The increasing integration of mobile cloud is helping many companies. Generating costs are high and hardware is expensive, and mobile cloud eliminates those costs. With the help of the mobile cloud, effort is saved and the work is done within the time limit cloud computing stretch to reduce the maintenance cost and enhance data safety and privacy. In the mobile cloud, a reduction in resources consumed is achieved by program architecture, support cloud, and mashup. This leads to the future generation of mobile applications that are highly dependent on the cloud.

EXERCISES

1. What are mobile web services?

2. What are XML-RPC protocols?

3. "Portability makes work easy and efficient." Explain.

4. What are the main differences between platform and infrastructure?

5. To what extent are cloud services different for mobile devices and desktop machines?

6. Which are the perfect lightweight data stream frameworks to execute latency-sensitive applications at the network edge?

7. How is low bandwidth a challenge to mobile cloud computing?

8. Name different QoS-aware protocols.

9. Explain DREAM algorithm.

10. How is CMReS algortihm related to mobile cloud computing security?

References

1. Kovachev, D., Renzel, D., Klamma, R., & Cao, Y. (2010, May). Mobile community cloud computing: emerges and evolves. In 2010 Eleventh International Conference on Mobile Data Management (pp. 393-395). IEEE.

2. Rodero-Merino, L., Caceres, J., Lindner, M., & Vaquero, L. (2009). A break in the clouds: towards a cloud definition. *ACM SIGCOMM Computer Communication Review*, 39(1), 50-55.

3. P. Mell and T. (2009). Grance, The NIST Definition of Cloud Computing. [Online]. Available: http://csrc.nist.gov/groups/SNS/cloud-computing/cloud-def-v15.doc

4. Shin, Y., Hur, J., Koo, D., & Yun, J. (2020). Toward Serverless and Efficient Encrypted Deduplication in Mobile Cloud Computing Environments. *Security and Communication Networks*, 2020.

5. Muralidhar, K., & Madhavi, K. (2020). Approaches to Address the Operational Limitations of MANETs through Ad Hoc Mobile Cloud Computing Paradigm. *International Journal of Interactive Mobile Technologies*, 14(9).

6. Kumar, J., Rani, A., & Dhurandher, S. K. (2020). Convergence of user and service provider perspectives in mobile cloud computing environment: Taxonomy and challenges. *International Journal of Communication Systems*, e4636.

7. Parajuli, N., Alsadoon, A., Prasad, P. W. C., Ali, R. S., & Alsadoon, O. H. (2020). A recent review and a taxonomy for multimedia application in Mobile cloud computing based energy efficient transmission. *Multimedia Tools and Applications*, 1-28.

8. Fernando, N., Loke, S. W., & Rahayu, W. (2013). Mobile cloud computing: A survey. *Future Generation Computer Systems*, 29(1), 84-106.

9. Dinh, H. T., Lee, C., Niyato, D., & Wang, P. (2013). A survey of mobile cloud computing: architecture, applications, and approaches. *Wireless Communications and Mobile Computing*, 13(18), 1587-1611.

10. Khan, A. N., Kiah, M. M., Khan, S. U., & Madani, S. A. (2013). Towards secure mobile cloud computing: A survey. Future Generation Computer Systems, 29(5), 1278-1299.

11. Othman, M., Madani, S. A., & Khan, S. U. (2013). A survey of mobile cloud computing application models. *IEEE Communications Surveys & Tutorials*, 16(1), 393-413.

12. Sanaei, Z., Abolfazli, S., Gani, A., & Buyya, R. (2013). Heterogeneity in mobile cloud computing: taxonomy and open challenges. *IEEE Communications Surveys & Tutorials*, 16(1), 369-392.

13. Huang, D. (2011). Mobile cloud computing. IEEE COMSOC Multimedia Communications Technical Committee (MMTC). *E-Letter*, 6(10), 27-31.

14. Rahimi, M. R., Ren, J., Liu, C. H., Vasilakos, A. V., & Venkatasubramanian, N. (2014). Mobile cloud computing: A survey, state of art and future directions. *Mobile Networks and Applications*, 19(2), 133-143.

15. Bahl, P., Han, R. Y., Li, L. E., & Satyanarayanan, M. (2012, June). Advancing the state of mobile cloud computing. In *Proceedings of the third ACM workshop on Mobile Cloud Computing and Services* (pp. 21-28).

16. Almusaylim, Z. A., & Jhanjhi, N. Z. (2020). Comprehensive Review: Privacy Protection of User in Location- Aware Services of Mobile Cloud Computing. *Wireless Personal Communications*, 111(1), 541-564.

17. Ibtihal, M., & Hassan, N. (2020). Homomorphic encryption as a service for outsourced images in mobile cloud computing environment. In *Cryptography: Breakthroughs in Research and Practice* (pp. 316-330). IGI Global.

18. Shamshirband, S., Fathi, M., Chronopoulos, A. T., Montieri, A., Palumbo, F., & Pescape, A. (2020). Computational intelligence intrusion detection techniques in mobile cloud computing environments: Review, taxonomy, and open research issues. *Journal of Information Security and Applications*, 55, 102582.

19. Le, D. N., Bhatt, C. M., & Madhukar, M. (Eds.). (2019). *Security Designs for the Cloud, IoT, and Social Networking*. John Wiley & Sons.

20. Cuervo, E., Balasubramanian, A., Cho, D. K., Wolman, A., Saroiu, S., Chandra, R., & Bahl, P. (2010, June). Maui: making smartphones last longer with code offload. In *Proceedings of the 8th international conference on Mobile systems, applications, and services* (pp. 49-62).

21. Zhao, X., & Okamoto, T. (2008, July). A device-independent system architecture for adaptive mobile learning. In 2008 Eighth IEEE International Conference on Advanced Learning Technologies (pp. 23-25). IEEE.

22. Yusoff, Z., & Dahlan, H. M. (2013, November). Mobile based learning: An integrated framework to support learning engagement through Augmented Reality environment. In *2013 International Conference on Research and Innovation in Information Systems (ICRIIS)* (pp. 251-256). IEEE.

23. Shail, M. S. (2019). Using micro-learning on mobile applications to increase knowledge retention and work performance: a review of literature. *Cureus*, 11(8).

24. Mitra, S., & Gupta, S. (2020). Mobile learning under personal cloud with a virtualization framework for outcome based education. Education and Information Technologies, 25(3), 2129-2156.

25. Al-Sheikh, M. A., & Ameen, I. A. (2020, July). Design of mobile healthcare monitoring system using IoT technology and cloud computing. In *IOP Conference Series: Materials Science and Engineering* (Vol. 881, No. 1, p. 012113). IOP Publishing.

26. Li, N. S., Chen, Y. T., Hsu, Y. P., Pang, H. H., Huang, C. Y., Shiue, Y. L., ... & Yang, H. W. (2020). Mobile healthcare system based on the combination of a lateral flow pad and smartphone for rapid detection of uric acid in whole blood. *Biosensors and Bioelectronics*, 164, 112309.

27. Varadan, V. K. (2021, March). Wearable and mobile healthcare nanosystems and their applications in medicine. In Nano-, Bio-, Info-Tech Sensors and Wearable Systems (Vol. 11590, p. 1159003). *International Society for Optics and Photonics*.

28. Aceto, G., Persico, V., & Pescapé, A. (2020). Industry 4.0 and health: Internet of things, big data, and cloud computing for healthcare 4.0. *Journal of Industrial Information Integration*, 18, 100129.

29. Massaro, A., Maritati, V., Savino, N., Galiano, A., Convertini, D., De Fonte, E., & Di Muro, M. (2018). A Study of a health resources management platform integrating neural networks and DSS telemedicine for homecare assistance. *Information*, 9(7), 176.

30. Haux, R. (2006). Health information systems–past, present, future. International journal of medical informatics, 75(3-4), 268-281.

31. Soroya, S. H., Farooq, A., Mahmood, K., Isoaho, J., & Zara, S. E. (2021). From information seeking to information avoidance: Understanding the health information behavior during a global health crisis. *Information Processing & Management*, 58(2), 102440.

32. Kurdi, H., Alshayban, B., Altoaimy, L., & Alsalamah, S. (2018). TrustyFeer: A subjective logic trust model for smart city peer-to-peer federated clouds. *Wireless Communications and Mobile Computing*, 2018.

33. Dinh, H. T., Lee, C., Niyato, D., & Wang, P. (2013). A survey of mobile cloud computing: architecture, applications, and approaches. *Wireless communications and mobile computing*, 13(18), 1587-1611.

34. Liu, Y., & Li, H. (2011). Exploring the impact of use context on mobile hedonic services adoption: An empirical study on mobile gaming in China. *Computers in Human Behavior*, 27(2), 890-898.

35. Cuervo, E., Balasubramanian, A., Cho, D. K., Wolman, A., Saroiu, S., Chandra, R., & Bahl, P. (2010, June). Maui: making smartphones last longer with code offload. In *Proceedings of the 8th international Conference on Mobile Systems, Applications, and Services* (pp. 49-62).

36. Prasad, M. R., Gyani, J., & Murti, P. R. K. (2012). Mobile cloud computing: Implications and challenges. *Journal of Information Engineering and Applications*, 2(7), 7-15.

37. Nikou, S., & Bouwman, H. (2014). Ubiquitous use of mobile social network services. *Telematics and Informatics*, 31(3), 422-433.

38. Baabdullah, A. M. (2020). Factors influencing adoption of mobile social network games (M-SNGs): The role of awareness. *Information Systems Frontiers*, 22(2), 411-427.

39. Zhang, Y., & van der Schaar, M. (2012). Peer-to-peer multimedia sharing based on social norms. *Signal Processing: Image Communication*, 27(5), 383-400.

40. Gawande, A., Clark, J., Coomes, D., & Wang, L. (2019, September). Decentralized and secure multimedia sharing application over named data networking. In *Proceedings of the 6th ACM Conference on Information-Centric Networking* (pp. 19-29).

15

BIG DATA IN CLOUD COMPUTING

PRASANT KUMAR PATTNAIK[1], DAC-NHUONG LE[2], SOUVIK PAL[3]

[1] KIIT, Deemed to be University, India
[2] Haiphong University, Haiphong, Vietnam
[3] Sister Nivedita University, Kolkata, India
 Email: patnaikprasant@gmail.com, nhuongld@dhhp.edu.vn, souvikpal22@gmail.com

Abstract
Current advancements in technology are increasingly digitizing our lives which has led to a rapid growth of data. Such multidimensional datasets are precious due to the potential of unearthing new knowledge and developing decision-making insights from them. Analyzing this huge amount of data from multiple sources can help organizations to plan for the future and anticipate changing market trends and customer requirements. While the Hadoop framework is a popular platform for processing larger datasets, there are a number of other computing infrastructures available for use in various application domains. The primary focus of the study presented in this chapter is how to classify major big data resource management systems in the context of cloud computing environment. We identify some key features which characterize big data frameworks as well as their associated challenges and issues. We use various evaluation metrics from different aspects to identify usage scenarios of these platforms. The study came up with some interesting findings which are in contradiction to the available literature on the internet.
Keywords: Big Data, cloud computing

15.1   Introduction to Big Data

Gartner defines big data as high-volume, high-velocity and/or high-variety information assets that demand cost-effective, innovative forms of information processing that enable enhanced insight, decision-making, and process automation. Big data is large sets of data (structured or unstructured) which are processed to gather information from it. There is a huge amount of data generated by companies every second which needs to be processed. So, big data will gather, store, and organize the data which will be further analyzed by data analysts [1, 2]. In other words, we say that Big Data is a large quantity of data, which can be processed for valuable information.

Building on Gartner's definition, the concept of big data and what it encompasses can be better understood with four Vs:

- *Volume*: The amount of data accumulated by private companies, public agencies, and other organizations on a daily basis is extremely large. This makes volume the defining characteristic for big data.

- *Velocity*: It's a given that data can and will pile up really fast. But what matters is the speed with which you can process and examine this data so that it becomes useful information.

- *Variety*: The types of data that get collected can be very diverse. Structured data contained in databases, and unstructured data such as tweets, emails, images, videos, and more, need to be consumed and processed all the same.

- *Veracity*: Because of its scale and diversity, big data can contain a lot of noise. Veracity thus refers to the certainty of the data and how your big data tools and analysis strategies can separate the poor quality data from those that really matter to your business.

Technology leaders also name a fifth V — value. But this one isn't inherent within the huge amounts of raw data. Instead, the true value of big data can only be realized when the right information is captured and analyzed to gain actionable insights [3, 4]. Big Data is characterized by 6 Vs as described in the following Figure 15.1.

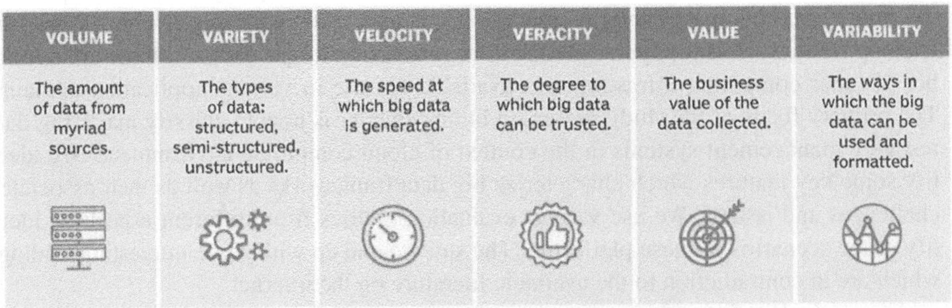

VOLUME	VARIETY	VELOCITY	VERACITY	VALUE	VARIABILITY
The amount of data from myriad sources.	The types of data: structured, semi-structured, unstructured.	The speed at which big data is generated.	The degree to which big data can be trusted.	The business value of the data collected.	The ways in which the big data can be used and formatted.

Figure 15.1: The six Vs of big data.

To get a better idea of how big data works, let's review some statistics [5]:

- Over 1 billion Google searches are made and 294 billion emails are sent everyday.

▪ Every minute, 65,972 Instagram photos are posted, 448,800 tweets are composed, and 500 hours worth of YouTube videos are uploaded.

▪ By 2020, the number of smartphone users could reach 6.1 billion. And taking the Internet of Things (IoT) into account, there could be 26 billion connected devices by then.

▪ The New York Stock Exchange generates about one terabyte of new trade data per day.

▪ Social Media: Statistics show that 500+ terabytes of new data get ingested into the databases of social media site Facebook every day. This data is mainly generated by photo and video uploads, message exchanges, comments, etc.

▪ A single jet engine can generate 10+ terabytes of data in 30 minutes of flight time. With many thousand flights per day, generation of data reaches up to many petabytes.

There are three forms of Big Data:

▪ *Structured*: Any data that can be stored, accessed and processed in the form of fixed format is termed "structured" data. Over a period of time, talent in computer science has achieved greater success in developing techniques for working with such kinds of data (where the format is well known in advance) and also deriving value out of it. However, nowadays, we can foresee instances where the size of such data grows to a huge extent, with typical sizes being in the rage of multiple zettabytes.

▪ *Unstructured*: This is any data of unknown form or structure classified as unstructured data. In addition to the size being huge, unstructured data poses multiple challenges in terms of its processing to derive value from it. A typical example of unstructured data is a heterogeneous data source containing a combination of simple text files, images, videos, etc. Today organizations have a wealth of data available to them but, unfortunately, they don't know how to derive value from it since this data is in its raw form or unstructured format [6].

▪ *Semi-structured*: Semi-structured data can contain both forms of data. We can see semi-structured data as being structured in form but it is actually not defined as such, e.g., a table definition in relational DBMS. An example of semi-structured data is the data represented in an XML file.

15.2   Big Data vs. Cloud Computing

There are eight major differences between big data and cloud computing [7], as given below and shown in Figure 15.2.

		Cloud Computing	Big Data
1	Definition	Provides resources (storage, computing, databases, monitoring tools, etc.) on demand	Provides a way to handle huge volumes of data and generate insights
2	Reference	It refers to internet services from SaaS, PaaS to IaaS	It refers to data, which can be structured, semi-structured, or unstructured.
3	How they are used	It uses wide range of network of cloud servers over the internet to analyze data and information.	It could be deployed either on-premise or cloud to discover undiscovered patterns and generate actionable insights
4	Formats	Cloud Computing is new paradigm to computing resources	It consists of all kind of data, which are in many different formats.
5	Use for	Use to store data and information on remote servers.	It is used to describe huge volume of data and information

Figure 15.2: Big data vs. cloud computing

- *Concept*: In cloud computing, we can store and retrieve the data from anywhere at any time. Whereas, big data is the large set of data which will be processed to extract the necessary information.

- *Characteristics*: Cloud computing provides the service over the internet, such as Software as a Service (SaaS), Platform as a Service (PaaS), and Infrastructure as a Service (IaaS). Whereas, there are some important characteristics of big data that can lead to strategic business moves, which are velocity, variety, and volume.

- *Accessibility*: Cloud computing provides universal access to the services. Whereas, big data solves technical problems and provides better results.

- *When to use*: A customer can shift to cloud computing when they need rapid deployment and scaling of the applications. The application deals with highly sensitive data and requires strict compliance with how things should be kept on cloud. Whereas, we can use big data for traditional methods and here frameworks are ineffective. Big data is not a replacement for relational database system, but rather solves specific problems related to large data sets, and most of the large data sets do not deal with small data.

- *Cost*: Cloud computing is economical as it has a low maintenance cost centralized platform, no upfront cost, and disaster safe implementation. Whereas, big data is highly scalable, has a robust ecosystem, and is cost-effective.

- *Job roles and responsibility*: The user of the cloud is the developer or office worker in an organization. Whereas, big data analysts in big data are responsible for analyzing the date of filing interesting sites and possible future trends.

- *Types and trends*: There are four types of cloud computing: public cloud, private cloud, hybrid cloud, and community cloud. Whereas, some important trends in big data technology are Hadoop, MapReduce, and HDFS.

- *Vendors*: Some of the vendors and solution providers of cloud computing are: Google, Amazon Web Service Microsoft, Dell, Apple, IBM. Whereas, some of the vendors and solution providers of big data are: Cloudera, Hortonworks, Apache, MapR.

In addition to the above comparison of big data and cloud computing, in order to better understand their differences some additional points regarding their features are given below.

The main focus of cloud computing is to provide computer resources and services with the help of network connection. While big data is about solving problems when a huge amount of data are generated and processed; in cloud computing, the data is stored in the servers maintained by different service providers. We can access this data with the help of the internet. However, big data breaks down a large amount of data and distributes it across different computer systems, where the data will be analyzed and processed [8].

The big data solutions can be deployed with the help of PaaS or SaaS; in SaaS various components or applications running on Hadoop are accessible. Hadoop is provided to customers in PaaS.

Big data utilizes the data generated before it is bought by an organization and provides insights which can benefit the business in the future. On the other hand, cloud computing is flexible and provides quick service with respect to it deployments, so that the streamlined operations of an organization go successfully.

15.3   Big Data and the Cloud

Big data projects typically get started with data storage and application of basic analytics modules. However, as you discover ways to extract data at a much larger scale, you will need to find better methods to process and analyze this data, which will likely require infrastructure upgrades [9].

You may add more capacity to your in-house data warehouse or power up more servers to cater to the rapidly increasing analytics requirements. But even with the boost of your on-premise systems, your infrastructure eventually may not be able to keep up.

This is where the cloud comes in, or more fittingly, when your big data goes to the cloud.

The benefits of moving to the cloud are well documented. But these benefits take on a bigger role when we talk of big data analytics.

Big data involves manipulating petabytes (and perhaps soon, exabytes and zettabytes) of data, and the cloud's scalable environment makes it possible to deploy data-intensive applications that power business analytics. The cloud also simplifies connectivity and collaboration within an organization, which gives more employees access to relevant analytics and streamlines data sharing.

While it's easy for IT leaders to recognize the advantages of putting big data in the cloud, it may not be as simple to get C-suite executives and other primary stakeholders onboard. But there's a business case to be made for the big data + cloud pairing because it gives executives a better view of the business and boosts data-driven decision making.

For instance, optimization of the supply chain and efficient tracking of defects – both principal concerns of a COO of a physical product company – is made easier with material data on hand. Data is also key for the CMO looking to increase customer engagement and loyalty, and for the CFO seeking new opportunities for cost reduction, revenue growth, and strategic investments [10].

And all of these insights can be easily presented to the CEO to inform fast, strategic decision making.

Whatever perspective you may have, big data complemented with an agile cloud platform can affect significant change in the way your organization does business and achieves your objectives.

Many enterprises are already making the move. A Forrester Research survey in 2017 revealed that big data solutions via cloud subscriptions will increase about 7.5 times faster than on-premise options.

15.4   Cloud Computing to Support Big Data

Cloud computing combines distributed computing resources into one virtual environment, providing big data analytics and solutions during the life cycles of big data. Three main categories of cloud computing services are: (1) Infrastructure as a Service (IaaS), (2) Software as a Service (SaaS), and (3) Platform as a Service (PaaS). Together with Data as a Service (DaaS), Model as a Service (MaaS) and Workflow as a Service (WaaS), cloud computing offers big data researchers the opportunity of anything as a service [11].

15.4.1   Cloud Storage for Big Data Storage

The characteristics of big data in high volume lead to challenges for data storage. Cloud computing's potential for unlimited storage support helps solve the volume challenge of big data, as the cloud provides virtually customizable storage with elastically expandable and reducible size. An alternative solution is Data Storage as a Service (DSaaS) enabled by block storage, which is the capability of adding external storages as "blocks." With block storage, it is possible to enlarge the storage size without physically loading hard drives. Virtually unlimited scalable storage offered by cloud computing grants users the capability of dynamic adjustment to satisfy the storage requirements of data with high volume and velocity. The modularized virtual resource offers effortless data sharing within production environments by allowing for an external data block to be detached and remounted from one machine to another. External data storage can be automatically backed up to prevent users from losing data, and backups that are securely saved at the back-end server can be easily transferred and restored. In addition, information security is guaranteed because the physical location cannot be obtained from the disk drive [12].

15.4.2   Cloud Computing for Big Data Processing

Processing large volumes of data requires dedicated computing resources, e.g., faster CPUs and networks and larger disks and RAMs. Cloud computing provides on-demand resources and delivers configurable resources, including mountable external storage spaces, computing resources (CPU, RAM), and network services. Traditionally, a computer uses approximately two-thirds of the power of a busy computer, and cloud computing has the potential to provide on-demand computing resources. Isolated virtual structures have been created for big data systems to enhance system stabilities, which can be easily managed in different file systems and replicated through backup images to provide fast configuration recovery [13]. The ability to replicate environments automates the expansion of compute nodes in virtual machine clusters, thereby efficiently utilizing resource pools to support big data analytics. With the foundational support of storage for big data, data processing inherits the advantages of fast data acquisition and relocation.

Although cloud computing could serve as an excellent infrastructure option for big data processing, several aspects should be considered to minimize the bottleneck effect for the general processing speed, such as the choice of cloud volume type according to I/O demand and cloud bandwidth selection according to application requirements.

15.4.3 Cloud Computing for Big Data Analytics

Popular big data analytical platforms such as Apache Hadoop are traditionally installed on physical machine clusters, resulting in a waste of computing resources due to hardware redundancy (CPU and RAM). With the virtual clusters provided by cloud computing through virtualization technology, distributed analytical platforms can be migrated to the virtual clusters from physical machine clusters, optimizing the usage of computing resources in an efficient manner [14].

With the aid of autoscaling and load balancing, deploying on-demand and scalable big data analytical platforms could easily provide resilient analytical frameworks and minimize waste of computing resources. Autoscaling supports parallel algorithms on distributed systems and architectures for scalability. It allows for the expanded resources to function when the algorithms or programs are enabled with parallel computing capability. Without it, public cloud providers such as AWS could not offer automatic scalability. The load balancer distributes workloads among virtual clusters and triggers autoscaling functions when analytics require higher computing configurations. The virtual system as a whole could dynamically fit higher computing requirements by launching more virtual duplications as needed. The load balancer acts as a virtual network traffic distributor and can be optimized to better allocate overall resources.

15.4.4 Cloud Computing for Big Data Sharing and Remote Collaboration

Traditional deployment of big data systems requires complicated settings and efforts to share data assets. It lacks access control and often leads to data security and data privacy issues. Cloud computing enhances the sharing of information by applying modern analytical tools and managing controlled access and security. Virtualization enables different parties to share data assets to achieve various goals and objectives under a centralized management system. With the support of cloud computing, it is possible to flexibly share data and remotely collaborate, which involve interdisciplinary collaborations and advanced workflows. Through data sharing, computational resource sharing, and production environment sharing, cloud computing can potentially be used to build a perceptual environment to support various businesses and applications [15]; unfortunately, workflow sharing remains challenging due to domain boundaries [16].

15.5 Opportunities and Challenges

Bringing big data to the cloud presents huge opportunities, but there are some challenges that need to be overcome. Let's go over the advantages first.

15.5.1 Pros of Putting Big Data in the Cloud

- *Requires zero CAPEX*: The cloud has fundamentally changed IT spending as organizations know it—and in a good way. As we mentioned earlier, big data projects require immense infrastructure resources, which traditionally would also mean high on-premise capital expenditure (CAPEX) investments [17]. But the cloud's infrastructure-as-a-service models have allowed companies to practically eliminate its biggest CAPEX expenses by shifting these into the operating expenditure (OPEX) column. So when you need to set up your database servers or data warehouses, you won't need to make massive upfront investments. This has been one of the most compelling benefits that has convinced businesses to migrate to the cloud.

- *Enables faster scalability*: Large volumes of both structured and unstructured data require increased processing power, storage, and more. The cloud provides not only readily-available infrastructure, but also the ability to scale this infrastructure really quickly so you can manage large spikes in traffic or usage.

- *Lowers the cost of analytics*: Mining big data in the cloud has made the analytics process less costly. In addition to the reduction of on-premise infrastructure, you can also save on costs related to system maintenance and upgrades, energy consumption, facility management, and more. You can also worry less about the technical aspects of processing big data and focus more on creating insights. Even better, the cloud's pay-as-you-go model is more cost-efficient, with little waste of resources.

- *Encourages an agile and innovative culture*: The ability to innovate is a mindset that should be cultivated within any enterprise. This type of culture can lead to creative ways of using big data to gain a competitive advantage, and the cloud makes it easier to spin up the necessary infrastructure to do so. When your team focuses on analyzing data instead of managing servers and databases, you can more easily and quickly unearth insights that can help you augment product lines, boost operational efficiency, improve customer service, and more.

- *Enables better business continuity and disaster recovery*: In cases of cyber attacks, power outages or equipment failure, traditional data recovery strategies will no longer do the trick. The task of replicating a data center, with duplicate storage, servers, networking equipment, and other infrastructure in preparation for a disaster is tedious, difficult, and expensive.

In addition, legacy systems often take a very long time to back up and restore. This is especially true in the era of big data, when data stores are so immense and expansive.

Having the data stored in cloud infrastructure will allow your organization to recover from disasters faster, thus ensuring continued access to information and vital big data insights.

15.5.2   Potential Challenges of Big Data in the Cloud

Migrating big data to the cloud presents various hurdles. Overcoming these require a concerted effort from IT leaders, C-suite executives, and other business stakeholders [18-20]. Here are some of the major challenges of big data cloud implementations:

- *Less control over security*: These large datasets often contain sensitive information such as individuals' addresses, credit card details, social security numbers, and other personal information. Ensuring that this data is kept protected is of paramount importance. Data breaches could mean serious penalties under various regulations and a tarnished company brand, which can lead to lost customers and revenue. While security should not be a hindrance to migrating to the cloud, you will have less direct control over your data, which can be a big organizational change and may cause some discomfort. To deal with this, be sure to carefully evaluate the security protocols and understand the shared responsibility model of your cloud service provider so you know what your roles and obligations are.

- *Less control over compliance*: Compliance is another concern that you'll have to think about when moving data to the cloud. Cloud service providers maintain a certain level of compliance with various regulations such as HIPAA, PCI, and many more. But similar to security, you no longer have full control over your data's compliance requirements.

15.6   Summary

For business and engineering, Big Data is used in the decision-making process to uncover useful insights concealed in the data. Cloud computing has aided the evolution of big data by providing computational, networking, and storage capacity while also posing processing issues. Innovation and competitiveness fueled by advances in cloud computing have resulted in the discovery of hidden information from data in the big data era. In this chapter, we've discussed big data applications in cloud computing, as well as the issues of storing, transforming, and processing data, as well as some good design concepts that could lead to more study.

EXERCISES

1. How is Hadoop related to big data?

2. Define HDFS and YARN, and talk about their respective components.

3. What is meant by commodity hardware?

4. Define and describe the term FSCK.

5. What is the purpose of the JPS command in Hadoop?

6. Why do we need Hadoop for big data analytics?

7. Explain the different features of Hadoop.

8. What is meant by indexing in HDFS?

9. What are edge nodes in Hadoop?

10. What are some of the data management tools used with edge nodes in Hadoop?

11. Explain the core methods of a reducer.

12. Discuss the different tombstone markers used for deletion purposes in HBase.

13. How can big data add value to businesses?

14. How do you deploy a big data solution?

15. How is NFS different from HDFS?

16. Explain "overfitting."

17. Name the three modes in which you can run Hadoop.

18. What is feature selection?

19. Name some outlier detection techniques.

20. Explain rack awareness in Hadoop.

21. Name the configuration parameters of a MapReduce framework.

22. What is a distributed cache? What are its benefits?

23. What is SequenceFile in Hadoop?

24. Name the common input formats in Hadoop.

25. What is the need for data locality in Hadoop?

26. What are the steps to achieve security in Hadoop?

27. How can you handle missing values in big data?

28. How is data analytics related to big data?

29. What kind of statistics have been used in big data?

30. What is the difference between horizontal and vertical partitioning?

References

1. Abolfazli, S., Sanaei, Z., Ahmed, E., Gani, A., & Buyya, R. (2013). Cloud-based augmentation for mobile devices: motivation, taxonomies, and open challenges. *IEEE Communications Surveys & Tutorials*, 16(1), 337-368.

2. Abouzeid, A., Bajda-Pawlikowski, K., Abadi, D., Silberschatz, A., & Rasin, A. (2009). HadoopDB: an architectural hybrid of MapReduce and DBMS technologies for analytical workloads. *Proceedings of the VLDB Endowment*, 2(1), 922-933.

3. Agrawal, D., Bernstein, P., Bertino, E., Davidson, S., Dayal, U., Franklin, M., ... & Widom, J. (2011). *Challenges and Opportunities with Big Data* 2011-1.

4. Agrawal, D., Das, S., & El Abbadi, A. (2011, March). Big data and cloud computing: current state and future opportunities. In *Proceedings of the 14th International Conference on Extending Database Technology* (pp. 530-533).

5. Assunção, M. D., Calheiros, R. N., Bianchi, S., Netto, M. A., & Buyya, R. (2015). Big Data computing and clouds: Trends and future directions. *Journal of Parallel and Distributed Computing*, 79, 3-15.

6. Aydin, G., Hallac, I. R., & Karakus, B. (2015). Architecture and implementation of a scalable sensor data storage and analysis system using cloud computing and big data technologies. *Journal of Sensors*, 2015. doi:10.1155/2015/834217.

7. Banditwattanawong, T., Masdisornchote, M., & Uthayopas, P. (2014, January). Economical and efficient big data sharing with i-Cloud. In *2014 International Conference on Big Data and Smart Computing (BIGCOMP)* (pp. 105-110). IEEE.

8. Chen, C. P., & Zhang, C. Y. (2014). Data-intensive applications, challenges, techniques and technologies: A survey on Big Data. *Information Sciences*, 275, 314-347.

9. Cuzzocrea, A., Fortino, G., & Rana, O. (2013, May). Managing data and processes in cloud-enabled large-scale sensor networks: State-of-the-art and future research directions. In *2013 13th IEEE/ACM International Symposium on Cluster, Cloud, and Grid Computing* (pp. 583-588). IEEE.

10. Dobre, C., & Xhafa, F. (2014). Parallel programming paradigms and frameworks in big data era. *International Journal of Parallel Programming*, 42(5), 710-738.

11. Ding, J. M., Jiang, Y., Wang, Q. X., Liu, Y. L., & Li, M. J. (2013). A data localization algorithm for distributing column storage system of big data. In *Advanced Materials Research* (Vol. 756, pp. 3089-3093). Trans Tech Publications Ltd.

12. Gui, Z., Yang, C., Xia, J., Huang, Q., Liu, K., Li, Z., ... & Jin, B. (2014). A service brokering and recommendation mechanism for better selecting cloud services. *PloS One*, 9(8), e105297.

13. Han, Q., Liang, S., & Zhang, H. (2015). Mobile cloud sensing, big data, and 5G networks make an intelligent and smart world. *IEEE Network*, 29(2), 40-45.

14. Joo, H., Hong, B., & Kim, S. (2012). Smart-contents visualization of publishing big data using NFC technology. In *Computer Applications for Graphics, Grid Computing, and Industrial Environment* (pp. 118-123). Springer, Berlin, Heidelberg.

15. Li, R., Asaeda, H., Li, J., & Fu, X. (2017). A distributed authentication and authorization scheme for in-network big data sharing. *Digital Communications and Networks*, 3(4), 226-235.

16. Yang, J., Wen, J., Jiang, B., & Wang, H. (2020). Blockchain-based sharing and tamper-proof framework of big data networking. *IEEE Network*, 34(4), 62-67.

17. Shi, X. (2021). Influence of Human Capital on Consumer Expenditure Under Big Data. In *2020 International Conference on Data Processing Techniques and Applications for Cyber-Physical Systems* (pp. 577-582). Springer, Singapore.

18. Khan, S., Shakil, K. A., & Alam, M. (2017). Big data computing using cloud-based technologies, challenges and future perspectives. *arXiv preprint arXiv:1712.05233*.

19. Wang, X., Yu, D., Zhang, F., & Li, X. (2021, June). Research on the Control System and Risk Management Based on Internet Big Data and Cloud Computing. In *Journal of Physics: Conference Series* (Vol. 1952, No. 4, p. 042086). IOP Publishing.

20. Ageed, Z. S., Zeebaree, S. R., Sadeeq, M. M., Kak, S. F., Yahia, H. S., Mahmood, M. R., & Ibrahim, I. M. (2021). Comprehensive survey of big data mining approaches in cloud systems. *Qubahan Academic Journal*, 1(2), 29-38.

PART IV

Cloud Computing Simulator Tools

16

CLOUDSIM: A SIMULATOR FOR CLOUD COMPUTING ENVIRONMENT

Dac-Nhuong Le[1], Souvik Pal[2], Prasant Kumar Pattnaik[3]

[1] Haiphong University, Haiphong, Vietnam
[2] Sister Nivedita University, Kolkata, India
[3] KIIT, Deemed to be University, India
Email: nhuongld@dhhp.edu.vn, souvikpal22@gmail.com, patnaikprasant@gmail.com

Abstract

Source:

- CloudSim is developed in the CLOUDS Laboratory, at the Computer Science and Software Engineering Department of the University of Melbourne.

- CloudSim Toolkit 3.0 was released in Jan 13, 2012.

Software License:

- The CloudSim Toolkit software is released as open source under Lesser General Public License (LGPL) license.

- Copyright: The CLOUDS Lab, The University of Melbourne, 2009 to date.

Downloaded Information:

- http://www.cloudbus.org/cloudsim

- https://code.google.com/p/cloudsim

Keywords: CloudSim, simulator

16.1 Introduction

In recent days, cloud computing emerged as the leading technology for delivering reliable, secure, fault-tolerant, sustainable, and scalable computational services, which are presented as software, infrastructure, or platform as services (SaaS, IaaS, PaaS). User applications have different composition, configuration, and deployment requirements. This chapter is concerned with the cloud-based simulator CloudSim; a new generalized and extensible simulation framework that enables seamless modeling, simulation, and experimentation of emerging cloud computing infrastructures and management services.

A suitable alternative is the utilization of simulation tools, which open the possibility of evaluating the hypothesis prior to software development in an environment where one can reproduce tests. Specifically in the case of cloud computing, where access to the infrastructure incurs payments in real currency, simulation-based approaches offer significant benefits, as it allows cloud customers to test their services in repeatable and controllable environment free of cost, and to tune the performance bottlenecks before deploying on real clouds. At the provider side, simulation environments allow evaluation of different kinds of resource leasing scenarios under varying load and pricing distributions. Such studies could aid the providers in optimizing the resource access cost with a focus on improving profits. In the absence of such simulation platforms, Cloud customers and providers have to rely either on theoretical and imprecise evaluations, or on trial-and-error approaches that lead to inefficient service performance and revenue generation.

The primary objective of this simulator is to provide a generalized and extensible simulation framework that enables seamless modeling, simulation, and experimentation of emerging cloud computing infrastructures and application services. By using CloudSim, researchers and industry-based developers can focus on specific system design issues that they want to investigate, without being concerned about the low-level details related to cloud-based infrastructures and services.

16.2 Main Features

The main features of CloudSim simulator [1] are as follows:

- Support for modeling and simulation of large-scale cloud computing data centers;

- Support for modeling and simulation of virtualized server hosts, with customizable policies for provisioning host resources to virtual machines;

- Support for modeling and simulation of energy-aware computational resources;

- Support for modeling and simulation of data center network topologies and message-passing applications;

- Support for modeling and simulation of federated clouds;

- Support for dynamic insertion of simulation elements, stop and resume of simulation;

- Support for user-defined policies for allocation of hosts to virtual machines and policies for allocation of host resources to virtual machines;

- Support for modeling and instantiation of large-scale cloud computing infrastructure, including data centers on a single physical computing node and Java virtual machine;

- A self-contained platform for modeling data centers, service brokers, scheduling, and allocations policies;

- Availability of virtualization engine, which aids in creation and management of multiple, independent, and co-hosted virtualized services on a data center node; and

- Flexibility to switch between space-shared and time-shared allocation of processing cores to virtualized services.

16.3 CloudSim Architecture

The multi-layered design of the CloudSim software framework and its architectural components are shown in Figure 16.1.

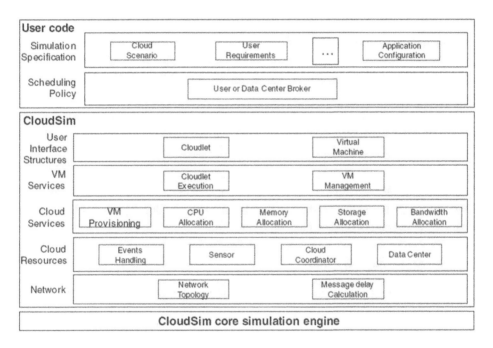

Figure 16.1: Layered architecture of CloudSim simulator.

Initial releases of CloudSim used SimJava as the discrete event simulation engine that supports several core functionalities, such as queuing and processing of events, creation of cloud system entities (services, host, data center, broker, VMs), communication between components, and management of the simulation clock. However, in the current release, the SimJava layer has been removed in order to allow some advanced operations that are not supported by it [1, 2].

The CloudSim simulation layer provides support for modeling and simulation of virtualized cloud-based data center environments, including dedicated management interfaces for VMs, memory, storage, and bandwidth. The fundamental issues, such as provisioning of hosts to VMs, managing application execution, and monitoring dynamic system state, are handled by this layer. A cloud provider, who wants to study the efficiency of different policies in allocating its hosts to VMs (VM provisioning), would need to implement his strategies at this layer. Such implementation can be done by programmatically extending the core VM provisioning functionality. There is a clear distinction at this layer related to provisioning of hosts to VMs. A cloud host can be concurrently allocated to a set of VMs that execute applications based on SaaS provider's defined QoS levels. This layer also exposes the functionalities that a cloud application developer can extend to perform complex workload profiling and application performance study. The topmost layer in the CloudSim stack is the User Code that exposes basic entities for hosts (number of machines, their specification, and so on), applications (number of tasks and their requirements), VMs, number of users and their application types, and broker scheduling policies. By extending the basic entities given at this layer, a cloud application developer can perform the following activities:

(i) Generate a mix of workload request distributions, application configurations;

(ii) Model cloud availability scenarios and perform robust tests based on the custom configurations; and

(iii) Implement custom application provisioning techniques for clouds and their federation.

As cloud computing is still an emerging paradigm for distributed computing, there is a lack of defined standards, tools, and methods that can efficiently tackle the infrastructure and application-level complexities. Hence, in the near future there will be a number of research efforts both in academia and industry toward defining core algorithms, policies, and application benchmarking based on execution contexts. By extending the basic functionalities already exposed to CloudSim, researchers will be able to perform tests based on specific scenarios and configurations, thereby allowing the development of best practices in all the critical aspects related to cloud computing.

16.3.1 Modeling the Cloud

The infrastructure-level services (IaaS) related to the clouds can be simulated by extending the data center entity of CloudSim. The data center entity manages a number of host entities. The hosts are assigned to one or more VMs based on a VM allocation policy that should be defined by the cloud service provider. Here, the VM policy stands for the operations control policies related to VM life cycle such as provisioning of a host to a VM, VM creation, VM destruction, and VM migration. Similarly, one or more application service can be provisioned within a single VM instance, referred to as application provisioning in the context of cloud computing. In the context of CloudSim, an entity is an instance of a component. A CloudSim component can be a class (abstract or complete) or set of classes that represent one CloudSim model (data center, host) [3, 4].

A data center can manage several hosts that in turn manage VMs during their life cycles. Host is a CloudSim component that represents a physical computing server in a cloud: it is assigned a pre-configured processing capability (expressed in millions of instructions per second—MIPS), memory, storage, and a provisioning policy for allocating processing cores to VMs. The host component implements interfaces that support modeling and simulation of both single-core and multi-core nodes.

The process of VM allocation (provisioning) creates VM instances on hosts that match the critical characteristics (storage, memory), configurations (software environment), and requirements (availability zone) of the SaaS provider. CloudSim supports the development of custom application service models that can be deployed within a VM instance and its users are required to extend the core cloudlet object for implementing their application services. Furthermore, CloudSim does not enforce any limitation on the service models or provisioning techniques that developers want to implement and perform tests with. Once an application service is defined and modeled, it is assigned to one or more pre-instantiated VMs through a service-specific allocation policy. Allocation of application-specific VMs to hosts in a cloud-based data center is the responsibility of a VM allocation controller component (called VmAllocationPolicy). This component exposes a number of custom methods for researchers and developers who aid in the implementation of new policies based on optimization goals (user centric, system centric, or both). By default, VmAllocationPolicy implements a straightforward policy that allocates VMs to the host on a first-come first-served (FCFS) basis. Hardware requirements, such as the number of processing cores, memory, and storage, form the basis for such provisioning. Other policies, including the ones likely to be expressed by cloud providers, can also be easily simulated and modeled in CloudSim. However, policies used by public cloud providers (Amazon EC2, Microsoft Azure) are not publicly available, and thus a pre-implemented version of these algorithms is not provided with CloudSim.

For each host component, the allocation of processing cores to VMs is done based on a host allocation policy. This policy takes into account several hardware characteristics, such as number of CPU cores, CPU share, and amount of memory (physical and secondary), that are allocated to a given VM instance. Hence, CloudSim supports simulation scenarios that assign specific CPU cores to specific VMs (a space-shared policy), dynamically distribute the capacity of a core among VMs (time-shared policy), or assign cores to VMs on demand.

Each host component also instantiates a VM scheduler component, which can either implement the space-shared or the time-shared policy for allocating cores to VMs. Cloud system/application developers and researchers can further extend the VM scheduler component for experimenting with custom allocation policies. Fundamental software and hardware configuration parameters related to VMs are defined in the VM class. Currently, it supports modeling of several VM configurations offered by cloud providers such as the Amazon EC2.

16.3.2 Modeling the VM Allocation

One of the key aspects that make a Cloud computing infrastructure different from a Grid computing infrastructure is the massive deployment of virtualization tools and technologies. Hence, compared with grids, clouds contain an extra layer (the virtualization layer) that acts as an execution, management, and hosting environment for application services. Hence, traditional application provisioning models that assign individual application elements to computing nodes do not accurately represent the computational abstraction, which is commonly associated with cloud resources. For example, consider a cloud host that has a single processing core. There is a requirement of concurrently instantiating two VMs on that host. Although in practice VMs are contextually (physical and secondary memory space) isolated, they still need to share the processing cores and system bus. Hence, the amount of hardware resources available to each VM is constrained by the total processing power and system bandwidth available within the host. This critical factor must be considered during the VM provisioning process, to avoid creation of a VM that demands more processing power than is available within the host. In order to allow simulation of different provisioning policies under varying levels of performance isolation, CloudSim supports VM provisioning at two levels: first, at the host level and second, at the VM level. At the host level, it is possible to specify how much of the overall processing power of each core will be assigned to each VM. At the VM level, the VM assigns a fixed amount of the available processing power to the individual application services (task units) that are hosted within its execution engine [5, 6].

16.3.3 Modeling the Cloud Market

The market is a crucial component of the cloud computing ecosystem; it is necessary for regulating cloud resource trading and online negotiations in a public cloud computing model, where services are offered in a pay-as-you-go model. Hence, research studies that can accurately evaluate the cost-to-benefit ratio of emerging cloud computing platforms are required. Furthermore, SaaS providers need transparent mechanisms to discover various cloud providers' offerings (IaaS, PaaS, SaaS, and their associated costs). Thus, modeling of costs and economic policies are important aspects to be considered when designing a cloud simulator. The cloud market is modeled based on a multi-layered (two layers) design. The first layer contains the economics of features related to the IaaS model such as cost per unit of memory, cost per unit of storage, and cost per unit of used bandwidth. Cloud customers (SaaS providers) have to pay for the costs of memory and storage when they create and instantiate VMs, whereas the costs for network usage are only incurred in the event of data transfer. The second layer models the cost metrics related to SaaS model. Costs at this layer are directly applicable to the task units (application service requests) that are served by the application services. Hence, if a cloud customer provisions a VM without an application service (task unit), then they would only be charged for the physical resources (i.e., the costs of memory and storage). This behavior may be changed or extended by CloudSim users.

16.3.4 Modeling the Network Behavior

Modeling comprehensive network topologies to connect simulated cloud computing entities (hosts, storage, end-users) is an important consideration because latency messages directly affect the overall service satisfaction experience. An end-user or a SaaS provider consumer who is not satisfied with the delivered QoS is likely to switch his/her cloud provider; hence, it is a very important requirement that cloud system simulation frameworks provide facilities for modeling realistic networking topologies and models. Internetworking of cloud entities (data centers, hosts, SaaS providers, and end-users) in CloudSim is based on a conceptual networking abstraction. In this model, there are no actual entities available for simulating network entities, such as routers or switches. Instead, the network latency that a message can experience on its path from one CloudSim entity (host) to another (cloud broker) is simulated based on the information stored in the latency matrix [7, 8].

16.3.5 Modeling a Federation of Clouds

In order to federate or inter-network multiple clouds, there is a requirement for modeling a CloudCoordinator entity. This entity is responsible not only for communicating with other data centers and end-users in the simulation environment, but also for monitoring and managing the internal state of a data center entity. The information received as part of the monitoring process, that is active throughout the simulation period, is utilized for making decisions related to inter-cloud provisioning. Note that no software object offering similar functionality to the CloudCoordinator is presently offered by existing providers, such as Amazon, Azure, or Google App Engine. Hence, if a developer of a real-world Cloud system wants to federate services from multiple clouds, they will be required to develop a CloudCoordinator component. By having such an entity to manage the federation of cloud-based data centers, aspects related to communication and negotiation with foreign entities are isolated from the data center core. Therefore, by providing such an entity among its core objects, CloudSim helps cloud developers in speeding up their application service performance testing.

The two fundamental aspects that must be handled when simulating a federation of clouds are communication and monitoring. The first aspect (communication) is handled by the data center through the standard event-based messaging process. The second aspect (data center monitoring) is carried out by the CloudCoordinator. Every data center in CloudSim needs to instantiate this entry in order to make itself a part of cloud federation. The CloudCoordinator triggers the inter-cloud load adjustment process based on the state of the data center. The specific set of events that affect the adjustment are implemented via a specific sensor entity. Each sensor entity implements a particular parameter (such as under provisioning, over provisioning, and SLA violation) related to the data center. For enabling online monitoring of a data center host, a sensor that keeps track of the host status (utilization, heating) is attached with the CloudCoordinator. At every monitoring step, the CloudCoordinator queries the sensor. If a certain pre-configured threshold is achieved, the CloudCoordinator starts the communication with its peers (other CloudCoordinators in the federation) for possible load-shredding. The negotiation protocol, load-shredding policy, and compensation mechanism can be easily extended to suit a particular research study.

16.3.6 Modeling Dynamic Workloads

Software developers and third-party service providers often deploy applications that exhibit dynamic behavior in terms of workload patterns, availability, and scalability requirements. Typically, cloud computing thrives on highly varied and elastic services and infrastructure demands. Leading cloud vendors, including Amazon and Azure, expose VM containers/ templates to host a range of SaaS types and provide SaaS providers with the notion of un-limited resource pool that can be leased on the fly with requested configurations. Pertaining to the aforementioned facts, it is an important requirement that any simulation environment supports the modeling of dynamic workload patterns driven by application or SaaS models. In order to allow simulation of dynamic behaviors within CloudSim, we have made a number of extensions to the existing framework, in particular to the cloudlet entity. They have designed an additional simulation entity within CloudSim, which is referred to as the Utilization Model, that exposes methods and variables for defining the resource and VM-level requirements of a SaaS application at the instance of deployment. In the CloudSim framework, utilization model is an abstract class that must be extended for implementing a workload pattern required to model the application's resource demand. CloudSim users are required to override the method, getUtilization(), whose input type is discrete time parameter and return type is percentage of computational resource required by the Cloudlet.

Another important requirement for Cloud computing environments is to ensure that the agreed-upon SLA in terms of QoS parameters, such as availability, reliability, and throughput, are delivered to the applications. Although modern virtualization technologies can ensure performance isolation between applications running on different VMs, there still exists plenty of scope for developing methodologies at the VM provisioning level that can further improve resource utilization. Lack of intelligent methodologies for VM provisioning raises a risk that all VMs deployed on a single host may not get the adequate amount of processor share that is essential for fulfilling the agreed-upon SLAs. This may lead to performance loss in terms of response time, time outs, or failures in the worst case. The resource provider must take into account such behaviors and initiate necessary actions to minimize the effect on the application performance. To simulate such behavior, the SLA model can either be defined as fully allocating the requested amount of resources or allowing flexible resource allocations up to a specific rate as long as the agreed-upon SLA can be delivered (e.g., allowing the CPU share to be 10% below the requested amount). CloudSim supports modeling of the aforementioned SLA violation scenarios. Moreover, it is possible to define particular SLA-aware policies describing how the available capacity is distributed among competing VMs in case of a lack of resources. The number of SLA violation events as well as the amount of resource that was requested but not allocated can be accounted for by CloudSim.

16.3.7 Modeling Data Center Power Consumption

Cloud computing environments are built upon an interconnected network of a large number (hundreds-of-thousands) of computing and storage hosts for delivering on-demand services (IaaS, PaaS, and SaaS). Such infrastructures in conjunction with a cooling system may consume an enormous amount of electrical power resulting in high operational costs. Lack of energy-conscious provisioning techniques may lead to overheating of cloud resources (compute and storage servers) in case of high loads. This in turn may result in reduced system reliability and lifespan of devices. Another related issue is the carbon dioxide (CO_2) emission that is detrimental to the physical environment due to its contribution in the greenhouse effect. All these problems require the development of efficient energy-conscious provisioning policies at resource, VM, and application level.

To this end, the CloudSim framework provides basic models and entities to validate and evaluate energy-conscious provisioning of techniques/algorithms. A number of extensions have been made to CloudSim for facilitating the above, such as extending the PE object to include an additional Power Model object for managing power consumption on a per-cloud-host basis. To support modeling and simulation of different power consumption models and power management techniques such as dynamic voltage and frequency scaling (DVFS), CloudSim provides an abstract implementation called PowerModel. This abstract class should be extended for simulating the custom power consumption model of a PE. CloudSim users need to override the method `getPower()` of this class, whose input parameter is the current utilization metric for cloud host and return parameter is the current power consumption value. This capability enables the creation of energy-conscious provisioning policies that require real-time knowledge of power consumption by cloud system components. Furthermore, it enables the accounting of the total energy consumed by the system during the simulation period.

16.3.8 Modeling Dynamic Entities Creation

Clouds offer a pool of software services and hardware servers on an unprecedented scale, which gives businesses a unique ability to handle the temporal variation in demand through dynamic provisioning or de-provisioning of capabilities from clouds. Actual usage patterns of many enterprise services (business applications) vary with time, most of the time in an unpredictable way. This leads to the necessity for cloud providers to deal with customers who can enter or leave the system at any time. CloudSim allows such simulation scenarios by supporting dynamic creation of different kinds of entities. Apart from the dynamic creation of user and broker entities, it is also possible to add and remove data center entities at runtime. This functionality might be useful for simulating dynamic environment where system components can join, fail, or leave the system randomly. After creation, new entities automatically register themselves in the Cloud Information Service (CIS) to enable dynamic resource discovery.

16.4   Design and Implementation of CloudSim

This section provides the finer details related to the fundamental classes of CloudSim, which are also the building blocks of the simulator [9-10]. The overall class design diagram for CloudSim is shown in Figure 16.2.

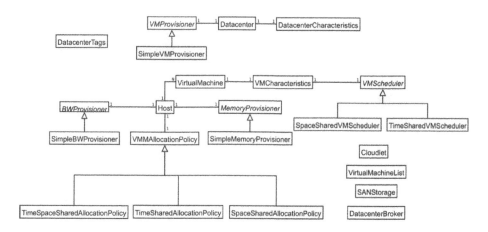

Figure 16.2: Class diagram of CloudSim.

BwProvisioner: This is an abstract class that models the policy for provisioning of bandwidth to VMs. The main role of this component is to undertake the allocation of network bandwidths to a set of competing VMs that are deployed across the data center. Cloud system developers and researchers can extend this class with their own policies (priority, QoS) to reflect the needs of their applications. The BwProvisioningSimple allows a VM to reserve as much bandwidth as required; however, this is constrained by the total available bandwidth of the host.

CloudCoordinator: This abstract class extends a cloud-based data center to the federation. It is responsible for periodically monitoring the internal state of data center resources and based on that it undertakes dynamic load-shredding decisions. Concrete implementation of this component includes the specific sensors and the policy that should be followed during load-shredding. Monitoring of data center resources is performed by the `updateDatacenter()` method by sending queries Sensors. Service/Resource Discovery is realized in the `setDatacenter()` abstract method that can be extended for implementing custom protocols and mechanisms (multicast, broadcast, peer-to-peer). Furthermore, this component can also be extended for simulating cloud-based services such as the Amazon EC2 load balancer. Developers aiming to deploy their application services across multiple clouds can extend this class for implementing their custom inter-cloud provisioning policies.

Cloudlet: This class models the cloud-based application services (such as content delivery, social networking, and business workflow). CloudSim orchestrates the complexity of an application in terms of its computational requirements. Every application service has a pre-assigned instruction length and data transfer (both pre and post fetches) overhead that it needs to undertake during its life cycle. This class can also be extended to support modeling of other performance and composition metrics for applications such as transactions in database-oriented applications.

CloudletScheduler: This abstract class is extended by the implementation of different policies that determine the share of processing power among Cloudlets in a VM. As described previously, two types of provisioning policies are offered: space-shared (CloudetSchedulerSpaceShared) and time-shared (CloudletSchedulerTimeShared).

Datacenter: This class models the core infrastructure-level services (hardware) that are offered by cloud providers (Amazon, Azure, App Engine). It encapsulates a set of compute hosts that can either be homogeneous or heterogeneous with respect to their hardware configurations (memory, cores, capacity, and storage). Furthermore, every datacenter component instantiates a generalized application provisioning component that implements a set of policies for allocating bandwidth, memory, and storage devices to hosts and VMs.

DatacenterBroker or Cloud Broker: This class models a broker, which is responsible for mediating negotiations between SaaS and cloud providers; and such negotiations are driven by QoS requirements. The broker acts on behalf of SaaS providers. It discovers suitable cloud service providers by querying the CIS and undertakes online negotiations for allocation of resources/services that can meet the application's QoS needs. Researchers and system developers must extend this class for evaluating and testing custom brokering policies.

The difference between the broker and the CloudCoordinator is that the former represents the customer (i.e., decisions of these components are made in order to increase user-related performance metrics), whereas the latter acts on behalf of the data center, i.e., it tries to maximize the overall performance of the data center, without considering the needs of specific customers.

DatacenterCharacteristics: This class contains configuration information of data center resources. Host: This class models a physical resource such as a compute or storage server. It encapsulates important information such as the amount of memory and storage, a list and type of processing cores (to represent a multi-core machine), an allocation of policy for sharing the processing power among VMs, and policies for provisioning memory and bandwidth to the VMs.

NetworkTopology: This class contains the information for inducing network behavior (latencies) in the simulation. It stores the topology information, which is generated using the BRITE topology generator.

RamProvisioner: This is an abstract class that represents the provisioning policy for allocating primary memory (RAM) to the VMs. The execution and deployment of VM on a host is feasible only if the RamProvisioner component agrees that the host has the required amount of free memory. The RamProvisionerSimple does not enforce any limitation on the amount of memory that a VM may request. However, if the request is beyond the available memory capacity, then it is simply rejected.

SanStorage: This class models a storage area network that is commonly ambient in cloud-based data centers for storing large chunks of data (such as Amazon S3, Azure Blob storage). SanStorage implements a simple interface that can be used to simulate storage and retrieval of any amount of data, subject to the availability of network bandwidth. Accessing files in a SAN at runtime incurs additional delays for task unit execution; this is due to the additional latencies that are incurred in transferring the data files through the data center's internal network.

Sensor: This interface must be implemented to instantiate a sensor component that can be used by a CloudCoordinator for monitoring specific performance parameters (energy consumption, resource utilization). CloudCoordinator utilizes the dynamic performance information for undertaking load-balancing decisions. The methods defined by this interface are: (i) set the minimum and maximum thresholds for performance parameter and (ii) periodically update the measurement. This class can be used to model the real-world services offered by leading cloud providers such as Amazon's CloudWatch and Microsoft Azure's Fabric Controller. One data center may instantiate one or more Sensors, each one responsible for monitoring a specific data center performance parameter.

VM: This class models a VM, which is managed and hosted by a cloud host component. Every VM component has access to a component that stores the following characteristics related to a VM: accessible memory, processor, storage size, and the VM's internal provisioning policy that is extended from an abstract component called the CloudletScheduler.

VmmAllocationPolicy: This abstract class represents a provisioning policy that a VM monitor utilizes for allocating VMs to hosts. The chief functionality of the VmmAllocationPolicy is to select the available host in a data center that meets the memory, storage, and availability requirement for a VM deployment.

VmScheduler: This is an abstract class implemented by a host component that models the policies (space-shared, time-shared) required for allocating processor cores to VMs. The functionalities of this class can easily be overridden to accommodate application-specific processor sharing policies.

Communication among Entities: The flow of communication among core CloudSim entities is discussed in Figure 16.3.

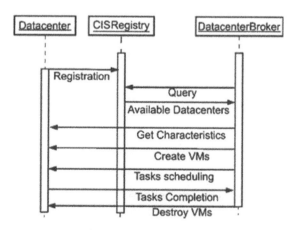

Figure 16.3: Flow of communications among CloudSim entities.

At the beginning of a simulation, each datacenter entity registers with the CIS Registry. CIS then provides information registry-type functionalities, such as matchmaking services for mapping user/brokers, requests to suitable cloud providers. Next, the DataCenter brokers acting on behalf of users, consult the CIS service to obtain the list of cloud providers who can offer infrastructure services that match application's QoS, hardware, and software requirements. In the event of a match, the DataCenter broker deploys the application with the CIS suggested cloud. The communication flow described so far relates to the basic flow in a simulated experiment. Some variations in this flow are possible depending on policies. For example, messages from brokers to datacenters may require a confirmation from other parts of the datacenter, about the execution of an action, or about the maximum number of VMs that a user can create.

16.5   Setting up Development Environments

This section teaches users how to install the CloudSim Simulator and the related OS and Development Environments.
   Supported OS [9, 10]:

- Windows XP (32-bit), Vista (32- or 64-bit), or Windows 7 (32- or 64-bit).

- Mac OS X 10.5.8 or later (x86 only).

- Linux (tested on Ubuntu Linux, Lucid Lynx).

Development environment (Eclipse based):

- Eclipse Classic (versions 3.5.1 and higher).

- JDK 1.6 or later.

- CloudSim tool kit.

The users may also use NetBeans IDE.

16.6   How to Use CloudSim with Eclipse

1. Decompress the CloudSim package in your directory of choice.

2. Open Eclipse.

3. In the Eclipse menu, select `New/Project...`

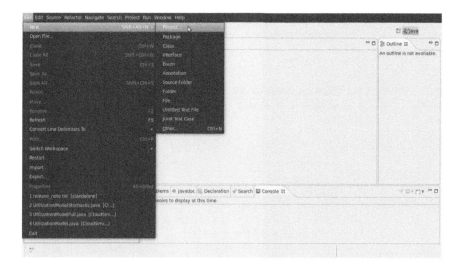

4. In the `Select a Wizard` window, select `Java Project` then click `Next`.

5. In the `Create a Java Project` window, fill in the field `Project name` with CloudSim. Then select `Create project from existing source`. In the `Directory` field, select the directory extracted from the CloudSim package. If you have more than one JVM, in this window you have to select Sun Java 6. Then, select `Finish` to complete project creation.

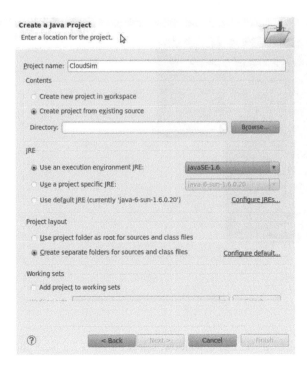

6. After these steps, you can navigate through CloudSim packages, and develop your own simulations using CloudSim.

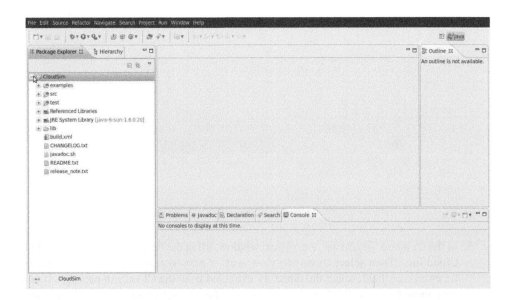

References

1. Rodrigo N. Calheiros, Rajiv Ranjan, Anton Beloglazov, César A. F. De Rose, And Rajkumar Buyya "CloudSim: A Toolkit for Modeling and Simulation of Cloud Computing Environments and evaluation of Resource Provisioning Algorithms" Software: Practice and Experience (SPE), Volume 41, Number 1, January, 2011, pp. 23 50.

2. Calheiros, Rodrigo N., Ranjan, Rajiv, Rose, César A. F. De and Buyya, Rajkumar. "CloudSim: A Novel Framework for Modeling and Simulation of Cloud Computing Infrastructures and Services." CoRR abs/ 0903.2525 (2009).

3. Buyya R, Ranjan R, Calheiros RN. Modeling and simulation of scalable Cloud computing environments and the CloudSim toolkit: Challenges and opportunities, Proceedings of the Conference on High Performance Computing and Simulation (HPCS 2009), Leipzig, Germany. IEEE Press: New York, U.S.A., 21-24 June 2009; 1-11.

4. Le, D. N., Kumar, R., Nguyen, G. N., & Chatterjee, J. M. (2018). *Cloud Computing and Virtualization*. John Wiley & Sons.

5. Calheiros, R. N., Ranjan, R., Beloglazov, A., De Rose, C. A., & Buyya, R. (2011). CloudSim: a toolkit for modeling and simulation of cloud computing environments and evaluation of resource provisioning algorithms. *Software: Practice and experience*, 41(1), 23-50.

6. Nguyen, H. H. C., Le, D. N., Van Son Le, & Nguyen, T. T. (2015, February). A New Technical Solution for Resource Allocation in Heterogeneous Distributed Platforms. In *ICADIWT* (pp. 184-194).

7. Barbierato, E., Gribaudo, M., Iacono, M., & Jakobik, A. (2019). Exploiting CloudSim in a multiformalism modeling approach for cloud based systems. *Simulation Modelling Practice and Theory*, 93, 133-147.

8. Gupta, K., & Johari, R. SORTIS: Sharing of Resources in Cloud Framework Using CloudSim Tool. In *International Conference on Innovative Computing and Communications* (pp. 835-843). Springer, Singapore.

9. https://github.com/Cloudslab/cloudsim

10. http://www.cloudbus.org/cloudsim/

17

OPENFAAS

PRASANT KUMAR PATTNAIK[1], DAC-NHUONG LE[2], SOUVIK PAL[3]

[1] KIIT, Deemed to be University, India
[2] Haiphong University, Haiphong, Vietnam
[3] Sister Nivedita University, Kolkata, India
 Email: patnaikprasant@gmail.com, nhuongld@dhhp.edu.vn, souvikpal22@gmail.com

Abstract
OpenFaaS[1] makes it easy for developers to deploy event-driven functions and microservices to Kubernetes without repetitive, boiler-plate coding. Package your code or an existing binary in a Docker image to get a highly scalable endpoint with autoscaling and metrics.

Highlights:

- Ease of use through UI portal and one-click install;

- Write functions in any language for Linux or Windows and package in Docker/OCI image format;

- Portable; runs on existing hardware or public/private cloud with Kubernetes or containerd;

- CLI available with YAML format for templating and defining functions;

- Autoscales as demand increases.

Keywords: OpenFaaS, simulator

---

[1] https://docs.openfaas.com/

17.1   Introduction

Serverless computing describes the concept of developing and running applications without having to worry about servers [1]. On a high level and from a developer point of view that might be the case, but the underlying serverless platform does of course still rely on servers of some kind.

In practice, serverless computing or function as a service (FaaS) is a layer of abstraction that hides away most of the operational aspects of running one or more applications. While all of the big cloud providers offer serverless products these days, one can also run a self-hosted serverless platform.

One example of an open-source serverless framework that's capable of running a private serverless platform is OpenFaaS. It is distributed under the MIT license and can be installed on any machine or cluster that's compatible with Docker Swarm and/or Kubernetes.

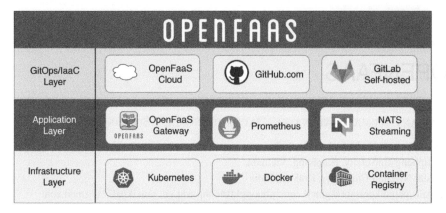

Figure 17.1: OpenFaaS.

The aim of this chapter is to provide step-by-step instructions on how to create and operate your own serverless platform using OpenFaaS.

17.2   OpenFaaS Architecture

The API Gateway[2] of OpenFaaS gives the opportunity to access the faas-provider from the outside. Tasks of the faas-provider are, for example, the creation of docker images out of functions, the deployment of functions or the removal of functions from the system. The gateway is realized as a REST API and is accessible via faas-cli, the provided UI, and simple http requests. With each deployed function the user can specify the amount of pods which should contain the function. One task of the gateway is to ensure autoscaling based on the users specification. During a function deployment it is possible to set some values like minimum/maximum amount of replicas or the scaling factor of functions. Those values are set in the yaml file of each function. The autoscaling is done with the help of Prometheus and the AlertManager in the case of an installation in Docker Swarm. If Open-

---

[2]https://docs.openfaas.com/architecture/gateway/

FaaS is installed inside a Kubernetes cluster, the built-in Horizontal Pod Autoscaler can be used.

Prometheus is an open source monitoring application which provides functions to get several metrics of your deployed functions inside OpenFaaS. One metric could be the rate of invocations of your function within a defined window [2, 3].

The AlertManager will read from the metrics retrieved by Prometheus and will inform the gateway if there is a need to scale functions. The rules for sending an alert are defined in a configuration file.

After receiving an alert from the AlertManager the Gateway will ensure that the concerned pods get scaled based on the given scaling factor. The component which will scale the pods is the faas-provider.

There is also the possibility to use Custom Resources[3] from Kubernetes to extend your Kubernetes API. With such an extension you can use Kubernetes to check logs, debug and monitor OpenFaaS functions. The OpenFaaS Operator inside the diagram is the Custom Resource. In order that the OpenFaaS Operator can do its job all necessary data is stored inside Secret, Deployment and Services.

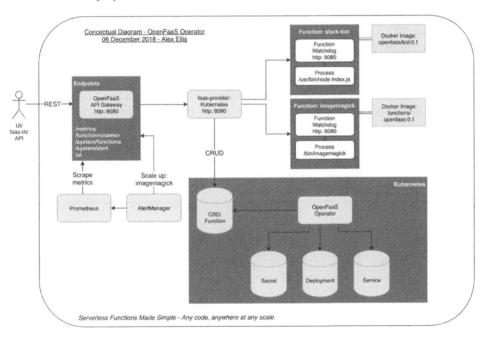

Figure 17.2: OpenFaaS architecture.

17.3 OpenFaaS Installation

OpenFaaS can run in a variety of environments. This guide walks you through how to install it on a developer computer or in-house development/test server, as well a more production-like environment [4, 5].

---

[3]https://kubernetes.io/docs/concepts/extend-kubernetes/api-extension/custom-resources/

17.3.1 Development Environment with Docker Swarm

Docker Swarm is a tool which makes it possible to create and manage multiple clusters of docker containers. Such a cluster is also called a swarm but we will use the term cluster to avoid confusion. One of Docker Swarm's features is to scale your cluster of docker containers. This means that the so-called swarm manager removes or adds nodes inside the cluster for a specific service.

As you can see in Listing 17.2, the first step is to create a master node with the Docker swarm mode but the version of the client and daemon API has to be at least 1.24. If you have more than one IP address you have to add the option `--advertise-addr`.

With that option you can apply an IP address to your master node or you can specify an interface. If you specify lo as interface the master node can only be reached inside that network interface.

Listing 17.1: Initialize the swarm

```
1  > docker swarm init # if you have a single IP address
2  > docker swarm init --advertise-addr <network adapter> # if you have more than one
```

In Listing 17.3 we just download the git repository of OpenFaaS, which can be updated with a simple git pull. After downloading the repository you have to execute the mentioned script below inside the root directory of the repository. This file deploys OpenFaaS inside your cluster and automatically generates admin credentials. If you want to set the password by yourself just change the value of secret inside `deploy_stack.sh`. This value can be found at line 32 but it's not recommended to modify this value. Just do it for local testing environments. After the first call of faas-cli login your hashed password will be written into `~/.openfaas/config.yml`.

Listing 17.2: Download OpenFaaS

```
1  > git clone https://github.com/openfaas/faas && cd faas
```

Listing 17.3: Deploy OpenFaaS in the swarm

```
1  > ./deploy_stack.sh # username: admin, password: randomly generated on the first run
2  > ./deploy_stack.sh --no-auth # no authentication
```

Now you are able to use the UI from OpenFaaS. The address shown in Listing 17.5 is used to access the UI.

Listing 17.4: Download OpenFaaS

```
1  http://127.0.0.1:8080
```

After your work is done you should remove OpenFaaS and all its containers which were created during installation. But before OpenFaaS gets removed, all deployed functions should first be removed. That's because all deployed functions run in a seperated Docker container and those won't be removed with the command which will remove OpenFaaS.

Listing 17.5: Download OpenFaaS

```
1  > faas-cli remove <function-name>
2  > docker stack rm func
```

17.3.2   Multi-Node Cluster with Docker Swarm

For testing OpenFaas in a multiple node scenario, we decided to make a cluster of Docker Swarm nodes in virtual machines. Using virtual machines for testing has the benefit that they can be easily ported to other physical hosts and in case of a malfunction we can reset them to a former snapshot without doing troubleshooting. As a virtualization platform we choose VirtualBox, but it is also possible to do this with every other available virtualization software.

We create a cluster with one master and two worker nodes. For that, three virtual machines with the latest Debian OS release were used. All the machines must be part of the same local network, either with the NAT Network option or the Network Bridge option of VirtualBox. After the machines are created and the OS is installed, all of them need Docker to be installed. On the master node, the swarm mode must be initialized as described in Listing 17.1. After initializing the swarm node, Docker returns a token, as shown in Listing 17.6, which is necessary for joining workers to the cluster.

Listing 17.6: Join Swarm Token
```
1  > faas-cli remove <function-name>
2  > docker stack rm func
```

The installation of OpenFaas on the master node can be done similar to that shown in Listing 17.2 and Listing 17.3. After the installation of OpenFaas is done, the worker nodes should join the swarm; to do this, the token from Listing 17.6 is needed. The command is shown in Listing 17.7.

Listing 17.7: Join Swarm Token
```
1  > docker swarm join --token "Token" "IP-AddressMasterNode"
```

To check if all the workers joined the swarm the command from Listing 17.8 can be used on the master node.

Listing 17.8: Show worker nodes
```
1  > docker node ls
```

The master node should now return the names of the joined workers; if it does, the setup of the cluster is done and functions can be deployed.

The described steps of installing and deploying OpenFaas can be transferred 1:1 to physical hosts insted of virtual machines, which makes it a good simulation of its own private hardware-based cluster. To remove a worker node from the cluster, the following command (Listing 17.9) must be used on the node:

Listing 17.9: Node leave swarm
```
1  > docker swarm leave
```

After that, the command from listing 10 should be used on the master node.

Listing 17.10: Master remove node
```
1  > docker node rm "NameOfTheNode"
```

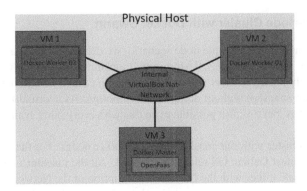

Figure 17.3: One host setup for the test cluster.

There are two possible options to run this test cluster on host systems. In the first one, all the virtual machines are running on the same physical host, as it is shown in Figure 17.2.

With this setup it is possible to simulate a cluster of multiple nodes on different machines on one physical host. The virtual machines are connected with a NAT Network which was created with VirtualBox. With this configuration, the machines can communicate with each other and with the host network, but from the host network, they are invincible.

The second option is to run the virtual machines on different physical hosts' systems. This is closer to an own hardware-based cluster, but it is independent from the hosts OS. The principle arcitecture is shown in Figure 17.3. In this schematic illustration, all virtual machines are on different physical hosts, but other configurations are also possible. For this setup it is important, to choose the Network Bridge functionality on the VM; with this option the machine acts like a independent host in the network. This is important, because the machines must communicate in the host network.

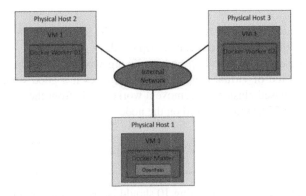

Figure 17.4: Multiple host setup for the test cluster.

17.3.3   Production Environment with Kubernetes

OpenFaaS is fully compatible with Kubernetes and can leverage many of its features for improved scalability and configurability. A production ready Kubernetes cluster typically provides a solid foundation for vertical scaling. If the cluster also has horizontal scaling in the form of cluster autoscaling,[4], OpenFaaS can virtually scale to infinity. (Provided you are willing to pay for it and your cloud provider doesn't run out of virtual machines.)

Figure 17.5: Kubernetes OpenFaaS.

FaaS is often hailed for its automatic scaling. But when you decide to run your own FaaS platform, scalability is likely limited by the underlying hardware. When combining OpenFaaS with Kubernetes and a cloud provider, you can cover the full spectrum of re-source requirements, from zero to serving one of the biggest websites on the internet or running compute-intensive parallelized scientific calculations.

This section will walk you through how to get a Kubernetes cluster with OpenFaaS up and running. This involves two major steps:

1. Creating a Kubernetes cluster.

2. Installing the necessary software components inside the Kubernetes cluster.

The process described in this installation guide will create a managed Kubernetes cluster on Microsoft Azure. However, we will give pointers as to what needs to be changed to use another cloud provider. The steps involving the installation of the actual software components for OpenFaaS should work on any Kubernetes cluster. This guide will walk you through the process command by command. If you're looking for a simpler and faster way you can find a mostly automated solution using Bash scripts in the accompanying GitHub repository.

17.3.3.1 *Prerequisites / Tool Chain*

To follow along with a Microsoft Azure account, a valid subscription is needed (a free

---

[4]Cluster autoscaling means worker nodes are created and destroyed automatically as workloads fluctuate.

trial is sufficient). Additionally, the following small selection of command-line tools are needed:

- Azure CLI [2] is needed to access your Microsoft Azure account from the command line. The simplest, although not recommended, way to install Azure CLI is to run:

Listing 17.11: Install Azure CLI

```
1  curl -L https://aka.ms/InstallAzureCli | bash
```

- Terraform [3] is an Infrastructure as Code tool. It can be used to create and destroy infrastructure like virtual machines, load balancers, block storage devices and many more with a range of providers such as Amazon Web Services, Google Cloud, Microsoft Azure, IBM Cloud, Scaleway and others. Although Terraform is not strictly necessary for a guide like this, using an Infrastructure as Code solution is more befitting to a production like setup. If preferred, you can use the graphical web interface of your cloud provider (https://portal.azure.com/ in our case) to create the required resources. Terraform is typically not provided by package managers and has to be downloaded as a binary from the official website (see listing 17.12)

Listing 17.12: Install the Terraform binary on Linux

```
1  > curl -O https://releases.hashicorp.com/terraform/0.12.0/terraform_0.12.0_l c
2  > inux_amd64.zip, unzip terraform_0.12.0_linux_amd64.zip
3  > sudo mv terraform /usr/local/bin/
```

- The Kubernetes command-line tool, kubectl [4], allows you to interact with Kubernetes clusters. Some Linux distributions provide a package for kubectl. There's also a Snap package. More information for your particular plattform can be found in the Kubernetes documentation.

- Helm [5] is a package manager for Kubernetes. It simplifies the installation of software that's comprised of multiple standalone components and assists with configuration management. For example, an application might consist of multple pods, which are collections of containers, some of which may require persistence storage and/or specific network configuration like exposing ports to a public network or load balancers. Helm packages are called charts and OpenFaaS provides an official Helm chart which is used in this guide. Helm is also not provided by package managers and has to be downloaded from the official website (see listing 17.13).

Listing 17.13: Install the Helm binary on Linux

```
1  > curl -O https://storage.googleapis.com/kubernetes-helm/helm-v2.14.0-linux- c amd64.tar.gz
2  > tar xfvz helm-v2.14.0-linux-amd64.tar.gz
3  > sudo mv linux-amd64/helm /usr/local/bin/
```

17.3.3.2 Creating the Kubernetes Cluster

First we need to log into Microsoft Azure using their command line tool by typing:

Listing 17.14: Log in to Microsoft Azure

```
1  > az login
```

This will open the Azure website in a browser window and ask you to enter your login information and confirm that you want to grant access to the Azure CLI. Next we need to create an Azure Service Principal. Microsoft defines a service principal as follows [6]: "An Azure service principal is an identity created for use with applications, hosted services, and automated tools to access Azure resources. This access is restricted by the roles assigned to the service principal, giving you control over which resources can be accessed and at which level. For security reasons, it's always recommended to use service principals with automated tools rather than allowing them to log in with a user identity."

This Service Principal requires a name and a password. It can be created with the command:

Listing 17.15: Create a Service Principal on Azure

```
1  > az ad sp create-for-rbac \
2  --name my-kubernetes-openfaas \
3  --password my-insecure-password
```

If you are copying and pasting commands from this guide please make sure to choose a more secure password. The output of that command will look something like this:

Listing 17.16: Example output after creating the Service Principal

```
1  {
2    "appId": "ff7043b8-99f3-9640-a673-e54f06e1416b",
3    "displayName": "my-kubernetes-openfaas",
4    "name": "http://my-kubernetes-openfaas",
5    "password": "my-insecure-password",
6    "tenant": "3ea17ddb-4ef6-4220-r2d2-c709799fb49a"
7  }
```

With the Service Principal created we can start configuring the Kubernetes cluster or Azure Kubernetes Service (AKS) as it's called by Microsoft. Instead of using the Azure website to create the cluster we will use Terraform (see 17.17). This follows the paradigm of having infrastructure as code. Create a folder for the Terraform files we are about to create. We are going to follow the best practices for Terraform and create the files `main.tf`, `output.tf`, `provider.tf` and `variables.tf`. For the contents of these files see Listing 17.17, Listing 17.18, Listing 17.19, and Listing 17.20 respectively.

Listing 17.17: Terraform main.tf

```
1   resource "azurerm_resource_group" "resource_group" {
2       name = "cc-project-resources"
3       location = "${var.location}"
4   }
5   resource "azurerm_kubernetes_cluster" "kubernetes_cluster" {
6       name = "cc-project-kubernetes"
7       location = "${azurerm_resource_group.resource_group.location}"
8       resource_group_name = "${azurerm_resource_group.resource_group.name}"
9       dns_prefix = "cc-project"
10      agent_pool_profile {
11      name = "default"
12      count = "${var.worker_pool_size}"
13      vm_size = "${var.worker_instance_type}"
14      os_type = "Linux"
15      os_disk_size_gb = 30
16  }
17  service_principal {
18      client_id = "${var.kubernetes_client_id}"
19      client_secret = "${var.kubernetes_client_secret}"
20  }
21
22  tags = {
23      Environment = "Production"
```

```
24    }
25    }
```

Listing 17.18: Terraform output.tf

```
1    output "client_certificate" {
2        value = "${azurerm_kubernetes_cluster.kubernetes_cluster.kube_config.0.cli cent_certificate}"
3    }
4
5    output "kube_config" {
6        value = "${azurerm_kubernetes_cluster.kubernetes_cluster.kube_config_raw}"
7    }
8
9    resource "local_file" "kube_config" {
10       content = "${azurerm_kubernetes_cluster.kubernetes_cluster.kube_config_raw}"
11       filename = "${path.module}//kubeconfig"
12   }
```

Listing 17.19: Terraform provider.tf

```
1    provider "azurerm" {
2        version = "=1.24.0"
3    }
```

Listing 17.20: Terraform variables.tf

```
1    variable "location" {
2        description="The Azure Region in which all resources in this example should
3        be provisioned"
4    }
5
6    variable "kubernetes_client_id" {
7        description = "The Client ID for the Service Principal to use for this Managed
8        Kubernetes Cluster"
9    }
10
11   variable "kubernetes_client_secret" {
12       description = "The Client Secret for the Service Principal to use for this Managed
13       Kubernetes Cluster"
14   }
15
16   variable "worker_instance_type" {
17       default = "Standard_D2s_v3"
18       description = "Type of Azure Compute instance you want as worker nodes"
19   }
20
21   variable "worker_pool_size" {
22       default = 1
23       description = "Number of Azure Compute instances you want running as worker nodes"
24   }
```

With all the necessary files created run:

Listing 17.21: Initialize Terraform

```
1    > terraform init
```

This will perform several initialization steps, e.g., downloading the Terraform module for Microsoft Azure.

For the next command there are three required and two optional parameters:

1. "`kubernetes_client_id`" — The ID of our Service Principal that was displayed after creating the Service Principal.

2. "`kubernetes_client_secret`" — The password of our Service Principal that we have chosen earlier.

3. "location" - An Azure region.

4. (optional) "`worker_pool_size`" — Number of Azure Compute instances you want running as worker nodes.

5. (optional) "`worker_instance_type`" — Type of Azure Compute instance you want as worker nodes.

The command will be similar to Listing 17.21. Before Terraform creates the resources we defined, it will present an overview of what resources are going to be created and prompt you to confirm their creation. The creation process typically takes between 5 and 10 minutes.

Listing 17.22: Let Terraform create the Kubernetes cluster
```
1   > terraform apply \
2       -var 'location = "North Europe"' \
3       -var 'kubernetes_client_id = "ff7043b8-99f3-9640-a673-e54f06e1416b"' \
4       -var 'kubernetes_client_secret = "my-insecure-password"'
```

You may start using your Kubernetes cluster now using the kubeconfig file that was created in the same directory as your Terraform files. For a quick check run:

Listing 17.23: Display a list of worker nodes (default is just a single node
```
1   > kubectl --kubeconfig=kubeconfig get node
```

Congratulations! You now have your own Kubernetes cluster. Before moving on to install OpenFaaS it is recommended to configure kubectl to look for the kubeconfig of the cluster we just created. This can be done in either of the following ways:

- Run export `KUBECONFIG=/path/to/your/kubeconfig`. This is limited to your current terminal window. When opening a new terminal window you would have to run the command again.

- Copy the kubeconfig file to `~/.kube/config` to permanently configure kubectl for your Azure Kubernetes cluster. Warning: this may overwrite an existing configuration.

17.3.4 Installing OpenFaaS Using Helm

Now that we have a Kubernetes cluster up and running we may proceed to install OpenFaaS. But there is one last intermediate step necessary. Installing the server-side component for Helm, the package management tool needed for installing OpenFaaS.

Azure Kubernetes Service uses Kubernetes' role-based access control (RBAC) by default. Thus we have to create a Service Account[5] and a Cluster Role Binding.[6]

The respective commands as well as the command for installing the server-side Helm component are listed in Listing 17.23. Note that Helm 3.0, which at the time of writing is still in alpha, will no longer have a server-side component. This guide is written for Helm versions 2.x.

---

[5] Kubernetes Authorization Overview https://kubernetes.io/docs/reference/access-authn-authz/authorization/
[6] Kubernetes RBAC https://kubernetes.io/docs/reference/access-authn-authz/rbac/

```
Listing 17.24: Installing the server-side Helm component
1   > kubectl -n kube-system create sa tiller
2   > kubectl create clusterrolebinding tiller \
3   --clusterrole cluster-admin \
4   --serviceaccount=kube-system:tiller
5   > helm init --wait --service-account tiller
```

For Helm to be able to find the OpenFaaS charts we need to add their repository by running:

```
Listing 17.25: Add the OpenFaaS repository to Helm
1   > helm repo add openfaas https://openfaas.github.io/faas-netes/
```

Now we can finally install OpenFaaS itself. As shown in listing 17.25, we will create a namespace, configure an admin password for OpenFaaS and deploy its Helm chart.

```
Listing 17.26: Installing OpenFaaS using Helm
1   > kubectl apply -f https://raw.githubusercontent.com/openfaas/faas-netes/mas cter/namespaces.yml
2   > kubectl -n openfaas create secret generic basic-auth \
3   --from-literal=basic-auth-user=admin \
4   --from-literal=basic-auth-password="my-openfaas-password"
5   > helm upgrade openfaas --install openfaas/openfaas \
6   --namespace openfaas \
7   --set basic_auth=true \
8   --set functionNamespace=openfaas-fn \
9   --set serviceType=LoadBalancer
```

To check whether OpenFaaS is running you may run:

```
Listing 17.27: Display a list of pods associated with the OpenFaaS
1   > kubectl --namespace=openfaas get deployments -l "release=openfaas, app=openfaas"
```

If the numbers in the columns "desired" and "available" are identical your OpenFaaS is ready.

Your OpenFaaS is publicly accessible on port 8080 via a load balancer that routes requests into your Kubernetes cluster. The IP of that load balancer is listed on the helm status page and can be extracted by running:

```
Listing 17.28: Terraform main.tf
1   > helm status openfaas | grep gateway-external
```

For instructions on how to use the OpenFaaS web interface or the OpenFaaS CLI refer to Section 17.3.4.

17.3.5   Install OpenShift

Grab the OpenShift client tools can find the latest from: https://www.okd.io/download.html.

```
Listing 17.29: Install OpenShift
1   export URL="https://github.com/openshift/origin/releases/download/v3.11.0/
2   openshift-origin-client-tools-v3.11.0-0cbc58b-linux-64bit.tar.gz"
3
4   curl -sSL -o openshift-client-tools.tgz $URL \
5    && tar -xvf openshift-client-tools.tgz \
6    && rm -rf openshift-client-tools.tgz
7
8   # Rename the destination folder:
9    && mv open* openshift
```

Make `oc` available via `PATH`

```
1  echo "export PATH=$PATH:'pwd'/openshift" | tee -a ~/.bash_profile
2  source ~/.bash_profile
```

Authenticate to the Docker hub

```
1  docker login
```

Install OpenShift

```
1  oc cluster up --skip-registry-check=true
```

This will take a few minutes

If you see an error / timeout at `run_self_hosted.go:181]` Waiting for the kube-apiserver to be ready then run the command again until it passes.

To access your OpenShift cluster, you can either access it via a browser on your local machine because port 443 is mapped locally, the URL is https://127.0.0.1:8443.

You can also access the API via `oc` installed in the footloose container, or download `oc` by adding the OpenShift client tools to your laptop.

This output shows you how to connect for the first time:

```
Listing 17.30: OpenShift
1   Login to server ...
2   Creating initial project "myproject" ...
3   Server Information ...
4   OpenShift server started.
5
6   The server is accessible via web console at:
7       https://127.0.0.1:8443
8
9   You are logged in as:
10      User: developer
11      Password: <any value>
12
13  To login as administrator:
14      oc login -u system:admin
```

Figure 17.6: OpenShift client tools.

Test your OpenShift cluster: Let's install OpenFaaS, which makes serverless functions simple through the use of Docker images and Kubernetes as a highly scalable control-plane. OpenShift is effectively a distribution of Kubernetes, so with some testing and tweaking everything should work almost out of the box.

17.4 Considerations

While the serverless platform we have created is a solid foundation for a production environment, there are things not in the scope of this guide that you should consider before using this Kubernetes + OpenFaaS combination in the wild.

All communication with the OpenFaaS gateway is unencrypted, both via the command line as well as the web interface. However, for advanced Kubernetes users it isn't too difficult to set up an ingress controller that supports SSL.

More things to consider are backups, disaster recovery, monitoring and alerting, fault tolerance, scalability, and others, just to name a few. Last but not least, it should be carefully examined whether OpenFaaS itself is ready for production.

17.5 Operation of OpenFaaS

The following sections will illustrate how to create, deploy, manage and use premade or self-made OpenFaaS functions by listing the most common and important commands and providing specific examples [6-10].

This guide assumes a locally running OpenFaaS installation on port 8080 similar to the instructions of Section 17.3.1. IP addresses and ports need to be adjusted if that is not the case.

17.5.1 Setup and Configuration of the OpenFaaS Command Line Tool

See listing 17.29 on how to install faas-cli. Running sh without root privileges will require additional manual configuration.

Listing 17.31: Install faas-cli
```
1  > curl -sSL https://cli.openfaas.com | sudo sh
```

Alternatively, you can download the latest release on the Github page of faas-cli[7] and place it in your PATH (/usr/local/bin for example.)

See listing 17.30 on how to log in into OpenFaaS from your command line.

Listing 17.32: Login to OpenFaaS with faas-cli
```
1  > faas-cli login --password-stdin # username 'admin' and default gateway
2  'http://127.0.0.1:8080' are implied
3  > faas-cli login --password-stdin --username <name> --gateway <gateway>
```

Important Warning: Do not manage functions with faas-cli in the OpenFaaS folder you cloned with git. It will deploy and try to stop functions which are included in the folder. This can lead to unexpected behavior and cli output.

---

[7]https://github.com/openfaas/faas-cli

17.5.2 OpenFaaS Store

OpenFaaS has an official function store with free functions. Listing 17.31 shows the cli commands which are necessary to list and deploy them. Store functions are a good way to test a new OpenFaaS installation because they can be deployed with having to know how to write a custom function.

```
Listing 17.33: Common commands for the OpenFaaS store
1  > faas-cli store list # list available functions
2  > faas-cli store inspect <function_name> # show information about a function of the store
3  > faas-cli store deploy <function_name> # deploy a function from the store
```

17.5.3 Management and Usage of Functions

Listing 17.32 shows the commands which are necessary for adding, removing and invoking functions.

```
Listing 17.34: Common commands for function management and usage
1  > faas-cli list # list deployed functions
2  > faas-cli store deploy <function_name> # deploy store function
3  > faas-cli deploy # deploy locally built functions or functions in docker images
4  > faas-cli invoke <function_name> # call a function
5  > faas-cli remove <function_name> # remove deployed functions
```

Deploy scans the current working directory for functions and tries to deploy them if no specific function configuration file or docker image is specified.

Invoke takes the input for the function call from STDIO. To circumvent this, a simple echo command which pipes its output into the input of faas-cli invoke can be used. See listing 17.33 for an example.

```
Listing 17.35: Example - Figlet function from the store
1  > faas-cli store deploy figlet
2  Deployed. 202 Accepted.
3  URL: http://127.0.0.1:8080/function/figlet
4  > faas-cli list
5  Function Invocations Replicas
6  figlet 0 1
7  > echo "Cloud Computing" | faas-cli invoke figlet
8     ___  _  _
9    / ___| | |  ___  _   _  __| |
10   | |   | |/ _ \| | | |/ _` |
11   | |___| | (_) | |_| | (_| |
12    \____|_|\___/ \__,_|_|\__,_|
13     ___  _  _
14    / ___|___  _ __ ___  _ __  _   _ _| |_(_)_ __   __ _
15   | |  / _ \| '_ ` _ \| '_ \| | | | __| | '_ \ / _` |
16   | | | (_) | | | | | | | | | | | |_| | | | | (_| |
17    _____/|_| |_| |_| .__/ \__,_|_|_|_| |_|\__, |
18   |_| |___/
19  > faas-cli remove figlet
20  Deleting: figlet.
21  Removing old function.
```

Listing 17.34 demonstrates a concrete example for deploying, calling and removing a function. For this example the Figlet function from the store is used. Figlet is originally a Unix command line tool which turns text into larger text banners. The Figlet function from the OpenFaaS store does the same.

```
Listing 17.36: Example - Calling a function with curl
1  > curl -X POST --data "OpenFaaS" http://127.0.0.1:8080/function/figlet
2
3   / _ \ _ _ __ _ _ | _ _|_ _ _ _ / __|
4  | | | | '_ \/ _ \ | '_ \| | | / _` |/ _`\__ \
5  | |_| | |_) |  __/ | | | |_| | (_| | (_| |_) |
6   \___/| .__/ \___|_| |_|_| \__,_|\__,_|___/
7        |_|
```

Functions are called with a http request. Instead of the faas-cli it is possible to call a function with the web UI of OpenFaaS or any http client (standalone or embedded in an application). Listing 17.34 demonstrates how a function is called with curl, a command line tool for sending data over the network.

17.5.4   Development of Functions

The quickest way to develop a function is starting with a template provided by OpenFaaS. These exist for several languages. Listing 17.35 lists two ways to view them: The first command just lists the available templates from the OpenFaas store (official, unofficial and incubating) and the second set of commands downloads the (official) templates into the working directory so that they can be used for the creation of a new function.

```
Listing 17.37: Listing available templates
1  > # View available templates from the store
2  > faas-cli template store list
3  > # Download the templates for offline access
4  > faas-cli template pul
```

Listing 17.36 illustrates how to create a new function. Create a bare function from a template first. The name can be freely chosen, the template name has to be valid template (like Python or Java). After the function is implemented, it can be built to a Docker image with the second command. OpenFaaS will create a build directory to store intermediate files which are necessary for the build. After the image is built successfully, it can be deployed with the last command.

```
Listing 17.38: Creating a function from a template
1  > faas-cli new <function_name> --lang=<template_name>
2  > # Implement your function before building it
3  > faas-cli build -f <function_name>.yml
4  > faas-cli deploy -f <function_name>.yml
```

17.5.5   Working with Docker Registries

Functions can be uploaded to and deployed from docker registries as seen in listing 17.37. As a prerequisite, the user has to be logged into docker on the command line and the image field of the yaml file of a function needs to point to a valid docker repository. If these criteria are met, the function can be uploaded as an image to the docker registry with `faas-cli` up which also deploys it after uploading. To deploy a function from a docker registry faas-cli deploy can be used. The image name must point to an image with a function while the name under which the function will be deployed can be chosen freely.

```
Listing 17.39: Working with docker registries
1  > # Make sure that you are logged in to the registry
2  > # Adjust the image name in the yaml file of the function
3  > faas-cli push -f <function_name>.yml
4  > faas-cli deploy --image <image_name> --name <any name>
```

17.5.6 Web UI

Basic tasks for managing functions can be done via the Web UI. You can use it to

- View running functions.

- Invoke functions.

- Deploy functions from the store or docker images.

- Stop functions.

References

1. Sarah Allen et al. CNCFWG-Serverless Whitepaper. In: (2018). https://github.com/cncf/wg-serverless/blob/master/whitepaper/cncf_serverless_whitepaper_v1.0.pdf.

2. Microsoft Coorporation. Microsoft Azure - Install the Azure CLI. Feb. 12, 2019. https://docs.microsoft.com/en-us/cli/azure/install-azurecli?view=azure-cli-latest.

3. Hashicorp. Terraform. May 29, 2019. https://www.terraform.io/.

4. Kubernetes. Install and Set Up kubectl. May 29, 2019. https://kubernetes.io/docs/tasks/tools/install-kubectl/.

5. Helm. Helm - The Package Manager for Kubernetes. May 29, 2019. https://helm.sh/.

6. Microsoft Coorporation. Create an Azure service principal with Azure Power-Shell. June 3, 2019. https://docs.microsoft.com/de-de/powershell/azure/create-azure-service-principal-azureps?view=azps-2.1.0.

7. https://docs.docker.com/engine/

8. https://prometheus.io/

9. https://docs.openfaas.com/deployment/docker-swarm/

10. https://docs.openfaas.com/deployment/troubleshooting/#i-forgot-my-gateway-password

17.5.6 Web UI

These tasks for managing functions can be done via the Web UI. You can use it to:

- View running containers.
- Invoke functions.
- Deploy functions from the .tar or .tar.gz image.
- Stop functions.

References

18

OPENNEBULA

Prasant Kumar Pattnaik[1], Dac-Nhuong Le[2], Souvik Pal[3]

[1] KIIT, Deemed to be University, India
[2] Haiphong University, Haiphong, Vietnam
[3] Sister Nivedita University, Kolkata, India
 Email: patnaikprasant@gmail.com, nhuongld@dhhp.edu.vn, souvikpal22@gmail.com

Abstract

OpenNebula is a simple, but powerful, open source platform to build and manage Enterprise Clouds. OpenNebula provides unified management of IT infrastructure and applications that avoids vendor lock-in and reduces complexity, resource consumption and operational costs.

Keywords: OpenNebula, simulator

18.1   Project Goal and Environment

This guide provides a complete step-by-step tutorial to set up an OpenNebula private cloud environment with one masternode and one workernode.

The masternode can manage multiple worker nodes, including network, storage and more. This environment can easily be extended by more workers if needed. Workernodes provide resources to host VMs. These resources can easily be assigned as needed. You will use the frontend which will be installed on the masternode to manage your worker node and hosted VMs.

In our project setup we used Ubuntu 18.04 as operating systems (OS). Therefore, slight differences could exist in the following commands, depending on your OS.

In our project setup we used VMWare Player Workstation to create VMs for master and worker nodes. This enables nested virtualization on the VMs. Furthermore, KVM was used as hypervisor for the VMs on the worker node.

18.2   Set Up Masternode with Frontend

18.2.1   Install Components

To start we need to download and install the necessary software components for the masternode. We use the sudo su command to execute all following commands with sudo privileges.

```
Listing 18.1: Install Components
1   sudo su
2   wget -q -O- https://downloads.opennebula.org/repo/repo.key | apt-key add -
3   echo "deb https://downloads.opennebula.org/repo/5.8/Ubuntu/18.04 stable opennebula"
4   > /etc/apt/sources.list.d/opennebula.list
5   apt update
6   apt-get install opennebula opennebula-sunstone opennebula-gate opennebula-flow
7   /usr/share/one/install_gems
```

18.2.2   Starting the Frontend

A default password is generated for the frontend. You can find it in the following file after "oneadmin:" which is the default username.

```
1   nano /var/lib/one/.one/one_auth
```

To change the password for the created linux user "oneadmin", execute the following command (as root).

```
1   passwd oneadmin
```

Next start OpenNebula and the frontend (called "Sunstone") service.

```
1   systemctl start opennebula
2   systemctl start opennebula-sunstone
```

To access the frontend open a browser and enter your masternode on Port 9869, which is used by default by OpenNebula. If you are working on the machine, just use localhost as computername.

```
1   http://<rechnername>:9869
```

You will see the login prompt. Use oneadmin and the password which you received earlier.

```
1 | Login: oneadmin, <generated password>
```

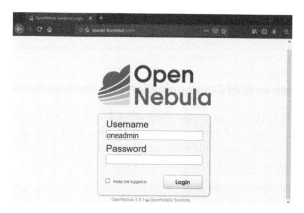

Figure 18.1: Sunstone login form.

You can change the default password of the webfrontend user in the user management section.

Figure 18.2: Change password of oneadmin or other users.

18.3 Set Up Worker Node with KVM

Depending on the hypervisor you want to use for your VMs you need to set up your worker node.

18.3.1 Install Components

```
     Listing 18.2: Install Components
1    sudo su
2    wget -q -O- https://downloads.opennebula.org/repo/repo.key | apt-key add -
3    echo "deb https://downloads.opennebula.org/repo/5.8/Ubuntu/18.04 stable opennebula"
4    > /etc/apt/sources.list.d/opennebula.list
5    apt-get update
6    apt-get install opennebula-node
7    service libvirtd restart
8    passwd oneadmin
```

18.3.2 Establish an SSH Communication Pipeline between Master and Worker

Your master needs to be able to access the worker through SSH passwordless. To enable this, login to your master and exchange communication keys with all worker nodes. Use the oneadmin user that the saved file has correct access rights. To make this step easier you can set the oneadmin password on all machines to the same string.

```
     Listing 18.3: Establish an SSH communication pipeline between Master and Worker
1    su oneadmin
2    ssh-keyscan <frontend-rechnername> <workernode-rechnername>
3    >> /var/lib/one/.ssh/known_hosts
4    scp -rp /var/lib/one/.ssh <workernode-rechnername>:/var/lib/one/
```

Confirm with your password previously set.
Test the SSH connection via terminal to be sure it works.

18.3.3 Network Configuration

Moreover, a bridge is needed on the worker node. In order to have a working network on the new VMs, the bridge must be created. One can do it in the /etc/network/interfaces file.

Here you must add the following text in order to have a working bridge (based on DHCP).

```
     Listing 18.4: Network configuration
1    auto br0
2    iface br0 inet dhcp
3    bridge_ports <network interface name>
```

Make sure that the network interface name (e.g., "eth0") is the one of your LAN connection. Also remember the name of the bridge, in this case "br0", which you may use in the Sunstone webfrontend for more advanced settings.

To check whether the bridge is working, you may use:

```
1    brctl show
```

18.4 Register Worker Node

You can do this step using the frontend:

```
1    Infrastructure -> Hosts
```

To add the worker use the plus symbol and enter the computername of the worker. If this step was successful the state should be 'ON' after several seconds.

Figure 18.3: Add worker node as host.

18.5   Deploy VM

Firstly, download a VM image from the OpenNebula AppStore via Sunstone-Frontend or upload an own image.

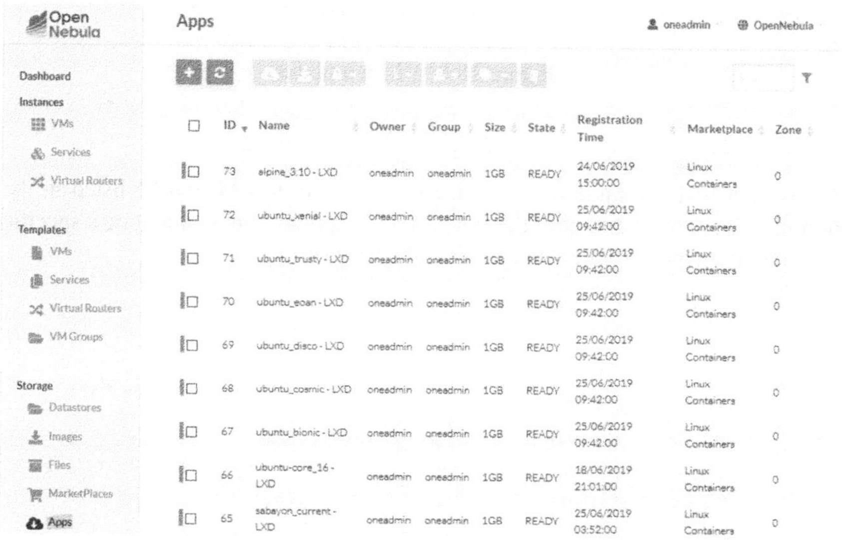

Figure 18.4: Apps that can be downloaded.

Afterwards click on VM Templates. You may use the predefined VM templates which are generated automatically if downloaded in the App Store. Otherwise, you can create an own VM template.

Figure 18.5: Available images that were downloaded.

Figure 18.6: VM templates.

To create a VM use the button `Instantiate`. Your VM will be listed in the `VMs` section in `Instances` and have the state `Pending` until you deploy it on a specific host. After deploying you can access via VNC in the browser.

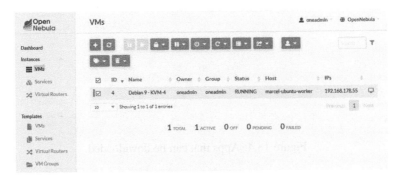

Figure 18.7: Running VM.

Figure 18.8: Accessing the VM via VNC.

References

1. University of Applied Sciences Frankfurt (2019), How to set up a basic private cloud environment with OpenNebula.

2. Milojicic, D., Llorente, I. M., & Montero, R. S. (2011). Opennebula: A cloud management tool. *IEEE Internet Computing*, 15(2), 11-14.

3. Toraldo, Giovanni. Opennebula 3 cloud computing. *Packt Publishing Ltd*, 2012.

4. Sotomayor, B., Montero, R. S., Llorente, I. M., & Foster, I. (2008). Capacity leasing in cloud systems using the opennebula engine.

5. Kostantos, K., Kapsalis, A., Kyriazis, D., Themistocleous, M., & da Cunha, P. R. (2013). OPEN-source IaaS fit for purpose: a comparison between OpenNebula and OpenStack. *International Journal of Electronic Business*, 11(3), 191-201.

6. Kessaci, Y., Melab, N., & Talbi, E. G. (2014). A multi-start local search heuristic for an energy efficient VMs assignment on top of the OpenNebula cloud manager. *Future Generation Computer Systems*, 36, 237-256.

7. Kalyanaraman, P., Jothi, K. R., Balakrishnan, P., Navya, R. G., Shah, A., & Pandey, V. (2020). Implementing Hadoop Container Migrations in OpenNebula Private Cloud Environment. *Role of Edge Analytics in Sustainable Smart City Development: Challenges and Solutions*, 85-103.

8. Belkadi, O., Laaziz, Y., Vulpe, A., & Halunga, S. (2019, November). An Integration of Open-Daylight and OpenNebula for Cloud Management Improvement using SDN. In *2019 27th Telecommunications Forum (TELFOR)* (pp. 1-4). IEEE.

9. https://github.com/OpenNebula

10. https://opennebula.io/

19

OPENSTACK

DAC-NHUONG LE[1], SOUVIK PAL[2], PRASANT KUMAR PATTNAIK[3]

[1] Haiphong University, Haiphong, Vietnam
[2] Sister Nivedita University, Kolkata, India
[3] KIIT, Deemed to be University, India
Email: nhuongld@dhhp.edu.vn, souvikpal22@gmail.com, patnaikprasant@gmail.com

Abstract

OpenStack is an open source platform, which offers powerful virtual servers and required services for cloud computing. It is mostly deployed as Infrastructure as a Service (IaaS), which aims to provide hardware tools and components for processing, storage, and networking resources throughout a data center.

OpenStack can be understood as a software platform that uses pooled virtual resources to build and manage clouds, both public and private ones. By default, OpenStack offers a couple of cloud-related services like networking, storage, image services, identity, etc., and can be clubbed with a few more to get a customized cloud optimization to support the cloud-native apps.

In this chapter, the reader will fully learn the basic needs and necessities of OpenStack; and a tutorial to install and get started with OpenStack will also be presented.

Keywords: OpenStack, simulator

19.1 OpenStack

Why should we adopt OpenStack? How does it fit our requirements? Here are a few reasons which answer our questions!

OpenStack is most importantly an open source environment that gives complete control over the cloud computation. Most of the platforms available in the market that help in virtualization and cloud computation are expensive and licensed. OpenStack can be installed free of cost and can be customized with the required services to suit the needs of the user. Hence, many corporations own their own version of OpenStack. Moreover, it can be scaled to any extent possible, making the jobs of the server admins easier. The OpenStack API is made robust and more flexible with improvements contributed by many developers across the world. This also ensures good community support. Many big shot companies in the IT world, like Huawei, Intel, Red Hat, have adopted OpenStack in their cloud management. Furthermore, most of us are unknowingly the users of OpenStack. Many cloud platforms have integrated OpenStack in their cloud toolkit by default. The OpenStack backend is ever growing, with more companies joining in every day!

19.2 Terminologies in OpenStack

The important terminologies that are repeatedly used in the rest of the module are discussed below in brief. These terminologies are important components of OpenStack architecture.

By default, OpenStack has many different moving parts. Besides, because of the open-source nature of the OpenStack, many developers can contribute to the addition of new components for the personalized application. But to clarify, the OpenStack community has declared around 9 components to be an integral part of OpenStack. They are:

- *Nova*: This is the fundamental computing engine of OpenStack. It manages a large number of virtual machines and other instances, which handle computing tasks.

- *Swift*: Swift is the storage system of OpenStack. It is used to store the objects and files. Instead of referring to the file and objects through the path, developers can instead refer to them through a unique identifier, which points to a file or piece of information and thereby allow the OpenStack to manage where to store the files. This reduces the effort of the developers to understand and worry about storage distribution. This also ensures that the data is being backed up in case of any failure of the machine or network loss.

- *Cinder*: This is known as the block storage component of OpenStack. This functions in a way that is analogous to the traditional ways of locating and accessing specific locations on a disk or a drive.

- *Neutron*: As the name suggests, this is the component that enables networking in OpenStack. It ensures that each component within the OpenStack is well connected with other components to establish good communication amongst them.

- *Horizon*: This is the dashboard of the OpenStack system. It provides all the possibilities for the system administrators to access and manage the cloud. This is the first component that everyone "sees" upon starting to use the OpenStack. Developers will be able to access and deal with all the components through the Application Programming Interface (API) also, while Horizon is the only place through which the system admins can interact with the OpenStack architecture.

- *Keystone*: This is the component that provides the identity services for all the users. It basically contains a central list of all the users of the OpenStack cloud mapped to the accessible services of the OpenStack. It provides a way for multiple access by allowing the developers to map their existing user access methods to Keystone.

- *Glance*: This provides the image services in OpenStack, where images refer to the virtual copies of the hard disks. Glance helps in allocating these images to be used as templates while assigning new virtual machine instances.

- *Ceilometer*: This provides telemetry services to its users. It performs a close regulation of each user's cloud components' usage and provides a bill for the services used. Think of the ceilometer as a component to meter the usage and report the same to individual users.

- *Heat*: This is that component of the OpenStack which allows developers to store the requirements of a cloud application in a file so that all the resources necessary for a program are available at hand. It thus provides an infrastructure to manage a cloud application. It is an orchestration instrument of OpenStack.

19.3   OpenStack Architecture

The basic components that make up the architecture of OpenStack are shown in Figure 19.1 and described below.

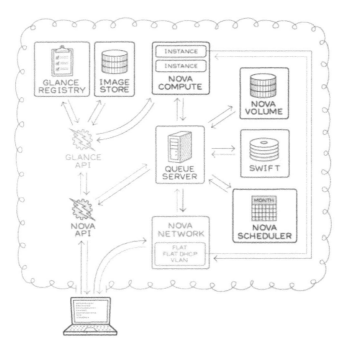

Figure 19.1: OpenStack architecture.

19.3.1 Compute (Nova)

Compute is one of the most important and mandatory components of OpenStack. It is basically a virtualization hypervisor. In a cloud computing environment, it acts as a controller, which manages all the resources in a virtual environment. It is also used to manage the high-performance bare metal configurations.

It is coded in Python and has utilized many predefined libraries to deliver robust functioning. The hypervisor technologies that might be used are Xen, KVM, and VMware, and this selection depends on the version of OpenStack used. SQL is used for database access.

The above scenario dissects the compute and the explanation of the scenario is given below.

Functionality:

- The nova-api handles the requests and responses from and to the end user.

- The nova-compute creates and destroys the instances as and when a request is made.

- Nova-scheduler schedules the tasks to the nova-compute.

- The glace registry stores the details of the image along with its metadata.

- The image store, stores the images predefined by the admin/user.

- The nova-network ensures the network connectivity and routing.

19.3.2 Networking (Neuron)

This is responsible for establishing a neuron structure between the components for better connectivity. It manages all the networking-related functionalities of the architecture as a whole. Starting from assigning and managing the IP addresses of the nodes to managing and implementing routing, it constitutes all.

19.3.3 Image

The instances of the virtual machines or the disk image are stored as images in glance image storage.

19.3.4 Object Storage (Swift)

This is the mountable storage unit of the architecture. It helps in data replication across the data center. The files and objects can be copied to multiple units with the help of this unit. The object storage units are replicated with every new server addition. It also stores the replicate content from all the active nodes and makes it available to the new clusters, ensuring a backup in case of any hardware failure or server loss.

19.3.5 Block Storage (Cinder)

Block storage provides persistent level storage facilities for cloud-oriented computing devices. It helps in the creation, addition, and removal of the new block devices in the server. It provides complete integration with the OpenStack, reducing the use of extraneous hardware components. It can be accessed and instructed using CLI or web-based services. Linux-based systems can go with Cloudbyte, EMC, Coraid, SAN Storage, etc.

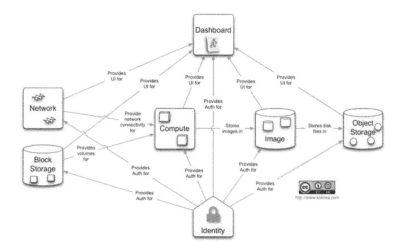

Figure 19.2: OpenStack object storage.

19.4   Logical Architecture

Understanding the logical architecture, besides the basic structural architecture, is essential to design, deploy and configure OpenStack.

OpenStack is made of all distinct services. Each of these services is internally configured to have one API service. Each API service is always looking for API requests and these requests when obtained are preprocessed and passed on to the other parts of the service.

The diagram below is a pictorial representation of the logical architecture in OpenStack.

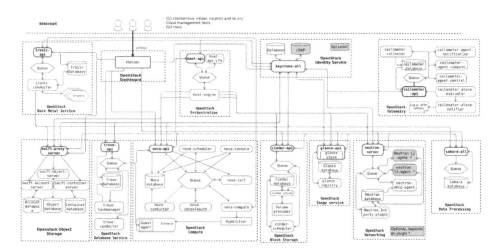

Figure 19.3: OpenStack logical architecture.

All services are authenticated through One Identity service (Keystone). Individual services generally interact with each other through the public APIs, except for a few, which require admin privileges.

For the inter-process communication within a service, AMQP message broker is used. The state of service will be stored and updated in the database.

When you are configuring your OpenStack cloud, you can choose the message broker and the database solution from a list of products/solutions available from the market, such as RabbitMQ, MySQL, MariaDB, and SQLite.

OpenStack can be accessed on Web User Interface through CLI or through API calls using tools like cURL or other plug-ins. Ultimately, all these REST API calls will allow access to the OpenStack services.

19.5 OpenStack Installation Guide

OpenStack, as an open source cloud computing platform, supports all cloud environments. It is contributed to by many developers across the world, leading to simple implementation with a rich set of features.

There are many versions of OpenStack available. Each of them differs in their installation and configuration by a few steps.

This section presents an informative tutorial that takes you through the steps required to install OpenStack. The instruction set is based on example architecture with minimalistic services. The following description is the basic setup requirement for all the versions of OpenStack installations.

19.5.1 Hardware requirements

An example of the components required for the OpenStack architecture is shown in Figure 19.4.

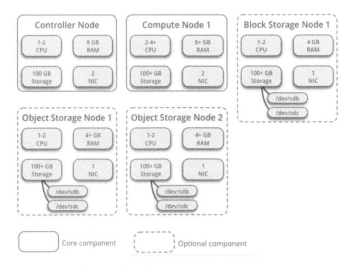

Figure 19.4: Hardware requirements.

Controller: The controller node mainly runs the following functionalities:

- Image Service

- Identity Service

- Management portions of :
  - Compute
  - Networking
  - Various networking agents
  - Dashboard

- Supporting services like SQL Database, message queue, NTP, etc.

- Controller node requires a minimum of two network interfaces.

Compute: The compute node basically runs the hypervisor portion. By default, it uses the KVM hypervisor. It also runs the Networking service agent that connects the instances to the virtual networks and also provides security through firewalling via security groups. More than one compute node can be deployed. A minimum of two network interfaces are required for each compute node.

Block Storage: The optional block storage requires a minimum of one network interface. It contains the disks for Block Storage and Shared File System services.

Production environment should have a separate storage network to increase efficiency. However, for the sake of simplicity, a management network is used between the compute nodes and the block storage.

Object Storage: Like the block storage, object storage is also optional and contains disks that are used for storing accounts, containers, and objects.

This service demands two nodes. Each node demands two network interfaces. More than one object storage service can be deployed in a system.

19.5.2   Networking requirements

There are two options available for networking. You can choose either of them. They are:

1. Provider Networks: The features of provider networking are given below:

   - They deploy the simplest OpenStack networking possible with Layer 2 (switching/bridging) services and VLAN segmentation networks.

   - They bridge the virtual network with the physical network infrastructure to enable the Layer 3 routing services.

   - They depend on the physical network infrastructure for Layer 3 routing services.

   - The instances are supplied with the IP address information through a DHCP service.

2. Self-Service Networks: This method of networking just augments the provider networking with the Layer 3 routing services, which enable the self-service networks (private networks). It basically uses overlay segmentation methods such as VXLAN

to include the services for private networks. It routes the virtual network to the physical network using NAT; and also draws a foundation for advanced services like LBaaS and FWaaS (see Figures 19.5 and 19.6).

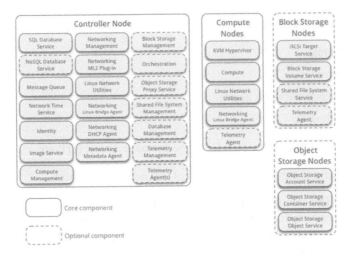

Figure 19.5: Networking option 1: Provider networks.

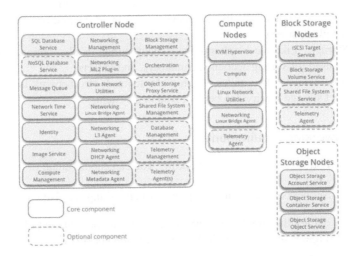

Figure 19.6: Networking option 2: Self-service networks.

Environment: This segment deals with configuring the controller node and a compute node within the example architecture.

Although many environments include Image service, Identity, Compute, at least one networking service, and the dashboard, the Object Storage service is capable of working independently. However, if you want to just try out the Object Storage service, ensure that the appropriate nodes are configured.

In order to configure nodes, use the account in admin privileges. To do this, either run commands as the "root" user or configure "sudo" utilities.

Before proceeding further, make sure that the hardware requirements are met.

Following are the requirements to make a proof-of-concept model for the OpenStack deployment with core services and CirrOS instances.

- Controller Node: 1 processor, 4 GB memory, and 5 GB storage.

- Compute Node: 1 processor, 2 GB memory, and 10 GB storage.

With an increase in the services added to the basic architecture, the hardware requirements also scale up to get the best performance.

To improvise the efficiency and reduce cluttering, minimal installation is recommended on your Linux distribution.

On each of the nodes, be sure to install a 64-bit version of your distribution.

For most of the application, a single partition on the disk is sufficient; however, for the extra additions like optional block storage, additional partition might be required. Try considering Logical Volume Manager (LVM) for such cases.

Many beginners decide on building each host as a virtual machine, for initial testing and trial sessions, mainly for two reasons:

- Only one physical server is sufficient to handle multiple nodes with any number of network interfaces.

- Periodic "snapshot" (history) will be marked during the installation process. Hence, you can always "roll back" to a working event, in case of any hiccups.

- However, the performance of hosts will suffer through VMs, particularly if, the hypervisor/processor is incapable of handling the nested VMs.

Security: While installing the OpenStack capabilities on your system, it is important to configure it for security during the process, so that all the computation on the cloud will be handled securely later. There are many security options available for the user such as password and policy.

Encryption: Additionally, the other services include the database server and message broker password security.

19.6   OpenStack Work

Cloud mainly provides computing for the end users in a remote environment, where they deploy the software programs and run them, instead of a physical environment that has more limitation in terms of capabilities and storage. OpenStack is considered an Infrastructure as a Service (IaaS), where it helps the users to easily add a new instance on which the cloud components can run. Basically, the infrastructure aims to provide a "platform" on which the developer can create and deploy software applications.

After understanding the layers of architecture, it is important to reconnect the dots and understand how OpenStack works!

Horizon is the face of the application environment. Everything a user needs to do should start with the dashboard, which is called Horizon. It is a simple graphical user interface which has the divided modules that perform a specific action.

As we know, every action on OpenStack works as a service API call. Every API call is first authenticated by Keystone for the permission availability. So, before you access the dashboard of OpenStack, you will have to authenticate yourself as a registered user, through your login credentials.

Once you successfully log in, you will see your dashboard with options to create new image instances, cinder, volumes and to configure network details.

The image instances are basically the instances of your virtual machines or environments on which you will configure the cloud. They can be Ubuntu, CirrOS, Red Hat, openSUSE, etc.

You can choose an instance and enter the details, such as the network configuration, to create a new one. This instance can be connected to new cinder instance or volumes to include any extra services. Remember that the creation of new image instance is also an API call.

Once an image is created, you can configure it and manage it through the CLI and add whatever data you want to add. You may even want to perform many extended operations on the instance created.

Any data computation performed on the cloud instance created will be stored along with its metadata in image architecture and other storage components, and thus in the associated databases.

You can even configure an instance to store the snapshots, where the state of the disk at any moment will be stored for future reference. This provision is available in the dashboard.

OpenStack is known as a platform to provide the cloud computing services. Amazon Web Services (AWS) is also known as a reliable and scalable platform for inexpensive cloud computing services. Both of these platforms are widely used by many shark companies for backend configuration. Considering the large-scale implementation, it is important for us to know which of the two solutions fit our need the best, before deciding to adopt one. The distinct differences of the two are given below. Go through each, then bank on one for the deployment.

Table 19.1: OpenStack vs. AWS.

Service	OpenStack	AWS
Compute Controller	Nova	EC2
Object Storage	Swift	S3
Identity & Access Management	Keystone	IAM
Image Catalog Service	Glance	AMI Catalog
Self-Service Portal	Horizon	Management Console
Virtual Networking	Quantum	VPC
Block Storage	Cinder	EBS
Templating & Orchestration	Heat	CloudFormation
Monitoring and Metering	Ceilometer	CloudWatch

References

1. Van, V. N., Long, N. Q., Nguyen, G. N., & Le, D. N. (2016). A performance analysis of openstack open-source solution for IaaS cloud computing. In *Proceedings of the Second Inter-*

national Conference on Computer and Communication Technologies (pp. 141-150). Springer, New Delhi.

2. Van, V. N., Long, N. Q., & Le, D. N. (2016). Performance analysis of network virtualization in cloud computing infrastructures on openstack. In *Innovations in Computer Science and Engineering* (pp. 95-103). Springer, Singapore.

3. Le, D. N., Kumar, R., Nguyen, G. N., & Chatterjee, J. M. (2018). *Cloud computing and virtualization.* John Wiley & Sons.

4. Seth, B., Dalal, S., Jaglan, V., Le, D. N., Mohan, S., & Srivastava, G. (2020). Integrating encryption techniques for secure data storage in the cloud. *Transactions on Emerging Telecommunications Technologies*, e4108.

5. Fifield, T., Fleming, D., Gentle, A., Hochstein, L., Proulx, J., Toews, E., & Topjian, J. (2014). *OpenStack Operations Guide: Set up and manage your openstack cloud.* O'Reilly Media, Inc.".

6. Markelov, A. (2016). *Certified OpenStack Administrator Study Guide.* Apress.

7. Khedher, O. (2015). *Mastering OpenStack.* Packt Publishing Ltd.

8. https://www:openstack:com

9. https://www:rdoproject:org/install/packstack/

10. https://mindmajix.com/openstack-tutorial

20

EUCALYPTUS

Souvik Pal[1], Dac-Nhuong Le[2], Prasant Kumar Pattnaik[3]

[1] Sister Nivedita University, Kolkata, India
[2] Haiphong University, Haiphong, Vietnam
[3] KIIT, Deemed to be University, India
 Email: souvikpal22@gmail.com, nhuongld@dhhp.edu.vn, patnaikprasant@gmail.com

Abstract

Eucalyptus is open source software for building Amazon Web Services (AWS)-compatible private and hybrid clouds computing environments, originally developed by the company Eucalyptus Systems. Eucalyptus is an acronym for Elastic Utility Computing Architecture for Linking Your Programs To Useful Systems. It enables pooling compute, storage, and network resources that can be dynamically scaled up or down as application workloads change.

Keywords: Eucalyptus, simulator

20.1 Introduction to Eucalyptus

20.1.1 Eucalyptus Overview

Eucalyptus is a Linux-based software architecture that implements scalable, efficiency-enhancing private and hybrid clouds within an enterprise's existing IT infrastructure. Because Eucalyptus provides infrastructure as a service (IaaS), you can provision your own resources (hardware, storage, and network) through Eucalyptus on an as-needed basis.

A Eucalyptus cloud is deployed across your enterprise's on-premise data center. As a result, your organization has full control of the cloud infrastructure. You can implement and enforce various levels of security. Sensitive data managed by the cloud does not have to leave your enterprise boundaries, keeping data completely protected from external access by your enterprise firewall.

Eucalyptus was designed from the ground up to be easy to install and non-intrusive. The software framework is modular, with industry-standard, language-agnostic communication. Eucalyptus is also unique in that it provides a virtual network overlay that isolates network traffic of different users as well as allows two or more clusters to appear to belong to the same local area network (LAN).

Eucalyptus is also compatible with Amazon's EC2, S3, and IAM services. This offers you hybrid cloud capability.

20.1.2 Eucalyptus Architecture

The Eucalyptus architecture is shown in Figure 20.1.

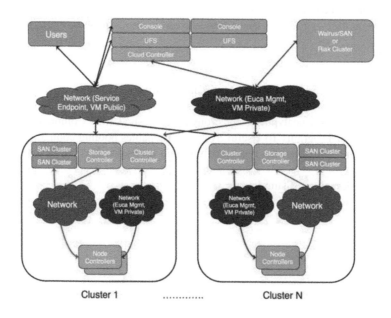

Figure 20.1: Eucalyptus architecture.

The cloud components: Cloud Controller (CLC) and Walrus, as well as user components: User-Facing Services (UFS) and the Management Console, communicate with cluster components: the Cluster Controllers (CCs) and Storage Controllers (SCs). The CCs and SCs, in turn, communicate with the Node Controllers (NCs). The networks between machines hosting these components must be able to allow TCP connections between them.

However, if the CCs are on separate subnets (one for the network on which the cloud components are hosted and another for the network that NCs use) the CCs will act as software routers between these networks in some networking configurations. Each cluster can use an internal private network for its NCs, and the CCs can route traffic from that private network to a network shared by the cloud components.

Virtual machines (VMs) run on the machines that host NCs. You can use the CCs as software routers for traffic between clients outside Eucalyptus and VMs. Or the VMs can use the routing framework already in place without CC software routers. However, depending on the Layer 2 isolation characteristics of your existing network, you might not be able to implement all of the security features supported by Eucalyptus.

Riak CS clusters provide an alternative to Walrus as an object storage provider. SAN clusters, available to Eucalyptus subscribers, are alternatives to direct-attached storage and Ceph as block storage providers.

20.1.3 Eucalyptus Components

This subsection describes the various components that comprise a Eucalyptus cloud.

The following Figure 20.2 shows a high-level architecture of Eucalyptus with its main components.

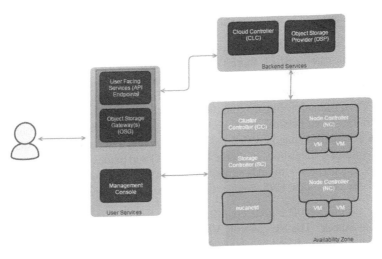

Figure 20.2: Eucalyptus components.

A detailed description of each Eucalyptus component follows.

- *Cloud Controller*: In many deployments, the cloud controller (CLC) service and the user-facing services (UFS) are on the same host machine. This server is the entry-point into the cloud for administrators, developers, project managers, and end-users. The CLC handles persistence and is the backend for the UFS. A Eucalyptus cloud must have exactly one CLC.

- *User-Facing Services*: The user-facing services (UFS) serve as endpoints for the AWS-compatible services offered by Eucalyptus: EC2 (compute), AS (AutoScaling), CW (CloudWatch), ELB (LoadBalancing), IAM (euare), and STS (tokens). A Eucalyptus cloud can have several UFS host machines.

- *Object Storage Gateway*: The object storage gateway (OSG) is part of the UFS. The OSG passes requests to object storage providers and talks to the persistence layer (DB) to authenticate requests. You can use Walrus, Riak CS, or Ceph RGW as the object storage provider.

- *Object Storage Provider*: The object storage provider (OSP) can be either the Eucalyptus Walrus backend, Riak CS, or Ceph RGW. Walrus is intended for light S3 usage and is a single service. Riak is an open source scalable general purpose data platform; it is intended for deployments with heavy S3 usage. Ceph RGW is an object storage interface built on top of Librados.

- *Management Console*: The Eucalyptus management console is an easy-to-use web-based interface that allows you to manage your Eucalyptus cloud. The management console is often deployed on the same host machine as the UFS. A Eucalyptus cloud can have multiple management console host machines.

- *Cluster Controller*: The cluster controller (CC) service must run on a host machine that has network connectivity to the host machines running the node controllers (NCs) and to the host machine for the CLC. CCs gather information about a set of NCs and schedule virtual machine (VM) execution on specific NCs. All NCs associated with a single CC must be in the same subnet.

- *Storage Controller*: The storage controller (SC) service provides functionality similar to Amazon Elastic Block Store (Amazon EBS). The SC can interface with various storage systems. Elastic block storage exports storage volumes that can be attached by a VM and mounted or accessed as a raw block device. EBS volumes can persist past VM termination and are commonly used to store persistent data. An EBS volume cannot be shared between multiple VMs at once and can be accessed only within the same availability zone in which the VM is running. Users can create snapshots from EBS volumes. Snapshots are stored by the OSG and made available across availability zones. Eucalyptus with SAN support provides the ability to use your enterprise-grade SAN devices to host EBS storage within a Eucalyptus cloud.

- *Node Controller*: The node controller (NC) service runs on any machine that hosts VM instances. The NC controls VM activities, including the execution, inspection, and termination of VM instances. It also fetches and maintains a local cache of instance images, and it queries and controls the system software (host OS and the hypervisor) in response to queries and control requests from the CC.

- *Eucanetd*: The eucanetd service implements artifacts to manage and define Eucalyptus cloud networking. Eucanetd runs alongside the CLC or NC services, depending on the configured networking mode.

20.2   Eucalyptus Installation

This section describes concepts and tasks you need to successfully install Eucalyptus.

20.2.1 System Requirements

To install Eucalyptus, your system must meet the baseline requirements described below.
   Compute Requirements:

- Physical Machines: All Eucalyptus services must be installed on physical servers, not virtual machines.

- Central Processing Units (CPUs): We recommend that each host machine in your Eucalyptus cloud contain either an Intel or AMD processor with a minimum of 4 2GHz cores.

- Operating Systems: Eucalyptus supports the following Linux distributions: CentOS 7 and RHEL 7. Eucalyptus supports only 64-bit architecture.

- Machine Clocks: Each Eucalyptus host machine and any client machine clocks must be synchronized (for example, using NTP). These clocks must be synchronized all the time, not only during the installation process.

- Machine Access: Verify that all machines in your network allow SSH login, and that root or sudo access is available on each of them.

Storage and Memory Requirements:

- Each machine in your network needs a minimum of 160GB of storage.

- We recommend at least 500GB for Walrus and SC hosts running Linux VMs. We recommend at least 250GB for Walrus and SC hosts running Windows VMs.

- We recommend 160GB per NC host running Linux VMs, and at least 250GB per NC host for running Windows VMs. Note that larger available disk space enables a greater number of VMs.

- Each machine in your network needs a minimum of 8GB RAM. However, we recommend more RAM for improved caching.

- Host machines running multiple services (e.g., CLC, CC and SC) likely need more than the minimum amounts of RAM and storage.

Network Requirements:

- All NCs must have access to a minimum of 1Gb Ethernet network connectivity.

- All Eucalyptus components must have at least one Network Interface Card (NIC) for a baseline deployment. For better network isolation and scale, the CC should have two NICs (one facing the CLC/user network and one facing the NC/VM network).

- For Edge networking mode, Eucalyptus needs at least one existing network.

- For VPCMIDO networking mode, Eucalyptus needs Midokura Enterprise MidoNet to be installed. For more information, see Install Midokura Enterprise MidoNet.

- The network connecting machines that host Eucalyptus components (except the CC and NC) must support UDP multicast for IP address 239.193.7.3. Note that UDP multicast is not used over the network that connects the CC to the NCs.

- Once you are satisfied that your systems requirements are met, you are ready to plan your Eucalyptus installation.

20.2.2 Services Placement

A Eucalyptus deployment includes user services (UFS and Management Console), as well as cloud services (Cloud Controller and Walrus) and one or more zones, each of which contains a Cluster Controller, a Storage Controller, and one or more Node Controllers (see Figure 20.3).

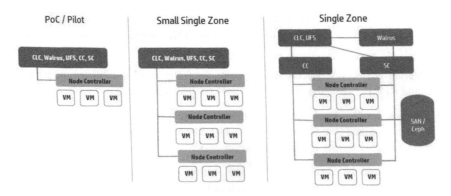

Figure 20.3: Eucalyptus services placement.

Cloud Services: The main decision for cloud services is whether to install the Cloud Controller (CLC) and Walrus on the same server. If they are on the same server, they operate as separate web services within a single Java environment, and they use a fast path for inter-service communication. If they are not on the same server, they use SOAP and REST to work together.

Sometimes the key factor for cloud services is not performance, but server cost and data center configuration. If you only have one server available for the cloud, then you have to install the services on the same server.

All services should be in the same data center. They use aggressive time-outs to maintain system responsiveness so separating them over a long-latency, lossy network link will not work.

User Services: The User Facing Services (UFS) handle all of the AWS APIs and provide an entry point for clients and users interacting with the Eucalyptus cloud. The UFS and the Management Console are often hosted on the same machine since both must be accessible from the public, client-facing network.

You may optionally choose to have redundant UFS and Management Console host machines behind a load balancer.

Zone Services: The Eucalyptus services deployed in the zone level of a Eucalyptus deployment are the Cluster Controller (CC) and Storage Controller (SC).

You can install all zone services on a single server, or you can distribute them on different servers. The choice of one or multiple servers is dictated by the demands of user workload in terms of number of instances (CC) and EBS volume access (SC).

Things to consider for CC placement:

- Place the CC on a server that has TCP/IP connectivity to the Eucalyptus frontend servers and the NC servers in its zone.

- Each CC can manage a maximum of 4000 instances.

Things to consider for SC placement:

- The SC host machine must always have TCP/IP connectivity to the CLC and be able to multicast to the CLC.

- The SC must have TCP/IP connectivity to the UFS/OSG hosts for uploading snapshots into the object store. (The SC does not require connectivity directly to users, it is an internal component and does not serve user EBS API requests; that job is done by the UFS.)

- The SC must be reachable via TCP/IP from all NCs in the zone within which the SC is registered. The SC and NC exchange tokens to authorize volume attachment, so they must be able to directly communicate. The SC provides the NCs with network access to the dynamic block volumes on the SC's storage (if the SC is configured for overlay local filesystem or DAS-JBOD).

- If you are a subscriber and use one of the Eucalyptus-provided SAN integration drivers, the SC must also have TCP/IP connectivity to the SAN device. The SC sends control messages to the SAN and acts as a proxy to upload snapshots from the SAN to the UFS/OSG.

- If you are going to use overlay local filesystem or DAS-JBOD configurations to export local SC storage for EBS, then SC storage should consist of a fast, reliable disk pool (either local file system or block-attached storage) so that the SC can create and maintain volumes for the NCs. The capacity of the disk pool should be sufficient to provide the NCs with enough space to accommodate all dynamic block volumes requests from end users.

Node Services: The node controllers are the services that comprise the Eucalyptus backend. All NCs must have network connectivity to whatever machine hosts their EBS volumes. This host is either a SAN or the SC.

20.2.3   Eucalyptus Features

Before installing Eucalyptus, we recommend that you think about the features you plan to implement with Eucalyptus. These features are detailed below.

- *Windows Guest OS Support*: This details what Eucalyptus needs in order to use Windows as a guest operating system.

- *SAN Support*: Eucalyptus includes optional, subscription only support for integrating enterprise-grade SAN (storage area network) hardware devices into a Eucalyptus cloud.

- *Availability Zone Support*: Eucalyptus offers the ability to create multiple local availability zones.

- *Object Storage*: Eucalyptus supports Walrus and Riak CS as its object storage backend. There is no extra planning if you use Walrus. If you use Riak CS, you can use a single Riak CS cluster for several Eucalyptus clouds. Basho (the vendor of Riak CS) recommends five nodes for each Riak CS cluster. This also means that you have to set up and configure a load balancer between the Riak CS nodes and the object storage gateway (OSG).

20.2.4 Networking Modes

Eucalyptus overlays a virtual network on top of your existing network. In order to do this, Eucalyptus supports these networking modes: Edge (AWS EC2 Classic compatible) and VPCMIDO (AWS VPC compatible).

These networking modes are designed to allow you to choose an appropriate level of security and flexibility for your cloud. The purpose is to direct Eucalyptus to use different network features to manage the virtual networks that connect VMs to each other and to clients external to Eucalyptus.

Eucalyptus networking modes are generally modeled after AWS networking capabilities. In legacy AWS accounts, you have the ability to choose EC2 Classic network mode or VPC network mode. New AWS accounts do not have this flexibility and are forced into using VPC. Eucalyptus VPCMIDO mode is similar to AWS VPC in that it allows users to fully manage their cloud network, including the definition of a Classless Inter-Domain Routing (CIDR) block, subnets, and security groups with rules for additional protocols beyond the default three (UDP, TCP, and ICMP) available in EC2 Classic networking.

Your choice of networking mode depends on the following considerations:

- Does your Eucalyptus cloud need to mimic behavior in your AWS account? If you need EC2-Classic behavior, select Edge mode. If you need EC2-VPC behavior, select VPCMIDO mode.

- Do you need to create security group rules with additional protocols (e.g., all protocols, RDP, XTP, etc.)? If so, choose VPCMIDO mode.

- If there is no specific requirement for either mode, then VPCMIDO mode is recommended given its flexibility and networking features.

20.2.5 Install Repositories

This subsection guides you through installing Eucalyptus from RPM package downloads.

The first step to installing Eucalyptus is to download the RPM packages. When you're ready, continue to Software Signing.

The following terminology might help you as you proceed through this section.

Eucalyptus open source software: Eucalyptus release packages include the freely available components, which enable you to deploy a Eucalyptus cloud.

Eucalyptus enterprise software: Paid subscribers have access to additional software features (for example, SAN support). If you are a subscriber, you receive an entitlement certificate and a private key that allow you to download Eucalyptus subscription software. (Everybody receives a GPG public key to be used to verify the software integrity.)

Euca2ools CLI: Euca2ools is the Eucalyptus command line interface for interacting with web services. It is compatible with many Amazon AWS services, so can be used with Eucalyptus as well as AWS.

RPM and YUM and software signing: Eucalyptus CentOS and RHEL download packages are in RPM (Red Hat Package Manager) format and use the YUM package management tool. We use GPG keys to sign our software packages and package repositories.

EPEL software: EPEL (Extra Packages for Enterprise Linux) are free, open source software, which is fully separated from licensed RHEL distribution. It requires its own package.

20.2.5.1 *Software Signing*

A number of GPG keys can be used to software packages and package repositories. The necessary public keys are provided with the relevant products and can be used to automatically verify software updates. You can also verify the packages or package repositories manually using the keys on this page. Use the rpm –checksig command on a download file to verify a RPM package for an Eucalyptus product.

```
1   rpm --checksig -v myfilename.rpm
```

Follow the procedure detailed on Debian's SecureApt web page to verify a deb package for an Eucalyptus product. Please do not use package signing keys to encrypt email messages.

20.2.5.2 *Install Eucalyptus Release Packages*

The prerequisite hardware and software should be in place and available to Eucalyptus.

1. Configure the Eucalyptus package repository on each host machine that will run a Eucalyptus service:

```
1   yum install http://downloads.eucalyptus.cloud/software/eucalyptus/
2   4.4/rhel/7/x86_64/eucalyptus-release-4.4-2.8.as.el7.noarch.rpm
```

   Enter y when prompted to install this package.

2. (Optional) If you are a Eucalyptus subscriber, you will receive two RPM package files containing your license for subscription-only services. Install these packages on each host machine that will run a Eucalyptus service. Install the license files to access the enterprise repository.

```
1   yum install eucalyptus-enterprise-license*.noarch.rpm
2   http://downloads.eucalyptus.com/software/subscription/
3   eucalyptus-enterprise-release-4.4-1.el7.noarch.rpm
```

3. Configure the Euca2ools package repository on each host machine that will run a Eucalyptus service or Euca2ools:

```
1   yum install http://downloads.eucalyptus.cloud/software/euca2ools/
2   3.4/rhel/7/x86_64/euca2ools-release-3.4-2.2.as.el7.noarch.rpm
```

   Enter y when prompted to install this package.

4. Configure the EPEL package repository on each host machine that will run a Eucalyptus service or Euca2ools:

   - For RHEL/CentOS 7.3

```
1   yum install http://dl.fedoraproject.org/pub/epel/
2   epel-release-latest-7.noarch.rpm
```

   Enter y when prompted to install this package.

   - For RHEL/CentOS 7.4 and higher

```
1   yum install epel-release
```

   Enter y when prompted to install this package.

5. If you are installing on RHEL 7, you must enable the Optional repository in Red Hat Network for each NC as follows:

- Go to http://rhn.redhat.com and navigate to the system that will run the NC.
- Click Alter Channel Subscriptions.
- Make sure the RHEL Server Optional check-box is selected.
- Click Change Subscriptions.

6. The following steps should be performed on each NC host machine.

    - Install the Eucalyptus Node Controller software on each NC host:

      ```
      1    yum install eucalyptus-node
      ```

    - Remove the default libvirt network. This step allows the eucanetd dhcpd server to start.

      ```
      1  virsh net-destroy default
      2  virsh net-autostart default --disable
      ```

    - Check that the KVM device node has proper permissions. Run the following command:

      ```
      1  ls -l /dev/kvm
      ```

    - Verify that the output shows that the device node is owned by user root and group kvm.

      ```
      1  crw-rw-rw- 1 root kvm 10, 232 Nov 30 10:27 /dev/kvm
      ```

      If your KVM device node does not have proper permissions, you need to reboot your NC host.

7. On each CLC host machine, install the Eucalyptus Cloud Controller software.

   ```
   1  yum install eucalyptus-cloud
   ```

8. Install the backend service image package on the machine hosting the CLC:

   ```
   1  yum install eucalyptus-service-image
   ```

   This installs worker images for both the load balancer and imaging services.

9. On the UFS host machine, install the Eucalyptus Cloud Controller software.

   ```
   1  yum install eucalyptus-cloud
   ```

10. (Optional) On the UFS host machine, also install the Management Console.

    ```
    1  yum install eucaconsole
    ```

    The Management Console can run on any host machine, even one that does not have other Eucalyptus services. For more information, see the Console Guide.

11. Install the software for the remaining Eucalyptus services. The following example shows services being installed on the same host machine. We recommend that you use a different host machine for each service, when possible:

    ```
    1  yum install eucalyptus-cluster eucalyptus-sc eucalyptus-walrus
    ```

12. This installs the cloud controller (CC), storage controller (SC), and Walrus Backend services. (Optional). If you are a subscriber and use a SAN, run the appropriate command for your device on each CLC host machine:

- For HP 3PAR SAN:

```
1  yum install eucalyptus-enterprise-storage-san-threepar-libs
```

- For NetApp SAN:

```
1  yum install eucalyptus-enterprise-storage-san-netapp-libs
```

- For Dell EqualLogic SAN:

```
1  yum install eucalyptus-enterprise-storage-san-equallogic-libs
```

13. (Optional) If you are a subscriber and use a SAN, run the appropriate command for your device on each SC host machine:

- For HP 3PAR SAN:

```
1  yum install eucalyptus-enterprise-storage-san-threepar
```

- For NetApp SAN:

```
1  yum install eucalyptus-enterprise-storage-san-netapp
```

- For Dell EqualLogic SAN:

```
1  yum install eucalyptus-enterprise-storage-san-equallogic
```

The package installation is complete.

20.3 Configure Eucalyptus

This section describes the parameters you need to set in order to launch Eucalyptus for the first time.

The first launch of Eucalyptus is different than a restart of a previously running Eucalyptus deployment in that it sets up the security mechanisms that will be used by the installation to ensure system integrity.

Eucalyptus configuration is stored in a text file, `/etc/eucalyptus/eucalyptus.conf`, that contains key-value pairs specifying various configuration parameters. Eucalyptus reads this file when it launches and when various forms of reset commands are sent the Eucalyptus components.

1. Configure SELinux: Security-Enhanced Linux (SELinux) is a security feature for Linux that allows you to set access control through policies. Eucalyptus 4.4 packages automatically install SELinux policy for Eucalyptus on RHEL 7 and CentOS 7. We recommend enabling SELinux on host systems running Eucalyptus 4.4 services to improve their security on RHEL 7. Enabling SELinux, as described in this topic, can help contain break-ins. You need to set Boolean values on Storage Controller (SC) and Management Console host machines. If your network mode is VPCMIDO, you also set a Boolean value on the Cloud Controller (CLC) host machines. To configure SELinux on Eucalyptus 4.4:

    (a) On each Storage Controller (SC) host machine, run the following command:

```
1 │ setsebool -P eucalyptus_storage_controller 1
```

This allows Eucalyptus to manage EBS volumes.

(b) On each Management Console host machine, run the following command:

```
1 │ setsebool -P httpd_can_network_connect 1
```

This allows the Management Console's HTTP proxy to access the back end.

(c) If your cloud uses VPCMIDO networking mode, on the Cloud Controller (CLC), run the following command:

```
1 │ setsebool -P httpd_can_network_connect 1
```

This allows the CLC's HTTP proxy to access the back end. SELinux is now configured and ready to use with your Eucalyptus 4.4 cloud.

2. Configure Network Modes: Eucalyptus overlays a virtual network on top of your existing network. In order to do this, Eucalyptus supports these networking modes: Edge (AWS EC2 Classic compatible) and VPCMIDO (AWS VPC compatible).

   ▪ Configure Edge Network Mode: This provides configuration instructions for Eucalyptus Edge network mode. Eucalyptus requires network connectivity between its clients (end-users) and the cloud components (e.g., CC, CLC, and Walrus).

   ▪ Configure VPCMIDO Network Mode: This provides configuration instructions for Eucalyptus VPCMIDO network mode. Eucalyptus requires network connectivity between its clients (end-users) and the cloud components (e.g., CC, CLC, and storage).

3. Create Scheduling Policy: This describes how to set up the Cluster Controller (CC) to choose which Node Controller (NC) to run each new instance.

   (a) In the CC, open the /etc/eucalyptus/eucalyptus.conf file.

   (b) In the SCHEDPOLICY=parameter, set the value to one of the following:

      ▪ GREEDY: When the CC receives a new instance run request, it runs the instance on the first NC in an ordered list of NCs that has the capacity to run the instance. At partial capacity with some amount of churn, this policy generally results in a steady state over time where some nodes are running many instances, and some nodes are running few or no instances.

      ▪ ROUNDROBIN (Default): When the CC receives a new instance run request, it runs the instance on the next NC in an ordered list of NCs that has capacity. The next NC is determined by the last NC to have received an instance. At partial capacity with some amount of churn, this policy generally results in a steady state over time where instances are more evenly distributed across the set of NCs.

   (c) Save the file.

20.4 Amazon Web Services Compatibility

Organizations can use or reuse AWS-compatible tools, images, and scripts to manage their own on-premises infrastructure as a service (IaaS) environment. The AWS API is implemented on top of Eucalyptus, so tools in the cloud ecosystem that can communicate with AWS can use the same API with Eucalyptus. In March 2012, Amazon Web Services and Eucalyptus announced details of the compatibility between AWS and Eucalyptus. As part of this agreement, AWS will support Eucalyptus as they continue to extend compatibility with AWS APIs and customer use cases. Customers can run applications in their existing data centers that are compatible with Amazon Web Services such as Amazon Elastic Compute Cloud (EC2) and Amazon Simple Storage Service (S3).

Eucalyptus 3.3 was released, featuring a new series of AWS-compatible tools. These include:

- *Autoscaling*: This allows application developers to scale Eucalyptus cloud resources up or down in order to maintain performance and meet SLAs. With autoscaling, developers can add instances and virtual machines as traffic demands increase. Autoscaling policies for Eucalyptus are defined using Amazon EC2-compatible APIs and tools.

- *Elastic Load Balancing*: This is a service that distributes incoming application traffic and service calls across multiple Eucalyptus workload instances, providing greater application fault tolerance.

- *CloudWatch*: This is a monitoring tool similar to Amazon CloudWatch that monitors resources and applications on Eucalyptus clouds. Using CloudWatch, application developers and cloud administrators can program the collection of metrics, set alarms and identify trends that may be endangering workload operations, and take action to ensure their applications continue to run smoothly.

Eucalyptus 4.4.5 (2018) is also the first private cloud platform to support Netflix's open source tools — including Chaos Monkey, Asgard, and Edda — through its API fidelity with AWS.

References

1. Eucalyptus Open Source Software License Agreement. http://www.eucalyptus.com/licenses/eucalyptus-software-license-agreement

2. Jonathan Gershater (August 24, 2012). Examining Excellent Eucalyptus. *Cloud Computing Journal*. Retrieved June 1, 2013.

3. Yohan Wadia (2012). The Eucalyptus Open-Source Private Cloud. *Cloudbook*. Archived from the original on May 27, 2013. Retrieved June 1, 2013.

4. Nurmi, D., Wolski, R., Grzegorczyk, C., Obertelli, G., Soman, S., Youseff, L., & Zagorodnov, D. (2009, May). The eucalyptus open-source cloud-computing system. In 2009 9th IEEE/ACM *International Symposium on Cluster Computing and the Grid* (pp. 124-131). IEEE.

5. Nurmi, D., Wolski, R., Grzegorczyk, C., Obertelli, G., Soman, S., Youseff, L., & Zagorodnov, D. (2008). Eucalyptus: A technical report on an elastic utility computing architecture linking your programs to useful systems. In *UCSB Technical Report*.

6. Cordeiro, T. D., Damalio, D. B., Pereira, N. C. V. N., Endo, P. T., de Almeida Palhares, A., Goncalves, G. E., ... & Mångs, J. E. (2010, November). Open source cloud computing platforms. In 2010 *Ninth International Conference on Grid and Cloud Computing* (pp. 366-371). IEEE.

7. Le, D. N., Kumar, R., Nguyen, G. N., & Chatterjee, J. M. (2018). *Cloud computing and virtualization*. John Wiley & Sons.

8. Duarte, A., Acevedo-Munõz, L., Gonçalves, C. I., Mota, L., Sarmento, A., Silva, M., ... & Valente, C. (2020). Detection of Longhorned Borer Attack and Assessment in Eucalyptus Plantations Using UAV Imagery. *Remote Sensing*, 12(19), 3153.

9. Bhan, R., Ahmad, M. S., Jain, M., Singh, A., Pamula, R., & Faruki, P. (2019, January). VM Availability in Presence of Malicious Attacks in Open-Source Cloud. In *2019 9th International Conference on Cloud Computing, Data Science & Engineering (Confluence)* (pp. 26-30). IEEE.

10. https://www.eucalyptus.cloud/

Glossary

Access Control Mechanisms: This is a privacy preserving access authenticated access control scheme for securing data in clouds that verifies the authenticity of the user without knowing the user's identity before storing information. Here only valid users are able to decrypt the stored information. It prevents reply attack, achieves authenticity and privacy. It is decentralized and robust, which allow multiple read and write, distributed access control and the identity of user is protected.

Accountability: Accountability is a component regarding privacy and security issues. Adequate information is required regarding how data is managed by the cloud providers so that they can maintain logging events like data access, data transmission or data modification. That's why, the governing organizations are enforcing the rules and regulations to maintain the accounting of access to the records.

ACID Transaction: ACID-based cloud databases are the strong follower of ACID transactions in order to retain and to protect the consistency of the database system.

ACID-Based Cloud Database: The traditional DBMSs come under ACID-based cloud databases. Commercially available DBMSs that fall under ACID-based cloud databases are: Amazon Relational Database System (RDS), Microsoft Azure SQL supporting SQL Server, and Amazon Machine Images which supports all traditional RDBMS (i.e., MySQL, Oracle, PostgreSQL, Sybase and so on.). Moreover, these databases are best suited for write-intensive database application like OLTP (online transaction processing).

Adaptation: Adaptation implies the ability of a system to adjust to bandwidth fluctuation without inconveniencing the user. In a mobile environment, adaptation is crucial because of intermittent disconnections and bandwidth fluctuations that arise due to handoff, obstacles, environmental noise, etc.

Agent-Based Layer: In agent-based layer, cloud agents are like brokers between virtual appliances layer and Business Service and Provider (BSP) layer. The main aim of the cloud agents is the optimal arrangement of VEEs into CSPs configured and managed by the service manager.

Amazon Elastic Compute Cloud: Amazon Elastic Compute Cloud (also known as EC2) is a commercial web service that allows users to rent computers on which to run and deploy their own.

Amazon Web Services: Amazon, being the first company to provide cloud services under the name Amazon Web Services (AWS) to external customers in 2006, has constantly expanded their service portfolio. The core of AWS is formed by the Xen-based cloud computing service called Elastic Compute Cloud (EC2). Currently, Amazon offers two structured database services: Amazon SimpleDB, a distributed non-relational data store, and Amazon Relational Database Service (RDS), a fully-featured relational database.

Aneka: Aneka cloud is an example of PaaS, which is a .NET-based platform which supports resource management and development. Each and every server acts like a cloud node and hosts Aneka container, which provides the infrastructure consisting of security and privacy, services for persistence, and control over communication.

App Engine: Google App Engine lets users run their Python program and Java applications on the cloud infrastructures supplied by Google. App Engine allows the users to deploy their applications to scale dynamically and it supports the need for data storage scaling up and down according to the requirements of the users.

Application Programming Interface (APIs): Cloud services need to build a standardized interface which would facilitate the customers to manage the relationships among financial management system, accounting management system, and renewal management system. A standard means a set of common, configurable and repeatable protocols which are determined and shared by some organizations. So these standardized platforms or interfaces help the cloud users avail the common instructions on how multiple applications or different data sources are able to interact with each other.

Architecture of Cluster Computing Environment: The components of a computer cluster include multiple standalone computers, an operating system, a communication or network software, and a high-performance interconnecting medium, middleware and different application.

Auditability Schemes: Auditing reduces the risk for customers as well as gives incentives to providers to improve their services. Auditability falls under the two following categories concerning the available schemes in auditability: private auditability and public auditability. Even though schemes with private auditability can attain higher scheme efficiency, public auditability permits anyone, not just the client (data owner), to deal with the cloud server for correctness of data storage while keeping no private information. Then, clients are able to pass on the evaluation of the service performance to an independent third-party auditor (TPA), without giving their computation resources. So, the types of auditing protocols can be categorized as Data owner auditing and Third-party auditing.

Auditing for Regulation or Compliance: A set of rules and principles are designed to govern or control the conduct for auditing. Compliance is concerned with legal issues, social activities, marketing strategies, and co-operative conduct. In every aspect of compliance, auditing is highly needed for maintenance of governing conduct. Auditing for regulations and compliance is also needed to restrict increasing complexity to comply with standards and to maintain the agreement for privacy laws.

Auditing for Risk and Governance: Governance is exceedingly concerned with the performance measurement and its strategies and risk management; and its proper administration is also an important issue of an IT landscape. Different management laws and policies, priorities, and resources are needed for the processes and alignment of customs, which are the basic functionalities of this category.

Auditing for Security: Security issues are a concern for auditing. In the administration of security, everyone should know the responsibilities of each designation. Technical auditing is also concerned with security issues. Physical resources are also in need of auditing for their priority, availability and cost complexity.

Auditing Service: Auditing service consists of a policy database, strategy rules engine, event processor, a query manager having two modules, i.e., Query Access Manager and Query Rules Manager, and an audit control module consisting of audit manager, audit trails, audit alerts and rules.

Authentication and Access Control Management: Authentication should have the responsibility for effective governance and proper management of their authenticated process. Access control management service enables policies and rules for access control in reply to a request from a client who is in need of resources; and this block should also be responsible for OS access control and network access control.

Backdoor and Debug Options: It is the common practice of developers to enable backdoor and debug options while publishing a website. This enables them to make developmental changes in the code and get them implemented in the website. Since these debug options facilitate backend entry to the developers, sometimes they are left enabled unnoticed. This may provide a hacker easy entry into the website and let him make changes at the website level.

Balanced Binary Tree Distribution: Balanced binary tree-based distribution is used for reducing the overhead of network congestion and allowing parallel transfers. Here all the computing nodes are set in balanced binary tree pattern making the source node as the root node.

Bandwidth Constrained, Variable Capacity Links: Wireless links have significantly lower capacity than their wired counterpart. Also, due to issues such as multiple access, fading, noise and interference conditions, the bandwidth of the wireless links can change arbitrarily with time.

BASE Transaction: According to Brewer, BASE transactions relax the ACID properties of consistency and isolation in favor of availability, graceful degradation, and performance.

Based on Availability and Partition Tolerance (AP): These systems ensure availability and partition tolerance primarily by achieving consistency [9]. Some of the available AP systems are Voldemort (key-value), Tokyo Cabinet (key-value), KAI (key-value), CouchDB (document-oriented), SimpleDB and many more.

Based on Consistency and Availability (CA): Here part of the database is not concerned about the partition tolerance and mainly the use of the Replication approach to ensure data consistency and availability.

Based on Consistency and Partition Tolerance (CP): This category of database systems not only stores data in the distributed nodes, but also ensures the consistency of these data, however this support is not good enough for the availability. The main CP systems are BigTable (column oriented), Hypertable (column oriented), HBase (column oriented), MongoDB (document), Terrastore (document), Redis (Key-value), Scalaris (key-value), MemcacheDB (key-value), Berkeley DB (key-value).

BGP Prefix Hijacking: Prefix hijacking is a type of network attack in which a wrong announcement related to the IP addresses associated with an Autonomous System (AS) is made. Hence, malicious parties get access to the untraceable IP addresses. On the internet, IP space is associated in blocks and remains under the control of ASs. An autonomous system can broadcast information of an IP contained in its regime to all its neighbors. These ASs communicate using the Border Gateway Protocol (BGP) model. Sometimes, due to some error, a faulty AS may broadcast incorrectly about the IPs associated with it. In such cases, the actual traffic gets routed to some IP other than the intended one. Hence, data is leaked to or reaches some other unintended destination.

Binary Translation: The VMM monitors the execution of guest operating systems; non-virtualized instructions executed by a guest operating system are replaced with other instructions.

Bottleneck Problem: Atomicity, consistency, and isolation are usually implemented in RDBMS using a central lock manager. For a distributed system, a central lock manager would be the bottleneck, because all database nodes would need to contact the lock manager for every operation.

Broadcasting: Efficient delivery of data simultaneously to hundreds of mobile users is possible in the mobile environment due to the fundamental broadcast nature of the underlying communication.

Broker Service: Cloud brokers are like the agents between the virtual environment and business service layer. The main goal of the cloud broker is to make optimal arrangement of virtual environment provided by CSPs which is configured and managed by the service manager.

Business Service Management: This block may help to manage the service orchestration, service conditions, and process management. Service manager should be able to derive a collection of desired resources and their configuration, and also placement constraints according to licensing, cost, confidentiality, etc. Process management has the authority to schedule and to manage the processes. Service manager also has the responsibility to monitor the deployed services and to adjust their capacity (number of VM instances).

Business Service Provider (BSP): The BSP layer consists of business service management (BSM), service-level agreement (SLA), service orchestration, and process management. The BSP layer provides common infrastructure elements for service-level management, metered usage, policy management, license management, and disaster recovery.

Business Service: The business service layer provides different aspects of business controls and conditions such as business service management, identity creation and validation, authentication and access control management, service-level agreement, and renewal service management.

CAPTCHA Breaking: CAPTCHAs were developed in order to prevent the use of internet resources by bots or computers. They are used to prevent spam and over-exploitation of network resources by bots. Even multiple web-site registrations, dictionary attacks, etc., by an automated program are prevented using a CAPTCHA. But recently it has been found that the spammers are able to break the CAPTCHA provided by the Hotmail and Gmail service providers. They make use of the audio system able to read the CAPTCHA characters for the visually impaired users and use speech-to-text conversion software to defeat the test. In yet another instance of CAPTCHA breaking, it was found that the net users are provided some form of motivation towards solving these CAPTCHAs by the automated systems, and thus CAPTCHA breaking takes place. Integration of multiple authentication techniques along with CAPTCHA identification (as adopted by companies like Facebook, Google, etc.) may be a suitable option against CAPTCHA breaking. Various techniques such as implementing letter overlap, variable fonts of the letters used to design a CAPTCHA, increasing the string length, and using a perturbative background can be used to avoid CAPTCHA breaking.

CAP Theorem: The CAP theorem was proposed by Dr. Eric Brewer, and is widely adopted today by large web companies (e.g., Amazon) as well as in the cloud database community. As it applies to a network, the acronym CAP stands for Consistency, Availability and Partition tolerance.

Centralized Distribution: Centralized distribution is a traditional approach. It can be implemented in a simple way so it can be easily used by users and administrators. The VM images are stored in the central NFS (network file server) server and the client nodes retrieve copies of VMs from the central node on demand. This type of multiple point-to-point transfer creates an inconsistent situation when a large number of clients want to access multi-terabyte files. So, client transfer should be synchronized.

Cloud Database: In cloud computing, users will access traditional as well as mobile database features through internet services provided by cloud computing over lightweight portable devices as well as through traditional desktop PCs without bothering about better CPU power and memory usage. Because the large volume of data will be stored in the cloud and are processed under many data grid servers, the users can access the cloud database through web services. Because of the many technological advancements of the communication network and portable devices, a huge mass of users can communicate by exchanging data continuously with the database in cloud regardless of their location.

Cloud Hypervisor: A cloud hypervisor is designed like a mainframe operating system that allows other operating systems to run on the same machine concurrently. It monitors the access of guest operating systems (users' operating systems). Hypervisor monitoring environment (HME) administers the system by letting the guest node enter the system and handling the memory management of the VMs. Hypervisor examples include VMware, Hyper-V, KMV, and Xen.

Cloud Platform Architecture: The base architecture of cloud is called cloud platform architecture, which includes the cloud service-oriented architecture. The cloud computing reference model groups the cloud computing functions and activities into sublayers.

Cloud Services: End-users or clients use the cloud services according to their needs. Cloud service providers (CSPs) deliver the service on an on-demand basis. The cloud service model consists of RaaS, IaaS, PaaS, and SaaS.

Cluster Computing Environment: A computer cluster can be defined as a set of loosely coupled computers working together in such a way that all the machines can be viewed as a single system image (SSI).

Cluster Grids: These are the simplest form of a grid environment which consists of multiple computer systems interrelated by means of a network. Cluster grids may include distributed workstations and servers, and it also contains centralized physical resources in a datacenter environment.

Column-Oriented: A column-oriented database uses Table as the data model, but does not support table association.

Community Cloud Computing Environment: In the case of joint venture application, the same cloud infrastructure needs to be constructed and shared by several organizations jointly, so that they may have use of the same framework as well as policies, services, requirements, applications, and concerns. Hybrid cloud is highly scalable and reduces cost complexity.

Computation Virtualization: Computation virtualization leads to virtualization of computing resources. Computing resources like server virtualization and operating system virtualization has enabled the transformation from server-centric traditional computing to network and internet-centric computing. Operating system and server virtualization create the virtual (logical) servers which are free from the constraints of the underlying physical location and physical infrastructure, and the virtualization may facilitate moving workloads from the source VM instance to target VM instance in real time, which is called live migration.

Computational Resources: Mechanisms are necessary for initiating programs and for monitoring and controlling the execution of the resulting processes. Management mechanisms that allow monitoring and control over the physical and computational resources allocated to processes are required, as are advanced reservation mechanisms. Enquiry functions are desirable for determining hardware and software characteristics as well as relevant state information such as current load and queue state in the case of scheduler-managed resources.

Confidentiality of Mobile Cloud-Based Data Sharing: The confidential data on mobile phones using cloud-based mobile device support might become public due to better access control and identity management. Cloud computing involves virtualization, and hence the need for user authentication and control across the clouds is high. The existing solutions are not able to handle the case of multiple clouds. Since data belonging to multiple users may be stored in a single hypervisor, specific segmentation measures are needed to overcome the potential weakness and flaws in hypervisor platform. Security challenges in a mobile cloud computing environment are slightly different as compared to the abovementioned network-related challenges. With applications lying in a cloud, it is possible for the hackers to corrupt an application and gain access to a mobile device while accessing that application. In order to avoid this, strong virus-scanning and malware protection software needs to be installed to avoid any type of virus/malware checking into the mobile system. Besides, by embedding device identity protection, like allowing access to the authorized user based on some form of identity check feature, unauthorized accesses can be blocked.

Consignment: After the transfer of all the VM states, OS instance and memory content, Host will get a message from the target host saying that host B has successfully received a consistent OS image. After getting this message, Host acknowledges the message as part of the commitment of the migration operation. Now the source host may discard and release the original VM at the source host, and the target host will become the primary host.

Consolidation: Various operating systems are able to run on the same particular server, reducing the requirement of a dedicated single machine to a particular application. New and existing applications are able to run simultaneously with their respective preloaded operating systems in multi-core servers which are combined with many threads of execution, which in turn saves space and also energy consumption in the datacenter. The new applications and new versions of existing applications can also be deployed without buying new hardware.

Constraints Allowed: Constraints provide one method of implementing business rules in the database. SQL implements constraint functionality in the form of primary key constraint, foreign key constraint, unique key and so on.

Cookie Poisoning: This involves changing or modifying the contents of cookie to have an unauthorized access to an application or to a web page. Cookies basically contain the user's identity-related credentials and once these cookies are accessible, the content of these cookies can be forged to impersonate an authorized user. This can be avoided either by performing regular cookie cleanup or implementing an encryption scheme for the cookie data.

CPU State Migration: Migration of CPU state concerns process migration. While migrating the CPU state, the process control block (PCB), the number of cores, processor speed, and required process-specific memory will all transfer from the source host to the destination host.

Customization: The system and computation resources must be extremely customizable when the cloud users rent resources from the providers. Customization leads to an atmosphere where users are allowed to deploy their applications onto cloud and resources are customized and configured according to the requirement of the users. For example, when an organization deploys more features and more clients for a certain amount of time, it needs more resources like more processing, bandwidth, computing resources and more CPU cores for that time period. And, consequently, all the resources are configured and customized with the features and the clients for that time span.

DaaS (Database as a Service): DaaS is a core service of cloud computing which provides two main database alternatives for the developers: Relational Cloud Database and Non-relational Cloud Database. Relational cloud database captures all the distributed relational database features like SQL-based query processing, optimization, etc. Some of the relational cloud databases are Amazon RDS and Azure SQL. Non-relational cloud database can have multiple data models, such as key-value-based, column-based, document-oriented and graph-based, to process the user queries. Popular non-relational cloud databases currently available are MongoDB, Amazon SimpleDB, Apache Cassandra and many others.

Data Latency: Data transfer in a wireless network is not as continuous and consistent as it is in the case of a dedicated wired LAN. And this inconsistency is largely responsible for longer time intervals for data transfer at times. Also, the distance from the source adds up to the longer time intervals observed in the case of data transfer and other network-related activities because of an increase in the number of intermediate network components.

Data Storage and Security in Cloud: Many cloud service providers provide storage as a form of service. They take the data from the users and store them in large data centers, hence providing users a means of storage. In spite of claims by the cloud service providers about the safety of the data stored in the cloud, there have been cases when the data stored in these clouds have been modified or lost due to some security breach or some human error.

Data Storage over IP Networks: Online data storage is becoming quite popular nowadays and it has been observed that the majority of enterprise storage will be networked in the coming years, as it allows enterprises to maintain huge chunks of data without setting up the required architecture. Although there are many advantages of having online data storage, there are security threats that could cause data leakage or data unavailability at crucial times. Such issues are observed more frequently in the case of dynamic data that keeps flowing within the cloud in comparison to static data. Depending upon the various levels of operations and storage provided, these networked devices are categorized into SAN (storage area network) and NAS (network-attached storage), and since these storage networks reside on various servers, there are multiple threats associated with them.

Database Auditing: Database auditing relates to observing a cloud database so that database auditors and administrators can take care of actions like access, modifications, and updating issues concerning database users. Database auditing is mainly query-based auditing. Queries are presented to the auditor one at a time; auditor checks if answering the current query (in combination with past answers) reveals any secret or forbidden information.

Denial of Service Attack: A denial of service (DoS) attack is an attempt to make the services assigned to the authorized users unavailable. In such an attack, the server providing the service is flooded by a large number of requests and hence the service becomes unavailable to the authorized user. Sometimes, when we try to access a site we see that due to overloading of the server with the requests to access the site, we are unable to access the site and observe an error. This happens when the number of requests that can be handled by a server exceeds its capacity. The occurrence of a DoS attack increases bandwidth consumption besides causing congestion, making certain parts of the clouds inaccessible to the users. Using an intrusion detection system (IDS) is the most popular method of defense against this type of attack. A defense federation is used for guarding against such attacks. Each cloud is loaded with separate IDS. The different intrusion detection systems work on the basis of information exchange. In case a specific cloud is under attack, the cooperative IDS alerts the whole system. A decision on trustworthiness of a cloud is taken by voting, and the overall system performance is not hampered.

Dependability on Hypervisor: A hypervisor controls all access to VMs and monitors the environment, so the hypervisor failing or crashing or an attack on it by hackers may lead to performance degradation.

Development Flexibility: A virtualized machine can host several versions of an operating system, allowing developers to test their programs in different OS environments on the same machine. In addition, with each application running in its own individual virtual partition, crashing in one virtual machine will not overthrow the system.

Device and Location Independency: Cloud service facilitates users accessing computation and hardware resources using only a web browser independent of their location or what kind of device they are using. A cloud infrastructure is situated offsite and accessed for resources via the internet by the cloud users. They can easily connect with the infrastructure and resources from anywhere regardless of their location.

Dictionary Attack: Data security in a cloud computing environment can be compromised by carrying out a dictionary or brute force attack. In a dictionary attack, the intruder makes use of all the possible word combinations which could have been successfully used to decrypt the data residing in/flowing over the network. This can be avoided by making use of a challenge-response system. In this protocol, the client is presented a challenge whenever it tries to access a network. It is then required to compute the response to the same and reply back to the server in order to be able to access the network. Response computation is a time-consuming process thus avoiding users being able to launch brute force or dictionary attacks in a short period of time, and hence ensuring security against the same.

Distributed Denial of Service Attacks (DDos): A DDoS attack may be called an advanced version of a DoS attack. It denies the important services running on a server by flooding the destination sever with large numbers of packets such that the target server is not able to handle it. However, unlike a DoS attack, a DDoS attack is relayed from different dynamic networks which have already been compromised. The attackers have the power to control the flow of information by allowing some information available at certain times. Thus, the amount and type of information available for public use is clearly under the control of the attacker. The DDoS attack is run by three functional units: a Master, a Slave, and a Victim. The Master is the attack launcher behind all the attacks causing DDoS, Slave is the network which acts like a launch pad for the Master. It provides the platform to the Master to launch the attack on the Victim. Hence, it is also called a co-ordinated attack. Basically a DDoS attack is operational in two stages: the first one being the intrusion phase where the Master tries to compromise less important machines to support flooding the more important one. The next one is installing DDoS tools and attacking the victim server or machine. Hence, a DDoS attack results in making the service unavailable to the authorized user similar to the way it is done in a DoS attack but different in the way it is launched. A similar case of a DDoS attack was experienced at the CNN news channel website leaving most of its users unable to access the site for a period of three hours. In general, the approaches used to fight the DDoS attack involve extensive modification of the underlying network. These modifications often become costly for the users. A swarm-based logic is used for guarding against the DDoS attack. This logic provides a transparent transport layer, through which the common protocols such as HTTP, SMTP, etc., can pass easily. The use of IDS in the virtual machine is proposed to protect the cloud from DDoS attacks.

Distributed Pattern-Based Environment: The virtual machine deployment pattern which helps the distribution of the virtual machine, making it more efficient by responding faster, minimizing communication latency, avoiding congestion and dynamic updation.

Distributed Resources of Physical Hosts: At the base level of the cloud stack, there are a pool of resources of physical hosts in the distributed manner. Physical hosts are nothing but a collection of processors, memory, CPU cores, and storage, which are provisioned to the user and logically presented as a several numbers of VMs through the process of resource virtualization.

Distributed Service Assurance Platform: This platform helps to create FCAPS (Fault, Configuration, Account, Performance, Security) virtual servers [6] that allow hosting the operating systems and executing the applications.

Distribution Between Cross Clouds: Multicast does well in LAN. But sometimes transfer is required beyond the LAN. For example, more than one private, physically distinguishable desktop cloud shares the same data and information and use the multicast distribution method. But transferring the data is forbidden by their network policy. To overcome this type of constraint, peer-to-peer or balanced binary tree distribution mechanisms are used over the common network linking those clouds.

DNS Attacks: The domain name server (DNS) performs the translation of a domain name to an IP address since the domain names are much easier to remember. Hence, DNSs are needed. But there are cases when having called the server by name, the user has been routed to some other malicious cloud instead of the one he asked for, and hence using an IP address is not always feasible. Although using DNS security measures, such as domain name system security extensions (DNSSEC), reduces the effects of DNS threats, there are still cases when these security measures prove to be inadequate when the path between a sender and a receiver gets rerouted through some malicious connection. It may happen that even after all the

DNS security measures are taken, the route selected between the sender and receiver causes security problems.

Document-Oriented: Document and key-value databases are very similar in structure, but the value of document database is semantic, and is stored in JSON or XML format. In addition, document databases generally contain a secondary index value to facilitate the upper application, but a key-value database does not.

Downtime: This is defined as the time between stopping the virtual machine on the source node and resuming it on the destination node. In live migration, downtime is an order of magnitude of milliseconds to seconds with respect to the application and memory size.

Dynamic Network Monitoring and Scalability: Applications running on mobiles in a mobile cloud computing platform should be intelligent enough to adapt to the varying network capacities and also should be accessible through different platforms without suffering any data loss. For example, sometimes a user while working on a smartphone may need to move on to a feature phone, and when he accesses the application through the smartphone, he should not encounter any data loss.

Dynamic Topologies: Since nodes are free to move arbitrarily, the network topology may change unpredictably.

Elasticity: Cloud computing provides the illusion of infinite physical and computing resources which are available on an on-demand basis.

Embedded: To get high performance and to reduce the time complexity, embedded hypervisors are integrated with processors on a separate chip.

Energy-Constrained Operation: The nodes in a MANET rely on battery power source. Mobile node batteries are small and normally store a very limited amount of energy. Inefficient network operations, such as routing, network initialization, etc., can rapidly drain the batteries. In this scenario, the most important critical system design criterion needs to be energy conservation.

Energy Efficiency: Cloud computing provides various types of on-demand services and running applications, but requires a lot of power. And hypervisor monitoring system also requires a huge amount of electricity to monitor the access to VMs. Therefore, energy efficiency is also a concern in cloud computing.

Enterprise Grids: An enterprise grid may be formed by combining multiple cluster grids. Multiple projects or departments can be enabled by enterprise grids to share computing and physical resources in a supportive way. Enterprise grids typically may have the resources from multiple administrative domains, but those are located in the same geographic location.

Evolution of Cloud Computing: The concept of cloud computing is not new. In fact, much of what we do on our computers today requires it. What is changing is the way that we look at what cloud computing is able to do for us today. The beginning of what is known as the concept of cloud computing can be traced back to the mainframe days of the 1960s, when the idea of "Utility Computing" was coined by MIT computer scientist and Turing award winner John McCarthy, who opined that "Computation may someday be organized as public utility."

False Resource Sharing: An attacker can use a virtual machine to broadcast a message containing false information about available resources, which can influence another virtual machine to migrate to the attacker VM.

Flexiscale: Flexiscale is a UK-based service provider offering services which are equivalent in nature to Amazon Web Services. The features of the virtual servers of this cloud provider are especially persistent storage by default, dedicated VLAN, fixed IP address, runtime adjustment of CPU, and a wider range of server size. Flexiscale cloud services also offers its service, which is priced by the hour.

Full Virtualization: Full virtualization requires a virtualizable architecture; the hardware is fully exposed to the guest OS which runs unchanged and this ensures that this direct execution mode is efficient. In full virtualization architecture, guest operating systems are provided with all the services given be physical computing systems, which include virtualized memory, virtual devices, and also virtual BIOS.

Global Grids: Global grids are a group of enterprise grids in which all of the enterprise grids have to agree upon different protocols and global usage policies, but not the essential way in which they are implemented. Computing and physical resources may be geographically distributed, and they are used for connecting different sites throughout the globe. Global grids provide the power of distributed resources to users anywhere in the world.

GoGrid: GoGrid allows its users to utilize a wide range of Windows and Linux images, with a range of fixed instance sizes. GoGrid also provides services like "value-added" stacks which are on top for various applications such as e-commerce, web hosting, and database services. It also provides a new feature which facilitates use by combining traditional dedicated hosts with the autoscaling infrastructure facility. Users can benefit from dedicated hosting combined with on-demand cloud infrastructure, which leads to the user getting the advantages of each paradigm of computing.

Google App Engine: The foundation of the Google App Engine (GAE) is fundamentally different from other cloud infrastructures, like, for example, Amazon's. This is because GAE does not provide bare VMs, but an application framework consisting of various services to build web applications. This is the reason why GAE is commonly termed Platform as a Service (PaaS), whereas the other cloud operators like Amazon and Microsoft provide Infrastructure as a Service (IaaS). Since GAE in general is targeted at scalable, distributed applications, there is no relational SQL-based database service in GAE.

Google Hacking: Google has emerged as the best option for finding details regarding anything on the internet. Google hacking refers to using Google search engine to find sensitive information that a hacker can use to his benefit while hacking a user's account. Generally, hackers try to discover security loopholes by probing Google for information about the system they wish to hack. After having gathered the necessary information, they carry out a hacking attack on the system concerned. In some cases, a hacker is not sure of the target. Instead he tries to discover the target, using Google, based on the loophole in the system he wishes to hack. The hacker then searches all the possible systems with such a loophole and finds those having loopholes he can exploit. A Google hacking event was observed recently when login details of various Gmail users were stolen by a group of hackers. This is the type of security threat that can be launched at the application level and cause system downtime, even disabling application access to authorized users. In order to avoid these threats, application security should be assessed at the various levels of the three service delivery models in cloud: IaaS, PaaS, and SaaS. In the case of an IaaS delivery model, cloud providers are mostly not concerned with the security policies applied by the customer and the application's management. The whole application runs on the customer's server on the cloud provider's infrastructure and is managed by them, and hence they are responsible for securing the application.

Governance: Governance deals with the manner in which something is regulated or governed, the system or criteria of regulations, the way it is managed. These serious issues should be taken into account and explicit attention should be given by the governmental organizations. Governance is exceedingly concerned with performance measurement and strategies relating to risk management; and its proper administration is also an important issue in the IT landscape. Different management laws and policies, priorities, and resources are needed for the processes, and alignment of customs is the fundamental role of governing organizations.

Grid Computing Environment: The term grid computing was first coined in the 1990s by Cart Kesselman and Ian Foster and succinctly defined as "coordinated resource sharing and problem solving in dynamic, multi-institutional virtual organizations."

Guest VM Attack: This is when an attacker uses virtual machine to broadcast a request to the network for an incoming virtual machine migration. Then the hypervisor maps between the virtual IP and the MAC addresses to the attacker's VM and the IP addresses address moves to a new MAC address of the attacker's VM. Then the attacker easily takes control of the requested migrating VM and can modify it.

Hardware-Assisted Virtualization: The shortcomings of paravirtualization have been raised due to modification of hardware that allows the guest operating system to make communication with the hypervisor without any modifications. These shortcomings may be overcome by hardware-assisted virtualization. Hardware-assisted guest operating system is capable of communicating directly with the hypervisor.

Heterogeneous Atmosphere: The structure of the distributed system (network latency, network topology, network connections, and total number of participating computers) is not predefined. The distributed system may consist of distinct kinds of computers and heterogeneous network links. While executing a program, the system structure may change in order to achieve the goal. This is known as heterogeneous atmosphere.

Hidden Field Manipulation: While accessing a web page, there are certain fields that are hidden and contain the page-related information basically used by developers. However, these fields are highly prone to attacks by hackers as they can be modified easily and posted on the web page. This may result in severe security violations.

Host Hypervisor: These kinds of hypervisors act as a separate software layer over both operating system and hardware to get improved performance.

Hybrid Cloud Computing Environment: A hybrid cloud is organized in a scenario where a private cloud is supplemented with resource and computing capability from public clouds. Hybrid cloud infrastructure comes up with a combination of public and private cloud.

Hypercalls: Hypercalls are a set of instructions which are able to make direct communication with the virtualization layer. Portability problems and low compatibility are shortcomings of the modification of the guest operating systems.

Hypervisor Administrator: In a cloud computing environment, hypervisor administrator may have the main responsibility to control access to VMs. It should monitor how the computing and system resources are distributed and circulated for virtualization and how virtual machines are mapped to the host machines so that the data and computing resources can easily be retrieved from the resource pool by the CSPs or the cloud user. In the booting time of the system, hypervisor is accessible and hypervisor administrator may regulate the allocation of system and computing resources and VMs are mapped to the host machine according to the need of the user or the application. Hypervisor administrator should have the capability to manage both the resources within the server (locally) as well as the resources located in the other servers connected to the network.

Hypervisor Monitoring Environment (HME): On top of the physical hosts is a hypervisor monitoring environment layer consisting of a hypervisor, resource virtualization, VMs, and hypervisor administrator. Suppose a cloud user needs an infrastructure-based service. For requesting infrastructure and resources, hypervisor is available from the time the system boots to manage the allocation of physical and computing resources to update the resource later across multiple VMs, which would be mapped depending on the availability of the physical hosts.

Hypervisor: Hypervisor is basically a mainframe operating system which allows other operating systems to run on the same system concurrently. Access to VMs are controlled by the hypervisor.

Hypervisor-Based Attack: As hypervisor controls all the access to VMs and monitors the environment, with malicious code the attacker's VM can legitimate the target hypervisor. So, an attacker VM can gain control over the destination hypervisor and other guest VMs.

Hypervisor-Based Virtualization Approaches: Hypervisor is a mainframe operating system which allows other operating systems to run on the same system concurrently. And its monitoring system monitors the access to virtual machines. Hypervisor is accessible at the booting time of the system to regulate the allocation of hardware infrastructure to the multiple VMs from the resource layer.

Identity Creation and Validation: Creation of user identity and its validation is the key responsibility of this block. When a new user comes up in the market, he needs to create his identity and this module may identify proper validation for deployment of user application.

Information Protocol: Information protocols are used to get information about the structure and states of resources like usage policy, current load and its configuration.

Infrastructure as a Service: Infrastructure as a Service (IaaS) deals with infrastructure on which RaaS may expand due to resource virtualization. IaaS provides virtualization technology which involves the provisioning of infrastructure to the cloud users.

Infrastructure-Based and Infrastructureless Database: The traditional databases deal with infrastructure-based environment. Hence, traditional database under infrastructure-based environment has many advantages like better data accessing speed, high bandwidth, higher energy backup, better computing units and device independence. On the other hand, it suffers from higher operational and maintenance costs.

Integration Platform as a Service: This block is responsible for integrating the resources for multiple applications and for the guest operating system. There are different kinds of guest operating systems; hence, this should be platform independent.

Isolated Guest Operating System-Based Virtualization: In this category, host OS runs on the hardware infrastructure. It supports multiple guest virtualized OS on the same physical server and is capable of maintaining isolation of different guest OS.

Joins and Triggers: Joins are used to relate information in different tables. A join condition is a part of the sql query that retrieves rows from two or more tables. An SQL join condition is used in the SQL WHERE clause of select, update, delete statements. Whereas a database trigger is procedural code that is automatically executed in response to certain events on a particular table or view in a database. The trigger is mostly used for maintaining the integrity of the information on the database

JSON: This stands for JavaScript Object Notation. It is a lightweight, text-based, language-independent data interchange format. Basically JSON syntax is used for exchanging and storing the text information. It is completely language independent, which makes it very easy and fast to parse the documents.

Key-Value-Based: The name itself signifies that it combines two entities; one is key, the other is a value associated with it. Here the query speed is faster than relational database, which supports huge data storage and better concurrency, etc.; query and modify operations for data through the primary key are supported as well. This category of database models is the origin of non-relational model and can be inherited by the rest of the data models.

KVM: A kernel-based virtual machine (KVM) is a hypervisor built right into the Linux kernel. It is similar to Xen in purpose but much simpler to get running. To start using the hypervisor, just load the appropriate KVM kernel modules and the hypervisor is up. As with Xen's full virtualization, in order for KVM to work, you must have a processor that supports Intel's VT-x extensions or AMD's AMD-V extensions. A KVM is a full virtualization solution for Linux. It is based upon CPU virtualization extensions (i.e., extending the set of CPU instructions with new instructions that allow writing simple virtual machine monitors).

Legacy Integration Services: This block may provide the services which can support integration of legacy or existing application. Support for inheritance or legacy of previous application is the key responsibility of that block.

Less Downtime: From the customer's point of view, live migration happens without any perceptible effect due to much less downtime. "Down-time" is defined as the time between stopping the virtual machine on the source node and resuming it on the destination node. In live migration, downtime is an order of magnitude milliseconds to seconds with respect to the application and memory size.

Life Cycle of Services in SOA: A service life cycle is required to understand the sequential activities, processes and the physical and computing resources necessary for designing, building, developing, deploying, and finally executing and delivering the services that make up an SOA.

Limited Physical Security: Mobile networks are prone to many more types of security threats than fixed cable networks, mainly due to the wireless transmissions and collaborative routing. There are increased possibilities of eavesdropping, spoofing, and denial-of-service attacks in these networks. Also, nodes are vulnerable to capture and compromise.

Live Migration Possible Attacks: In the live migration scheme, lack of appropriate access policy and some certain rules for different kinds of security loopholes help an attacker carry out attacks such as a guest VM attack, false resource sharing, denial-of-service attack and so on.

Live Migration Process: Live migration is the process in which the states and memory contents of virtual machines are transferred from the source host to destination host via the network.

Live Migration: In the flow of the rapid use of virtualization, migration procedure has been enhanced due to the advantages of live migration such as server consolidation and resource isolation. Live migration of virtual machines is a technique in which the virtual machine seems to be active and gives responses to end-users all the time during the migration process. Live migration facilitates energy efficiency, online maintenance, and load balancing.

Load Balancing: A virtual machine is migrated one node to another to share the scheduled workload, so as to optimize the consumption of available CPU resources.

Load-Distribution-Based Environment: Load distribution is required when a particular host faces a huge workload, i.e., a huge number of client requests, which leads to performance degradation. Then the requests need to be transferred to another host or another data center to distribute the workload. In the virtualization environment, the load balancer has the responsibility to reduce the load overhead and that leads to classification of load-balancing approaches.

Location Awareness: A handheld device equipped with global positioning system (GPS) can provide information about the current location of a user. Many applications ranging from strategic to personalized services require or get added value by location-based services. For example, while a person is on the move.

Low Performance: It is very time-consuming and costly to achieve serializability during concurrent execution in ACID-based database transaction.

Management Protocols: Management protocols are used for negotiating access to the shared physical resources, specifying resource requirements, and monitoring the operations to be performed. A protocol may also monitor the current status of an operation while executing and controlling the operation.

Maturity: Since NoACID-based cloud databases only emerged a few years ago, they have a small set of users and clients. However, due to their popularity in current situations it is in the process of being standardized, as many projects and researches are continuing with this field.

Migration and Cloning: Virtual machine migration is a cloud infrastructure capability that is gradually becoming more utilized. It is the key feature of virtualized technologies. Virtual machine live migration is basically transferring its instances, including the operating system, runtime memory pages, and active CPU states, from a source host to the destination host. Virtual machines, each having their own operating systems and applications, do respective tasks, like self-contained packages, which have been called "decoupled from the hardware." It is relatively easy to move a VM from one host physical machine to another host machine that is either currently running or will be running or booted up after placing the new VMs, as well as recovering from hardware failure.

Minimizing Investment Expenditures: If an organization wants to build new business applications with minimum investment on computing and hardware resources for supporting its clients, the organization might rent the computing and system resources on a per-hour or per-storage-unit basis from a cloud service provider who provides this type of service.

Mobile Computing: Mobile computing is widely described as the ability to compute and communicate while on the move. Mobile computing means, two separate and distinct concepts: mobility and computing. Computing denotes the capability to automatically carry out certain processing. Mobility, on the other hand, provides the capability to change a portable location during communication and computing. The main advantage of this mobility is the flexibility that it provides to the user. The user need not necessarily sit in front of his desktop, but can either move locally or even to far away places.

MongoDB: This is a schemaless document-oriented database developed by 10gen and an open source community. The name MongoDB comes from "humongous." The database is intended to be scalable and fast and is written in C++. In addition to its document-oriented database features, MongoDB can be used to store and distribute large binary files like images and videos.

Multicast: Multicasting is an efficient way to distribute VMs. In multicast, the information or data is transmitted to a required group of destination nodes in s single transmission. Packets are sent in a group, so it can minimize the CPU load but increase the packet loss probability. It works best in local area network (LAN).

Multiple Data Models: NoACID-based cloud databases are not restricted for use only in a single data model, as ACID-based cloud databases usually are. They may use several data models, like key-value-based, column-oriented, document-oriented, and graph-based data models, for storing and retrieval of data from the data store.

Multi-tenancy: Multi-tenancy is an extremely obligatory concern in clouds, which allows sharing of resources and costs across multiple users. Multi-tenancy refers to a principle in software architecture where a single instance of the software runs on a server, serving multiple client organizations (tenants). It brings service providers several benefits, such as centralization of infrastructure in different locations with minimized costs and increment of utilization and efficiency with high peak load capacity. Tenancy information, which is stored in a separate database but altered concurrently, should be well maintained for isolated tenants. Otherwise some problems such as data protection will arise.

MVCC: Multiversion concurrency control (MVCC or MVC) is a concurrency control method which is used by database management systems. It is an advanced technique which is used to improve the performance of the database in multi-user environment. MVCC provides concurrent access to the database, which helps to implement transactional memory.

Native Hypervisor: This type of hypervisor is designed to reside directly over the hardware platform for providing better performance.

Network Accessibility: The internet has been a major factor in the evolution of cloud computing and without having the network (internet) access it would not be possible to access the mobile cloud, limiting the available applications that can be used.

Network Virtualization: Network virtualization is involved in implementing virtual networks within the physical server for switching between all the virtual servers, instead of multipathed or multiplexed network channels, by directly trunking them to WAN transport. Multiple HBAs and NICs may be needed for each application connected with a high-speed single Ethernet connection.

No Joins and Triggers: NoACID-based cloud databases lose the concept of association data through joins and imposing some sort of validation and restriction to access the data through triggers.

Normalization: This encompasses a set of procedures designed to eliminate simple domains (non-atomic values) and the redundancy (duplication) of data, which in turn prevents data manipulation anomalies and loss of data integrity.

On-Demand Migration: The downtime period of source CDS node may be reduced by the use of an on-demand migration approach, where a minimal amount of data of the UDB is migrated to the destination node to avoid the disruption of services. Once the UDB comes online at destination node the corresponding transaction starts executing. But the only problem is that if the transaction requires the data, which has not been migrated to the destination, then an expensive cache miss occurs. The post-migration overhead will increase with the increase in warm-up time for caching the data at destination, due to which the on-demand migration approach also does not fit for live migration.

Operational Environment: The operational category involves the virtual machine migration technique which concerns the transfer of the instances of the virtual machines from the local sites to the remote sites and is able to run there.

Paravirtualization: Paravirtualization is a process that is used to virtualize a guest OS. It is mainly helpful because it provides better performance than hardware-assisted or full virtualization. The reasons for adopting paravirtualization are as follows: firstly, some features of the hardware can't be virtualized. Secondly, it is used to present users with a simpler interface. Paravirtualization demands that the guest OS be modified to run under the VMM; also, the guest OS code must be ported for individual hardware platforms.

Peer-to-Peer Computing: This is a technique in which every computer shares physical resources and services by directly exchanging between the systems and each computer can act as servers and clients for the other computers connected to the network. Which computer can act as a client or server depends on what role is most trustworthy and efficient for the network. In peer-to-peer computing, content is typically exchanged in a direct way based on the fundamental internet protocol (IP) of the network. The main advantage of peer-to-peer (P2P) computing is that there is a chance of central point of failure and decentralized coordination maintains the consistency of the global state.

Peer-to-Peer Distribution: This is a decentralized approach. There is no centralized server, every node in the system works as a server or client. Every VM node may act as sender or receiver or sender and receiver both. It is possible to make multiple transfers of different files to the same node. BitTorrent protocol is an example of peer-to-peer distribution.

Performance Measurement Service: Service providers should have the capabilities to maintain a management system that monitors the access to data centers and IT services. The management system monitors the services, measures the performance, reduces the time delays, and optimizes the services.

Performance Measurements and Update Configuration: Virtual servers have the responsibility of managing performance measurements, performance optimization, fault management and reliability and accounting. This block allows the service developers to make self-managed and self-configuring business workflows.

Personalization: Services in mobile environment can be tailored according to the user's profile. This is required to let the users easily avail information with handheld devices.

Platform and OS Usage and Services: In this block, virtual servers may load and host the preferred choice of operating systems that allow loading and executing the user application. In a cloud platform, application developers create and deploy applications and do not necessarily need to know the underlying resources or infrastructure.

Platform as a Service: Platform as a service (PaaS) has the capability to provide independent platform having deployment capabilities, which may be capable of executing multiple applications on a single platform concurrently.

Platform Service: Platform service should have ability to create FCAPS-oriented (Fault, Configuration, Account, Performance, and Security) virtual servers which should allow hosting the guest operating systems and executing user applications.

Privacy-Preserving Data Integrity Checking: This is a privacy-preserving remote data integrity checking protocol with data dynamics and public verifiability. The protocol provides public verifiability without the help of a third-party auditor. It doesn't leak any private information to the third party, which provides good performance without the support of the trusted third party and provides a method for independent arbitration of data retention contracts. But it has unnecessary computation and communication costs.

Privacy-Preserving Public Auditability for Storage Security: This allows a third-party auditor to confirm the integrity of dynamic data stored in the cloud. This scheme achieves both public auditability and dynamic data operations. The protocol was designed to achieve security and performance guarantees like public auditing, storage correctness, privacy preservation, batch auditing, and light weight. The method is found to be scalable and efficient, which provides a complete outsourcing solution and integrity checking and thus saves the amount of auditing time. It relies on third-party auditors and has the use of expensive modular exponentiation operations, which lead to storage overhead on server and extra communication cost.

Privacy: Privacy is the right and obligation of individuals and organizations with respect to the collection, use, retention, and disclosure of personal information. Privacy control allows the person to maintain a degree of intimacy. Privacy protects the honest use of personal information of cloud users. Privacy breaches may create a lot of problems for cloud users.

Private Cloud Computing Environment: When clients want to secure their own data but still need to gain cloud infrastructure, they need for private cloud.

Proactive Maintenance: A cloud system should take the kinds of actions that are intended to cause changes, rather than just reacting to change. In case of failures, live migration facilitates proactive maintenance that helps to resolve the internal potential problem of a cloud system before the disruption of service occurs.

Process Virtual Machine: A process virtual machine, sometimes referred to as an application virtual machine, runs as a normal application process inside operating systems and also supports a single process. It is created when that particular process is started and also destroyed when it ends. The process VM aims to provide a platform-independent programming environment which abstracts away the details of the underlying infrastructure or hardware or operating system, and also allows a program to execute in the same way on any platform. A process VM is able to provide a high-level abstraction, which is that of a high-level programming language. Process VMs are implemented using an interpreter; performance comparable to compiled programming languages is gained by the use of just-in-time compilation.

Prompt Access for Supporting Business Agility: One of the most appreciable reimbursements of cloud infrastructure services is to append or add new infrastructure capacity swiftly at minimal cost. Generally, self-service provisioning of resources allows users to access the resources in a self-service manner without any human interaction. Hence, automated self-service leads to more flexible cloud infrastructure.

Public Cloud Computing Environment: According to Armbrust *et al.*, public cloud has made the cloud available in a pay-as-you-go manner to the general public. In this public cloud model, the hardware and computing resources and also same infrastructure is used by multiple users.

Public Verifiability (PV) for Storage Security: To ensure the correctness of data, the service providers allow a third-party auditor to work on behalf of the cloud consumer, to check the integrity of the stored data in the cloud. This scheme ensures that the storage at the client side is minimal, which will be helpful for thin clients.

Query Integrity/Keyword Searches: The query integrity and keyword search scheme is used to check the privacy in cloud. An efficient privacy-preserving keyword search scheme (EPPKS) is used in cloud computing that allows a service provider to participate in partial decipherment and enables them to search the keywords on encrypted files. It makes use of an efficient privacy-preserving keyword search scheme. It provides protection of user data privacy, queries privacy, and supports keyword searches on encrypted data. It has been found to be efficient, practical and provably and semantically secure.

Query Language: During transaction processing a user can interact with the database only by using the structured query language (SQL).

Rackspace Cloud Service: Rackspace provides infrastructure service that offers fixed instances of virtual machines in the cloud. It offers a wide range of pre-made Linux-based images. In this cloud, RAM measures user-requested images. Like GoGrid, Rackspace servers combine dedicated hosts with cloud infrastructure to facilitate the use of all the features of automated cloud computing. It offers features such as enabling static (fixed) IP address, load balancing, and persistent storage.

Relational and Non-Relational Database: A relational database is one that complies with the relational rules of tables as described by Codd (i.e., relational algebra and relational calculus). The set of tables building the database are related to each other (if at all) through a primary key/foreign key structure. For example, a student table may have student ID as its primary key, at the same time a department table contains student ID as a foreign key which defines the relation between the two. In relational databases predefined schemas and SQL queries are mainly used for storing and retrieving the information. Recently, there has been a surge of alternative technologies for large-scale analytic processing in cloud computing environment, most of which are not based on the relational model. For this reason, distributed file systems together with MapReduce have become strong competitors of relational database systems that analyze large data sets, exploiting parallel processing. Moreover, progress is being made on using MapReduce to evaluate relational queries. Hence, many non-relational databases have been developed. Some of the important features of non-relational databases are that they are schema free, horizontally scalable, enhanced data modeling and representation, faster computations. Non-relational databases are not fully adhering ACID transactions during write/update operations. Some of the popular non-relational DBMSs are MongoDB, Cassandra, CouchDB, Amazon SimpleDB and Redis.

Relational Data Model: To store and retrieve data from the data store, these databases only use the relational data model. Data can be stored here in the form of tables (i.e., combination of rows and columns).

Renewal Service Management: It is responsible for renewal of policies, rules, and access controls. Validation and updated SLAs should also be under the renewal service. This service is basically a smooth interacting medium for internet-centric places of business where both clients and CSPs could interact for their business and IT Infrastructure.

Replication: In the case of distributed cloud databases, replication means that a data item is stored on more than one node. This is very useful to increase read performance of the database, because it allows a load balancer to distribute all read operations over many machines. It is also very advantageous in that it makes the cluster robust against failures of single nodes. If one machine fails, then there is at least another one with the same data which can replace the lost node.

Resources as a Service (RaaS): At the bottom-most layer of the cloud service stack, there is a collection of physical resources, such as storage, servers, bandwidth, data center space, and networks, which may be accessed and shared by multiple users.

Resource Virtualization: The concept of virtualization is the most important basic sub-block of the cloud framework. Virtualization is the process by which we can hide the underlying infrastructure by inserting a logical layer. The three basic resources, i.e., computation, network, and storage, are virtualized and represented logically in this layer. Resource virtualization can be considered one of the most important layers of cloud stack. The basic concept of virtualization is to hide underlying infrastructure by creating a logical interface which helps the customers deploy their application onto their respective VMs so that the resources can be easily provisioned to users.

RPDC: A remote data possession checking (RDPC) scheme is efficient in terms of computation and communication; it allows verification without the need for the challenger to compare against the original data; it uses only small challenges and responses, and users need to store only two secret keys and several random numbers.

Scalability: This means that an application is capable of scaling itself when more users and more applications are added and also when the configuration of application or application requirements changes. It should be capable of releasing the resources when the users or applications are freed from the service.

Scheduling-Based Environment: This scheduling-based category focuses on how the virtual machines are scheduled in different scheduling algorithm by the VMM according to the request of the cloud user.

Security: Security is improved due to centralization of data, which prevents loss of control over certain sensitive data.

Self-Service Provisioning of Resources: Consumers or cloud subscribers of cloud services expect instant access to resources when they need them. Cloud users simply request a certain amount of services, storage, processing capabilities, and computing services from the CSPs. And for servicing that request, CSPs must provide an atmosphere that provides self-service access.

Separate Participation: This is an instance where each individual computer has its distinct participation and has a limited view of the complete system. Each computer only knows some module or some part of the whole program or input.

Service Analysis: This is the analytical study of a particular business process, which rationalizes the capabilities of different fields of business service like service contracts, agreements, globalization, etc. Driven by the different strategies and policies of the service provider, a business case is established that will be used in future stages.

Service Consumption: This can be understood by its name alone. A business service is consumed by the users through web services; whenever service providers validate some business services, the customers as well as the providers maintain some regulations such as security policies, service dependencies, agreement-level policies, resource provisioning rules, service syntax and semantics, and also capability.

Service Decommissions: In this phase of the cycle, data are transferred and unused data are cleaned up. An acknowledgment message is also transferred from the user and even from the related organization's end. As there are changes in different business strategies, service providers try their best to provide better services. Furthermore, this phase also has the ability to decommission services.

Service Development: After the analysis phase, the development phase is there to create the business service required by the customers. It is the phase where service developers write the coding part, which leads to the rationalization of different contracts and business services implemented through this phase. Service developers also create the web-based interface through which the customers can easily get the services.

Service-Level Agreement (SLA): SLA management is a key aspect of business service. It is concerned with business-aligned rules and policies. Distributed resources like network, storage and network are provisioned but should not be the cause of an SLA violation of any application executing with greater than predefined threshold line. Hence, the service agreement should be maintained to keep the rules of an organization.

Service-Level Agreement (SLA) Auditing: In the business service provider (BSP) layer, SLAs are concerned with business-oriented agreements and laws. So, in every level of agreements, auditing is highly required to maintain proper usage of laws and terms and conditions.

Service Operation: This is a key phase in the life cycle. Various types of activities are performed by the Management API, which are the management infrastructure responsible for the following operations: metered usage of services, performance optimization, service updating, enabling authentication, authorization procedure, maintaining data privacy, generating business strategies, providing dynamic provisioning, monitoring transactions, reporting, and keeping metadata.

Service-Oriented Architecture (SOA): This is a paradigm for organizing and utilizing distributed capabilities that may be under the control of different ownership domains.

Service Provisioning: When testing phase is completed, service is ready for use and the service is provisioned to the users.

Service Testing: This is the phase which comes after the development phase and it contains test-data module for testing purposes. In this phase, in-progress software can be periodically checked for errors, regressions, and also for debugging. Sometimes, performance testing and functional testing is also done in this phase for maintaining quality of service (QoS).

Service Creation Platform: This block may provide the tools which can be used for creation of applications. Applications are termed as a collection of services that can be created and distributed over the virtual servers created and controlled by the Platform service.

Service Delivery Platform: This can be defined as a workflow engine that should be capable of execution of the application and should be able to manage the orchestration of multiple distributable workflow elements.

Sharding: The term sharding derives from the noun "shard," as it means that the data inside a database is split into many shards, which can be distributed over many nodes. The data partitioning can, for example, be done with a consistent hash function that is applied to the primary key of the data items to determine the associated shard.

Sniffer Attacks: These are launched by applications which can capture packets flowing in a network and if the data that is being transferred through these packets is not encrypted, it can be read. There is a chance that vital information flowing across the network can be traced or captured. A sniffer program, through the NIC (Network Interface Card), ensures that the data/traffic linked to other systems on the network also gets recorded. This can be achieved by placing the NIC in promiscuous mode by which it can track all data flowing on the same network. A malicious sniffing detection platform based on ARP (address resolution protocol) and RTT (round-trip time) can be used to detect a sniffing system running on a network.

Software as a Service: This is used for applications delivered by the service provider in a particular cloud infrastructure. The applications are accessible from various devices via a user interface like web-based mail.

Software Service: This layer may provide ready-to-use software service and the clients need not incur any overhead costs for buying and maintaining the software. Cloud users need not to know the underlying architecture of cloud infrastructure; they just use and access the software.

Software-Oriented Service: This module provides ready-to-use software service. The end users do not incur any overhead costs for purchasing and maintaining the software.

SQL-Based and NoSQL-Based Database: SQL is an ANSI (American National Standards Institute) standard language for accessing and manipulating databases. All the relational DBMSs are tightly coupled with SQL, hence it also is known as SQL-based DBMS.

Standardized Platform: Each organization has its own APIs, services, policies, and different rules and regulations. So, in a cloud platform, it's quite difficult to maintain a combination of all those things from various organizations; and interoperability of all the applications is also a mammoth task.

Stop and Copy: Stop and Copy is the simplest way of migrating UDB. Initially the source CDS node stops serving the UDB and copies the data to destination CDS node and then restarts the UDB transactions at destination CDS node. This approach also has some limitations such as the overall system downtime (due to the stopping of source CDS node) increases with the increase of UDB size. Apart from that, the entire database cache is lost due to restarting the transaction at destination node so that the post-migration overhead time is highly increased to warm up the cache. Because of these weaknesses this method is not well suited for live migration.

Storage Migration: To maintain VM migration, the system has to provide each VM with a location-independent, consistent vision of the file system that is accessible on all hosts. Each VM uses its own virtual disk, to which the corresponding file system is mapped, and transfers the contents of the virtual disk to the source machine. We depend on the storage area networks (SAN) or NAS to permit us to migrate connections to the storage devices. This phenomenon allows us to migrate a disk by reconnecting to the disk on the target machine.

Storage Virtualization: The key driver of storage virtualization, storage networking, and server virtualization are fiber channel (FC) and FC-based storage area networks (FC-SAN), which facilitate storage connectivity (very high speed) and storage solutions like point-to-point replication and serverless backup.

Structured and Unstructured Database: The labels "structured data" and "unstructured data" are often used ambiguously by different interest groups; and often used lazily to cover multiple distinct aspects of the issue. In reality, there are at least three orthogonal aspects to structure: the structure of the data itself, the structure of the container that hosts the data, and the structure of the access method used to access the data.

System Virtual Machine: A system virtual machine enables one computer to behave like two or more computers by sharing the host hardware's resources. Multiple VMs, each of which run their own OS (this operating system is called guest operating system), are frequently utilized in server consolidation, where different cloud services that are used to execute on separate machines to avoid interference, are instead run in individual VMs on the same physical machine. The requirement to execute multiple operating systems was the actual inspiration for virtual machines, as it permitted time-sharing a single computer between numerous single-tasking operation systems. In some cases, a system virtual machine can easily be measured as a generalization of the idea of virtual memory that historically preceded it. The use of virtual machines to support different guest OSs is becoming popular in embedded systems; a typical use is to support a real-time operating system at the same time as a high-level OS such as Linux or Windows.

Traditional Approach: In the traditional approach, there are mixed hardware environment, multiple management tools, frequent application patching and updating, complex workloads, and multiple software architecture. In comparison, the cloud data center is a far better approach with homogeneous environment, standardize management tools, minimal application patching and updating, simple workloads and single standard software architecture.

Transaction-Based Environment: This category deals with different architecture-based virtualizations and deployment of different operating systems and new applications.

Ubiquity: The dictionary meaning of ubiquity is "present everywhere." Mobile computing allows a user to perform computation from anywhere, at anytime.

For example, a business executive can receive business notifications and issue business transactions as long he/she is in wireless coverage area.

Unicast Distribution: Unicast distribution distributes the VM images in a sequential order to the destination nodes even in remote sites. But it is very time-consuming and faces network congestion.

User Application-Based Virtualization: In this category, virtualization is done according to the users' on-demand requirements and is hosted on top of the host OS. Upon getting a request, emulation of VM containing its own guest OS and related applications is carried out by this virtualization method so that users can get their specific on-demand service from the emulated VMs.

Utility Computing: This can be defined as a service provisioning model where a service provider makes computing resources and infrastructure management available to the customer as needed. This approach is like pay-per-use or metered service, which means a customer can pay only for the internet service, file sharing, web site access, and other applications they use.

Virtual Appliances: Virtual appliances run with the APIs (application programming interface) of various customer service providers (CSPs) or platforms. It is an instance of virtual environment extension (VEE). Cloud applications are deployed as virtual appliances to make management better.

Virtual Machine (VM): Virtual machines are like the the user interface, which have their own operating system (guest OS) hosted by the host OS. Instead of interacting with a single computer, VMs have the capability to facilitate the aggregation of system and computing resources from multiple machines, and present a consistent and unified view to the users and the applications. The basic responsibility of VMs is to support multiple OS and application instances and to provide greater scalability.

Xen: It is a virtual machine monitor (VMM) or hypervisor developed by the Computer Laboratory at the University of Cambridge, United Kingdom, in 2003. Since 2010 Xen has been free software, developed by the community of users and licensed under the GNU General PublicLicense (GPLv2). It makes it possible to run many instances of an operating system or indeed different operating systems in parallel on a single machine (or host). Xen is the only type-1 hypervisor that is available as open source.

Authors

Souvik Pal
Associate Professor
Department of Computer Science and Engineering
Sister Nivedita University, Kolkata, India

Souvik Pal is an Associate Professor in the Department of Computer Science and Engineering at Sister Nivedita University (Techno India Group), Kolkata, India. Prior to that, he was associated with Global Institute of Management and Technology; Brainware University, Kolkata; JIS College of Engineering, Nadia; Elitte College of Engineering, Kolkata; and Nalanda Institute of Technology, Bhubaneswar, India. Dr. Pal received his MTech, and PhD degrees in the field of Computer Science and Engineering from KIIT University, Bhubaneswar, India. He has more than a decade of academic experience. He is author or co-editor of more than 15 books from reputed publishers, including Elsevier, Springer, CRC Press, and Wiley, and he holds three patents. He is serving as a Series Editor for "Advances in Learning Analytics for Intelligent Cloud-IoT Systems," published by Scrivener-Wiley Publishing (Scopus-indexed); "Internet of Things: Data-Centric Intelligent Computing, Informatics, and Communication," published by CRC Press, Taylor & Francis Group, USA; "Conference Proceedings Series on Intelligent Systems, Data Engineering, and Optimization," published by CRC Press, Taylor & Francis Group, USA; Dr. Pal has published a number of research papers in Scopus / SCI/SCIE Journals and conferences. He was the organizing chair of RICE 2019, Vietnam; RICE 2020 Vietnam; ICICIT 2019, Tunisia. He has been invited as a keynote speaker at ICICCT 2019, Turkey, and ICTIDS 2019, 2021 Malaysia. He has also served as Proceedings Editor of ICICCT 2019, 2020; ICMMCS 2020, 2021; ICWSNUCA 2021, India. His professional activities include roles as Associate Editor, Guest Editor, and Editorial Board member for more than

100+ international journals and conferences of high repute and impact. His research area includes cloud computing, big data, internet of things, wireless sensor network, and data analytics. He is a member of many professional organizations, including MIEEE; MCSI; MCSTA/ACM, USA; MIAENG, Hong Kong; MIRED, USA; MACEEE, New Delhi; MI-ACSIT, Singapore; and MAASCIT, USA.

Dac-Nhuong Le
Associate Professor in Computer Science
Faculty of Information Technology
Haiphong University, Haiphong, Vietnam

Dac-Nhuong Le received a MSc and PhD in computer science from Vietnam National University, Vietnam in 2009 and 2015, respectively. He is an Associate Professor in Computer Science, Dean of Faculty of Information Technology, Haiphong University, Vietnam. He has a total academic teaching experience of 15+ years with many publications in reputed international conferences, journals and online book chapter contributions (Indexed by SCIE, SSCI, Scopus, ACM, DBLP). His areas of research include soft computing; network communication, security and vulnerability; network performance analysis and simulation; cloud computing; IoT; and biomedical image processing. His core work is in network security, soft computing and IoT and biomedical image processing. Recently, he has been on the technique program committee, the technique reviews committee, and was the track chair for international conferences under Springer-ASIC/LNAI Series. Presently, he is serving on the editorial board of international journals and has authored/edited 20+ computer science books by Springer, Scrivener-Wiley, IET, CRC Press.

Prasant Kumar Pattnaik
Professor, School of Computer Engineering
Kalinga Institute of Industrial Technology (KIIT)
Deemed to be University, India

Prasant Kumar Pattnaik has a PhD in Computer Science, and is a fellow IETE member and a senior IEEE member, is a professor at the School of Computer Engineering, KIIT Deemed to be University, Bhubaneswar, India. He has more than a decade of teaching and research experience. Dr. Pattnaik has published a number of research papers in peer-reviewed international journals and conferences. His areas of research are computer networks, data mining, cloud computing, and mobile computing. He has authored many computer science books in the fields of data mining, robotics, graph theory, Turing machine, cryptography, security solutions in cloud computing, mobile computing, and privacy preservation.

Printed and bound by CPI Group (UK) Ltd, Croydon, CR0 4YY

27/10/2024

14580478-0005